MODERN HUMANITIES RESEARCH ASSOCIATION

TUDOR & STUART TRANSLATIONS

VOLUME 16

General Editors
ANDREW HADFIELD
NEIL RHODES

ROBERT GARNIER IN ELIZABETHAN ENGLAND

MARY SIDNEY HERBERT'S *ANTONIUS*

and

THOMAS KYD'S *CORNELIA*

ROBERT GARNIER IN ELIZABETHAN ENGLAND

MARY SIDNEY HERBERT'S *ANTONIUS*

and

THOMAS KYD'S *CORNELIA*

Edited by

Marie-Alice Belle and Line Cottegnies

MODERN HUMANITIES RESEARCH ASSOCIATION
2017

Published by
The Modern Humanities Research Association
Salisbury House
Station Road
Cambridge CB1 2LA
United Kingdom

First published 2017

ISBN 978-1-78188-632-8 (hbk)
ISBN 978-1-907322-67-9 (pbk)

Copies may be ordered from www.tudor.mhra.org.uk

MHRA TUDOR AND STUART TRANSLATIONS

For details of published and forthcoming volumes please visit our website:

www.tudor.mhra.org.uk

TABLE OF CONTENTS

GENERAL EDITORS' FOREWORD

The aim of the *MHRA Tudor & Stuart Translations* is to create a representative library of works translated into English during the early modern period for the use of scholars, students and the wider public. The series will include both substantial single works and selections of texts from major authors, with the emphasis being on the works that were most familiar to early modern readers. The texts themselves will be newly edited with substantial introductions, notes, and glossaries, and will be published both in print and online.

The series aims to restore to view a major part of English Renaissance literature which has become relatively inaccessible and to present these texts as literary works in their own right. For that reason it will follow the same principle of modernisation adopted by other scholarly editions of canonical literature from the period. The series will have a similar scope to that of the original *Tudor Translations* published early in the last century, and while the great majority of the works presented will be from the sixteenth century, like the original series it will not be rigidly bound by the end-date of 1603. There will, however, be a very different range of texts with new and substantial scholarly apparatus.

The *MHRA Tudor & Stuart Translations* will extend our understanding of the English Renaissance through its representation of the process of cultural transmission from the classical to the early modern world and the process of cultural exchange within the early modern world.

Andrew Hadfield
Neil Rhodes

NOTE ON THIS EDITION

All quotations from the classics are excerpted from the Loeb standard editions. Robert Garnier's text is that of the 1585 *Tragédies*. References to Shakespeare are from the Oxford edition of the complete works. See textual notes for editorial principles and final bibliography for complete references.

All translations from the French or from the Latin are ours, unless specified. Where relevant, we have also included translations from important early modern sources (North's Plutarch, Marlowe's translation from Lucan's *Pharsalia*, etc.), because they represented important cultural references for the early modern reader — and translator.

INTRODUCTION

CRITICAL AND HISTORICAL BACKGROUND

In his 2010 study of the *French Origins of English Tragedy*, Richard Hillman proposed a new way of documenting the significance of French neoclassical precedents to the development of English tragedy. Instead of tracing 'influences' or focusing on 'sources' only, he persuasively argued, one should be considering the multi-faceted and 'dynamic imaginative engagement of late sixteenth- and seventeenth-century English dramatists and audiences with French texts and contexts'.[1]

Translation lies at the heart of such engagement, and in a context of ongoing cultural and literary exchanges between England and France,[2] Robert Garnier's tragedies elicited particular interest on the part of English dramatists. His tragedies have been identified as a diffuse 'influence' on the development of English tragedy, and as topical sources for many Elizabethan plays.[3] With two of his plays translated in quick succession, Garnier was the best-known French playwright of the period in England: *Antonius* and *Cornelia* were only preceded by Arthur Golding's translation of a sacred play by

[1] Richard Hillman, *The French Origins of English Tragedy* (Manchester: Manchester University Press, 2010), p. 1. The traditional approach he seeks to counter is exemplified by Alexander Witherspoon's *The Influence of Robert Garnier on Elizabethan Drama* ([Hamden]: Archon Books, 1968 [1924]), and, to a lesser extent, Kenneth Muir's *The Sources of Shakespeare's Plays* (London: Methuen, 1977).

[2] As documented by the following works, among others: Deanne Williams, *The French Fetish from Chaucer to Shakespeare* (Cambridge: Cambridge University Press, 2004); *French Essays on Shakespeare and His Contemporaries*, ed. by Jean-Marie Maguin and Michèle Willems (Newark: University of Delaware Press, 1995); *Representing France and the French in Early Modern English Drama*, ed. by Jean-Christophe Mayer (Newark: University of Delaware Press, 2008); Hassan Melehy, *The Poetics of Literary Transfer in Early Modern France and England* (Farnham: Ashgate, 2010); *French Connections in the English Renaissance*, ed. by Catherine Martin and Hassan Melehy (Burlington, VT: Ashgate, 2013); Anne E. B. Coldiron, *English Printing, Verse Translation, and the Battle of the Sexes, 1476–1557* (Farnham: Ashgate, 2009); *The Culture of Translation in Early Modern England and France, 1500–1660*, ed. by Tania Demetriou and Rowan Tomlinson (Basingstoke and New York: Palgrave Macmillan, 2015); and Warren Boutcher, *The School of Montaigne* (Oxford: Oxford University Press, 2016).

[3] See Witherspoon, but also Frederick Boas's edition of the *Works of Thomas Kyd* (Oxford: Clarendon, 1901) (hereafter Boas), and, more recently, Howard Norland, *Neoclassical Tragedy in Elizabethan England* (Newark: University of Delaware Press, 2009).

Théodore de Bèze in 1577. Only Corneille would attract more interest from English readers, but not until much later, in the 1640s and 1650s.[4] The attraction may have been motivated by Garnier's high profile in French literary and courtly circles. As Anne Lake Prescott puts it, he represented in many ways the 'high-fashion' of French Renaissance culture.[5] Fusing classical historical sources with contemporary Humanist poetry and thought, his reinterpretation of the Senecan tragic model represented one of the first and most successful contributions to early modern French drama — one that would have a lasting influence on the high genre of the 'tragédie classique'. What is more, his dramatizations of ancient history, most often through the eyes of an illustrious *femme forte*, were explicitly designed as mirrors in which audiences could contemplate the main moral and political concerns of their times.[6]

Such literary, intellectual and political considerations were clearly relevant in the later years of Elizabeth's reign, and it is not surprising that the first English translation of Garnier's theatre originated in one of the most influential literary and political milieux, that of the Sidney-Pembroke 'circle' (see below for discussion). In 1592 Mary Sidney Herbert, Countess of Pembroke, sister to the recently deceased courtier and poet Sir Philip Sidney, published her translation of Garnier's *Marc Antoine* (first published in 1578) under the title *Antonius, A Tragedie*. In William Ponsonby's elegant quarto, the play was published as a companion piece to Sidney Herbert's translation of Philippe de Mornay's *Discourse of Life and Death*; it was reprinted separately in 1595 as *The Tragedy of Antonie* (see textual notes for details). It was probably in response to the 1592 volume that Thomas

---

[4] Arthur Golding's *A Tragedie of Abrahams Sacrifice* (London: Thomas Vautroullier, 1577) appears to have been the first English translation of a French tragedy. The influence of Jodelle can be traced in Samuel Daniel's *Cleopatra*, for example, but arguably through Garnier. On this point, see in particular Richard Hillman, 'The French Accents of Seneca on the Tudor Stage', in *New Perspectives on Tudor Cultures*, ed. by Mike Pincombe and Zsolt Almasi (Newcastle-upon-Tyne: Cambridge Scholars, 2012), pp. 244–62.

[5] Anne Lake Prescott, 'Mary Sidney's French Sophocles: The Countess of Pembroke reads Robert Garnier', in *Representing France and the French in Early Modern English Drama*, ed. by Mayer, pp. 68–89 (p. 76).

[6] Garnier himself terms his tragedy *Cornélie* 'a poem all too well fitting the miseries' of his time ('poeme à mon regret trop propre aux malheurs de nostre siecle'). Robert Garnier, *Tragédies de Robert Garnier Conseiller du Roy, Lieutenant general Criminel au siege Presidial & Senechaussee du Maine* (Paris: Mamert Patisson Imprimeur du Roy, chez Robert Estienne, 1585), p. 36r (hereafter Garnier).

Kyd, best known for his *Spanish Tragedy*, and long recognized as one of the 'pioneering figures'[7] of the English tragic tradition, published in turn a translation of Garnier's *Cornélie*, a tragedy originally composed in 1572 and predating *Marc Antoine*. The 1594 volume, simply entitled *Cornelia*, was reissued in 1595 with the fuller title *Pompey the Great, his faire Corneliaes Tragedie: Effected by her Father and Husbandes down-cast, death and fortune*.

Although composed and printed within a very short time span, and in response to the same French dramatic model, these two translations have encountered quite different critical fortunes. Sidney Herbert's *Antonius* was followed by a whole series of plays about the civil wars of Rome, including (besides Kyd's play) Samuel Daniel's 1594 *Cleopatra*, which, if we are to believe its preface, was commissioned by the Countess, and, later, of course, Shakespeare's *Antony and Cleopatra* (1607).[8] Although Sidney Herbert's translation then suffered from an eclipse of close to four hundred years, she has more recently attracted a great deal of critical attention, especially in the last twenty-five years or so, in her various capacities as a poet, a patron, and a translator, in the context of renewed interest in early modern women's writing. *Antonius* has been edited several times since the nineteenth century, with six editions in quick succession between 1990 and 2005. It can now be taught in universities, but its importance as a translation has not always been given its full due. By contrast, the reception of Kyd's *Cornelia* has been rather chequered, at least by modern standards: while *Cornelia* was included in the many editions of Robert Dodsley's *Select Collection of Old Plays* (first published 1744), and in Frederick Boas's 1901 Oxford edition of *The Works of Thomas Kyd* (reissued in 1955), no new edition of Kyd's translation has been published since.[9]

Besides this unbalanced reception history, critics discussing both plays together have long tended to pit them the one against the other in (over-)convenient binaries: Sidney Herbert's allegedly faithful approach to Garnier has thus been routinely contrasted with the liberties Kyd took with the French text.[10] While Sidney Herbert has

---

[7] Lukas Erne, *Beyond The Spanish Tragedy: A Study of the Works of Thomas Kyd* (Manchester: Manchester University Press, 2002), p. x.

[8] See 'Literary Influence', below.

[9] An original-spelling edition of Thomas Kyd's *Works* in two volumes is currently in preparation under the direction of Brian Vickers. See textual notes for more details on eighteenth- and nineteenth-century editions of *Cornelia*.

[10] See Witherspoon, p. 94, and Norland, *Neoclassical Tragedy*, pp. 219–20 in particular.

been portrayed as a scrupulous and scholarly translator, Kyd has been presented as another case of 'small Latin and less Greeke' on the English stage.[11] Some feminist readings have pictured Sidney Herbert's translation activities as a typically female, domestic practice, whereas Kyd's engagement with Senecan 'closet drama' has often been read as an anomaly in the career of an otherwise celebrated dramatist writing mainly for the 'public' stage.[12]

Perhaps the only common point to be found in such readings of *Antonius* and *Cornelia* is a general tendency to represent both endeavours as of relatively minor importance: translation still tends to be presented as an ancillary practice, only motivated by the ideological limitations imposed on women by early modern patriarchy, or by pecuniary necessity.[13] The usual description of both

[11] Boas is particularly scathing in his evaluation of Kyd's 'mistakes', 'mistranslations' and 'blunders' in the notes to his edition (pp. 414–36).

[12] Feminist readings of Sidney Herbert's translation as a domestically oriented practice include Tina Krontiris, *Oppositional Voices: Women as Writers and Translators of Literature in the English Renaissance* (London: Routledge, 1992), p. 64–77; Karen Raber, 'Domestic drama: The Politics of Mary Sidney's *Antonie*', in *Dramatic Difference: Gender, Class, and Genre in the Early Modern Closet Drama*, ed. by Raber (Newark: University of Delaware Press, 2001), pp. 52–110; and Alison Findlay, *Playing Spaces in Early Women's Drama* (Cambridge: Cambridge University Press, 2006), pp. 28–30. On the perception of *Cornelia* as an 'oddity' in Kyd's career, see e.g. Norland, *Neoclassical Tragedy*, p. 226, Erne (who calls the play 'the odd man out among Kyd's plays'), *Beyond the Spanish Tragedy*, p. 214, and Iris Oberth, 'Appropriating France in Elizabethan drama: English Translations of Robert Garnier's Plays', in *Elizabethan Translation and Literary Culture*, ed. by Gabriela Schmidt (Berlin: De Gruyter, 2013), pp. 275–98 (p. 293).

[13] The early feminist perception of translation as a practice embraced by women because they did not have access to more authorial forms of textual production — see Margaret Hannay, *Silent But for the Word: Tudor Women as Patrons, Translators, and Writers of Religious Works* (Ohio: Kent State University Press, 1985) — has been thoroughly critiqued in recent years. See for example Brenda Hosington and Hannah Fournier, 'Translation and Women Translators', in *The Encyclopedia of Women in the Renaissance: Italy, France and England*, ed. by Diana M. Robin, Anne Larsen and Carole Levin (Santa Barbara: University of California Press, 2007), pp. 369–72; Danielle Clarke, 'Translations', in *The Cambridge Companion to Early Modern Women's Writings*, ed. by Laura Knoppers (Cambridge: Cambridge University Press, 2010), pp. 167–80; Marie-Alice Belle, 'Locating Women's Translations in Early Modern England and France', *Renaissance and Reformation*, 35.4 (2012), 5–24; or Patricia Pender, *Early Modern Women's Writing and the Rhetoric of Modesty* (London: Palgrave Macmillan, 2012), pp. 16–35. Concerning Kyd's pecuniary difficulties, they were certainly real in 1592–93, but some critics have tended to take Kyd's modesty topos literally and to consider his apology for the 'rough and unpolished' nature of his work as an indication that it was hastily composed. Boas also misreads Kyd's mention of spending 'a winter's week with desolate Cornelia'

plays, which were never performed, as early examples of 'closet drama', primarily intended for private reading among a literary elite,[14] has further contributed to their marginalization. Long portrayed as part of a reactionary attempt led by Sidney Herbert to 'reform' the public stage along the lines of Sir Philip Sidney's *Defence of Poesie*, *Antonius* and *Cornelia* have thus been relegated to the peripheries of literary history. Such a view was summed up, as late as 2006, in David Bergeron's characterization of the Garnier translations as 'a kind of cottage industry [...] [T]he true course of English drama passed them by; theirs, as it turned out, represented a program of the past, not the future charted by Marlowe and Shakespeare'.[15]

More recent reappraisals, however, have challenged the relatively marginal position long attributed to both texts, and although no critical consensus has emerged on either play, recent studies on the Garnier translations by Sidney Herbert and Kyd do converge on a number of points.

First, following Mary Ellen Lamb's seminal 1981 challenge to the 'myth' of a concerted attack on the public stage on the part of the Countess of Pembroke and a closed circle of authors,[16] critics have re-examined the immediate material and social contexts surrounding the 'Englishing' of Garnier's plays. While acknowledging the importance of the precedent set by the Countess of Pembroke, as a poet and a patron, in translating Garnier's *Marc Antoine*, recent studies have found both translations to originate, not in an elitist 'conspiracy' of playwrights led by Sidney Herbert, but rather within the rich and complex Elizabethan system of literary patronage and publication — one where manuscript circulation and print production, private reading and courtly entertainment, as well as

---

as an indication that it was composed in a week, while Kyd actually refers to the reading of the play. See Boas, p. lxii and Norland, *Neoclassical Tragedy*, pp. 218–19.

[14] See especially Raber, or, for a more balanced approach, Marta Straznicky, '"Profane Stoical Paradoxes": *The Tragedie of Mariam* and Sidneian Closet Drama', *English Literary Renaissance*, 24.1 (1994), 104–34; and *Privacy, Playreading, and Women's Closet Drama 1550–1700* (Cambridge: Cambridge University Press, 2004), especially pp. 49–50.

[15] David M. Bergeron, *Textual Patronage in English Drama, 1570–1640* (Aldershot: Ashgate, 2006), pp. 86–87.

[16] Mary Ellen Lamb, 'The Myth of the Countess of Pembroke: The Dramatic Circle', *The Yearbook of English Studies*, 11 (1981), 194–202, and more recently Hillman, '"De-centring the Countess's Circle": Mary Sidney Herbert and Cleopatra', *Renaissance and Reformation / Renaissance et Réforme*, 28.1 (2004), 61–79.

support for literary experimentation and public performance, often overlapped.[17]

Besides, critics have demonstrated a growing awareness of the nature of translation in the early modern period, not as a passive or mechanical activity but as a form of collaborative authorship, including in translations by women. As Danielle Clarke forcefully argued in her 1997 essay on Sidney Herbert's *Antonius*, to limit one's reading of translated texts to 'the isolation of a specifically feminine subjectivity', or to the 'nitty-gritty of the linguistic transformations performed' by translators is to show both historical and critical neglect for the 'methods and purposes of Renaissance translation.'[18] Such an oversight is gradually being corrected, as instead of focusing on the (female) translator's coy 'faithfulness' or blatant 'mistakes', scholars now comment more on the authorial and ideological strategies underlying each writer's appropriation of the original. In the case of Sidney Herbert, this new perspective is perhaps best exemplified by Eve R. Sanders' characterization of the Countess's textual and intellectual engagement with Garnier as an authorial, as well as interpretive, act.[19] A similar approach to Kyd's rendering of Garnier was proposed as early as 1979, with Josephine Roberts and James Gaines' depiction of Kyd's departures from the French as conscious, poetically motivated 'amendments'— a reading more recently relayed by Erne's call for the literary rehabilitation of Kyd's last and 'maturest' tragedy.[20]

[17] See for example Henry Woudhuysen, *Sir Philip Sidney and the Circulation of Manuscripts, 1558–1640* (Oxford: Clarendon Press, 1996), Eve R. Sanders, *Gender and Literacy on Stage in Early Modern England* (Cambridge: Cambridge University Press, 1998), pp. 89–137, Edward Wilson-Lee, 'Women's Weapons: Country House Diplomacy in the Countess of Pembroke's French Translations', in *The Culture of Translation*, ed. by Demetriou and Tomlinson, pp. 128–44; and Erne, *Beyond the Spanish Tragedy*, pp. 203–16. On patronage, see also Richard A. McCabe, *'Ungainefull Arte.' Poetry Patronage, and Print in the Early Modern Era* (Oxford: Oxford University Press, 2016).

[18] Danielle Clarke, 'The Politics of Translation and Gender in the Countess of Pembroke's *Antonie*', *Translation and Literature*, 6 (1997), 149–66 (p. 150). See also Suzanne Trill, 'Sixteenth-century Women's Writing: Mary Sidney's *Psalmes* and the "Femininity of Translation"', in *Writing and the English Renaissance*, ed. by Suzanne Trill and William Zunder (London: Longman, 1996), pp. 140–58.

[19] Sanders for example characterizes Sidney's 'revisionary reading of the character of Cleopatra [as a way of] assuming the anti-conventional role of writer-translator' (p. 92).

[20] See, respectively: Josephine Roberts and James Gaines, 'Kyd and Garnier: The Art of Amendment', *Comparative Literature*, 31.2 (1979), 124–33; and Erne, *Beyond the Spanish Tragedy*, p. 214.

Taking Sidney Herbert's and Kyd's translation strategies seriously has in turn enabled scholars to explore their underlying intellectual, political and ideological motivations, and to situate them within the wider historical and political context of the 'nasty nineties', a period obscured by ongoing political and religious conflict in Continental Europe, and by constitutional and dynastic uncertainties at home.[21] The treatment of Garnier's Roman characters and historical events in Sidney Herbert's *Antonius* and Kyd's *Cornelia* has long been considered solely in terms of Shakespeare's potential sources (for *Antony and Cleopatra* and *Julius Caesar*, respectively). More specific attention to the political and ideological issues at stake in the appropriation of Catholic Garnier's political reading of Roman history has reframed the critical discussion, and spurred exciting — if unresolved — debates. Among the main questions discussed are the relationship of both Kyd's and Sidney Herbert's translations to the philosophical traditions of the *ars moriendi* and of the 'advice to the Prince'; their potential encoding along the lines of Sidney Herbert's well-known support for the Protestant cause, or, more radically, of contemporary Republican discourse; and, more generally, their common concern with a politically 'ambiguous' context undermining the triumphant eschatologies offered by the official discourse on the legitimacy of divinely-appointed monarchs.[22]

Such readings have significantly shifted the debate from the somewhat claustrophobic 'closet' of Senecan drama[23] to a consideration of the transnational exchanges, both intellectual and literary, that underlie the 'Englishing' of Garnier's plays. What has long been considered a 'domestic' enterprise emerges in this light as part of a

---

[21] See for example Anne Lake Prescott, 'Mary Sidney's "Antonius" and the Ambiguities of French History', *The Yearbook of English Studies*, 38.1 (2008), 216–33; Curtis Perry, 'The Uneasy Republicanism of Thomas Kyd's *Cornelia*', *Criticism*, 48.4 (2008), 535–55; and Daniel Cadman, *Sovereigns and Subjects in Early Modern Neo-Senecan Drama: Republicanism, Stoicism and Authority* (Farnham: Ashgate, 2015), pp. 23–68. The 'nasty nineties' expression is Patrick Collinson's, first coined in 'Ecclesiastical Vitriol: Religious Satire in the 1590s and the Invention of Puritanism', in *The Reign of Elizabeth I: Court and Culture in the Last Decade*, ed. by John A. Guy (Cambridge: Cambridge University Press, 1995), pp. 150–70.

[22] These issues are all discussed in detail below, pp. 67–72.

[23] As Coburn Freer wittily pointed out: 'the term [closet drama] would seek not only to define but to kill. Nothing can live much less grow in a closet; and closets are usually full of objects we cannot use' ('Mary Sidney, Countess of Pembroke', in *English Women Writers of the Renaissance and Reformation*, ed. by Katharina Wilson (Athens: University of Georgia Press, 1987), pp. 481–521 (p. 484).

culture of translation rooted in the practices of literary hospitality and intellectual 'civil conversation' inherited from Humanist culture.[24] While the actual relationship of Sidney Herbert's *Antonius*, and Kyd's *Cornelia*, to the literary programme suggested in Philip Sidney's *Defence of Poesie* remains yet to be fully demonstrated, what is clear is that the linguistic, metrical, and dramatic experimenting in both plays cannot be considered the isolated poetical musings of a self-absorbed elite. Indeed, as demonstrated by North's 1579 Plutarch, famously translated from Jacques Amyot's *Vies des hommes illustres* (1559),[25] or by Spenser's translations of du Bellay's poetry in his 1591 *Complaints*, translators participating in the appropriation and adaptation of Continental writings often self-consciously advertised the cultural and linguistic trajectories involved in the 'Englishing' of their sources.[26] Thus, the fashioning of England's literary idiom through translation and imitation, even in its more experimental forms, was conceived of and presented as part of a European, and indeed increasingly competitive, cultural dialogue. In this light, Sidney Herbert's French-inspired syntax and diction, and Kyd's engagement with Garnier's learned, neoclassical drama, are surely to be read in terms of the transnational European culture, or the intellectual and literary 'cosmopolitanism', to use Robert Stillman's term, of the late sixteenth century.[27]

Our main objective in offering a new edition of both plays together is to build on these important critical developments. The apparatus of textual and critical notes offered here aims to situate each text within the wider context of England's literary exchanges with France, the development of English neoclassical drama, and the complex system of patronage and literary production in and around the 'Sidney circle'. Our purpose in so doing is to set the distinctive translation practices encountered in Sidney Herbert's *Antonius* and Kyd's

---

[24] See Demetriou and Tomlinson's introduction to *The Culture of Translation*, p. 36 in particular.

[25] Plutarch, *The Lives of the Noble Grecians and Romanes*, trans. by John North (London: Thomas Vautroullier and John Wright, 1579), hereafter North.

[26] Another important case of transnational cultural translation is that of Hoby's *Courtier*, as revealed by Anne Coldiron's recent analyses. See her 'Form[e]s of Transnationhood: The Case of John Wolfe's Trilingual *Courtier*', *Renaissance Studies*, 29.1 (2015), 103–24; and *Printers Without Borders: Translation and Textuality in the Renaissance* (Cambridge: Cambridge University Press, 2015), pp. 160–98.

[27] Robert Stillman, *Philip Sidney and the Poetics of Renaissance Cosmopolitanism* (Aldershot: Ashgate, 2008).

Cornelia against the rich and rapidly shifting background — be it intellectual, material, political or religious — of the late Elizabethan era.

In order to identify such translation strategies, we have systematically checked the English text against its French counterpart, which has not always been the case in recent editions of *Antonius*. While we do indicate significant departures from Garnier in the text of the English translations, our approach differs from that of the Oxford editions of *Antonius* and *Cornelia* (by Margaret Hannay et al. and Frederick Boas, respectively) in that we do not necessarily focus on issues of faithfulness — or its critical correlative, 'fluency' or 'effectiveness' — nor do we aim to offer a qualitative evaluation of each translator's textual or interpretive performance.[28] By alerting the reader to additions and omissions in the English text, as well as shifts in language, tone, style or focus, our aim instead is to highlight the various ways in which each translator appropriated Garnier's neoclassical aesthetics, engaged with his moral and political interpretation of Roman history, reshaped his characters and gave them a distinctive, English voice, thus making them relevant in the literary, political and ideological context of the 1590s.

This edition is also the first to offer detailed information on the classical sources used by Garnier and his translators, including of course Seneca's tragedies and Plutarch's *Lives*, but also hitherto unnoticed references to major epic poems such as Lucan's *Pharsalia*, Virgil's *Aeneid*, and Lucretius' *De Rerum Natura*, as well as lyric poetry (Horace's *Odes*) and philosophical writings (mainly Seneca's epistles). We have followed in many places the leads offered in Jean-Claude Ternaux's critical editions of Garnier's plays and in previous editions of both translations.[29] In others, we have attended to the echoes and textual parallels present in the translations only, for, as will be apparent, Sidney Herbert and Kyd often elaborate on their French sources with the help of well-known classical passages and topoi. This, again, has not been done in a mere *Quellenforschung*

---

[28] See for example the section entitled 'Fidelity to Originals', in *The Collected Works of Mary Sidney Herbert, Countess of Pembroke*, ed. by Margaret P. Hannay, Noel J. Kinnamon and Michael G. Brennan (Oxford: Clarendon Press, 1998), I, pp. 147–228 (hereafter *CW*); and notes in Boas, pp. 414–36.

[29] Robert Garnier, *Marc Antoine*, ed. by Jean-Claude Ternaux (Paris: Classiques Garnier, 2010); Robert Garnier, *Cornélie: Tragédie*, ed. by Jean-Claude Ternaux (Paris: Champion, 2002). See textual notes on the various available editions of the Garnier translations (especially Sidney Herbert's).

spirit, but because Garnier and his translators constantly engage in a dialogical relationship with classical precedents, re-working and re-writing ancient texts. Highlighting these practices seemed all the more important to us as the crucial links between neoclassical drama and Humanist imitation and commonplacing have often been neglected by critics of *Antonius* and *Cornelia* — which has sometimes resulted in critical misrepresentations of Sidney Herbert's and Kyd's elaborate reading and writing habits (see discussion below). Many Elizabethan readers were actually quite familiar with the sources we trace here, either through the reading regimen of Humanist education, or thanks to the many classical translations published in the Tudor age. One cannot overemphasize the importance of North's 1579 Plutarch, which truly built a bridge between French and English readers of Garnier's drama, since Amyot's text, which was North's acknowledged source, also provided Garnier with much of his material, and some of his actual phrasing.[30] Other Tudor translations of the classics were part of the same literary culture shared by contemporary readers of *Antonius* and *Cornelia*, such as the Seneca translations of the 1560s,[31] or Marlowe's partial version of Lucan's *Pharsalia*, which was only published in 1600, but which was clearly known to Kyd.[32]

Readers will find further suggestions in the footnotes as to the intertextual links established by both translators with contemporary literary works and translations. Echoes in Garnier of French poets of the *Pléiade* (du Bellay's *Antiquitez de Rome* more specifically) were not lost to Elizabethan literary circles, as Spenser's English version of du Bellay's collection, already circulating in manuscript, was published in 1591 together with his *Complaints*.[33] Similarly, reminiscences of Ariosto, of Alciato's book of emblems and other elements of European literary culture were also probably just as vivid

[30] This is clearly documented in Ternaux's editions of both plays.

[31] Several translations of Seneca's plays were published in the late 1550s and early 1560s, and were later bound together into Thomas Newton's volume, *Seneca his tenne tragedies* (London: Thomas Marsh [for Thomas Newton], 1581). See James Ker and Jessica Winston's edition, *Elizabethan Seneca: Three Tragedies* (Tudor and Stuart Translation Series, London: MHRA, 2012), and discussion below.

[32] Marlowe and Kyd actually shared writing rooms in the early 1590s — which allegedly led to Marlowe's 'atheistic' papers becoming mixed with Kyd's, resulting in the latter's imprisonment and torture in 1593. See Erne, *Beyond the Spanish Tragedy*, p. 208.

[33] On the manuscript circulation of the translations, see Woudhuysen, p. 174.

for the Elizabethan reader familiar with Harington's celebrated translation of the *Orlando Furioso* (published in 1591), or with Whitney's popular *Choice of emblems* (1586). Such intertextual references are to be read in terms of the culture of patronage in the Sidney Herbert milieu: Spenser's *Complaints*, for instance, were specifically dedicated to the Countess of Pembroke as an elegiac tribute to Sir Philip Sidney. They also offer valuable insight into the way Garnier's text was 'transplanted' — to use a common Renaissance metaphor for translation — within the Elizabethan literary idiom, and its intellectual, religious and political contexts.

Finally, while offering modernized spelling and punctuation, this edition pays close attention to the textual and material features of the texts, as they were first made available to the Elizabethan public. We have provided notes to clarify some of the more stylistically intricate or grammatically challenging passages; we also document first occurrences — some of which are not recorded in the *OED* — and signal neologisms coined by Kyd and Sidney Herbert, thus underscoring their respective contribution to the vibrant debates of the 1580s and 1590s on linguistic innovation and experimentation.[34] In terms of the original typeset, we have used italics to identify the lines marked in both translations as moral *sententiae*, in keeping with the Humanist printing tradition for moral, and more specifically Senecan, drama.[35] We have also reproduced the original *mise en page*, especially in the choruses,[36] in order to highlight the poetical and metrical forms variously explored by Sidney Herbert and Kyd in their adaptation of Garnier's innovative dramatic model.

ROBERT GARNIER AND FRENCH NEOCLASSICAL TRAGEDY

As has long been established, the source text for both Sidney Herbert's and Kyd's translations is that of the 1585 edition of Garnier's *Tragédies*.[37] First published separately in 1574 and 1578

---

[34] First occurrences differ from neologisms in that they refer to words which already exist, but in different acceptions or with different grammatical functions.

[35] See G. K. Hunter, 'The Marking of Sententiae in Elizabethan Printed Plays, Poems, and Romances', *The Library*, 6.3/4 (1951), 171–88.

[36] Note, however, that for the sake of consistency, we have slightly modified the indentation system in the 1594 edition of *Cornelia* in order to harmonize it with that used in *Antonius*.

[37] For Sidney Herbert, see *CW*, p. 147; for Kyd, see Gassner's edition (*Cornelia von Thomas Kyd*, Munich: Wolf und Sohn, 1894), p. vi.

respectively, the tragedies of *Cornélie* and *Marc Antoine* were gathered, together with *Porcie* (1568), in Garnier's 1580 *Les Tragédies de Robert Garnier*. An enlarged edition dedicated to Henri III appeared in 1582, but it was only in 1585 that the canonical version of Garnier's texts was published, as the last revised edition of his texts before his death.[38] This elegant duodecimo edition opens with a portrait of the author, a dedication to Guy du Faur de Pibrac, and a long poem to the King, in which Garnier praises Henri III both as a providential ruler sent by God to end France's wars of religion, and as a trustworthy guide for his own poetical endeavours. In the subsequent prefatory pieces, the *Pléiade* poets Pierre de Ronsard, Joachim du Bellay, Jean-Antoine de Baïf and other literary figures (such as the late Robert Estienne the younger) join to celebrate Garnier's talent as a poet, a Humanist, and a tragic author. As Anne Lake Prescott notes, the image of Garnier conveyed in this edition is that of an 'urbane [poet], political, court-connected, learned but not academic, and read by his friends as politically relevant to a nation at war with itself'.[39]

Born in 1544, Garnier was trained as a lawyer, and served as '*avocat du roi*' in Paris before obtaining a position as a senior magistrate (*Maréchal de la sénéchaussée*) for his native province of Maine in 1574, a position he held until his death in 1590.[40] In 1585, just one year after his *Tragédies* volume was published, he rose to one of the highest public offices as member of the *Grand Conseil du Royaume*. Through most of his career as a civil servant, he expressed strong support for the Catholic regimes of Charles IX and Henri III. Conventional praises of the divine nature of monarchy and of the role of the king as a buttress against civil unrest abound in the dedications of his works, as well as in his official poems, such as his 1567 *Hymne à la monarchie*, and his occasional sonnets for the 1574 *Tombeau* of Charles IX. Although in the late 1580s Garnier was to become a supporter of the (ultra-) Catholic League led by Guise, his consistent denunciations of the bloody excesses of civil war — especially in the

[38] See note 5. Although a further edition of the *Tragédies* was published in Toulouse in 1588, it is faulty and does not correspond to Garnier's final revisions. See *Marc Antoine*, ed. by Ternaux, p. 24.

[39] Lake Prescott, 'Mary Sidney's French Sophocles', p. 74.

[40] The biographical information here and below is taken from Marie-Madeleine Mouflard's *Robert Garnier (1545–1590): la vie* (La Ferté-Bernard, Sarthe: R. Bellanger, 1961) and Henri Chardon, *Robert Garnier, sa vie, ses poésies inédites* (Paris: Slatkine, 1970).

plays published immediately after the St Bartholomew's Day massacre in 1572 — tend to position him as a moderate.[41]

The development of his literary career is due in great part to his connection with Humanist and court circles. Garnier established himself in Paris in the 1560s and was quickly distinguished for his poetic, oratory and dramatic talent. Through Ronsard, he became acquainted with the *Pléiade* group of poets at the court of Charles IX, and his plays were both printed and performed to great critical acclaim over the following decades. While his early work mostly focuses on Roman history, he also adapted Greek tragedies for the French stage (*Hippolyte*, 1573; *La Troade*, 1579; *Antigone*, 1580). He is mostly remembered, however, for his Biblical tragedy *Les Juifves* (1583), and for his Ariosto-inspired *Bradamante* (1582), which represents the first French instance of a tragicomedy.[42]

Together with *Porcie*, *Cornélie* and *Marc Antoine* belong to Garnier's early experiments with Senecan drama. From this classical precedent, Garnier inherits a five-act structure punctuated by choruses, as well as a relatively static narrative model in which characters are shown to react to events that largely take place offstage. The action starts *in medias res*, and scenes develop according to two main patterns: either they revolve around descriptive or expressive monologues by main characters; or they stage a debate — typically between a key figure and his/her confidante (see Act IV in both plays) — punctuated by Seneca's signature feature of *stichomythia*, a quick-paced, either witty or emotionally-charged exchange between the speakers. While clearly steeped in the imitation of Seneca's drama, Garnier's *Cornélie* and *Marc Antoine* also draw from Greek dramatic sources, especially in the choruses, in which various echoes of Sophocles and Euripides can be heard.[43]

Garnier's appropriation of the ancient tragic model was not without precedent. Following Lazare de Baïf's seminal translations from the Greek in the 1530s, the renaissance of the tragic genre in France was marked in the 1550s by a wave of plays either directly imitated from Seneca, such as Jean de la Péruse's *Médée* (1553), or based on the Senecan model, as in the case of Jodelle's tragedies *Cleopâtre*

---

[41] On Garnier's politics, see Gillian Jondorf's seminal study, *Robert Garnier and the Themes of Political Tragedy in the Sixteenth Century* (London: Cambridge University Press, 1969).

[42] See Mouflard, *passim*.

[43] *Marc Antoine*, ed. by Ternaux, pp. 19–23.

Captive (1552) and *Didon se Sacrifiant* (*c.* 1560, published 1574), or in Grévin's *La Mort de César* (1561).[44] All based on classical historical or literary sources, these plays embody the literary ambitions of the *Pléiade* group: as is well known, du Bellay's 1549 *Defence et Illustration de la langue française* had advocated the turning of classical material into French tragedies as one of the privileged means by which poets could fully 'illustrate' the riches and dignity of French as a literary language.[45]

In many ways, Garnier's trilogy of *Porcie*, *Cornélie* and *Marc Antoine* represents a continuation of the programme initiated by his *Pléiade* predecessors. Garnier seems to advertise this aspect in the argument to his plays, where he openly recognizes his debt to ancient historiographers, in particular Plutarch and Dio Cassius.[46] But he really proves a master of Humanist *imitatio* in his way of weaving well-known dramatic, lyrical and epic topoi — whose origins, this time, are left for the reader to recognize — into the poetic fabric of his plays. For example, the Messenger's speech in Act V of *Cornélie*, a long description of the final battle between Scipio's and Caesar's troops, complete with embedded speeches from the generals of each camp, represents an artful collage of epic topoi taken from Homer's *Iliad*, Virgil's *Aeneid* and Lucan's *Pharsalia*. Similarly, Cleopatra's last words in *Marc Antoine* unmistakably echo those uttered by Dido — Virgil's own Cleopatra figure — in Book IV of the *Aeneid*. Other instances abound, demonstrating the importance of literary *imitatio*, both to Garnier's writing practices, and to the modes of reception it entailed from the more educated members of his audience.

The poetical and metrical features of Garnier's Roman plays also reflect the literary activities of *Pléiade* poets and dramatists in the previous few decades. Garnier's experiments with various metrical forms and stanzaic structures in the choruses of *Cornélie* and *Marc Antoine* are clearly meant as a response to the metrical virtuosities displayed by Jodelle or Grévin in their own neoclassical tragedies.[47] Furthermore, his dramatic idiom integrates elements of contemporary

---

[44] Florence de Caigny, *Sénèque le Tragique en France (XVIe–XVIIe siècles): Imitation, traduction, adaptation* (Paris: Classiques Garnier, 2011), pp. 19–55.

[45] See *Marc Antoine*, ed. by Ternaux, p. 20.

[46] Garnier, *Tragédies*, pp. 39v and 75v respectively.

[47] On metrical innovation and variety in Renaissance French drama, see for example Franck Lestringant, 'Le vers de théâtre au XVIe siècle', *Cahiers de l'Association Internationale d'Études Françaises*, 52.1 (2000), 267–78. Many thanks to Anne Graham and John Nassichuk for alerting us to this aspect of Garnier's work.

lyric poetry, in particular the neo-Petrarchan mode developed in the 1540s by Maurice Scève's *Délie*, among others, and which was still very much in favour in the 1570s. Most striking in this respect is the portrayal of Cleopatra's beauty in *Marc Antoine* in II. 2, which follows the details given in Plutarch's *Life of Antony* as well as the conventional rhetoric of neo-Petrarchan love poetry.

Yet by casting his Roman plays as products of the latest Humanist and literary developments, Garnier was also able to distance himself from his immediate predecessors, in particular Jodelle. As Ternaux and others have noted, Garnier innovates by adopting a more flexible approach to the limits of time and place which Jodelle, following Aristotle, had established at a strict twenty-four hours.[48] More importantly perhaps, Garnier takes full advantage of the static nature of Senecan drama to stage human emotion and provoke pathos, not so much through plot developments or unexpected *coups de theâtre*, but through extended dialogues and soliloquies. This feature, which has long been recognized as Garnier's most important contribution to the development of French neoclassical tragedy,[49] is most visible in *Marc Antoine* — Garnier's direct response to Jodelle's precedent. While Jodelle's *Cléôpatre Captive* exploited the literary and interpretive tradition representing Cleopatra as a scheming, deceitful temptress, Garnier's slow-paced tragedy allows a more sympathetic portrait to emerge. Not only is the Egyptian queen presented as a faithful wife to Antony (*Marc Antoine*, II. 2), but she is also depicted as a tender mother: in the opening lines of Act V, her distress at abandoning her children is evoked in a long, moving, highly rhetorical complaint.[50]

Pathos, however, is not an end in itself. In keeping with Humanist poetics, Garnier's appeal to his audience's emotions serves a clear didactic function. The audience is made to pity the 'cruel fate' ('cruelle fortune') of Mark Antony and Cleopatra, but also to behold the consequences of Antony's self-indulgence and of Cleopatra's despair. Conversely, the spectacle of Cornelia's endurance in the face of public and domestic calamity offers an example of the trials and final triumph of the Stoic mind over the odds of fortune. The moral

---

[48] See *Marc Antoine*, ed. by Ternaux, p. 21.

[49] See for example Florence Dobby-Poirson's analyses in *Tyrans et victimes: le pathétique chez Robert Garnier* (Paris: Champion, 2006), especially ch. 3, pp. 147–289.

[50] Garnier, p. 105v.

lessons to be learnt from these classical *exempla* are made explicit in the choruses, which often adapt ancient themes to a more Christian ethos. For instance, Seneca's Stoic ideal of aligning one's will with the immutable fates is expressed in the unmistakably Catholic terms of the individual's submission to a benevolent providence.[51] Such lessons are also highlighted throughout the printed volume by the use of double inverted commas at the beginning of lines in order to identify them as didactic *sententiae*. This common practice, which was inherited from the first Humanist editions of Seneca's tragedies,[52] is liberally used by Garnier (and his printers) to emphasize moral commonplaces such as Fortune's fickleness, the virtues of Stoicism, the alienating power of love, or the disastrous consequences of tyranny and ambition.

The political implications of such a didactic reading of classical history are made quite explicit by Garnier himself. In the first edition of *Cornélie* he states that the bloody visions of civil war evoked in his tragedy have no other function than to reflect the disorders which France has just witnessed.[53] Through such a statement, which is repeated in the 1585 edition dedicated to Henri III, Garnier frames his tragedies in terms of the '*conseil au prince*' tradition — and indeed, as Wilson-Lee has recently noted, the issue of monarchs listening to counsel features prominently in his Roman plays.[54] Garnier's condemnation of excessive pleasure, or *libido vivendi*, in *Marc Antoine* could possibly apply to Henri III, who was known (and criticised, even among faithful Catholic subjects) for his voluptuous habits and lavish court entertainments.[55] Similarly, Garnier's portrayals of Caesar, in *Cornélie*, and of Augustus, in *Marc Antoine*, as hubristic tyrants speak to contemporary anxieties about the potential abuse of power at the hands of absolute monarchs.[56] Some critics have even suggested a topical reading of *Marc Antoine* as a

[51] See on this point Louise Frappier, 'Sénèque revisité: la topique de la Fortune dans les tragédies de Robert Garnier', *Études françaises*, 44.2 (2008), 69–83. For the Protestant re-interpretation of this theme by Sidney Herbert and Kyd, see below.
[52] Hunter, 'The Marking of Sententiae', p. 171.
[53] Robert Garnier, *Cornélie, Tragédie* (Paris: Robert Estienne, 1574), sig. A3v.
[54] Wilson-Lee, p. 137.
[55] *Marc Antoine*, ed. by Ternaux, pp. 12–14.
[56] See e.g. *Marc Antoine*, ed. by Ternaux, p. 14, but also Louise Frappier, 'L'exemplarité de Jules César dans la tragédie humaniste: Muret, Grévin, Garnier', *Tangence*, 104 (2014), 107–36.

pièce à clef,[57] but the complexities of Garnier's characterization seem to foreclose univocal interpretations.

In fact, one of the distinct features of the Senecan mode is that it allows playwrights — and their audiences — to address complex moral and political issues from a variety of standpoints. With their dialogic structure, Garnier's plays thus stage a number of traditional Humanist debates, such as the conflict between reason and passion (*Marc Antoine*, Act I and *Cornélie* II.1); the advantages of clemency vs repression when dealing with one's enemies (Act IV in both plays); the evils of disordered political ambition; the temptation of suicide vs the Christian 'good death' (Cleopatra vs Cornelia). More sensitive political and philosophical problems are also explored in both plays, such as the questions of tyrannicide and the 'just war', which are broached in both plays, but even more particularly in *Porcie* and *Cornélie*; the validity of providential readings of history (*Cornélie*, *Marc Antoine*); and the related issues of personal agency and free will. In these last two instances, Garnier frames the debate in terms of the traditional opposition between the Stoic and Epicurean schools of philosophy, but he is obviously also addressing the deep political and religious rift between French Catholics and Huguenots — a conflict which would remain unresolved for decades, despite Garnier's sunny celebration of Henri III as a harbinger of civil concord and virtue in the dedication to his 1585 *Tragedies*.

Of course, the decision to translate Garnier was ultimately Sidney Herbert's and Kyd's, and we will discuss their potential motivations below, but their interest in Garnier's theatre should also be linked to the wider cultural context of Elizabethan neoclassical drama. As is well known, Elizabeth's reign was marked by a revival of the Senecan tragic model, at once in the form of learned, neo-Latin drama composed and performed in the context of the Universities,[58] and in a series of vernacular translations and stage productions. First originating in academic circles and published separately in the 1550s and 1560s, versions of the Senecan tragic corpus by Jasper Heywood, John Studley and others continued to appear in print through the latter half of the sixteenth century. They were included most notably in

---

[57] See Ternaux's discussion of Mouflard's parallel between Cleopatra and Mary Stuart (*Marc Antoine*, pp. 14–17).

[58] See Norland, *Neoclassical Tragedy*, and 'Neo-Latin Drama in Britain', in *Neo-Latin Drama and Theatre in Early Modern Europe*, ed. by Jan Bloemendal and Howard B. Norland (Leiden: Brill, 2013), pp. 471–544.

Newton's 1581 volume *Seneca His Tenne Tragedies*.[59] The impact of these translations on the development of English Senecan drama is well documented.[60] It is significant that the first performances of Norton and Sackville's *Gorboduc* at the Inner Temple (1561) coincided with the wave of translations mentioned above, and, while generally following the general structure and pace of Senecan drama, the tragedy was also seminal in adapting ancient themes and topoi to the early modern English dramatic form. In the 1590s, at a time when England looked to France for metrical and generic models for poetry (one need only think of contemporary translations of Bèze, du Bellay, or du Bartas into English),[61] one can easily see how Garnier's innovative handling of the Senecan precedent could prove attractive to authors and translators such as Sidney Herbert and Kyd.

Sidney Herbert's *Antonius* and Kyd's *Cornelia* were also produced in a context of great dramatic and poetic interest in the Roman civil wars. Samuel Daniel's *Cleopatra* (1594) is perhaps the most closely related example, but a number of plays staged or published in the wake of the Garnier translations attest to an increased attention in late Elizabethan England to that specific chapter of Roman history. Examples include a 1595 university play entitled *Caesar and Pompey*; Brandon's *Tragedy of Octavia* (1598, never performed), and of course Shakespeare's *Julius Caesar* (1599) and *Antony and Cleopatra* (1607).[62] Other, non-theatrical productions also focussed

---

[59] As discussed in Ker and Winston, *Elizabethan Seneca*, pp. 1–3.

[60] See the seminal studies by Elizabeth M. Spearing, *The Elizabethan Translations of Seneca's Tragedies* (Cambridge: Hefper and Sons, 1912) and H. B. Charlton, *The Senecan Tradition in Renaissance Tragedy* (Manchester: Manchester University Press, 1946), but also G. K. Hunter, *Dramatic Identities and Cultural Tradition: Studies in Shakespeare and His Contemporaries: Critical Essays* (New York: Barnes & Noble Books, 1978), and Gordon Braden, *Renaissance Tragedy and the Senecan Tradition: Anger's Privilege* (New Haven and London: Yale University Press, 1985).

[61] See Golding's 1577 translation of Théodore de Bèze's *Abraham Sacrifiant* as *A Tragedie of Abrahams Sacrifice* (London: Thomas Vautroullier, 1577), or, closer to Herbert Sidney and Kyd, Spenser's 1591 'Ruines of Rome', translated from du Bellay's *Antiquitez de Rome*, and Joshua Sylvester's translations from du Bartas's *La Sepmaine*, published from 1596 onwards, and later collected in the volume *Bartas: his deuine weekes and workes* (London: Humphrey Lownes, 1605).

[62] A survey of contemporary classical translations, as well as plays pertaining to the Roman civil war, is to be found in Freyja Cox Jensen, *Reading the Roman Republic in Early Modern England* (Leiden: Brill, 2012), pp. 63–69. See also pp. 134–39 and 163–86 on the Pompey/Caesar and Antony/Cleopatra episodes, respectively. Another significant precedent is to be found in Thomas Lodge's *The Wounds of Civil War*, a play about the war between Marius and Sulla which stages Pompey, among other

on that theme, such as the 1587 augmented edition of William Baldwin's *Myrroure for magistrates* (first published 1559), which comprised a tragic poem by John Higgins on 'Caius Julius Caesar',[63] and, although it was only to appear in 1600, Marlowe's translation of the first book of Lucan's *Pharsalia*, which was probably composed in the 1580s and which circulated in manuscript form.[64]

Such an emphasis on the end of the Roman republic has widely been interpreted as a reflection of contemporary concerns about the threat of civil war, and the future of the English monarchy at the end of Elizabeth's reign. Curtis Perry notes for instance how, in the late 1580s and 1590s, English political writings often turned to Roman themes — and the fall of the Republic in particular — as 'a kind of political science laboratory for thinking through problematic questions about liberty and governance, republic and empire'.[65] Garnier's plays, which were themselves composed in a context of constitutional crisis, provided choice material for that kind of experimenting. In the following sections we will highlight the impact of such cultural and historical circumstances on Sidney Herbert's and Kyd's translation strategies, as they illuminate both translators' responses to Garnier's re-writing of Roman history, and their common rootedness in the cultural, philosophical and ideological debates of late Elizabethan England.

MARY SIDNEY HERBERT'S *ANTONIUS*

The Context

At the time when Mary Sidney Herbert proudly endorsed her translation of Garnier's *Marc Antoine*, published in 1592, as having been written 'at Ramsburie, 26. of November 1590', she was almost thirty.[66] These were extremely eventful years for her. She was at the

key characters, published in 1594, the same year as Kyd's *Cornelia* (although it may have been performed as early as the 1580s). See Andrew Hadfield, *Shakespeare and Republicanism* (Cambridge: Cambridge University Press, 2005), p. 66ff.

[63] As noted by Domenico Lovascio, 'Julius Caesar's "Stony Heart": Thomas Kyd's *Cornelia* and the *Mirror for Magistrates*', *Notes and Queries*, 59.1 (2012), 52–53.

[64] It was actually entered in the Stationers' Register in September 1593, just a few months before Kyd's *Cornelia* (Erne, *Beyond the Spanish Tragedy*, p. 208).

[65] Perry, p. 539. For responses to Lucan in the period, see also Edward Paleit, *War, Liberty, and Caesar: Responses to Lucan's 'Bellum Ciuile', ca. 1580–1650* (Oxford: Oxford University Press, 2013).

[66] For a full biography, see Margaret P. Hannay, *Philip's Phoenix: Mary Sidney, Countess of Pembroke* (Oxford: Oxford University Press, 1990).

head of a large aristocratic household, a mother, a respected patron, as well as an author. But these were also tragic years on a personal plane: between 1584 and 1590 she lost in quick succession her daughter Katherine (in 1584), her father, mother and brother (in 1586), and two of her uncles.[67] Her activities as an author and a translator in the early 1590s included successively the completion of the *Psalms* begun by her brother Philip, the composing of elegies to his memory, as well as translations of Petrarch. As Philip Sidney's literary executor, she had also been working on the edition of *Arcadia* (published in 1593), and presumably of his *Defence of Poesie* (1595).[68]

The story of Antony and Cleopatra had already been the subject of at least six plays written on the Continent, in Italian, French, and Spanish, since 1550,[69] but this was its first dramatic appearance in the English language. The story was well known through its sources, Plutarch in particular, and the craze for pictorial representations of Cleopatra's suicide to which these sources gave rise in the sixteenth century.[70] Garnier, who found his inspiration in Jodelle's *Cléopâtre captive* (first performed in 1553), chose a particular segment of the well-known historical episode: the play begins just after Antony's defeat at Actium;[71] then follows his suicide (off-stage). The play ends just as Cleopatra announces her own suicide, after she has lifted her lover's body into her monument.

The translation and publication of *Antonius* was an unprecedented gesture for a woman of Sidney Herbert's rank, especially as it represented a departure from the culture of manuscript circulation in

---

[67] Hannay, *Philip's Phoenix*, p. 59.

[68] There were two editions of *The Defence of Poesie*, one, authorized, by William Ponsonby and one, suppressed, by Richard Olney. On the rivalry between the two publishers, see Woudhuysen, pp. 232–34, and Michael Brennan, 'William Ponsonby: Elizabethan Publisher', *Analytical and Enumerative Bibliography*, 7 (1984), 91–110.

[69] These included, among others, Alessandro Spinello, *Cleopatra* (1550), Cesare de Cesari, *Cleopatra* (1552), Etienne Jodelle, *Cléopâtre captive* (1553), Giambattista Giraldi Cinthio, *Cleopatra* (1583), and Nicolas de Montreux, *Cleopâtre* (1592). See, among others, Richard Hillman, *French Reflections in the Shakespearean Tragic* (Manchester: Manchester University Press, 2012), pp. 94–149.

[70] See above for more on the sources. Cleopatra's suicide was a particularly popular theme in Renaissance Italian and French painting (see e.g. Giampatrino, 'Le suicide de Cléopâtre mordue par un aspic', Musée du Louvre, Paris, first half of the sixteenth century).

[71] For the sake of consistency, we will call the character Antony rather than Antonius (given that Sidney Herbert is the only one to use the latter form, and not even consistently) in this introduction.

which she was steeped.[72] Neither her *Psalms* nor her rendering of Petrarch's *Triumph of Death* appeared in print, but *Antonius* was published under her own name, and, perhaps more to the point, without any of the usual prefatory disclaimers of modesty. This assertive gesture seems to indicate, contrary to a critical commonplace that is dying hard, that, for Sidney Herbert at least, translation carried a strong authorial dimension.[73] *Antonius* was first published in 1592 by William Ponsonby, one of the leading stationers at the time, whose work was to become closely associated with the Sidney circle.[74] In the 1592 volume the play was printed as a companion piece for a work which would have resonated with political importance in the context of the early 1590s, Philippe de Mornay's *A Discourse of Life and Death*. It was published again (perhaps even more intriguingly) on its own in 1595 — the very year of the posthumous edition of Sidney's *Defence of Poesie*, also issued by Ponsonby.

The association of *Antonius* with Philippe de Mornay's treatise is significant in a variety of ways. Both Mornay and Garnier represented leading figures in the contemporary French literary landscape, in their respective capacities as a Huguenot theologian and philosopher on the one hand, and as a celebrated playwright on the other. Sidney Herbert was obviously in tune with current, sophisticated trends in Continental literature. The association with de Mornay also shows that translation for Sidney Herbert was inseparable from patronage

---

[72] The only available female precedent was perhaps Jane Lumley's translation of Euripides' *Iphigenia At Aulis*, which also tackles contemporary political issues, and which stages women's agency within the domestic sphere as counsellors to powerful kinsmen. See Jaime Goodrich, 'Returning to Lady Lumley's Schoolroom: Euripides, Isocrates, and the Paradox of Women's Learning', *Renaissance and Reformation*, 35.4 (2012), 97–118. But the play remained in manuscript, and is therefore not quite comparable with Sidney Herbert's bold venture into vernacular, contemporary drama. On Sidney Herbert and manuscript production, see Hannay, 'Mary Sidney and Scribal Publication', in *Women's Writing and the Circulation of Ideas: Manuscript Publication in England, 1550–1800*, ed. by George Justice and Nathan Tinker (Cambridge: Cambridge University Press, 2002), pp. 17–49.

[73] See discussion above, pp. 1–6.

[74] Ponsonby had just published Spenser's *Faerie Queene* in 1591, and was to become the 'official' stationer for the Sidneys, even becoming involved in various lawsuits with other printers who issued unauthorized versions of the works of Sir Philip Sidney. On relationships between booksellers and the publication of Spenser and Sidney, see Woudhuysen, p. 24, and Andrew Hadfield, *Edmund Spenser: A Life* (Oxford: Oxford University Press, 2012), p. 368. See also Anne Russel, 'The Politics of Print and *The Tragedie of Antonie*', *Research Opportunities in Renaissance Drama*, 24 (2003), 91–100.

and family and diplomatic alliances. An indefatigable upholder of European Protestantism, and a diplomat active in Henri IV's cause, Philippe de Mornay (1549–1623) was also a personal friend of Philip Sidney's, and had been a protégé of the Sidney family for many years, after he fled to England to escape the 1572 St Bartholomew's Day massacre. Philip Sidney had translated the first books of his *Traité de la vérité de la religion chrétienne*;[75] and here Mary Sidney Herbert was following in his footsteps, clearly fashioning herself as her brother's successor in the defence of the Protestant cause.[76] According to some critics the 1592 volume should thus be read primarily as a memorial to Philip Sidney. While the translation of de Mornay may be interpreted as Sidney Herbert's attempt to emulate her brother,[77] *Antonius* could also be seen as relevant to Philip's ideas about tragedy, which only appeared in print in 1595.[78] Moreover, the play's focus on loss and mourning, through the dramatization of Cleopatra's undying grief at the death of her lover, might have appealed to a mourning Sidney Herbert.[79]

But juxtaposing Garnier with de Mornay in the same volume might still seem rather paradoxical. As seen above, Garnier had been a moderate Catholic until he joined the League in 1590. He supported the Catholic King Henri III, to whom he dedicated the 1585 edition used by Sidney Herbert and Kyd. Sidney Herbert's choice might also appear all the more peculiar as the two texts are generically very

---

[75] *A Woorke concerning the trewnesse of the Christian religion, written in French* (London: for Thomas Cadman, 1587).

[76] See on this Roger Kuin, 'Life, Death, and the Daughter of Time: Philip and Mary Sidney's Translations of Duplessis-Mornay', in *French Connections in the English Renaissance*, ed. by Catherine Gimelli Martin and Hassan Melehy (Farnham and Burlington: Ashgate, 2013), pp. 143–60.

[77] Diane Purkiss argues that Sidney Herbert's choice is 'part of her self-fashioning as the sister, image, and literary heir of her brother Philip Sidney'. Introduction, *Three Tragedies by Renaissance Women*, ed. by Diane Purkiss (London: Penguin, 1998), p. xx.

[78] If there was a manuscript circulation of the *Defence* at all, it seems to have been restricted to a very limited circle. See *Index of English Literary Manuscripts*, ed. by Peter Beal (London, Mansell and New York: R. R. Bowker Company, 1980), I, 1450–1625, Part 2, pp. 484–85.

[79] Mary Ellen Lamb, 'The Countess of Pembroke and the Art of Dying', in *Women in the Middle Ages and the Renaissance: Literary and Historical Perspectives*, ed. by Mary B. Rose (Syracuse: Syracuse University Press, 1986), pp. 207–26 (p. 209). Some critics have argued (rather unnecessarily) for an incestuous element in Sidney Herbert's attachment to her brother. See Hillman, 'De-centring the Countess' Circle', pp. 66–67 in particular. See also Deborah Uman, *Women as Translators in Early Modern England* (Newark: University of Delaware Press, 2012), p. 88.

different, even, as Wilson-Lee puts it, 'unrelated by genre and subject matter and indeed so opposed in the ideological position they represent as to make the discernment of any coherent position on the part of the translator very tricky'.[80]

Recent critics have tried to resolve this paradox by showing that both works complement each other in their condemnation of the nefarious consequences of the passions, in particular in a ruler, and their concern with the nature of the good death.[81] Mary Ellen Lamb thus interprets the play as part of a diptych on the *ars moriendi*, and, more precisely, as an indirect application of de Mornay's neo-Stoic treatment of the theme in his *Discourse of Life and Death* — although, as discussed below, it might be problematic to describe Cleopatra's suicide as an example of a Stoic death.[82] Beyond the complexities associated with Cleopatra's tragic figure, both translations in the 1592 volume can thus best be seen as belonging to the wider genre of counsel, perhaps for the benefit of Queen Elizabeth herself. There might be more than a mere coincidence in the fact the Queen paid a visit to Ramsbury only a couple of months after the book was published, in the summer of 1592.[83] This context should naturally encourage readers to remain attuned to the political and religious undertones of Sidney Herbert's text, but without ever forgetting that *Antonius* is the translation of a text by Garnier. As such, it needs to be interpreted in its own terms — not as a completely original work, but as a way of engaging with and mediating Garnier's own text in a creative way.[84] This caveat cannot be overemphasized, for it is all too easy to overlook the play's nature as a translation.[85]

[80] Wilson-Lee, p. 129. On this point, see also Lake Prescott, 'Mary Sidney's French Sophocles', p. 68.

[81] See Hillman, *French Reflections*, pp. 94–149, p. 101 in particular, and Wilson-Lee, *passim*.

[82] Mary Ellen Lamb, *Gender and Authorship in the Sidney Circle* (Madison: University of Wisconsin Press, 1990), pp. 129–30. Wilson-Lee comments that it is difficult to see how Sidney Herbert could have openly sympathized with controversial Cleopatra's plight (p. 136).

[83] Wilson-Lee suggests that Sidney Herbert might have had the book on display at the time of the Queen's visit (p. 132).

[84] Barry Weller suggests that it ought to be read as a 'kind of collaboration between Garnier and Sidney'; 'Mary Sidney Herbert, Countess of Pembroke: *Antonius* (1592)', in *The Ashgate Research Companion to the Sidneys, 1500–1700, vol. 2*, ed. by Margaret P. Hannay, Michael G. Brennan and Mary Ellen Lamb (Farnham and Burlington: Ashgate, 2015), pp. 199–210 (p. 202).

[85] When Uman reads the play as feminist memorializing of a strong woman by herself or as staging a critique of male heroism, these are two points not attributable to

A Blueprint for the Reform of the English Stage?

Even if Witherspoon's early assessment of Sidney Herbert's social snobbery is clearly outdated,[86] *Antonius* is still often read as an elitist form of closet drama, written in opposition to the popular drama destined for the public stage. Yet as early as 1981, Mary Ellen Lamb's seminal study firmly opposed the 'myth' of Pembroke as the ringleader of a concerted effort to 'reform' the popular stage.[87] More recently, work by Lukas Erne and Daniel Cadman, among others, has shown that the two forms should be considered as 'complementary rather than antagonistic in the influence they exerted'.[88] The Herbert family actually patronized contemporary stage productions, and Mary's husband Henry Herbert supported the creation of the company of 'Pembroke's Men' in 1591. Members of the family, including Mary Sidney Herbert, arranged for both private and public theatrical performances to take place, and finally her own sons, William and Philip, were the 'incomparable pair of brethren' to whom Shakespeare's first folio was dedicated. Sidney Herbert was by no means an enemy of the stage.[89]

One way of re-framing the debate about the alleged 'reform' of English drama by Sidney and her circle is to re-examine the assumptions it carries — sometimes erroneously — about the nature of 'closet drama'. This term, used to describe all forms of unperformed drama, seems to have appeared in nineteenth-century critical discourse to designate plays written to be read, not performed.[90] By extension, it has been applied to plays which for many different reasons were never performed, either because they were published when the theatres were closed (between 1642 and

Sidney Herbert (Uman, pp. 83–84). As noted by Norland in particular, Kontikis and Raber also tend to present the play at times as an original work by Sidney Herbert (Norland, *Neoclassical Tragedy*, p. 206).

[86] Witherspoon notoriously described the play as 'of a clique and for a clique' (p. 183).

[87] Lamb, 'The Myth of the Countess of Pembroke'.

[88] See Erne, *Beyond the Spanish Tragedy*, p. 212 and Daniel Cadman, '"Quick Comedians": Mary Sidney, Samuel Daniel and the *Theatrum Mundi* in Shakespeare's *Antony and Cleopatra*', *Actes des congrès de la Société française Shakespeare*, 33, 2015 <http://shakespeare.revues.org/3536> [accessed 1 March 2016].

[89] For more connections with the theatrical world, see *CW*, pp. 37–38; see also *Selected Works*, p. 45. For a tantalizing anecdote about a performance of *As You Like It* at Wilton, in the presence of Shakespeare, see Hannay, *Philip's Phoenix*, p. 122.

[90] *Blackwood's Edinburgh Magazine*, vol. XI, January–June 1822 (Edinburgh and London: William Blackwood and T. Cadell, 1822), p. 448.

1660, for instance), or because they were never intended to be performed, as was the case for dramatic pamphlets of the revolutionary period, for dramatic poetry like Milton's *Samson Agonistes*, or again, for the kind of drama that was specifically meant to be read — which the French would call 'théâtre à lire' and the Germans 'Lesedrama' in the nineteenth century. The term is also often used in England to describe drama that was meant for the private (or semi-private) sphere, and was read or performed in a domestic context, for instance, rather than on the public stage. In such cases, the implication has often been derogatory.[91] Academic and school drama is also often described as 'closet drama'.

But how closeted is closet drama, then, if it does imply a public performance of sorts? It seems that the term is too inclusive, and has acquired connotations that need to be unravelled. It seems to carry the implication that the only form of drama that is viable, or worthwhile, is the one that is performed 'in public', in a commercial theatre, in front of a paying and socially-mixed audience — preferably 'popular' (as opposed to aristocratic). But to categorize Garnier's drama, or even Seneca's, as 'closet drama' in this sense is erroneous: firstly because a play like *Marc Antoine* was performed in Garnier's own lifetime,[92] and written with performance in mind, and secondly because there were many dramatic forms in Elizabethan England other than the plays performed on the so-called 'public' stage: pageants, masques and drama staged at court or in the city, in aristocratic households, or in academic contexts, or in the Inns of Court. Moreover, and although the debate has been lively among specialists, according to Classicist Florence Dupont, even Seneca's theatre was meant to be 'performed'.[93] The misunderstanding proceeds, she argues, from a modern confusion about the meaning of performance: recitation in a public context (in front of an audience) was a codified form of Roman *ludus*, and, as such, perfectly qualifies as performed drama.

---

[91] Jonas Barish, 'The Problem of Closet Drama in the Italian Renaissance', *Italica*, 71.1 (1994), 4–31 (in particular p. 28), Marta Straznicky, 'Closet Drama', in *A Companion to Renaissance Drama*, ed. by Arthur F. Kinney (Oxford: Oxford University Press, 2002), pp. 416–29 and Straznicky, 'Recent Studies in Closet Drama', *English Literary Renaissance*, 28 (1988), 142–60.

[92] See *Marc Antoine, Hippolyte*, ed. by Raymond Lebègue (Paris, Belles Lettres, 1974), pp. 217–18, and discussion above.

[93] Florence Dupont, *Les Monstres de Sénèque* (Paris: Belin, 1995), p. 6, note 3.

The term 'closet drama' to describe 'Senecan drama' in England is thus misleading, when used indiscriminately to lump together various forms of early modern dramatic forms that were not performed on the public stages of the paying theatres. It also rests on a misunderstanding about the nature of continental neoclassical drama. If there is no evidence that *Antonius* or *Cornelia* were ever staged, new work by Yasmin Arshad suggests that Daniel's tragedy *Cleopatra* was probably privately performed in Lady Anne Clifford's household (with Lady Anne as Cleopatra).[94] Alison Findlay, Stephanie Hodgson-Wright, and Gweno Williams have further challenged the idea that plays like *Antonius* are 'unperformable'.[95] When in 1592 William Gager dedicated his university play *Ulysses Redux* to Sidney Herbert, probably as a bid for patronage, he perhaps also recognized some deeper affinity between his own neoclassical vernacular play and Sidney Herbert's precedent.[96] There is no evidence that Sidney Herbert considered her play as written only to be read (silently or collectively), and never to be performed or given a form of recitation, 'in public' by one or, rather, several 'Actors', as she calls the characters of the play, following Garnier (p. 74v). In her version of the Argument, which is substantially different from the French, she adds a reference to the stage, as if she had some kind of spatialized performance in mind: '*The stage supposed Alexandria*'.[97] It is not known what form of entertainment she devised for Elizabeth I on the latter's visit to Ramsbury in the summer of 1592, but it can be surmised that at the very least she presented a copy of the book to the Queen.[98] *Antonius* thus allowed Sidney Herbert to experiment with

---

[94] See Yasmin Arshad, Helen Hackett and Emma Whipday, 'Daniel's *Cleopatra* and Lady Anne Clifford: From a Jacobean Portrait to Modern Performance', *Early Theatre*, 18.2 (2015), 167–86 (pp. 168 and 171). See also Yasmin Arshad, 'The Enigma of a Portrait: Lady Anne Clifford and Daniel's *Cleopatra*', *The British Art Journal*, 11.3 (2011), 30–37.

[95] See for instance Alison Findlay and Stephanie Hodgson-Wright, with Gweno Williams, *Women and Dramatic Production 1550–1700* (London: Longman, 2000).

[96] Norland, *Neoclassical Tragedy*, p. 204. According to the ESTC, in a variant dedication, the play is dedicated to Thomas Sackville, one of the authors of *Gorboduc*.

[97] See below, p. 93.

[98] For a reception of Elizabeth devised by another woman, Lady Russell, also in 1592, see Peter Davidson and Jane Stevenson, 'Elizabeth I's Reception at Bisham (1592): Elite Women as Writers and Devisers', in *The Progresses, Pageants, and Entertainments of Queen Elizabeth*, ed. by Elizabeth Archer, Elizabeth Goldring and Sarah Knight (Oxford: Oxford University Press, 2007), pp. 207–26 (pp. 223–24). For the Penshurst manuscript of the *Psalms* as a presentation copy for Elizabeth on

genre and explore a neoclassical vein that was familiar in the academic milieu, but not on the contemporary 'public' stage; as such, it can be read as part of an attempt to diversify English drama by looking towards the Continent for inspiration.

With its classical inspiration and its didactic and heroic undertones, it is not difficult to see how *Antonius* could be relevant to Philip Sidney's ideas about tragedy. But is it an illustration of the serious, neoclassical drama that he might have had in mind? In *The Defence of Poesie*, written perhaps as a response to Stephen Gosson's dedication of his anti-theatrical *The Schoole of Abuse* (London: for Thomas Woodcock, 1579),[99] Sidney offers a measured defence of the public stage against accusations of immorality. Theatre, he claims, far from being an invitation to immoral behaviour, can purge spectators from evil passions, precisely because it showcases their nefarious consequences. Because tragedy also shows tyrants, it also serves to arouse a horror of tyranny in the beholder's mind. Sidney famously praised Thomas Norton and Thomas Sackville's *Gorboduc* (1565) as being 'full of stately speeches and well sounding Phrases, clyming to the height of *Seneca* his style, and as full of notable moralitie, which it doth most delightfully teach, and so obtayne the very end of Poesie'.[100] But he also deplored the absence of the unities of time and place, in deference to Aristotle, and railed against plays that spanned decades and covered several continents within the narrow space of a performance.[101] The dramatic structure of *Antonius* corresponds almost perfectly to what Sidney might have had in mind: as a neoclassical tragedy that finds its inspiration both in Seneca and Jodelle, it follows the unities of action, time and place.[102] It privileges poetry and narrative: events happen offstage and are narrated and commented on onstage. The play could be said to fulfil the moral

---

another visit, see Michael Brennan, 'The Queen's Proposed Visit to Wilton House in 1599 and the "Sidney Psalms"', *Sidney Journal*, 20.1 (2002), 27–53.

[99] Gosson thought it immoral to show illicit passions on the stage, but was not hostile to reading drama. See Stephen Gosson, *Playes confuted in five Actions* (London, 1582), sigs E6r–v.

[100] Philip Sidney, *The defence of poesie* (London: [Thomas Creed] for William Ponsonby, 1595), sig. [I4]v. On the political implications of *Gorboduc*, see, among others, Jessica Winston, 'Expanding the Political Nation: Gorboduc at the Inns of Court and Succession Revisited', *Early Theater*, 8.1 (2005), 11–34.

[101] '[I]t is very defectious in the circumstances, which grieveth me, because it might not remain as an exact model of all tragedies. For it is faulty both in place and time, the two necessary companions of all corporal actions' (Sidney, ibid.).

[102] See above, p. 15, for Garnier's freer interpretation of these rules than Jodelle's.

function that Philip Sidney ascribed to drama, by highlighting the tragic outcome of a self-destructive relationship between Cleopatra and Antony, and showcasing the rise of a cynical tyrant, Octavius.

There is no evidence, however, of Sidney Herbert's *avowed* desire to reform the public stage as such. The lines that Daniel wrote in his dedication to Sidney Herbert of his own sequel, *Cleopatra* (1594), have repeatedly been produced to prove the existence of a concerted plan to reform the stage, because they seem to point to a whole band of armed pens in league to fight barbarism:

> Now when so many pennes (like Speares) are charg'd
> To chace away this tyrant of the North:
> *Gross Barbarism*, whose powre growne far inlarg'd,
> Was lately by thy valiant Brothers worth
> First found, encountred, and provoked forth.[103]

But read in context, the passage does not refer specifically to drama: it is an allegory of the English language, and perhaps of English literature, in relation to the cultural supremacy of Italy and France.[104] 'This tyrant of the North' alludes to contemporary commonplaces on the uncouth nature of the English language, with its Anglo-Saxon, non-Latinate roots, a cliché which Daniel was to challenge in his 1603 *Defence of ryme*.[105] The passage should be read within the context of contemporary debates on English language and diction, which tended to merge (more or less paradoxically) an acute concern for the perceived backwardness of the English tongue, and a nationalistic defence of its potential for linguistic and stylistic renewal. We know that Philip and Mary Sidney were deeply concerned with such issues. In particular, Mary Sidney Herbert's translation of the Psalms,[106] as she took over from her brother, was an experimental work both in terms of metre and of style, and so is *Antonius*.[107]

---

[103] 'Dedication', *Delia and Rosamond augmented* (London: [James Roberts and Edward Allde] for Simon Waterson, 1594), sig. H5v.
[104] See also Hannay, *Philip's Phoenix*, pp. 121–22.
[105] See Samuel Daniel, *A Defence of ryme* (London: for Edward Blount, 1603).
[106] For an assessment of Sidney Herbert's translation of the Psalms, see *CW*, p. 151, Hannibal Hamlin, *Psalm Culture and Early Modern English Literature* (Cambridge: Cambridge University Press, 2004), p. 96, and Danielle Clarke, 'The Psalms of Mary Sidney, Countess of Pembroke', in *The Ashgate Research Companion to the Sidneys Volume II*, ed. by M. Hannay et al., pp. 295–310.
[107] Cleopatra is characterized in the play (following Plutarch) by her gift in languages and rhetorical skills. Margaret Ferguson suggests that she could be read here as standing for two strong women skilled in the art of translation, Herbert herself and,

Clearly, then, Sidney Herbert was not out to wage a war against the popular stage. Both she and her family in general had an interest in staged drama; furthermore, had she been looking for a literal demonstration of Philip Sidney's ideal of a didactic, exemplary form of drama, *Marc Antoine* might not actually represent the most obvious choice: the protagonists, Antony and Cleopatra, tread a thin line between infamy and heroism, and the moral 'lesson' of the tragedy is particularly ambiguous. In Plutarch, Antony is condemned for his philandering, and Cleopatra is presented as an unashamed seducer. Garnier's depiction of the lovers is more nuanced, and more problematic as a result. Sidney Herbert does nothing to simplify the moral complexity of the play, or the generic tensions between epic and tragic that result from this ambivalence.

'Queen most lamentable': Sidney Herbert's Cleopatra

While Sidney Herbert's treatment of Cleopatra clearly reflects her occasional embarrassment at the rather *risqué* nature of the love affair staged in the play, the lack of critical consensus about this point is a measure of the complexity of both the play and Sidney Herbert's translation strategies. At the risk of exaggerating the creative aspect of the translation, and of projecting current agendas onto the text, feminist critics have often noted that with Cleopatra Sidney Herbert chose a strong female character, a flamboyant queen and a loyal lover — a perspective that tends to displace Antony as the tragic hero of the play.[108] Victor Stretkowicz notes for instance that 'there can be no doubt that its portrayal of Cleopatra as an unwavering and loyal wife, alienated by an Antony who misunderstands her motives, makes a bold feminist statement.'[109] But the ambiguities of the early modern reception of Cleopatra's character should not be underplayed. In Garnier's tragedy, Cleopatra is depicted as an ambivalent character only partially redeemed by grief and her undying love for Antony. Perhaps in an attempt to rehabilitate her, and obviously to comply with French norms of 'bienséance' (decorum) on the stage, Garnier chooses to represent her as Antony's wife. This marriage is mentioned

beyond her, Elizabeth I. See Margaret Ferguson, 'Sidney, Cary, Wroth', in *A Companion to Renaissance Drama*, ed. by Kinney, p. 491.

108 Clarke, 'The Politics of Translation', *passim*.

109 Victor Skretkowicz, 'Mary Sidney Herbert's *Antonius*, English Philhellenism and the Protestant Cause', *Women's Writing*, 6.1 (1999), 7–25 (p. 7). For Sidney Herbert's attraction to Cleopatra, see also Lamb, *Gender and Authorship*, pp. 115–45.

in Suetonius and Dio Cassius,[110] but not in the other sources, which, on the contrary, underline the illegitimate nature of the love affair between Antony and Cleopatra. Plutarch's description of the status of this relationship is equivocal: he points out that before marrying Octavia, Antony 'denied not that he kept Cleopatra; but so did he not confess that he had her as his wife'.[111] While the emphasis on marriage is essential to Garnier for reasons of decorum, it also enriches his characterization of the heroine. Garnier's Cleopatra is thus a learned woman (as in Plutarch), an affectionate mother, a faithful wife and a passionate lover. These aspects uneasily coexist in the same character, and Sidney Herbert's translation clearly shows evidence of tension and anxiety — especially when it comes to the sexual nature of the two characters' relationship.

For several critics, including Sanders, Sidney Herbert made a conscious decision to 'enhance Garnier's portrayal of Cleopatra as a figure of heroic stature.'[112] This they see, for instance, in her subtle revision of Garnier's Argument, which places a greater emphasis on Cleopatra's role: '*she not daring to open* [the tomb] *lest she should be made prisoner to the Romans and carried in Caesar's triumph, cast down a cord from an high window, by the which (her women helping her) she trussed up Antonius half dead, and so got him into the monument*'.[113] Where Garnier had described this as a group scene, Sidney Herbert enhances Cleopatra's agency, and turns her women into mere accessories. Returning to Garnier's main source, Plutarch (in North's translation, as is shown by the word 'trussed'), she also adds details about Cleopatra's reasons for withdrawing into the tomb, thus explaining the apparent irrationality of Cleopatra's actions. The dual nature of Cleopatra's character as a queen and a lover is further

---

[110] Suetonius, *Life of Augustus* LXIX, in *Lives of the Caesars*, vol. 1, trans. by J. C. Rolfe, Loeb Classical Library 31 (Cambridge, MA: Harvard University Press, 1914). This would have been marriage according to Egyptian law, and would not have been recognized as such by Rome.

[111] North, p. 984.

[112] Sanders, p. 114. Raber sees this as a 'sanitization' of the character of Cleopatra (p. 62). See also Lamb, *Gender and Authorship*, p. 132, for the 'suppression of Cleopatra's sexual nature'; and Krontiris, 'Mary Herbert: Englishing a Purified Cleopatra', in *Readings in Renaissance Women's Drama: Criticism, History, and Performance 1594–1998*, ed. by S. P. Cerasano and Marion Wynne-Davies (London and New York: Routledge, 1998), pp. 156–66.

[113] In the French: 'fut tiré tout sanglant par Cleopatre & ses deux femmes, puis couché honorablement sur un lict, & ensepulturé' (Garnier, pp. 75r–v). See Sanders, pp. 114–15.

highlighted at the end of the play, where Sidney Herbert clearly responds to Garnier's intertextual reference to Book IV of Virgil's *Aeneid.* In V. 154–68, Garnier gives his heroine the very words uttered by the dying queen of Carthage, Dido, who was considered at the time to represent at once a poetical double of the historical Cleopatra, and a tragic figure of discarded love. By directly translating from the *Aeneid* in the corresponding passage, Sidney Herbert re-activates the Dido/Cleopatra parallel, and casts her Cleopatra as an example of the devastating consequences of passion, especially in a queen. By emphasizing Cleopatra's status as a ruler, Sidney Herbert simultaneously shifts the focus away from the purely personal dimension of Antony and Cleopatra's love affair, and away from the rather macabre emphasis in the French text on Antony's bloody corpse and the way it is handled. By highlighting the epic undertones of Garnier's source, Sidney Herbert could be seeking to restore decorum — which Garnier's baroque aesthetic often threatens to breach. She also asserts the heroic status of Cleopatra and puts her on a par with Antony, Garnier's eponymous hero and main tragic character. But by subtly reminding her readers of the historical context and of the political implications of Cleopatra's conduct, she also re-frames her death as a specifically tragic event, in a moment that could otherwise appear as the acme of an essentially personal, passionate drama.

Sidney Herbert's anxieties about Garnier's treatment of Cleopatra are apparent — together with her own subtle re-orientation of the text — at various points in the play. Garnier's insistence on Antony and Cleopatra's married status is clearly an issue with Sidney Herbert, and she slightly twists the text in some places to avoid mentioning it. In her final speech, for instance, Cleopatra stages herself as Antony's tragic widow, 'veuve de son amour' (literally 'widowed from his love'); this simply becomes 'without his love'. Sidney Herbert also downplays a number of direct allusions to sexuality, adultery or even the female body. Caesar's judgmental mention of Cleopatra's children as 'jumeaux d'adultère' (literally 'adultery's twins', p. 99v) is thus rendered as 'Cleopatra's brats' (IV. 76). In the Argument again, Sidney Herbert adds a reference to Antony's *political* motivation for marrying Octavia ('*who for knitting a straighter bond of amity between them, had taken to wife the sister of Caesar*', Argument, 3–4), effectively neutralizing the part played by her beauty in the match, contrary to what Plutarch insinuates.[114] While

[114] See North, p. 984.

the interpolation obviously clarifies the historical background of the affair,[115] it also carries moral judgment. As Norland has noted, Sidney Herbert condemns Antony's philandering by adding, in a passage highly reminiscent of Plutarch, but notably missing in the French original, that he '*return*[*ed*] *to his former loves, without any regard of his virtuous wife Octavia*'.[116]

But as both Norland and Hillman have noted, it is chiefly with respect to Cleopatra's sensuality (and body) that Sidney Herbert shows the most consistent line of intervention.[117] Garnier's mention of Cleopatra's 'entrailles' (bowels or womb) is thus rendered as her 'breast' ('A thousand sobs I from my breast will tear', IV. 231). Sidney Herbert fails to translate the uncommon image in Garnier of the dried-out 'veins' ('veines') of Cleopatra's eyes, choosing instead the more common image 'conduits' (V. 125). She thus expurgates the implicit but disturbing image of Cleopatra shedding tears of blood, a choice consistent with the tendency not to emphasize Cleopatra's physiological presence. References to the power of Cleopatra's beauty are similarly downplayed or neutralized. In a passage where Garnier repeats the word 'beauté' as the cause of Cleopatra's demise, Sidney Herbert uses instead a synecdoche referring to her 'face'. Charmion praises her 'lovely face' (for 'aimable beauté'), and Cleopatra's anaphoric repetition in the next two lines sounds, as a consequence, slightly less immodest than in Garnier, as it draws the reader's attention away from her sensuous body to her 'face too lovely': 'My face too lovely caused my wretched case. | My face hath so entrapped, so cast us down' (II. 2. 43, 44–45).[118] Later, Sidney Herbert chooses the noncommittal word

[115] Antony' marriage to Octavia was designed to help stabilize the situation after the second triumvirate fell through in 36 BC, and to secure peace between Caesar and Antony as they divided the Roman world between them both.

[116] Argument, ll. 10–11. See North, p. 986, and analysis in Norland, *Neoclassical Tragedy*, p. 207.

[117] It should be noted that Sidney Herbert is 'emphatically white-skinned', as Joyce Green MacDonald remarks, and her skin is twice compared to alabaster (as in II. 2. 35). See *Women and Race in Early Modern Texts* (Cambridge: Cambridge University Press, 2002), p. 37. On race in the early modern representations of Cleopatra, see Pascale Aebischer, 'The Properties of Whiteness: Renaissance Cleopatras from Jodelle to Shakespeare', *Shakespeare Survey*, 65 (2011), 221–38.

[118] Garnier, p. 83r. The passage possibly echoes Marlowe's lines about Helen of Troy's face in *Dr Faustus* (scene 13), although the play was published later (*The Tragicall History of D. Faustus*, London: V. S. for Thomas Bushell, 1604), sig. [E4]v).

'force' (II. 2. 43) for Garnier's 'beauté', and renders the evocative expression 'frians attraits' (literally 'seductive charms') as 'winning parts'.[119] Although Hillman's judgemental assessment of Sidney's translation as 'flattening and restraining the more extravagant impulses of the original' is too extreme,[120] it is fair to say that the force of the erotic passion between the two characters is attenuated in some instances.

It might therefore seem paradoxical to attribute Sidney Herbert's interest in the play, as many critics have done, to her fascination with a 'heroic' Cleopatra, or even to a desire to illustrate Philip Sidney's ideas about the 'moralization' of the English stage. Even readings of Cleopatra's death as an example of Stoic suicide are subject to caution, as her characterization in Garnier as a passionate woman committing suicide to fulfil her love to her 'husband' and lover rather seems to align her with anti-Stoic heroines such as those portrayed in Ovid's highly-popular *Heroides*.[121] Like the complaint of a new Dido — but this time Ovid's Dido, explicitly staged as a counter-narrative to Virgil's tragic figure — Cleopatra's last words in the play hardly plead for a Stoic containment of grief and passion, as she is shown fainting over Antony's body:

> A thousand kisses, thousand thousand more,
> Let you my mouth for honours farewell give,
> That in this office weak my limbs may grow,
> Fainting on you, and forth my soul may flow. (V. 205–08)

---

[119] Sidney Herbert, II. 2. 332; Garnier, p. 87v.

[120] Hillman, *French Reflections*, pp. 130–31. Garnier's text can hardly be described as extravagant or impulsive, and as shown here (and in much of the critical literature written on the text), Hillman's assessment of Sidney Herbert as 'not up to the challenge' seems erroneous.

[121] Cf. *The Heroycall Epistles of the Learned Poet Publius Ovidius Naso In English Verse*, trans. by George Tuberville (London: Henry Denham, 1567), often reprinted. Cleopatra is not included in the collection, but it is clear that the *Heroides* as a collection of epistles by fictional writing women became models of female lyricism. On English responses to the *Heroides*, see Georgia Brown, *Redefining English Literature* (Cambridge: Cambridge University Press, 2004), p. 44; Michael L. Stapleton, 'Edmund Spenser, George Tuberville, and Isabella Whitney Read Ovid's *Heroides*', *Studies in Philology*, 105.4 (2008), 487–519; John Kerrigan, *Motives of Woe: Shakespeare and 'Female Complaint': A Critical Anthology* (Oxford: Oxford University Press, 2013); and Line Cottegnies, 'The Sapphic Context of Lady Mary Wroth's *Pamphilia to Amphilanthus*', in *Women and the Poem in Seventeenth Century England: Inheritance, Circulation, Exchange*, ed. by Susan Wiseman (Manchester: Manchester University Press, 2013), pp. 60–76.

Here, again, that Sidney Herbert might have seen this as improper or problematic can be perceived in a slight departure from the French. Garnier's last lines, 'mon corps affoiblissant | Defaille dessus vous, mon ame vomissant' ('[let] my body growing weak, | faint over you, my soul spewing forth', p. 108v), suggests a rather indecorous passage from life to death, as the word 'vomir' (to spew out) graphically describes the violent, organic expulsion of the soul out of the body. Garnier has 'my body' as the grammatical subject of the word 'vomir', and he actually repeats the word twice within a few lines. In the first occurrence, Cleopatra's breast is said to spill out red hot coals ('la braise | Que vomist ma poitrine ainsi qu'une fournaise', ibid.) — an image evoking an erupting volcano. Sidney Herbert attenuates the violence of Garnier's image by turning the sentence around: Cleopatra's breast no longer breeds and churns out hot coals, but instead, coals 'from [her] breast, as from a furnace, rise' (v. 194). A similar effect can be perceived in the final lines of the text. Garnier strikingly ends the play on a dissonant gerundive, 'vomissant', an active verb that again makes Cleopatra appear as a Gorgon-like fury, spewing out her life in her excessive grief. The dissonance of this agony is downplayed in Sidney Herbert's version, which reintroduces a more peaceful form of closure. Her Cleopatra is shown as ready to fade away: 'forth my soul may flow'. By replacing 'vomissant' with 'flow', and relying on assonance and fluid alliteration, Sidney reintroduces harmony in Garnier's highly dissonant ending. The disquieting, morbid suggestion of an orgasmic embrace with Antony's corpse, suggested in the French ('mon corps affoiblissant | Defaille dessus vous'), is also softened into a more conventional, if still potentially erotic, evocation of Cleopatra fainting with grief, her limbs 'growing weak' over Antony's corpse.

Even if Sidney Herbert extenuates the violence of the original denouement, her portrayal of the dying Cleopatra hardly fits the usual depiction of the Stoic death, therefore. Cleopatra can perhaps be seen more as an anti-model, a ruler incapable of keeping her passions in check, in spite of the neo-Stoic maxims distilled in the play by her followers and the Chorus. If Cleopatra's death is what drew Sidney Herbert to the play, then it must have been as an antithesis of the good death advocated in de Mornay's treatise (in the 1592 volume), and as an eloquent illustration of the tragic consequences of passionate attachment.

Experimenting with Translation

Critics usually agree to characterize Sidney Herbert's translation as rather literal, so literal in fact that it could 'constitute a reliable crib for Garnier's French', according to Freer,[122] and a work 'almost designed', in Gavin Alexander's words, 'for the intellectual pleasure of parallel-text appreciation.'[123] The Oxford editors consider her a faithful and accurate translator, an assessment echoed by Braden, who describes *Antonius* as a 'meticulous' work.[124] While opinions vary as to the literary value and 'effectiveness' of such a practice,[125] it is probably best to approach it here, not in the light of modern categories such as faithfulness or fluency, but in terms of Elizabethan conceptions of translation — and more particularly, its important literary function in Sidney Herbert's milieu.

Apart from one obvious mistake, which seems to proceed from a simple misreading,[126] all other departures from Garnier show an active intervention on the part of the translator. Far from seeing translation as ancillary, Sidney Herbert obviously had a high opinion of her task as a translator. She seems to have consulted a wide range of sources, as evidenced in the footnotes of our edition. As noted above, she went back to North's 1579 Plutarch — but not to Dio Cassius, as is confirmed by her omission of Dio's name in her translation of Garnier's Argument — to complete the Argument and elucidate some references. She also clearly had her classics close at hand, especially Seneca, Virgil and Horace, as well as contemporary authors such as Alciato, Ariosto (the latter most probably in Sir John Harington's celebrated 1591 translation) and Spenser. Following

---

[122] Quoted in *CW*, p. 150 n. 5.

[123] Gavin Alexander, 'Review of *The Collected Works of Mary Sidney Herbert, Countess of Pembroke*, ed. Margaret P. Hannay, Noel J. Kinnamon, and Michael G. Brennan. Oxford: Clarendon Press, 1998', *Translation and Literature*, 8.1 (1999), 78–91 (p. 79).

[124] See *CW*, p. 150, and Gordon Braden, 'Tragedy', in *The Oxford History of Literary Translation in English, Volume II: 1550–1660*, ed. by Gordon Braden, Robert Cummings and Stuart Gillespie (Oxford: Oxford University Press, 2010), pp. 261–79 (p. 274).

[125] Hillman is perhaps the most extreme in his judgment, as he calls the translation 'woolly' and considers that it 'teeter[s] [...] on the brink of Pyramus-and-Thisbe-like parody' (*French Reflections*, p. 131). See also Lisa Hopkins, '*A Midsummer Night's Dream* and Mary Sidney', *English Language Notes*, 41.3. (2004), 23–28 (p. 27). Norland is more representative in considering the translation faithful but flat (*Neoclassical Tragedy*, p. 226).

[126] See *Antonius*, p. 117, n. 18.

typical Elizabethan practices when translating the classics, she repeatedly elucidates references that might be considered obscure or difficult. For instance, she paraphrases Garnier's 'Levant' as 'the morning beams' (I. 154), perhaps in an attempt to disambiguate 'levant' (where the sun rises) from the specific geographic entity of the eastern Mediterranean 'Levant'.[127] She adapts several classical references, substituting for instance a better-known Trojan river (Scamander) for another (Simoïs) in II. 1. 55, which, although directly from Homer, might not have been so very well-known. Several mythological references to classical gods or deities are similarly simplified.[128]

More significantly, perhaps, she works as a fully-fledged editor. In II. 2 she regularizes speech headings in four instances to reduce the number of interlocutors interrupting Cleopatra, thus effecting an important redistribution of text.[129] This was perhaps motivated by reasons of enhanced decorum, or dramatic realism, given that some of these interruptions are very short, but it is also consistent with Garnier's own practice in most of the scene. Sidney Herbert's editorial interventions can be even more ambitious. In the Chorus of Act III (442–46) she slightly reorganizes and regularizes Garnier's syntactic and metrical pattern, turning the initial rhyming couplet of the stanza into an independent syntactic unit, to match the subsequent quatrain. Another instance of regularization and clarification is to be found in III. 229–30, where she adds two lines to complete a thought left unfinished by Antony in Garnier.

Moreover, far from offering a mere clarification of Garnier's complex text, Sidney Herbert's translation actively engages with contemporary debates on the linguistic and poetic capacity of the English language. In keeping with her well-known metrical experimentations in translating the Psalms,[130] in *Antonius* she

---

[127] Ibid., p. 102, n. 34.

[128] See also the paraphrase of Garnier's obscure 'Edonides' as 'Bacchus' priests' (I. 78), with the help of North's Plutarch; Garnier's reference to 'Canusium wool' is glossed as 'wool of the finest fields' (IV. 398); 'l'onde Canopide' is similarly simplified into 'Nilus' (II. 2. 110). See Sanders, p. 109, and more generally pp. 107–17. Sidney Herbert obviously had a solid knowledge of Garnier's classical sources to do this.

[129] Lines 41, 161, 163, 173–78 and 262 in II. 2 are attributed to a different follower of Cleopatra's than in the original.

[130] See e.g. Hannibal Hamlin, who notes for instance that one of the extant MS copies of the Sidney Psalter expressly advertises the experimental nature of the enterprise (p. 121); and Seth Weiner, 'The Quantitative Poems and the Psalm Translations: The

explores and expands the English potential for a Latinate diction, lexicon and syntax. While she probably used dictionaries like Holyband's *The Treasure of the French tong* (1580), her lexicon is richer and more polyglot than what was usually prescribed. She does not hesitate, for instance, to create Latinate neologisms, some of which are not recorded in the *OED*. This edition identifies thirty first-usage credits in *Antonius*.[131] Loanwords from the French are frequent, such as 'impack' for 'empaqueter' (IV. 287), 'buriable' for the French neologism 'sépulturable' (V. 6), 'frizzed' for 'refrisez' (V. 47). A similar pattern of analogical word-creation gives rise to words such as 'overlive', used in the sense of 'survivre' (survive). Her penchant for compactness also leads her to create striking new compound words, such as 'life-dead' (IV. 303) or 'self-cruel' (II. 2. 199).

It is important here to situate such linguistic creativity in a context of ongoing debates about the import of so-called 'inkhorn' terms, either from Latin or from French, which represented the main languages of translation in the early modern period.[132] While some lamented the 'barbaric' roots of Anglo-Saxon, and thus stressed the need to enrich it by creating new words modelled on Latin or romance languages, such imports also created a great deal of anxiety about the potential corruption of English identity that the linguistic influence thus given to Continental — and worst of all, Catholic — cultures could provoke.[133]

Place of Sidney's Experimental Verse in the Legend', in *Sir Philip Sidney: 1586 and the Creation of a Legend*, ed. by Jan van Dorsten, Dominic Baker-Smith, and Arthur F. Kinney (Leiden: Brill, 1986), pp. 193–220.

[131] The Oxford edition mentions twenty-seven first-usage credits in *OED* (*CW*, p. 65). 'Pell mell', which is listed as one, is attested in North's Plutarch, however (*OED*). See list of first occurrences below.

[132] French in particular figures as the second language, after Latin, from which translations are produced in the period 1476–1640, according to the statistics made available by Brenda Hosington's catalogue of printed translations in Britain, *Renaissance Cultural Crossroads* (<http://www.hrionline.ac.uk/rcc/> [accessed 1 July 2016]). See on this point *The Culture of Translation*, ed. by Demetriou and Tomlinson, p. 5 (although the 1660 date they give as a *terminus ad quem* should be corrected to 1640).

[133] An influential case of association between linguistic and moral corruption is to be found in Roger Ascham's *The Schoolemaster* (London: John Daye, [1570]), which crystallizes contemporary anxieties about the '*inglese italianato*' (the italianate Englishman) losing both his linguistic and national identities by extensive contact with a foreign culture. See Rhodes' Introduction to *English Renaissance Translation Theory*, ed. by Neil Rhodes with Gordon Kendal and Louise Wilson (London: MHRA, 2013), pp. 43–45.

While such anxieties are widely expressed in translation prefaces throughout the early modern period,[134] they seem to re-surface in the 1590s, following for example Puttenham's *The arte of English poesie* (London: Richard Field, 1589), condemning excessive use of imported polysyllabic words, or Nashe's satiric comments in the preface to Robert Greene's *Menaphon* (London: T[homas] O[rwin] for Sampson Clarke, 1589). Philip Sidney, on the contrary, saw the capacity of the English language for compound words as a positive trait, and one that actually aligned English with ancient Greek.[135] While Sidney Herbert does not expressly position herself in the debate, her practices clearly indicate that she favoured a cosmopolitan approach to the English language, one that matched her outlook on translation as an act of 'cultural hospitality'[136] as well as a source of linguistic and literary enrichment.

Sidney Herbert is also creative in her handling of Garnier's prosody. Her choice of pentameter as an equivalent for the French alexandrine creates effects of compression and greater concision than in the original text. As Braden comments, 'conjunctions, articles, and pronouns have a way of disappearing to give much of the blank verse a distinctive muscularity'.[137] At times, she audaciously re-frames English syntax and grammar to match Garnier's metrical and stylistic features, in particular his use of parallels and symmetrical structures. Such is the case in a distinctive passage in Act I in which Sidney Herbert combines Latinate syntax and analogical word-formation to mimetically echo her French original:

---

[134] See Rhodes, ibid. and Massimiliano Morini, *Tudor Translation in Theory and Practice* (Farnham: Ashgate, 2006), pp. 37–38.

[135] He actually calls it 'one of the greatest beauties [that] can be in a language'; Sidney, *Defence*, sig. L1v.

[136] As noted by Wilson-Lee, pp. 132–33. On the debates of the 1590s concerning neologisms and the enrichment of the English tongue, see for example Richard Foster Jones's classic study, *The Triumph of the English Language: A Survey of Opinions Concerning the Vernacular from the Introduction of Printing to the Restoration* (Stanford: Stanford University Press, 1951). A comprehensive study of the actual expansion of the English language through foreign imports and coinages can be found in Terttu Nevalainen, 'Early Modern English Lexis and Semantics', in *The Cambridge History of the English Language, Volume III: 1476–1776*, ed. by Roger Lass (Cambridge: Cambridge University Press, 1999), pp. 332–458.

[137] Braden, 'Tragedy', p. 274. Sanders also comments on Sidney Herbert's elision of conjunctions (p. 111).

So long thou stay'st, so long thou dost thee rest,
So long thy love with such things nourished
Reframes, reforms itself and stealingly
Retakes his force and rebecomes more great. (I. 97–100)[138]

Her fascination with the balancing effects that are characteristic of Garnier's style is also exemplified in the Chorus of Roman Soldiers (Act IV) commenting on the dire consequences of the civil war:

Shall never we this blade
Our blood hath bloody made
Lay down? These arms down lay
As robes we wear alway?
But as from age to age
So pass from rage to rage? (IV. 370–75)

Sidney Herbert follows the rhyme pattern of the French, but employs trimeters instead of Garnier's octosyllabic lines, and for the sake of brevity, resorts this time to native, English diction. She renders 'Republique' as 'state', replaces 'cuirace' with the more generic 'arms', and translates the adverb 'éternellement' as the intensifying repetition 'from rage to rage'. Four repetitive patterns are added by Sidney Herbert, a chiasmic variation on 'lay down' / 'down lay', the repetitive 'from rage to rage', and two polyptotons: 'never' / 'ever' and 'blood' / 'bloody'. Together these amendments result in a simpler, alliteration-crammed chorus, which arguably tends to make her complaint of the people against their leaders more effective than Garnier's original. Such a tendency to 'clarify and simplify' has often been remarked on by recent criticism, and, while her style is still too ornate to be described as 'Attic',[139] her translation does demonstrate a rejection of copiousness. Together with the strong syntactic and metrical structure she imports from the French, and her blending of Latinate and native diction, her translation, attentive to prosody, lexicon and rhythm, manifests the experimental spirit that animated fellow poets and translators — like Philip Sidney and Edmund Spenser — in her literary milieu.

---

[138] Compare with Garnier: 'Tandis tu fais sejour, tandis tu te reposes, | Et tandis ton amour, nourry de telles choses, | Se refait, se reforme, et peu à peu reprend | Sa puissance premiere, et redevient plus grand.' ('Now you stay, now you rest, | and meanwhile your love, nourished with such things, | grows strong again, renews and regains | its initial force, and grows greater again', p. 77v)
[139] Skretkowicz, p. 14.

Perhaps the most notable aspect of Sidney Herbert's practice of translation as metrical experiment is to be found in her handling of Garnier's choruses. As noted above, Garnier's metrical choices in the choruses were part of a movement derived from the works of Ronsard and other members of the *Pléiade* group, keen on expanding the register of French dramatic metre. In the four choruses of the play, Garnier departs from the alexandrine; he mainly turns to octosyllables, a traditional French lyric metre, and, more unexpectedly, to heptasyllables in the chorus to Act II. Stanza structures and rhyme arrangements vary through the play (eleven stanzas of eight or eleven lines for Acts I and II, sixteen stanzas of six lines in Act III, and ten stanzas of eight lines in Act IV), but they follow regular but differing patterns. Sidney Herbert follows Garnier in experimenting with metric, rhyme and verse patterns in the choruses, although in the rest of the play she chooses blank pentameters as an equivalent for his rhymed (in either rhyming couplets or alternate rhymes) alexandrines.

The outcome is surprisingly varied. She turns Garnier's octosyllables into iambic trimeters in Act I; in Act II she renders the original heptasyllables with an unusual, seven-syllable trochaic line. She scrupulously reproduces the stanzaic structure of all choruses, but uses a whole gamut of rhyme patterns and introduces subtle variants. The chorus of Act I thus takes up the eight-line stanza of the French, but complicates the original structure by adopting a complex rhyme pattern that varies from stanza to stanza. Instead of the simple crossed rhyme of the original (*ababcdcd*), Sidney Herbert's version shows a variation on a more complex pattern (*abcdadcb*) — except stanzas 8 to 10 which adopt yet another arrangement (*abacdcdb*). She closely follows the French in the chorus of Act II, with its odd eleven-line stanza divided into two quatrains (rhyming *ababcddc*) and a tercet (rhyming *ece*). She introduces a simple variant in the tercet (*ece* or *ede*), however, in almost perfect alternation. The choruses of Acts III and IV, respectively in iambic tetrameters and trimeters, follow the French rhyme schemes even more closely (respectively *aabccb* and *aabbcdcd*), although in Act IV rhyming couplets replace Garnier's combination of rhyming couplets and crossed rhymes. Finally, with no chorus at the end of Act V, Cleopatra's last, dying speech is obviously endowed with special status in Garnier. This is reflected in the prosody, with ten stanzas of eight alexandrines in rhyming couplets. Sidney Herbert shows her awareness of the solemnity of the moment by departing, this time, from Garnier's regular rhyme scheme and introducing rhyming couplets at the end of each stanza, thus endowing Cleopatra's last words with a poise and harmony greater than in the original.

Far from being 'woolly' or literal-minded, as some have claimed, Sidney Herbert's translation thus reveals a spirit of experimentation consistent with what she achieved in the *Psalms*, and which is characteristic of the Sidney circle more generally.[140] As such, it places her indeed 'at the forefront of reformers of English dramatic rhetoric and style', in a context of linguistic exchange and cultural dialogue with contemporary French literary models.[141]

'Bellona's Bloody Trade': The Politics of Antonius

Early modern readers were trained to read literary works for political allegory. A copy of George Chapman's *The conspiracie and tragoedie of Charles Duke of Byron* (1625) owned by Philip Herbert, Mary Sidney Herbert's son, contains marginalia that draw analogical correspondences between the text and the current political situation.[142] As noted long ago by A. H. Tricomi, such practices suggest 'a *tradition* of [early modern] reformist political drama', partly originating in Sidney.[143] In an age steeped in classical literature and obsessed with civil unrest, the civil wars of Rome naturally offered a major cultural reference, and Sidney Herbert would not have ignored the play's relevance to the contemporary French as well as English contexts.[144] For some critics, the play — and its 1592 publication — should even be read as a strong political intervention in contemporary

---

[140] See e.g. Glenn S. Spiegel, 'Perfecting English Meter: Sixteenth-century Theory and Practice', *Journal of English and Germanic Philology*, 79 (1980), 192–209, and Robert Kilgore, 'Poets, Critics, and the Redemption of Poesy: Philip Sidney's Defence of Poesy and Metrical Psalms', in *The Sacred and Profane in English Renaissance Literature*, ed. by Mary A. Papazian (Newark: University of Delaware Press, 2008), pp. 108–31.

[141] Skretkowicz, p. 13.

[142] Hannay, *Philip's Phoenix*, p. 129.

[143] Albert H. Tricomi, 'Philip, Earl of Pembroke and the Analogical Way of Reading Political Tragedy', *Journal of English and Germanic Philology*, 85 (1986), 332–45 (p. 345).

[144] See for example Lake Prescott, 'Mary Sidney's French Sophocles', p. 69, Oberth, pp. 284–86, and Paulina Kewes, '"A Fit Memorial for the Times to Come": Admonition and Topical Application in Mary Sidney's *Antonius* and Samuel Daniel's *Cleopatra*', *The Review of English Studies*, 63.259 (2012), 243–64 (p. 247 in particular). Hillman sees the political significance of *Antonius* as being general rather than particular, however. See Richard Hillman, 'De-centring the Countess's Circle', the chapter 'Nursing Serpents: French Ripples within and beyond the "Pembroke Circle"', in *French Reflections*, pp. 94–149, and Lamb, *Gender and Authorship*, pp. 115–45.

political and diplomatic issues, with Sidney Herbert positioning herself as a royal counsellor.[145]

The play's emphasis on reason over emotion, and on public duty over private relationships could certainly resonate as a gentle warning to a queen who was notorious for entertaining favourites — the literature of counsel is full of such admonition. But there is also room for a more topical kind of application of the play's philosophical and political themes. Considering the play's connection with de Mornay's work, it is worth noting that the latter (who had already served as Henri de Navarre's unofficial ambassador to England in 1577–1579) was again present in England, this time as Henri IV's ambassador, in early 1592. His task was to try and convince Elizabeth I to send more troops to help the Protestant Henri IV — who was to abjure Protestantism only the following year — to counterbalance Spain's support of the French Catholic party.[146] But Elizabeth was reluctant to do so, as she was already helping the Dutch to fight Spain.[147] For Sidney Herbert, to publish her version of de Mornay's work at this specific juncture, together with *Antonius*, could not but represent a politicized gesture stemming at once from her family's long support of international Protestantism, and from the specific context of Mornay's 1592 diplomatic mission.

In such a context, Garnier's focus on the horrors of civil strife takes a particular relief. Most striking in this respect is the chorus of Roman soldiers lamenting the civil war, which, as noted above, Sidney Herbert re-works for poetic and expressive effect:

Shall ever civil bate
Gnaw and devour our state?
[…]
Our hands shall we not rest
To bathe in our own breast? (IV. 368–69, 376–77)

[145] See e.g. Wilson-Lee (p. 129 in particular), or Jaime Goodrich, *Faithful Translators: Authorship, Gender, and Religion in Early Modern England* (Evanston: Northwestern University Press, 2014), pp. 107–43. On Sidney Herbert as royal counsellor, see also Hannay, '"Princes You As Men Must Dy": Genevan Advice to Monarchs in the *Psalmes* of Mary Sidney', *English Literary Renaissance*, 19.1 (1989), 22–41.

[146] See Wilson-Lee, pp. 130–31.

[147] In 1578 de Mornay had incurred Elizabeth's displeasure by urging against the match with the Catholic Duc d'Anjou. On his manoeuvring, see Elizabeth A. Pentland, 'Philippe Mornay, Mary Sidney, and the Politics of Translation', in *Women's Writing / Women's Work in Early Modernity*, *Early Modern Studies Journal*, 6 (2014), 66–99.

Such a lament must have struck a particularly sensitive chord for contemporary witnesses (or survivors, like de Mornay) of the St Bartholomew's Day massacre, and for a family who had lost a hero to the cause. Of course, Garnier had written the work in a different context, as a moderate supporter of the League in the late 1570s, but this message was still meaningful for England in the early 1590s.

Garnier's lament on the civil wars of Rome could indeed be read in the 1590s as a strong political warning for England, and for Elizabeth in particular, as the ageing Queen refused to name her successor, raising acute fears of a succession crisis — especially among Protestants.[148] In 1594, only two years after *Antonius* was published, a treatise attributed to the Jesuit Robert Persons would suggest that the direct heirs to the Lancastrian line (and therefore to the throne of England) were none other than Philip II and his daughter, the Infanta.[149] In this atmosphere, rife with rumours and paranoia, it is easy to see how the chorus of defeated Egyptians in Act II of Garnier's *Marc Antoine* could speak to the contemporary situation, as they lament their loss of freedom under the yoke of a foreign prince:

But if force must us enforce,
Needs a yoke to undergo,
Under foreign yoke to go
Still it proves a bondage worse,
And doublèd subjectìon
See we shall, and feel, and know,
Subject to a stranger grown. (II. 2. 416–22)

Here, again, Sidney Herbert enhances the original themes of bondage and tyrannical rule through specific rhetorical strategies. The expressive polyptoton 'force' / 'enforce' is hers, as is the mournful emphasis on suffering expressed in 'we shall, and feel, and know' (II. 2. 421), where Garnier only had: 'Et double sugection | Sentons en nostre courage | D'une estrange nation' ('we feel in our hearts | our double subjection | to a foreign nation', p. 89r). Such an emphasis

[148] See Clarke, 'The Politics of Translation', *passim*.

[149] Anon., *A conference about the next succession of the crowne of Ingland ... Published by R. Doleman* (Imprinted at N. with Licence [Antwerp], 1594). The text is more likely to be perhaps by William Allen and Sir Francis Englefield according to *ESTC*. See also *Doubtful and Dangerous: The Question of Succession in Late Elizabethan England*, ed. by Susan Doran and Pauline Kewes (Manchester: Manchester University Press, 2014).

could be read as an echo of the contemporary anti-tyrannical discourse supported by the Sidney circle — as witnessed by Philip Sidney's comment in the *Defence* that tragedy should teach spectators how to hate tyrants.[150] It could also be linked with de Mornay's potential implication in the famous anti-tyrannical Huguenot tract, *Vindicae, contra tyrannos* (1579), which lays the legal and theological foundations for political resistance to unjust kings.[151] But the bloodthirsty Roman tyrant Octavius, whose conquest over Egypt the chorus mourns, could also stand here for Philip II, ever ready to attack England and revenge the 1588 Armada defeat.[152]

That Octavius could be read as a double for Philip II in this passage is further supported by a covert allusion to Catholicism, surreptitiously introduced by Sidney Herbert in the same chorus. The vanquished Egyptians finally prophesize the future downfall of Rome at the hand of a 'barbarous prince':

> One day there will come a day
> Which shall quail thy fortune's flower,
> And thee ruined low shall lay
> In some barb'rous prince's power;
> When the pity-wanting fire
> Shall, O Rome, thy beauties burn,
> And to humble ashes turn
> Thy proud wealth and rich attire,
> Those gilt roofs which turret-wise,
> Justly making envy mourn,
> Threaten now to pierce skies. (II. 445–56)

Sidney Herbert amplifies Garnier here, turning his 'envious spires' ('pointes envieuses', p. 89v) into an elaborate allegorical personification of envy. More importantly perhaps, she re-activates and exploits

[150] As discussed above, p. 27. See Cadman, *Sovereigns and Subjects*, pp. 1–12 in particular, and on the politicization of *The Defence of Poesie* see Stillman, pp. 169–216. Neither Mary Sidney Herbert nor *Antonius* is mentioned in this study of Sidney's politics, however.

[151] See *Vindicae, Contra Tyrannos*, ed. by George Garnett (Cambridge: Cambridge University Press, 1994), introduction, pp. lv–lxxxvi, and Blair Worden, *The Sound of Virtue: Philip Sidney's Arcadia and Elizabethan Politics* (New Haven: Yale University Press, 1996), pp. 281–94.

[152] Kewes, 'A Fit Memorial', p. 245. See also Jane Pettegree's analysis in *Foreign and Native on the English Stage, 1588–1611: Metaphor and National Identity* (London: Palgrave Macmillan, 2011), pp. 29–33.

the intertextual connections at play in her original. In his evocation of the classical topos of Rome toppled by her own pride, Garnier echoes fellow poet du Bellay's *Antiquitez de Rome* (1558), Sonnet 7 in particular. As already noted, du Bellay's sonnet cycle was translated by Spenser, and dedicated to Sidney Herbert in the 1591 volume of *Complaints*, which Spenser explicitly presents as a memorial tribute to Sir Philip Sidney. As recent criticism has demonstrated,[153] Spenser's translation re-interprets Garnier's original meditation on vanity and decay with a specific, anti-Catholic bias. The Rome whose pride and fall is evoked in Spenser's translation is Catholic Rome, the whore of Babylon already denounced in his earlier translations from du Bellay's *Songe* for the English version of Jan van der Noot's anti-Catholic *Theatre for worldlings*.[154] Sidney Herbert's translation clearly echoes Spenser's rendering of Sonnet 7, especially l. 5: 'Triumphant arcks, spyres neighbours to the skie ...'.[155] It also carries similar anti-Catholic implications, as it singularly dresses Rome in 'rich attire' (l. 452), a detail added by the translator which inevitably evokes the rich vestments of the clergy in the Roman church — and the outrage they provoked, along with Rome's 'proud wealth', in contemporary Protestant discourse.

Sidney Herbert's ideological and cultural re-framing of Garnier's play is finally perceptible in the way she handles the neo-Stoic material in *Marc Antoine*. This tradition was clearly important to her — de Mornay's *Discourse of Life and Death* consists of a neo-Stoic admonition against the snares of passion, and a warning against the vanity of worldly life in the *contemptu mundi* tradition.[156] Garnier's tragedy, although stemming from a different ideological quarter, owed much to this neo-Stoic tradition, and to Seneca in particular, from

---

[153] On Spenser's Protestant re-writing of du Bellay, see Anne E. B. Coldiron, 'How Spenser Excavates Du Bellay's *Antiquitez*', *Journal of English and Germanic Philology*, 101 (2002), 41–67; Hassan Melehy, 'Antiquities of Britain: Spenser's *Ruines of Time*', *Studies in Philology*, 102 (2005), 159–83; and Stewart Mottram, 'Spenser's Dutch Uncles: The Family of Love and the Four Translations of *A Theatre for Worldlings*', in *Translation and the Book Trade in Early Modern Europe*, ed. by José María Pérez Fernández and Edward Wilson-Lee (Cambridge: Cambridge University Press, 2014), pp. 164–84.

[154] See Mottram, pp. 164–84.

[155] Edmund Spenser, *Complaints. Containing sundrie small poemes of the worlds vanitie* (London: for William Ponsonby, 1591).

[156] See Cadman, *Sovereigns and Subjects*, pp. 9–12. Note that the original *Discourse* was published with a selection of maxims from Seneca, which Sidney Herbert chose not to include in her 1592 translation.

whom he borrows many of his *sententiae*. Like de Mornay, Garnier lays the emphasis on the overbearing power of ambition and love, and reminds his audience of the frailty and vanity of human life. If recent criticism has mainly focussed on Cleopatra, it is actually Antony who seems to have stood as the main 'lamentable' example of the destructive power of unruly passion for contemporary readers. In a 1593 comment, Gabriel Harvey opposes 'the furious Tragedy *Antonius* [...] a bloudy chaire of estate' to the 'divine *Discourse of Life and Death* [...] a restorative Electuary of Gemmes',[157] thus indicating that the play was indeed read as a companion piece for de Mornay's treatise, but also that it called for a symbolic antidote. In contemporary moral discourse, as in printed anthologies of commonplaces, Antony was often portrayed as an exemplum of passionate excess and intemperance. In a 1598 collection of literary commonplaces, *Politeuphuia*, Antony's fate illustrates the sinful lure of despair, although it is not possible to know whether the compiler, Nicholas Ling, had Garnier's play in mind: '*Anthony*, when he heard that *Cleopatra* had killed her selfe: sayd, dye, *Anthony*, what lookest thou for.'[158] Finally, the popular 1600 anthology *Bel-vedére, or The Garden of the Muses*, compiled by John Bodenham, includes an unattributed entry which also singles out Mark Antony for his passionate unruliness: '*Marke Anthonie* disgrac'd his former fame, | By not restraining his affections.'[159] In Sidney Herbert's volume, Antony must clearly be seen as an example of the worldly life denounced in de Mornay's treatise.[160]

While her characterization of Antony clearly matches such a perception, here again the translation brings the moral point home by subtly adapting it to the main tenets of English Calvinism. In the chorus to Act I that follows Antony's lament on the irresistible power of his passion for Cleopatra, her inconstancy, and his lost glory, Garnier develops the neo-Stoic topos of man's misery and frailty as a mere toy to fickle Fortune. While Sidney Herbert faithfully renders

[157] Gabriel Harvey, *A New Letter of Notable Contents With a Straunge Sonet, Intituled Gorgon, or the Wonderfull Yeare* (London: John Wolfe, 1593), sigs A4v–B1.
[158] Nicholas Ling, *Politeuphuia, Wits Commonwealth* (London: for Nicholas Ling, 1598), p. 272.
[159] John Bodenham, *Bel-vedére, or, The Garden of the Muses* (London: F. K. for Hugh Astley, 1600), p. 164.
[160] See for instance Elaine V. Beilin, *Redeeming Eve: Women Writers of the English Renaissance* (Princeton, Princeton University Press, 1987), pp. 128ff.

most of the speech, she gives a distinctly Calvinistic inflection to the philosophical commonplace:

> Nature made us not free
> When first she made us live:
> When we began to be,
> To be began our woe. (I. 173–76)

The word 'free' does not feature in the original, which is phrased in much more general terms: 'Nature en naissant nous fait estre | Sugets à les souffrir toujours' ('Nature subjects us from birth | ever to suffer them [i.e. mishaps]', p. 78v). Similarly, Sidney Herbert amplifies the Stoic doctrine of necessity in II. 2, by having Charmion emphasize the pre-determined course of human affairs, just slightly more so than in the French:

> Things here below are in the heav'ns begot,
> Before they be in this our world born,
> And never can our weakness turn awry
> The stayless course of powerful destiny. (II. 2. 97–100)

Garnier had more neutrally pointed to how things are 'ordained' in heaven before they happen here below.[161]

The Christianization of neo-Stoic maxims in the play leads to more unresolved tensions, some of which are actually more tangible in *Antonius* than in Garnier's original. For instance, the translation seems to reflect Sidney Herbert's unease towards some of the most explicitly theological, potentially sacrilegious references to Antony and Cleopatra's love as divine or saintly in Garnier. References to love as a form of idolatry are thus discreetly expurgated or banalized: when Antony describes his obsession with Cleopatra's 'false idol' ('son idole faux', p. 91r), Sidney Herbert simply describes how 'her image haunts [his] mind' (III. 48). Cleopatra's 'saintly face' ('face sainte', p. 88r) becomes 'her face' (II. 2. 327); 'her divine spirit' ('esprit divin', p. 88r) turns into 'her celestial sprite' (II. 2. 334), while her description of their love as 'saintes amours' (p. 86v) is simply turned into 'our true love' (II. 2. 272).

But it is mainly as regards the vexed issue of suicide that one gets a vivid sense of Sidney Herbert's ambivalence towards the French

[161] 'Les choses d'ici bas sont au Ciel ordonnees | Auparavant que d'estre entre les hommes nees' ('Things here below are in heaven ordained, | even before they are born among men', p. 84r).

text. While she remains on the whole faithful to the play's classical approach to suicide as an honourable and virtuous act under certain conditions — which is essential to the historical episode — Sidney Herbert's text also mirrors the Christian condemnation of suicide as a mortal sin.[162] The point is made at length in de Mornay's *Discours*, and it is easy to see how Antony's suicide could represent the epitome of the 'despairing' death explicitly condemned in the last lines of de Mornay's treatise (here in Sidney Herbert's translation):

> Neyther ought wee to flye death; for it is childish to feare it: and in flieng [*sic*] from it, wee meete it. Much lesse to seeke it, for that is temeritie: nor every one that would die, can die. As much despaire in the one, as cowardise in the other: in neither any kinde of magnanimitie.[163]

Sidney Herbert's version of the Argument is indicative of her response to this difficult topic. She passes over the details of Antony's self-inflicted agony, and altogether omits the original mention of his servant Eros's own suicide.[164] In the course of the play, she also attenuates the gruesome details of Eros's death, who in Garnier's text is said to have 'spewed out his blood and soul and dropped dead at [Antony's] feet' ('Il vomit sang & ame, & cheut à ses pieds mort', p. 102r). Sidney Herbert smoothes out the rather bold zeugma ('sang & ame'), and simply writes that he 'ending life fell dead before his feet' (IV. 260). As noted above, she also leaves out the very same verb ('vomir') in the last lines of the play evoking Cleopatra's own imminent death.[165] By attenuating in both cases the most violent aspects of suicide, Sidney Herbert may be reacting against Garnier's exuberant, baroque aesthetic; but she also censors out details which could potentially arouse the audience's pity towards such 'un-magnanimous' examples of the sin of despair.

If the ambiguities of Sidney Herbert's response to her original slightly complicate her representation of Antony and Cleopatra, her bold choice to adapt Garnier's new tragic medium for the English public should not be underestimated: this was a new genre, which

[162] In many respects this tension is already present in Garnier. See Clarisse Liénard, 'Le suicide dans les tragédies de Robert Garnier: les influences néo-stoïciennes', *Seizième siècle*, 6 (2010), 51–61.
[163] *A Discourse of Life and Death*, sigs E2v–E3.
[164] See Sanders, p. 108 and Oberth, p. 287, for a similar interpretation.
[165] As discussed above, p. 34.

turned tragedy into an aesthetic, morally ambivalent form investigating the passion of love and its deadly consequences — and made tragic heroes of guilty lovers. *Antonius* thus presents both a moral condemnation and a glorification of Antony and Cleopatra's love. While this had been done in other genres, from epic to lyric, since Virgil's *Aeneid* (Book IV in particular), it was unprecedented in dramatic form in England. The final publication of the play as a separate text, independently from de Mornay's treatise, and in an attractive octavo, only makes this 'invention' more resounding. With the complex tragedy of Antony and Cleopatra, Sidney Herbert was offering to the English public the first modern tragedy of passion, without any excuse or disclaimer. This would not be lost on Shakespeare, who would follow suit with his own *Antony and Cleopatra*.

THOMAS KYD'S *CORNELIA* (1594)

Circumstances and Publication

Cornelia was composed and published in the last year of 'industrious' Kyd's busy life as a public playwright.[166] We know little about his early years, other than that he was born in 1558, and that he entered Richard Mulcaster's newly founded Merchant Taylors' School in 1565, at a time when Edmund Spenser (four years his senior) was also a student there.[167] Although there is no record of Kyd receiving a University education, Mulcaster's Humanist curriculum included a thorough study of Latin classics, Greek poetry, and the Hebrew Bible.[168] It was also at Merchant Taylors' that Kyd had his first experiences with the theatre: every year, students performed plays in Latin and English at court, and it can be supposed that Kyd participated in such activities. He might also have acted in the plays performed at Merchant Taylors' Hall in 1574.[169] In the years

[166] This was how Dekker described him; Thomas Dekker, *A Knight's Conjuring* (London, T[homas] C[reede] for William Barley, 1607), sig. K4v.
[167] A detailed biography can be found in Arthur Freeman, *Thomas Kyd, Facts and Problems* (Oxford: Oxford University Press, 1967). See also Boas, pp. xii–xxvi and Erne, *Beyond the Spanish Tragedy*, pp. 1–13.
[168] See William Barker, 'Merchant Taylors' School', in *The Spenser Encyclopaedia*, ed. by A. C. Hamilton, P. Cheney et al. (Toronto: Toronto University Press, 1990), pp. 468–69 and John Wesley, 'Mulcaster's Boys: Spenser, Andrewes, Kyd', unpublished PhD thesis, University of St Andrews, 2008.
[169] On Kyd's early theatre experience, see Erne, *Beyond the Spanish Tragedy*, pp. 1–2.

1583–1585, he appears to have contributed, this time as a playwright, to the repertoire of the Queen's men, together with Thomas Watson and Thomas Achelley, although none of the texts he wrote for this company are now extant.[170]

As is well known, Kyd's great dramatic success was his 1587 *Spanish Tragedy* (subsequently published in 1592), which attracted much critical attention from his contemporaries, and was regularly performed (sometimes in a revised form) well into the seventeenth century. Its influence on the tragedies of Marlowe, Shakespeare, Chapman and others is well documented.[171] Several other plays have also been attributed to him, such as the tragedy *Don Horatio*, probably composed as a companion piece to *The Spanish Tragedy*, and later adapted by the Children of the Chapel as *The first part of Ieronimo* (published in 1604); a tragedy of *Hamlet*, now lost but probably known to Shakespeare; and the play *Soliman and Perseda* (published in 1592), which Kyd adapted from a French novella by Jacques Yver.[172] But Kyd's literary production was not limited to playwriting. In 1588, he published *The Householder's Philosophy*, a translation of Tasso's prose treatise *Il Padre di Famiglia*, and, as we know from a letter to Lord Puckering in 1593, he projected a narrative poem on the conversion of Saint Paul, which never materialized.[173]

Cornelia was licensed on January 26, 1594, as 'a book called *Cornelia*, Thomas Kydde being the author',[174] and printed by James Roberts for Nicholas Ling and John Busby later in the year. Kyd's name does not appear on the title page, although the dedication is signed with his initials and his full name appears on the last page. The volume was published at a time when Kyd was still under the cloud

[170] Erne, *Beyond the Spanish Tragedy*, pp. 1–2.

[171] Erne, *Beyond the Spanish Tragedy*, pp. 4–6; see also pp. xv–xvii for a chronology of Kyd's plays.

[172] Both *Don Horatio* and *The Spanish Tragedy* were acted at the Rose by Strange's Men in 1592; see Erne, *Beyond the Spanish Tragedy*, pp. 37–42 for a discussion of the links between both plays. On the lost *Hamlet* play and Shakespeare, see also Erne, *Beyond the Spanish Tragedy*, pp. 5–7 and 146–58. *Soliman and Perseda* was adapted from *Le Printemps d'Yver* (1572), translated into English by Henry Wotton in 1578 as *A courtlie controuersie of Cupids cautels*. On Kyd's role in the writing of various anonymous plays, see Erne, *Beyond the Spanish Tragedy*, pp. 200–24; Brian Vickers, 'Thomas Kyd, Secret Sharer', *TLS*, April 18 (2008), 13–15; and Macdonald P. Jackson, 'New Research on the Canon of Thomas Kyd', *Research Opportunities in Medieval and Renaissance Drama*, 47 (2008), 107–27.

[173] Erne, *Beyond the Spanish Tragedy*, p. 220.

[174] Boas, p. lxxiv.

of the accusations levelled against him in the so-called 'Dutch Church Libel' scandal. In 1593, an anonymous blank-verse tract that openly threatened Flemish and French Protestant refugees was posted in Austin Friars, and Kyd was suspected of being its author when 'vile hereticall Conceiptes' were found among his papers.[175] Although he claimed that the incriminating documents were not his, but Marlowe's, with whom he had shared writing rooms a couple of years before, he was imprisoned in May 1593, and subsequently tortured. In the letters he wrote to Sir John Puckering, Lord Keeper, in an attempt to clear his name after his release, he mentions that the accusations caused him to lose the protection of his long-time patron (who remains unnamed). As has often been noted, the publication of *Cornelia* in the early months of 1594 most certainly represents a desperate bid for patronage, at a time of 'privy broken passions', as Kyd laments in the dedicatory epistle of his translation.

The dedicatee of the 1594 volume is Bridget Fitzwalter, Countess of Sussex (1575–1623), wife to Robert Radcliffe, the newly created 5th Earl of Sussex. Both were well-known literary patrons. In 1592 Robert Greene dedicated his *Philomela* to her, giving his poem the subtitle of *The Lady Fitzwa*[*l*]*ter's Nightingale*; in one of the prefatory poems to his 1611 translation of the *Iliad*, George Chapman commends himself to the Earl, 'with duty always remembered to his honoured Countess'.[176] Since Kyd, in turn, reminds his addressee of her 'favours past', it has been suggested that he was perhaps employed by Henry Radcliffe, 4th Earl of Sussex, as a secretary or a tutor in the 1580s, and that his acquaintance with the Countess dated back to that time.[177] Considering that the 4th Earl died in December, 1593, the play's emphasis on '*desolate Cornelia*', a '*fair precedent of honour, magnanimity, and love*' mourning the death of her father Scipio, made Kyd's translation a suitable gift for the Countess at a time of private loss for the Radcliffes — the 4th Countess also died within the same month. Such circumstances seem actually to have motivated one of Kyd's departures from Garnier's text. In Act V, as Cornelia laments the death of her father Scipio ('Mais qu'ay-je fait

---

[175] According to the fragment preserved in Harleian MS. 6848, fols 187–89; see Freeman, p. 26.

[176] Robert Greene, *Philomela, The Lady Fitzvvaters nightingale* (London: Edward White, 1592); George Chapman's Homer, *The Iliads of Homer Prince of Poets* (London: R[ichard] F[ield] for Nathaniel Butter, 1611), sig. [Gg7]r.

[177] See on this point Freeman, pp. 34–37.

d'horrible, helas! Qu'ay-je commis | Pour te perdre, mon pere, entre tes ennemis?'),[178] Kyd expands the passage with four additional lines that could be read as a eulogy for the departed Earl:

Thy death, dear Scipio, Rome's eternal loss,
Whose hopeful life preserved our happiness
Whose silver hairs encouraged the weak
Whose resolutions did confirm the rest[.] (v. 361–64)

The connection with the Sussex family seems to be further emphasized in the second, posthumous reissue of *Cornelia* by Nicholas Ling the following year, with the new, expanded title of *Pompey the Great his fair Corneliaes Tragedie: Effected by her Father and Husband's downe-cast, death, and fortune. Written in French, by that excellent Poet Ro*[*bert*] *Garnier; and translated into English by Thomas Kid*. The title page displays the same decorative knot as the one that appears on John Busby's 1594 edition of Thomas Drayton's epic poem *Matilda*, explicitly celebrating 'the faire and chaste Daughter of the Lord Robert Fitzwalter' and 'the true glory of the House of Sussex'.[179] By displaying a similar device on the title page of the 1595 edition, Ling, who had a long working relationship with Busby, as witnessed by their collaboration on the 1594 volume, must have sought to situate the new edition within the orbit of the interconnected and influential Sidney, Harington, and Fitzwalter families.[180] Drayton's *Matilda*, for instance, was dedicated to Lucy Harington, countess of Bedford, first cousin to Philip Sidney and Mary Sidney Herbert, and a major patron of late Elizabethan poetry and drama.[181]

---

[178] 'But what horrible deeds have I done, alas! | What have I done to lose you, my father, among your enemies?' (Garnier, p. 70v).

[179] Thomas Drayton, *Matilda The faire and chaste daughter of the Lord Robert Fitzwater* (London: John Busby, 1594).

[180] As Juliet Fleming has recently argued, decorative flowers and knots could serve to 'mark a book as belonging to a particular genre or kind, as having come from a particular print shop, [or] as being the work of a particular author or coterie'. See her 'Changed Opinion as to Flowers', in *Renaissance Paratexts*, ed. by Helen Smith and Louise Wilson (Cambridge: Cambridge University Press, 2011), pp. 48–64 (p. 63). On the relationship between Ling and Busby, see Gerald D. Johnson, 'John Busby and the Stationers' Trade', *The Library*, Sixth Series, 7.1 (1985) 1–15.

[181] Drayton, *Matilda*, sig. A2r. On Lucy Harington, Countess of Bedford and her ties to the Sidney 'circle', see e.g. Julie Crawford's *Mediatrix: Women, Politics, and Literary Production in Early Modern England* (Oxford: Oxford University Press, 2014), which discusses at length the interconnected social and family dynamics of female authorship and patronage in the late Elizabethan period.

It has often been suggested that Kyd's choice of the Countess of Sussex as a dedicatee for his translation was but a *pis aller*, and that the patron he must originally have had in mind was the Countess of Pembroke: not only does Kyd translate the prequel to Sidney Herbert's *Antonius*, but he also announces his next translation project to be Garnier's *Porcie* — which would have completed the 'Englishing' of Garnier's trilogy first initiated by Sidney Herbert in 1592. As seen above, this was also the year in which Daniel dedicated his own sequel to *Antonius*, *The tragedie of Cleopatra*, to the Countess of Pembroke. A few years after Sir Philip Sidney's much lamented death, it would have been suitable to present the character of Cornelia, a virtuous matron mourning the death of her kinsmen fighting against tyranny, as a noble precedent for the Countess's public grieving. Such a portrayal would have been in keeping with Sidney Herbert's own translation of Petrarch's *Triumph of Death* (probably composed in the early 1590s), and with the wave of elegiac verse that continued to be dedicated to her in the years following her brother's death, such as Spenser's 1591 volume of *Complaints*.

According to Erne, however, the unnamed patron whom Kyd declares to have lost in the wake of the 1593 scandal was none other than Henry Herbert, Earl of Pembroke.[182] The Pembroke and Sussex families were deeply connected, not only in terms of family ties — the 3rd Countess of Sussex was Frances Sidney, Philip and Mary Sidney's aunt — but also through their activities as patrons of literary and dramatic productions in the 1580s and 1590s. If one accepts Erne's conclusion that Kyd was employed as a playwright for Pembroke's men until his imprisonment in 1593, it should also be noted that the company was taken over by the 5th Earl of Sussex in the very same year.[183] This, in turn, may have motivated Kyd's attempt to gain patronage from the Sussex family. Finally, given the close ties between both families, one can suppose that, by dedicating *Cornelia* to the Countess of Sussex, Kyd was almost certain to attract the attention of the Countess of Pembroke.

---

182 Erne, *Beyond the Spanish Tragedy*, p. 229.

183 See Andrew Gurr, *The Shakespearian Stage 1574–1642* (Cambridge: Cambridge University Press, 2003 [1992]), pp. 40–41.

Translation as Cultural Appropriation: Kyd's Garnier and the 'English Seneca'

Kyd seems to have been aware of Garnier's drama long before the 1590s, and at least from the time he was composing *The Spanish Tragedy*. It has long been noted, for instance, that the General's depiction of the battlefield in *The Spanish Tragedy* I. 2 is imitated from the Messenger's speech in Act V of *Cornélie* — which, according to Boas, probably underlies Thomas Nashe's derogatory comment, in his preface to Robert Greene's *Menaphon* (1589), on those who 'spend two or three howers in turning French *Doudie*'.[184] Nashe similarly mocks 'those that thrust Elysium into Hell',[185] probably referring to Kyd's unorthodox depiction of the classical underworld in the Induction to the *Spanish Tragedy*. But while the topography of the ancient Hades evoked by Andrea's ghost obviously differs from Virgil's authoritative precedent in Book VI of the *Aeneid*, such a departure has recently been shown to represent not so much a misreading of classical sources as Kyd's conscious response to Garnier's own re-writing of the episode in *Cornélie*, III. 1.[186] While echoes of *Cornélie* have also been detected in *Soliman and Perseda*,[187] Kyd's reading of Garnier was clearly not limited to that play. As Frank Ardolino has recently argued, the distinctly Christian and eschatological overtones of the revenge theme as staged by Kyd originate in Garnier's own biblical tragedy, *Les Juifves*, also contained in the 1585 volume of *Les Tragédies*.[188]

Such a long and fruitful engagement with Garnier's drama is probably what makes Kyd's *Cornelia* 'more than a translation'.[189] As has often been noted, and will appear even more clearly in the footnotes to this edition, Kyd often rewrites his French source, and departs from it at various levels. Sizable omissions are rare. Apart from a four-line stichomythic exchange in III. 2, probably removed in order to quicken the pace of the scene, the only omissions that exceed two lines concern two poetic conceits. In III. 2 Garnier evokes the bodies of the worthies fallen during battle, and how they have become

[184] Quoted in Boas, p. xxi.
[185] Ibid.
[186] Erne, *Beyond the Spanish Tragedy*, pp. 53–54.
[187] See for example Boas, pp. lvii, 437, and 439.
[188] Frank Ardolino, 'The Influence of Robert Garnier's *Les Juifves* on Kyd's *The Spanish Tragedy*', *Notes and Queries*, 62.1 (2015), 64–66.
[189] Erne, *Beyond the Spanish Tragedy*, p. 209.

food ('pasture') for birds and fish in the sea: 'pasture des oiseaux, | Pasture des poissons qui rament sous les eaux' ('now food for birds, | food for the fish that row under the sea', p. 52v). Kyd only keeps the first part of the simile and leaves out Garnier's antithesis (fowl / fish), as well as the baroque conceit of fish 'rowing' ('rament') undersea. Similarly, in III. 3, Garnier has Cornélie resort to the topos of the world turned upside down, common in French Humanist poetry, with beasts grazing from the sea and fish spawning on land.[190] Here, again, Kyd omits Garnier's expressive paradox, perhaps because such rhetorical devices were less common in the English poetic repertoire than in the French, and thus seemed unsuitable for the evocation of Cornelia's undying sorrow.

There are a few substantial additions, such as the four lines in praise of Scipio quoted above, and, more importantly perhaps, an eighteen-line nightscape at the very beginning of Act III, which Erne deems 'characteristic of Kyd', both in terms of metrics and of rhetorical skill.[191] The choruses are also frequently modified, with Kyd paraphrasing or re-arranging Garnier's material to suit his own rhetorical devices or his choice of metre. Such is the case for example in Act I, where Kyd contracts Garnier's original octaves to accommodate his own variation on the rhyme royal stanza, and reorganizes the original material and rhyme patterns accordingly (see below). Often, a metaphor or comparison in the original is replaced by another metaphor or allusion. One of Garnier's favourite metaphors, for instance, is the one that compares the battlefield to a grim harvest, with soldiers falling like sheaves upon the ground. Although Kyd does translate the metaphor in many instances, he does not sustain it throughout the play, and replaces it in one instance with a more familiar simile implying native English gorse (I. 217). In a similar vein, Kyd often clarifies Garnier's imagery by glossing or simplifying the underlying historical or mythological references. He erases for example Garnier's erudite mention of Clotho ('la sévère Clothon'), one of the Parcae whose function is to 'unravel the fatal skein of life' ('despecer de mes jours le fatal peloton', p. 51v), and simply refers to 'sweetest death | dissolv[ing] the fatal trouble' of Cornelia's life (III. 1. 108–09). Most of the time, however, Kyd intervenes at word-

[190] 'Plustot dedans la mer les animaux paistront, | Et les poissons flottans sur la terre naistront' ('Sooner will beasts graze upon the sea, sooner will fish be born floating on land', p. 55v).

[191] Erne, *Beyond the Spanish Tragedy*, p. 214.

or sentence-level, thereby operating subtle shifts of perspective that sometimes alter Garnier's characterization, and often open new interpretive avenues.

While some of Kyd's departures from the French clearly result from some misreading of the original, critics have long been rather unfair towards Kyd's alleged 'blunders' and 'mistakes'.[192] As Roberts and Gaines have convincingly argued, most of his 'amendments' should not, in fact, be considered as interpretive or linguistic mistakes, but rather as the result of Kyd's translation of Garnier's tragedy into his own poetic and dramatic idiom. This process of linguistic and imaginative transformation is perhaps best exemplified in Kyd's rendering of the line 'Des effroyables nuits où les trépassés vont', which evokes the ghosts of the deceased wandering at night, as: 'Of dead-sad Night, where sins doe mask unseen' (II. 20). The conventional reading of Kyd's translation is that he mistook the French term 'les trépassés' for its English cognate, 'trespasses' (sins).[193] Yet Kyd correctly translated other occurrences of the term in the play, which shows that he was aware of its meaning, but probably took advantage of the interpretive possibilities made available to the English ear.[194] After all, the image of sins 'masking unseen' by night was already part of the metaphorical fabric of his plays: in *The Spanish Tragedy* (II. 1. 24), Hieronimo exclaims: 'O heavens, why made you night to cover sinne?'[195] More generally, the language of 'sins' and 'hell' is consistent with one of Kyd's most noticeable patterns of 'amendment' of his French source, i.e. the almost systematic Christianization of references to pagan gods and the classical underworld. Thus Pluto's 'shady cave' ('caverne ombreuse') in Garnier becomes 'gaping fire'; and Garnier's generic evocation of the 'torments' Pluto has in store ('tous les tourments de son abisme') takes on a distinctively Christian connotation as Kyd specifies: 'all the plagues that fiery Pluto hath | The most outrageous sinners laid upon' (I. 206–07).

[192] See above, p. 4.
[193] See Boas, p. 417 and Witherspoon, p. 96.
[194] Roberts and Gaines offer a systematic study of Kyd's rendering of 'trépas' and 'trépassés', which they conclude by noting that: 'If we consider all the appearances of the 'trespas' group in Garnier's *Cornélie* and their treatment in Kyd's version, we find that Kyd often chooses to rework them, but that he definitely knows their meaning' (p. 126).
[195] See Roberts and Gaines, pp. 126–27.

Kyd was not alone in adopting such practices: the transformation of the 'horror and pity' of ancient tragedy into the Christian language of sin and retribution was a key feature of early modern English neoclassical drama, and of Senecan plays in particular.[196] As recent criticism has established, this tendency is exemplified in the learned, Latin university plays of William Gager and others.[197] It is also particularly visible in the English translations of Seneca's tragedies that circulated in Elizabethan England. Jasper Heywood and John Studley often followed the precedent set by Erasmus in his Latin translations of Euripides by openly highlighting their interventions in the fabric of Seneca's plays, and they rewrote whole passages (typically the choruses) to align them with contemporary moral commonplaces, or make them compatible with Christian doctrine.[198] The importance of such precedents for the Elizabethan genre of the revenge tragedy, and for Kyd's *Spanish Tragedy* in particular, is well known.[199] In the case of *Cornelia*, it helps explain Kyd's translation of many mythological references — some of them more obscure than others — into the more familiar poetic and religious language of English Senecan drama.

The subliminal presence of Garnier's theatre in Kyd's own dramatic production further seems to indicate that, beyond the circumstantial association it allowed him with the Sidney Herbert milieu, there was something specific to be found in the French precedent. Frank Ardolino has noted that Garnier's *Les Juifves* exerted a seminal influence in Kyd's *Spanish Tragedy*, in that it 'plac[ed the Senecan theme of] revenge within a divine context'.[200] Although not

---

[196] See on this point Norland, 'Gager's *Ulysses Redux*: Tragoedia Nova', in *'Divers Toyes Mengled': Essays on Medieval and Renaissance* Culture, ed. by Michel Bitot, Roberta Mullini and Peter Happé (Tours: Publications de l'Université François Rabelais, 1996), pp. 199–210.

[197] A detailed analysis is to be found in Norland, *Neoclassical Tragedy*, and 'Neo-Latin Drama in Britain'; see also Tania Demetriou, 'Periphrōn Penelope and her Early Modern Translations', in *The Culture of Translation*, ed. by Demetriou and Tomlinson, pp. 86–111.

[198] See *The sixt tragedie of ... Seneca*, 'To the Reader'. Jasper Heywood explicitly modifies the choruses in Seneca's *Troas*. Erasmus had explained his approach to translation, and the changes he made to Euripides' choruses, in the preface to the second edition of his *Iphigenia* (1507), addressed to William Warham. See *The Correspondence of Erasmus, 1501 to 1514*, trans. by R. A. B. Mynors and D. F. S. Thomson (Toronto: University of Toronto Press, 1975), pp. 208–09.

[199] See Erne, *Beyond the Spanish Tragedy*, pp. 80–84.

[200] Ardolino, p. 66.

directly religious in theme, *Cornélie* also re-articulates ancient tropes on the mutability of Fortune, the dangers of hubris, or the relative advantages of mercy and justice, in distinctly Christian — albeit Catholic — terms, thus providing a textual and cultural intermediary between classical tragedy and the early modern imagination. As Hillman has pointed out, Garnier offered Elizabethan playwrights an important precedent for the 'skewing of Seneca to incorporate [contemporary] anxieties, both political and metaphysical'.[201] More specifically, through his connection with the *Pléiade* poets and other contemporary French Humanists, Garnier was closely engaged in the early modern neo-Stoic movement, whose aim was precisely to reconcile ancient Stoicism — as exemplified in Cicero's and Seneca's philosophical writings — and Christian doctrine.[202] While Elizabethan translators of Seneca often had to heavily edit the original text in order to make it relevant, or even acceptable, to the English reader, Kyd's evocation of 'sins', 'heaven' and 'hell', only furthered and amplified a process of cultural adaptation — and more specifically, the Christianizing of ancient themes — that was already at work in the French source.[203]

Another feature in Garnier that converged with the early modern English reception of Senecan drama was his strong emphasis on moral *exempla*. Following common practice in early modern editions of Seneca, and, perhaps more pointedly, the precedent established by Sidney Herbert's *Antonius*, both editions of *Cornelia* use italics to indicate didactic *sententiae*. Again, Kyd highlights the moral applications of the text by adapting some of the original commonplaces with the help of contemporary English cultural references. In III. 2, instead of Garnier's tale, taken from Aeschylus, of the shepherd who reared a wolf cub, Kyd mentions Aesop's fable of the farmer and

[201] Hillman, 'French Accents', p. 242. See also *French Origins* for further parallels between Garnier's historical plays and English Senecan drama, especially *Gorboduc* (p. 38).

[202] See on this point Cadman, who also notes the pivotal role of France as the European centre of Humanist neo-Stoicism (*Sovereigns and Subjects*, pp. 47–49), or Liénard. Lazare de Baïf, who signs one of the laudatory poems in the 1585 *Tragédies*, was also well-known for his attempt to integrate the ancient tragic model with Christian themes.

[203] Note also that when compared to contemporary translations of Seneca's tragedies, Kyd's departures from the French original are minor, a fact overlooked by earlier editors and commentators, especially Boas and Witherspoon, who ignored early modern approaches to translation and favoured a Romantic-inspired focus on literal accuracy.

the snake, which was certainly more familiar to the Elizabethan public.[204] Similarly, Garnier's somewhat erudite evocation of 'boules mouvantes' in reference to the rotation of the planets in the chorus to Act II is rendered by a more pedestrian comparison to a game of bowls, a popular pastime in Tudor England, and one that was commonly alluded to in Elizabethan plays.[205] There are also many echoes of the Geneva Bible to be found in Kyd's *Cornelia*: see for example his rendering of Garnier's 'sur la terre globeuse' ('on the earth's globe') as 'underneath the sun' in Act II (252), or the maxims '*Judge others as thou wouldst be judged again;* | *And do but as thou wouldst be done unto*', in the chorus to Act I (128–29).[206] In Act V, Kyd combines Garnier's evocation of Orestes, a classical topos for remorse, with a Christian focus on the 'remembrance of our former sins' originating, not in the French source, but most probably in the *Book of Common Prayer*'s order of the Holy Communion:

> As when Alecto in the lowest hell
> Doth breathe new heat within Orestes' breast,
> Till outward rage with inward grief begins,
> A fresh remembrance of our former sins. (V. 225–28)[207]

Such devices pertain to the process of cultural translation that sprang directly from the didactic reading and re-casting of classical sources and literary commonplaces as moral examples for the English audience to ponder and follow.[208]

---

[204] Aesop's fables were part of the Elizabethan school curriculum. See Peter Mack, *Elizabethan Rhetoric: Theory and Practice* (Cambridge: Cambridge University Press, 2004), p. 35.

[205] It can be found, for example, in Shakespeare's *Richard II* (III. 3) or, later, in John Webster's *The White Devil* (I. 2). In Webster's *The Duchess of Malfi*, Bosola compares fate to a game of tennis by likening men to 'the starres tennys-balls' (*The Tragedy of the Dutchesse of Malfy* [London: Nicholas Okes for John Waterson, 1623], p. 94).

[206] Compare with Matthew 7. 2: 'For with what judgment ye judge, ye shall be judged' and 7. 12: 'therefore whatsoever ye would that men should do to you: even so do ye to them' (Geneva Bible). Garnier has: '[les Dieux] veulent que l'on juge un autre par soymesme | Et comme nous ferons qu'on nous face de mesme' ('[the Gods] want us to judge others as we would ourselves, | and, as we will treat others, so to be treated in our turn', p. 42r).

[207] Compare with the wording of the 'General Confession' in the 1559 *Book of Common Prayer*: 'the remembrance of them [our sins] is grievous unto us; the burden of them is intolerable'.

[208] As Norland puts it, English translators 'read Seneca through Christian eyes, which led them to omit pagan ritual and occasionally to introduce Christian doctrine as they

'Desolate Cornelia': Pathos and Exemplarity

As noted above, a distinctive character of Garnier's play is its static plot, and its primary emphasis on declamation rather than onstage action. Following Cicero's long speech in Act I lamenting the end of the Republic, Act II thus foregrounds Cornelia's own complaint on the death of Pompey, whom she wishes to join in death. Act III opens on a similar note, with a first scene showing Cornelia and the Chorus debating the themes of Fortune and heaven's indifference to human suffering, and a second scene staging her despair and thirst for revenge at the arrival of Pompey's former attendant carrying his ashes. Act IV is dominated by political themes, with Brutus and Cassius discussing Caesar's ambitious rise to power, and the legitimacy of tyrannicide in such cases, before giving way to Caesar's own triumphant exchanges with Antony. Act V reverts to Cornelia's perspective, as she hears news of the defeat of Pompey's camp led by her father Scipio, whose suicide she mourns, and briefly thinks of emulating; she finally decides to live, both to honour his memory and to see him avenged.

As a direct consequence of Garnier's own focus on the eponymous character, it is generally agreed that one of the main contributions made by Kyd's *Cornelia* to Elizabethan drama is 'the portrayal of emotion', both through the play's sustained focus on its main character, and through the staging of 'various interlocutors [whose interactions with Cornelia] provide a model for the depiction of emotional responses'.[209] Garnier's emphasis on Cornelia's suffering and endurance is highlighted in Kyd's dedication, where he presents the Roman heroine as a '*fair precedent of honour, magnanimity, and love*'.[210] He further underscores her exemplarity in the Argument of the play by developing Garnier's reference to 'la misérable Cornélie' into '*this most fair and miserable lady*'.[211] The portrayal of Cornelia as an example of virtue obviously has to do with the didactic reading of the tragedy expected in an early modern context, as well as with the dedication of the translation to the Countess of Sussex; but Kyd

interpret particular figures and situations as "mirrors" or cautionary exempla of morality' (*Neoclassical Tragedy*, p. 67).

209 Norland, *Neoclassical Tragedy*, p. 233. See also his 'Englishing Garnier: Mary Sidney's *Antonie* and Daniel's *Cleopatra*', in *Tudor Theatre: Emotion in the Theatre / L'Émotion au théâtre*, ed. by André Lascombes (Bern: Peter Lang, 1996), pp. 159–76.

210 Dedication, l. 15.

211 The Argument, l. 33.

also facilitates the audience's empathy with '*desolate Cornelia*' by effectively responding to Garnier's poetics of pathos. Cornelia's opening speech in Act II retains the highly rhetorical features of its original, replicating its anaphoric structure and embedded clauses, and expanding on Garnier's allusion to Cornelia's successive husbands (Crassus and Pompey), not so much for the sake of clarification as for rhetorical and pathetic effect:

And will ye needs bedew my dead-grown joys
[...]
O eyes, and will ye ('cause I cannot dry
Your ceaseless springs), not suffer me to die?
[...]
O then, shall wretched I — that am but one,
Yet once both theirs — survive, now they are gone?
(II. 1–4, 29–30)

Similar effects can be found in Cornelia's response to the news of Scipio's death in Act V, with Kyd not unexpectedly turning to familiar rhetorical topoi and metaphors ('my enflamed blood' for 'mon sang', p. 70v),[212] and stressing the theme of revenge ('to venge this outrage, or revenge my wrongs') where Garnier has Cornelia contemplate death ('ou pour clore mes jours', 'or to close my days', ibid.):

O miserable, desolate, distressful wretch,
Worn with mishaps, yet in mishaps abounding!
What shall I do, or whither shall I fly
To venge this outrage, or revenge my wrongs?
Come, wrathful Furies with your ebon locks,
And feed yourselves with mine enflamèd blood! (V. 338–43)

Finally, where Garnier's text seemed to offer the full range of the poetics of grief, from mourning to despair, and from revenge to virtuous resolution, Kyd actually provides a new, lyric dimension to the staging of Cornelia's 'desolation' in an eighteen-verse addition at the beginning of Act III. The passage is set apart from the rest of the text by its original metrical structure (as discussed below), as well as its flowing verse and skilful handling of anaphora ('Whose mournful passions dull the morning joys | Whose sweeter sleeps are turned to

[212] Compare with Hieronimo's 'enflamed thoughts' in *The Spanish Tragedy*, III. 2. 18.

fearful dreams | And whose first fortunes …', III. 1. 15–17) and anadiplosis ('dews him with her tears, | Sweet tears of love, remembrancers to time; | Time past with me …', III. 1. 12–14).[213] It also subtly interweaves mythological references ('Cynthia', 'Clitie', 'Cytherea') with homely English imagery ('the cheerful cock', 'the country wench', 'remembrancers').

However rhetorically and poetically artful such passages may be, the portrayal of emotion cannot be dissociated from its didactic function; and Cornelia's outbursts of grief are used to address common topics of moral philosophy. For example, Cicero, who in Act II advises Cornelia not to 'transpose' (i.e. get beside) herself with grief, stands — somewhat expectedly — as a stern moralist. In an exchange that rehearses the main tenets of Stoicism and simultaneously echoes Cicero's own writings and Horace's moral odes, he answers Cornelia's death wish by advocating the virtues of constancy and steadfastness, and by emphasizing the Stoic (and Christian) principle of conforming one's mind to divine will: '*Death's always ready, and our time is known | To be at heav'n's dispose, and not our own*' (II. 288–89).[214] Similarly, in Act III, the Chorus's attempt to mitigate Cornelia's despair as she narrates her encounter with Pompey's ghost takes the shape of the common philosophical debate on the nature of dreams, with the material essence of Pompey's ghost being dismissed by the Chorus as a trick played by devilish spirits on 'pensive minds': '*To pensive minds deceived with their shadows, | They counterfeit the dead in voice and figure, | Divining of our future miseries*' (III. 1. 131–33).

The didactic nature of such passages is underscored by the use of italics and by the choruses, which, according to the Senecan model, rehearse and clarify the lessons to be derived from such philosophically complex exchanges. Kyd also intervenes by using couplets, instead of blank verse, to help identify didactic passages (as above), and even sometimes by altering the very fabric of the text. In the chorus to Act I, which focuses on the fickleness of Fortune and the rise and fall of the great, he departs from Garnier in order to combine the Stoic notion of *ataraxia*, or freedom from all human passions, with a moralizing emphasis on 'chasten[ing one's] desire':

[213] Erne (*Beyond the Spanish Tragedy*, p. 71) identifies a similar use of anadiplosis in *The Spanish Tragedy*, II. 1. 119–29.

[214] On Garnier and French neo-Stoicism, see above, pp. 57–58.

'He lives more quietly whose rest is made, | And can with reason chasten his desire' (151–2).[215]

Cornelia's own virtues in her various capacities as a widow, a mother, and a daughter are also emphasized throughout the play, which ends on her decision to live on in spite of her many losses, thus casting her as an example of female fortitude. Garnier's characterization does not, however, restrict her to the domestic sphere. As noted above, one of Garnier's major (if unacknowledged) sources is Lucan's *Pharsalia*, in which Cornelia rises to epic status through two major speeches (in *Pharsalia* VIII. 639–61 and IX. 55–109, respectively) which echo Lucan's own description of Pompey's defeat as a political catastrophe of cataclysmic magnitude. Cornelia's lament on her 'secret cross' in Act II (61–64) is clearly indebted to Lucan, as is her mention of the jealousy of Pompey's first wife, Julia, in Act V (374–77). Virgil's *Aeneid* also provides an important subtext for Cornelia's evocation of Pompey's death in Act II (186–90), and for her account of his ghost's apparition in III. 1 (75–105), which are respectively modelled on Aeneas' descriptions of the ghosts of Creusa and of Hector in Book II of the *Aeneid*.

The epic undertones of Garnier's tragedy are not lost on Kyd, who is known to have drawn on similar sources for his *Spanish Tragedy*.[216] In fact, he tends to throw such intertextual and intergeneric connections into relief. For example, he frames Cornelia's report of Pompey's assassination with the added exclamation, 'grief to hear, and hell for me to speak' (II. 201), which is not in the original, but echoes Virgil's 'horresco referens' ('I shudder at the words'), as uttered by Aeneas in his tale of the fall of Troy (*Aeneid*, II. 204). Kyd also follows Garnier in ending the ghost's speech, as reported by Cornelia in III. 1, with the traditional formula 'he said', usually used in epic poetry to conclude embedded speeches.[217] Finally, he shows his alertness to Garnier's epic subtext in the Messenger's speech in Act V, by sometimes departing from the French original to follow its classical sources instead — more than once borrowing from Christopher Marlowe's translation of *Pharsalia* I. Such poetical allusions have significant political implications (which are discussed

[215] Compare with Garnier: 'Celuy commande plus, qui vit du sien contant' ('He has more power, who can be content with his lot', p. 42r).

[216] Eugene Hill, 'Senecan and Virgilian Perspectives in *The Spanish Tragedy*', *English Literary Renaissance*, 15 (1985), 143–65.

[217] See also V. 147: 'This said.' (Garnier: 'Ainsi dist', p. 67v).

below), but they are also important in terms of characterization, as they add a further dimension to the staging of 'desolate' Cornelia's grief. Recent criticism has indeed tended to limit Kyd's rendering of Cornelia's tragic figure to the representation of human emotions, which is in keeping with the traditional association of *Cornelia* with domestically (and female-) oriented 'closet-drama'. Yet a closer look at his translation strategies shows how Kyd consistently highlights Cornelia's heroic stature, and frames her grief in the very terms of Garnier's classical epic sources. This in turn reveals a richer engagement than has been hitherto noticed on Kyd's part, not only with Garnier's elaborate practices of literary composition and imitation, but also with the political undertones of the play, as the audience is constantly reminded of the heroine's association with the great epic poems on the rise and fall of Rome.[218]

Linguistic and Metrical Innovation in Cornelia

While deeply rooted in the literary, intellectual and ideological contexts of its time, Kyd's translation is also linguistically and metrically innovative. Such aspects have often been discussed in the case of Sidney Herbert's own translation — because of her well-known interest in metrical experimentation, as noted above — but they have rarely been noticed in relation to Kyd.[219] Only recently has Erne pointed to the quality of Kyd's versification, which he considers more mature than in Kyd's earliest plays, in which, he notes, the verse is usually 'heavily end-stopped'.[220] In *Cornelia* Kyd shows great versatility in dealing with Garnier's often metrically and grammatically intricate sentences. Sometimes he enhances the dramatic effect of Garnier's style by turning long, run-on sentences into terse, pithy statements, as is the case in Cicero's opening monologue, for instance (see in particular I. 34–37). At other times he exploits the expressive potential afforded by run-on lines to enhance Cornelia's laments (as noted above); to support the rhetorical efficacy of embedded speeches (see for example Scipio's speech,

---

[218] These are explored in further detail in Belle, '"Comme espics dans les plaines": Patterns of Translation of Robert Garnier's Epic Similes in Thomas Kyd's *Cornelia* (1594)', *Renaissance and Reformation*, 40.3 (2017), forthcoming.

[219] At least in the plays' modern reception; see below.

[220] Erne, *Beyond the Spanish Tragedy*, p. 210. Note however that Kyd had already integrated the Senecan feature of stichomythia in his dramatic idiom, and he shows again his mastery of the device in *Cornelia* (with a few exceptions: he clearly uses 'you know' as a filler in IV. 1. 99 and IV. 2. 125).

v. 112–18); or to convey a sense of confusion, as in the Messenger's account of the battle in Act v.[221]

Like Sidney Herbert, Kyd also innovates in his rendering of Garnier's choruses, which are composed in a variety of metrical forms. Following Garnier, Kyd departs in those passages from the usual narrative verse — i.e. blank verse for Kyd as an equivalent for Garnier's alexandrines. While the rhyme schemes in the English choruses often vary from those of the original, Kyd offers a consistent adaptation of Garnier's syllabic metre into English accented forms. Octosyllables are usually rendered as iambic tetrameters, and the alternating octosyllabics and hexasyllables in the five-line stanzas of the Act III chorus are translated in a matching pattern of alternating iambic tetrameters and dimeters. In the latter case, while Garnier's stanza was quite commonly employed in French lyric poetry,[222] such a pattern was almost unprecedented in England.[223] Kyd's experimental approach to metrics is also illustrated in the chorus to Act I, where he compresses Garnier's eight-verse octosyllabic stanzas into an uncommon variation on the rhyme royal stanza. Instead of adopting the usual *ababbcc* rhyme pattern, Kyd creates an enclosed rhyme quatrain (*ababccb*), thus at once adding to the majesty of the rhythm by slowing down the end of the stanza, and integrating Garnier's own ending rhyme pattern (*ababcddc*) into the native English form. Another instance of metrical innovation is to be found at the beginning of Act III, where, as noted above, Kyd's added eighteen lines blend with the six lines given to Cornelia by Garnier, to create an almost self-contained complaint in a rare variety of sextets combining blank verse quatrains with rhyming couplets.

Such examples of metrical variety and innovation are unmatched in any of Kyd's plays, which tends to demonstrate that he was aware, not only of Garnier's own metrical innovations, but of the metrical virtuosity displayed by Sidney Herbert in *Antonius* as well as in the Psalm translations. But his choice of metre and his skilful handling

[221] See for example, v. 183–87: 'Bellona fired with a quenchless rage | Runs up and down', etc.

[222] See Philippe Martinon, *Les Strophes: étude historique et critique sur les formes de la poésie lyrique en France depuis la Renaissance* (Geneva and Paris: Slatkine, 1989), pp. 194–95.

[223] A similar combination — although with a different arrangement of lines — is to be found, for example, in Philip Sidney's translation of Psalm 38. One of Daniel's choruses in *Cleopatra* (1594) also features irregular metre, but he uses the much more common ballad metre, combining tetrameters and trimeters.

of verse-forms to match the diverse themes and moods expressed in the choruses show that, rather than simply replicating or adapting Garnier's metrical forms, he used them to dramatic purposes, thus exploiting to the full the resources afforded by the French model of Senecan tragedy.

Another feature that aligns Kyd's translation with contemporary efforts to enrich the English literary repertoire — including Sidney Herbert's precedent — is the amount of word-creation that results from his 'Englishing' of Garnier. Although his translation style, as noted, is quite different from that of the Countess, similar patterns are discernible. Kyd coins a number of English equivalents to more or less transparent French words, for instance 'linsel' (from 'linceuil', or shroud) or 'souspirable' (literally from the French: worth sighing over, i.e. lamentable).[224] Like Sidney Herbert, he favours compound words, perhaps because they facilitate the compression of Garnier's sense that a blank-verse translation necessitates, like 'dead-grown', 'slow-paced' or 'swift-foot' (the latter being used as an adjective). Intensive prefixes are also used, as in 'surcloy' or 'overmourn'. Some of his more creative neologisms seem to have been produced for the needs of expressiveness, for example 'outlaunch', which combines the image of an effusion of blood (out-), with the medical 'launching', or lancing (i.e. piercing), of a wound.

While the number of *OED* entries in which *Cornelia* features is surprisingly high (see section on neologisms below), the overall diction of the play is less markedly Latinate than Mary Sidney Herbert's, as Kyd tends to tap the Anglo-Saxon roots of the English language.[225] In the context of contemporary debates on word-creation, and the often-reviled import of Latinate or foreign 'inkhorn terms' that marked the 1590s,[226] it might be tempting to situate Kyd on the side of the defenders of English diction, and thus pit his native, fluent language against the more 'Frenchified' poetics of Sidney Herbert's *Antonius*. Yet Kyd's French-derived, rare coinages (such as 'souspirable') seem to preclude such a theoretical positioning on his part.[227] His general tendency to translate Garnier into 'common'

[224] See also his frequent use of 'signorize' (from the Italian), a word he already employed in his translation of Tasso's *Padre di Famigila* (see Boas, p. 415 n. 55).

[225] See for instance his coinage 'madding' in relationship to the goddess of war Bellona (v. 185), which is a transposition of Virgil's epithet 'furens', i.e. raving.

[226] As discussed above, p. 37.

[227] One should also note the potential influence of Richard Mulcaster, since Kyd was educated at Merchant Taylors' School. In his *First part of the elementarie* (1582)

English (as opposed to foreign, 'curious' terms, as critics called them at the time), is perhaps best understood as a result of an internalization of Garnier's poetic idiom over the course of the years.

Kyd's contribution to the expansion of the English language and metre is thus averred, and should not simply be seen as a tribute to the Sidney Herbert milieu and their well-known experiments with metre and form. With the play's exploration of the poetics of grief through the character of Cornelia, its subtle responses to the generic tensions of Garnier's play, and its political astuteness in interweaving the French source with contemporary English concerns, the fine metrical and linguistic fabric of Kyd's last tragedy clearly belies enduring perceptions of the translation as hurried and derivative. As such, it firmly establishes it as part of Kyd's canon of original works — and of Elizabethan neoclassical tragedy.

A 'Mirror for Magistrates'? Ideological, Political and Religious Contexts

Kyd's engagement with the political themes in Garnier's rendering of the Roman civil wars has attracted considerable critical attention over the last decade. This is indeed a central aspect of Garnier's tragedies; in *Cornelia* the issues of freedom, tyranny, and just war are discussed at length, first through Cicero's long lament on the end of the Republic in Act I, and in the course of Act IV, which pits Brutus and Cassius' exchange on Caesar's hubris and the legitimacy of tyrannicide against Caesar's own blasphemous assertion of his personal 'pleasure' ('one man's pleasure', IV. 1. 3) over the common good. As noted above, such issues were crucial in the context of Elizabeth's late reign, and Kyd highlights their relevance to contemporary debates. For example, as Perry has shown, Kyd systematically re-casts complaints by Garnier's characters about the loss of Republican freedom in terms of the English discourse on the ancient liberties traditionally guaranteed by common law.[228] This he does for example by translating Garnier's 'république' as 'commonwealth' ('Now we have lost our conquered liberty, | Our

Mulcaster defends the dignity of the English tongue and its capacity, 'bycause it is conversant with so manie people', to assimilate other languages, 'to make a foren word, an English denison'. *The first part of the elementarie vvhich entreateth chefelie of the right writing of our English tung, set furth by Richard Mulcaster* (London: Thomas Vautroullier, 1582), p. 83.

[228] See Perry, pp. 543–44 in particular.

commonwealth', III. 1. 30–31), for instance, and by inserting the adjective 'ancient' in front of the noun 'liberté' where Garnier had none. Such is also the case in Cicero's lament in Act I: 'We live despoiled and robbed by one | Of th'ancient freedom wherein we were born' (I. 120–21).[229]

Intertextual references added or highlighted by Kyd also contribute to the re-framing of Garnier's tragedy in terms of contemporary political discourse. The subliminal presence of Lucan's *Pharsalia* I at key moments in the play is highly suggestive here. For instance, in his rendering of Cicero's invective against Caesar's hubris in Act III, Kyd departs from Garnier, who compares Caesar to a bright, yet short-lived fire, that suddenly dies out ('et puis il tombe mort', 52v). Kyd writes instead that the 'flaming blaze [...] Still darting sparkles, till it find a train | To seize upon, and then it flames a[g]ain' (III. 2. 25–30). In this he seems to follow Lucan's own comparison of Caesar to a lightning bolt (*Pharsalia*, I. 150–57), as translated by Marlowe: 'raging shoots | Alongst the air and nought resisting it | Falls, and returns, and shivers where it lights'.[230] Marlowe's Lucan also seems to be the subtext of Kyd's rendering of Caesar's revealing statement in IV. 2: 'For as I am inferior to none, | So can I suffer no superiors.' (Marlowe: 'Pompey could bide no equal, nor Caesar no superior'.[231]) As Freyja Cox Jensen has shown, the association of Caesar with 'poisoned ambition' (I. 24) was commonplace in contemporary readings, and, more specifically, dramatizations of the Roman civil wars.[232] Kyd emphasizes this trait, not only by effectively rendering the rhetorical force of Cicero's condemnations in Acts I and III, and the barbed repartees of plotting Brutus and Cassius in Act IV, but also by re-activating Garnier's politically charged sources.

But Kyd's characterization of Caesar as a tyrant is not solely indebted to Lucan. As Lodovico Lovascio has recently noted, Kyd's added mention of Caesar's 'stony heart' in Act V could very well represent a reminiscence of Caesar's 'tragedy' in the 1587 enlarged edition of the *Mirour for magistrates*:

---

[229] See also IV. 49–50: '[Brutus]: … suffer not | His ancient liberty to be repressed'.

[230] *Lucans first booke translated line for line, by Chr*[*istopher*] *Marlow*[*e*] (London: Peter Short, 1600), sig. B3r. See Belle, 'Comme espics dans les plaines'.

[231] Ibid.

[232] Freyja Cox Jensen, 'From Pharsalus to Philippi: Stories of Pompey and Caesar', in *Reading the Roman Republic*, pp. 125–61.

But sith my whole pretence was glory vain,
To have renown and rule above the rest,
Without remorse of many thousands slain
[…]
I deem therefore my stony heart and breast
Received so many wounds for just revenge.[233]

This in turn would contribute to anchoring Kyd's translation in the genre of 'Advice to the Princes', which commonly highlighted the didactic dimension of ancient historical figures by turning them into examples of Biblical virtues. As North noted in the dedication of his 1579 Plutarch to Queen Elizabeth: 'if they have done this for heathen Kings, what should we doe for Christian Princes? If they have done this for glorye, what should we doe for religion? If they have done this without hope of heaven, what should we doe that looke for immortalitie?'[234] For Caesar's 'stony heart' also echoes Ezekiel 36. 26 in the Geneva Bible, and God's promise to turn 'stony hearts' into hearts of flesh. The allusion is all the more intriguing as it could be applied both to condemn the unwillingness of tyrants to listen to words of wisdom,[235] and to announce a brighter dynastic future, in which kings (or indeed queens) would rule with 'hearts of flesh'. Such a perspective is also hinted at when Kyd rephrases Cornelia's wish to see her kinsmen avenged ('*Je descendrai joyeuse, ayant ains que mourir* | *Obtenu le seul bien que je peux requerir*') in words highly reminiscent of Simeon's canticle celebrating the advent of the Messiah: 'I'll down with joy, because before I died, | Mine eyes have seen what I in heart desired'.[236]

The conflation in Kyd's translation of Christian themes and political discourse has complex ramifications. According to Perry, the Christian perspective introduced by Kyd's added references to the Bible serves simultaneously to underline and to destabilize the

[233] John Higgins, 'Caius Julius Caesar', quoted by Lovascio, p. 52. Compare with Kyd: 'His stony heart, that ne'er did Roman good, | Would melt with nothing with their dearest blood' (v. 272–73).
[234] North, sigs *2r–v.
[235] Wilson-Lee emphasizes the importance of the theme of counsel in Garnier's plays — and in Sidney Herbert's translation in particular, as discussed above (pp. 137–39).
[236] Compare with Luke 2. 29–30: 'Lord, now lettest thou thy servant depart in peace, according to thy word, for mine eyes have seen thy salvation' (Geneva Bible). Garnier is more generic: 'Je descendrai joyeuse, ayant ains que mourir | Obtenu le seul bien que je peux requerir' ('I will down with joy, having obtained, before I died, | the only thing I could request', p. 55r).

parallels that the reader may want to establish between the political issues discussed in the play, and its late Elizabethan context.[237] While from a political perspective the end of the Roman republic embodied the demise of 'ancient liberties', from an eschatological perspective the Empire was traditionally celebrated as the time ordained for the birth of Christ. The ambiguities involved in this twofold approach to history have been unravelled by Cadman, who notes how Caesar's discourse conflates the Stoic theme of submitting to Fate with the Christian perspective on providence as a benevolent force leading history to its completion: 'Heaven sets our time, with heav'n may nought dispense [...] Fortune and the heavens have care of us' (IV. 2. 147–49).[238] This, he notes, creates an unresolved tension between the anti-tyrannical ideas expressed by Brutus and Cassius in IV. 1 and the religious and philosophical qualities of Caesar's discourse in the mirroring scene (IV. 2).[239] Rather than reading the play as a plain 'mirror' of the times — as Garnier described his play to his royal dedicatee — one can only agree with Perry's suggestion that the conflation of Roman history, Christian providentialism, English traditional political thought and Continental republicanism be read as a multi-faceted commentary on this troubled period, and an invitation to explore, from a variety of perspectives, the vexed political debates of the 1590s.

Another way of understanding Kyd's interweaving of political and religious themes is to relate them to the ambiguities that also surface in Mary Sidney Herbert's own translation of Garnier. Sidney Herbert's support for the Huguenot cause is inscribed in the 1592 volume, not only through the pairing of *Antonius* with de Mornay's *Discourse of Life and Death*, but also through topical allusions reminding her audience of the Sidneys' continuing support for continental Protestantism — be it through diplomatic, military, or literary means.[240] Kyd's emphasis on the defence of 'ancient liberties' naturally chimes in with the anti-tyrannical stance displayed in Sidney Herbert's translation. But other associations come to mind. As noted above, Sidney Herbert's *Antonius* echoes Spenser's translations of du

---

[237] Perry, pp. 546ff.

[238] See also the chorus celebrating the advent of peace with Caesar's 'happy race' (IV. 2. 178–79), and affirming Jove's protection over humankind in a passage marked as *sententiae* (IV. 2. 200–04).

[239] Cadman, *Sovereigns and Subjects*, pp. 51–53.

[240] See above, pp. 41–47.

Bellay's poetry, first in Jan van der Noot's *Theatre for Worldlings*, then in the 1591 *Complaints* dedicated to the Countess,[241] but these works have never been discussed in connection with *Cornelia*. Yet allusions to both can be identified in Kyd's translation: the Chorus in III. 2 makes it clear that Fortune 'tyrannize[s] [...] o'er the world and wordlings' (147–48, Kyd's addition), and the recurring theme of Rome's self-induced ruin is consistently rendered in terms that suggest close familiarity with Spenser's *Ruines of Rome*.[242] Spenser's mediation is noteworthy here, not only because of his association with the Sidney Herbert milieu, but also because of the cultural and ideological translation he achieves, as he re-invests du Bellay's lament on Rome's lost grandeur with Puritan topoi on the decay of Catholic Rome, and the impending advent of the new Jerusalem.[243] The intertextual links established in Kyd's translation, and the ensuing association of the tragic topos of the fall of Rome with the anti-Catholic providentialism of Protestant discourse, thus realign Garnier's themes of fall and mutability with the eschatological and political perspectives of Spenser's poetry — and their echoes in Sidney Herbert's *Antonius*.

Besides the associations they provide with Kyd's immediate precedent, the connections established here between classical sources, anti-tyrannical political discourse, and Protestant readings of history are finally significant when it comes to locating *Cornelia* within Kyd's dramatic corpus. On the basis of the traditional opposition between 'popular' plays, usually exemplified by *The Spanish Tragedy*, and learned, Senecan 'closet' drama, *Cornelia* has often been considered as an 'oddity' in Kyd's career.[244] Yet, not only did Garnier's Humanist drama provide an important inspiration for Kyd's *Spanish Tragedy*, the latter also displays thematic traits and intertextual strategies that actually converge with those identified here. Hill's seminal reading of the Virgilian sources of *The Spanish*

---

[241] See above, pp. 44–45, in this edition and Lake Prescott, 'Mary Sidney's French Sophocles', p. 82.

[242] In II. 267–74 for example, Cicero evokes Rome's pride and subsequent fall in terms similar to the passage of *Marc Antoine* discussed above (see p. 44), which echoes du Bellay's *Antiquitez de Rome*. Kyd re-activates the intertextual connection with a reference to Spenser's rendering.

[243] On Spenser's Protestant re-writing of du Bellay, see above, p. 45.

[244] Erne, *Beyond the Spanish Tragedy*, p. 211. Norland calls it 'something of a mystery' (*Neoclassical Tragedy*, p. 226). On the problems raised by the term 'closet drama', see above, pp. 24–27.

Tragedy has shown it to be a subtle and learned work, an 'anti-*Aeneid*' that ironically exploits the dynastic associations of the epic genre to prophesize the fall of the Spanish Catholic empire and Britain's future glory.[245] More recently, Ardolino's focus on the influence of Garnier's *Les Juifves* on the *Tragedy* has also revealed how, by exploiting the Biblical language of the French play, Kyd was able to stage Hieronymo's revenge in terms of the conflict between England and Spain, and to portray the demise of the Catholic powers as another 'fall of Babylon' (*Spanish Tragedy*, IV. 1. 195). With its strong connection with Lucan's 'anti-*Aeneid*' and its echoes of apocalyptic Protestant discourse, *Cornelia* not only confirms Kyd's dramatic interest in Garnier's theatre,[246] but also his desire to integrate contemporary political and religious discourses into the repertoire of English tragedy. The play's focus on Cornelia's mourning and the general loss of 'ancient liberties', which sounds a rather pessimistic note, especially in comparison with the triumphant providentialism of the *Spanish Tragedy*, could certainly be interpreted as a reflection of Kyd's own troubled circumstances at the time of composition; it also offers a vivid commentary on the political and dynastic uncertainties of the late Elizabethan era.

ROBERT GARNIER IN ELIZABETHAN ENGLAND: LITERARY RECEPTION AND INFLUENCE

The two plays gathered in this volume were decisive in acclimatizing neoclassical French tragedy in England, and directly inspired a series of Roman plays in English, performed or unperformed, as will be discussed below. Ironically enough, they did little to enhance the reputation of Robert Garnier himself in England in the early modern period — or later. Although *Antonius*, after four hundred years of eclipse, has finally received the critical attention it deserves, and is now commonly read and taught, it is often treated more as an original work (alongside works by other women writers) than as a translation.[247]

---

[245] Hill, 'Senecan and Virgilian Perspectives', p. 164: 'Far from being a native pot-boiler, *The Spanish Tragedy* is a deeply conscious work [...] [T]he Vergilian material hints to the audience at something none of the characters is able to see: the transmission of Empire can happen again'.

[246] Cadman likewise argues that *Cornelia* should be read as 'a crystallisation of Garnier's influence rather than as evidence of Kyd's defection from one aesthetic campaign to another' (*Sovereigns and Subjects*, p. 46).

[247] See the Routledge anthology in which *Antonius* is the only translated text (*Renaissance Drama by Women*, ed. by S. P. Cerasano and Marion Wynne-Davies

While this is a reflection of the way women's literary history has been reconstructed in the last forty years or so, it is also a paradox that we need to keep in mind when digging for evidence of its literary reception.

Kyd's *Cornelia* has not had the same luck, however, although Erne's recent call for a new edition of Kyd's works, 'beyond the *Spanish Tragedy*', indicates that its revival is perhaps at hand.[248] The relative neglect that the play has suffered since the beginning of the twentieth century could be explained by two main factors, the first being the impact of Romanticism on late nineteenth-century approaches to translation, which valued linguistic accuracy (hence Boas's and Witherspoon's comments);[249] the second being a renewed interest in revenge tragedy, and Kyd's *Spanish Tragedy* in particular, among modernist critics such as T. S. Eliot — which relegated *Cornelia* to a secondary place in the canon of Kyd's works.[250] But such attitudes to *Cornelia* are only relatively recent. Kyd's translation seems to have received more attention than *Antonius* in Sidney Herbert's own time, if we are to judge its impact, so to speak, by the number of quotations included in printed collections of common-places. It was also singled out in Robert Dodsley's eighteenth-century *Select Collection of Old Plays* as one of the better products of the Elizabethan stage, and was reprinted through to the end of the nineteenth century, thanks to its inclusion in the many re-issues of Dodsley's popular collection.[251]

[London and New York: Routledge, 2013 [1996]]) or the Penguin edition of early modern women authors, where Sidney Herbert's translation is paired with Jane Lumley's *Sophocles* (ed. by Purkiss).

[248] Erne, *Beyond the Spanish Tragedy*, p. 8.

[249] As noted above, pp. 6 and 56.

[250] In his seminal 1919 essay '*Hamlet* and His Problems', in *The Sacred Wood: Essays in Literature and Criticism* (London: Methuen, 1920). Kyd's *Tragedy* is also famously alluded to in *The Waste Land*. On Eliot's re-fashioning of the early modern literary canon, see Steven Matthews, *T. S. Eliot and Early Modern Literature* (Oxford: Oxford University Press, 2013).

[251] Dodsley includes Kyd 'amongst the better poets of his time', and (rather surprisingly for us) adds: 'but whether he printed any thing besides this play, I cannot tell'. Robert Dodsley, *A Selection Collection of Old Plays, Volume the Eleventh* (London: Printed for R. Dodlsey, 1744), p. 64. Of course, the French source of the play and its neoclassical model were more tasteful for eighteenth century criticism, shaped as it was by the influence of French classicism, as demonstrated in particular by the wave of translations and imitations of Corneille and Racine from the 1650s onwards. Collier's 1825 edition seems to imply that *Cornelia* is the only play of Kyd's to have escaped 'ridicule' (1825, p. 237), but the editor of the 1874 edition,

Early Print History and Reception

The immediate reception of *Antonius* is difficult to assess, although Ponsonby's second edition of the play as a small, attractive octavo in 1595 under the title *The Tragedie of Antonie*, and no longer as a companion piece for *The Discourse of Life and Death*, seems to indicate that the play was in high demand.[252] By 1595 Henri IV of France had converted to Catholicism and it might have been seen as politic by the bookseller to disentangle the play from the name of a Frenchman closely associated with the French king, and from partially obsolete political associations. The translation of the treatise would be reissued separately, however, in 1600, and several times again in the early years of the seventeenth century.[253] But it might be more than a coincidence that 1595 was also the year in which Ponsonby finally published Sir Philip Sidney's *Defence of Poesie*, which immediately sold out and led to a second edition in the same year.[254] The dual 1595 publication could have been a way for the bookseller — or Sidney Herbert herself — to suggest an intrinsic link between both texts.

The second edition of *Antonius* also comes after the publications in quick succession, all in 1594, of Kyd's *Cornelia*, Shakespeare's *Titus Andronicus* and Daniel's *Cleopatra*, the latter of which was presented as an ostentatious homage to Sidney Herbert. In fact, the new title of *Antonius* as *The Tragedie of Antonie*, with the Englishing of the hero's name (although the character is still called Antonius in

W. Hazlitt, sounds more sceptical about the value of the play (1874, p. 176). See bibliography for a full list of editions of Dodsley's *Selection of Old Plays*.

[252] On the difficulty of establishing correlations between number of editions and popularity, see Alan B. Farmer and Zachary Lesser, 'What Is Print Popularity? A Map of the Elizabethan Book Trade', and Neil Rhodes, 'Shakespeare's Popularity and the Origins of the Canon', in *The Elizabethan Top Ten: Defining Print Popularity in Early Modern England*, ed. by Andy Kesson and Emma Smith (Farnham: Ashgate, 2013), pp. 19–54 and 101–122, respectively. According to Farmer and Lesser's criteria, however, a reprint at such close range can almost certainly be considered a sign of popularity (p. 28).

[253] Sidney Herbert's translation of de Mornay went through five separate editions in the early years of the seventeenth century, which shows that Henri IV's conversion to Catholicism did not long alienate the reading public against his former ambassador, whose loyalty to Protestantism remained unflagging. The treatise was published by Ponsonby in 1592 and 1600, then, after his death, by Matthew Lownes in 1606, 1607 and 1608. On Ponsonby and his successors, see Hadfield, *Edmund Spenser*, p. 368.

[254] See note 68 on Olney's rivalling publication as *An apologie for poetrie* (which was suppressed).

the dramatis personae, speech headings and running titles), is a possible tribute to Daniel's *Cleopatra*. Published (in 1594 and 1595) as part of a volume entitled *Delia and Rosamond augmented. Cleopatra*, Daniel's tragedy was however introduced with a separate title page boasting *The tragedie of Cleopatra*. Daniel's works seem to have sold very well, and, although never printed on its own, the play was published at least eleven times between 1594 and 1623.[255] Daniel, who had taken up residence at Wilton in the early 1590s,[256] dedicated his tragedy to his great patron Sidney Herbert, suggesting that he only wrote it at her prompting, as a sequel to *Antonius*.[257]

Sidney Herbert's elegant little 1595 volume, with lace ornaments at the top and bottom of each page, has paradoxically done better in terms of survival than the first edition, with eleven extant copies, in spite of its very small octavo size (which made it ineligible for being bound in collective volumes of play-texts), against the four extant copies of the 1592 edition — but this is still better than some of Shakespeare's quartos. Contemporary testimonies about the reception of the play are scant. As a patron of many authors, Sidney Herbert is often praised for her wit and generosity in the period, but the play is rarely mentioned. Francis Meres thus praises 'learned *Mary*, the honorabl [*sic*] Countesse of *Pembrooke*, the noble Sister of immortall sir *Philip Sidney*, [who] is very liberall vnto Poets; besides shee is a most delicate Poet, of whom I may say, as *Antipater Sidonius* writeth of *Sappho*,' but has nothing to say about *Antonius*.[258] Gabriel Harvey's guarded appreciation of the play in 1593 (quoted above) is one of the few comments we have by a contemporary reader, although William Covell also wrote approvingly of 'well graced Anthonie', which 'deserveth immortall praise, from the hand of that divine Lady, who, like Corinna contending with Pindarus was oft victorious'[259] —

---

[255] W. W. Greg, *A Bibliography of the English Printed Drama to the Restoration, Vol. I* (London: for the Bibliographical Society at the University Press, Oxford, 1939), pp. 216–19. On the complex process of revisions imposed on the play, see e.g. Russell Leavenworth, *Daniel's Cleopatra: A Critical Study* (Salzburg: Universität Salzburg, Salzburg Studies in English Literature n°3, 1974), pp. 16–18.

[256] See Hannay, *Philip's Phoenix*, p. 125.

[257] *Delia and Rosamond*, sig. [H5]r.

[258] Francis Meres, *Wits common wealth The second part. A treasurie of diuine, morall, and phylosophicall similies, and sentences, generally vsefull* (London: William Stansby, to be sold by Richard Royston, 1634), p. 630. For more contemporary comments, see Margaret Hannay, *Philip's Phoenix*, p. 141.

[259] William Covell, *Polimanteia* ([Cambridge and London]: Printed by John Legate [and J. Orwin in London], 1595), sig. R2v. For Harvey, see above, p. 46.

a rather noncommittal comment which could address the elegant ('well-graced') material features of the 1595 edition rather than the play itself.

Library catalogues or inventories of the period rarely mention plays by their titles, but we know from a list of 169 plays (bound in several volumes) which was compiled in 1609 that Sir John Harington, the translator of Ariosto, possessed copies of both *Antonius* and *Cornelia*.[260] A reconstructed catalogue of Drummond of Hawthornden's extensive library, which comprised many French books (but few plays), indicates that not only did he own a copy of *Antonius*, but also of Kyd's *Cornelia*, as well as an edition of Garnier's tragedies in French.[261] There might also have been a copy of *Antonius* in the Countess of Bridgewater's London library, since it included an undated copy of de Mornay's *Discourse of Life and Death*.[262] But Sidney Herbert's play was not readily anthologized in

[260] See his list of eleven bound volumes of plays in British Museum Add. MS. 27 632, fol. 43. See also F. J. Furnivall, 'Sir John Harington's Shakspeare Quartos', *Notes & Queries*, s-7.IX (May 1890), 382–83; Alan H. Nelson, 'Shakespeare and the Bibliophiles: from the earliest years to 1616', in *Owners, Annotators and the Signs of Reading*, ed. by Robin Myers, Michael Harris and Giles Mandelbrote (London: British Library, 2005), 49–73; and the digitized image of a page in Harington's manuscript catalogue of plays, presented in the virtual exhibition by a team of experts from the Folger Library, *Shakespeare Documented*: <http://www.shakespeare documented.org/exhibition/document/sir-john-haringtons-catalogue-plays-ownership-shakespeare-quartos> [accessed 25 June 2016]. The presence of *Antonius* is interesting here, because it must have been separated from de Mornay's *Discourse* to be bound with other plays, which indicates a different kind of appropriation.

[261] *The Library of Drummond of Hawthornden*, ed. by Robert H. Macdonald (Edinburgh: Edinburgh University Press, 1971), pp. 194 and 208. Drummond also owned Alexander's *Monarchicke Tragedies* and Greville's *Mustapha* (pp. 187, 195) and two editions of Sidney's *Defence of Poesie* (p. 201), not to mention three Shakespeare quartos.

[262] Heidi Brayman Hackel, *Reading Material in Early Modern England: Print, Gender, and Literacy* (Cambridge: Cambridge University Press, 2005), p. 278. The inventory is dated 1627–1633. For Brayman, it is likely that this was the edition that included the play, because the Countess's collection of playtexts was extensive (p. 249). The Folger library also holds a manuscript precis of Sidney Herbert's translation of de Mornay's *Discourse* in the hand of Elizabeth Ashburnham Richardson, 1st Lady Cramond (1576/7–1651) (Folger MS V. a. 511, fols 84r–85v). It is not known which edition of the *Discourse* she used. See Margaret P. Hannay, 'Elizabeth Ashburnham Richardson's Meditation on the Countess of Pembroke's *Discourse*', *EMS*, 9 (2000), 114–28, and for a reprint, *Selected Works of Mary Sidney Herbert, Countess of Pembroke*, ed. by Margaret P. Hannay, Noel J. Kinnamon and Michael G. Brennan (Tempe: Arizona Center for Medieval and Renaissance Studies, 2005), pp. 130–35. For other evidence of appropriation by contemporary readers,

the printed collections of commonplaces of the period, even those with a strong dramatic or poetic bias. A notable exception is John Bodenham's 1600 collection, *Bel-vedére*, the preface of which mentions 'Mary, Countesse of Pembroke' among the 'right Honourable persons', including Sir Philip Sidney, whose works ('out of sundry things extant, and many in privat') have been tapped for his miscellany; Bodenham then includes a dozen passages from *Antonius* — without acknowledging his debt. They consist of rather aphoristic passages, often drawn from the play's *sententiae* and sometimes quoted approximately.[263] This apparent lack of popular interest is somewhat puzzling, given the popularity of Kyd's *Cornelia* and of Daniel's *Cleopatra* in some of these miscellanies.[264] Is it because she was considered as being apart from the mainstream conversation? Her gender and status, singled out by Bodenham in *Bel-vedére*, might have granted her a peculiar position among the community of contemporary authors in the eyes of the compilers, especially as both the reissues of de Mornay's *Discourse* and her completion of the Sidney *Psalms* enhanced her reputation as a religious author. As reflected in Gabriel Harvey's awareness of the potential moral ambivalence of the play, however, *Antonius* might have in fact given little scope for anthologizing in commonplace books that looked for clear moral teachings and easily detachable passages, ready for neat classification and re-use.

Cornelia's early print history is also somewhat chequered, although for very different reasons. The 1594 edition of *Cornelia* seems to have

---

see the personalized edition of a 1600 edition of the *Discourse* now at the Folger (STC 18139 copy 2) which contains seventeen additional manuscript pages with quotations and verse about death in the hand of 'Jeff. Gilbert' (signed 1605).

263 Bodenham, *Bel-vedére*, sigs A4v–[A5]. The extracts were obviously chosen for their pithy, aphoristic nature. Two examples will suffice to illustrate Bodenham's practice: the following quotation was integrated into the section 'Of Kings and Princes': '*Sleeplesse suspition, pale distrust, cold feare, | Alwaies with princes company doth beare*' (*Bel-vedére*, p. 60; close to *Antonius*, III. 169–70); while this second one appeared in the section 'Of Authority': '*When one selfe-power is common made to two, | Their duties they nor suffer nor will doe*' (*Bel-vedére*, p. 196; close to *Antonius*, IV. 146–47). Other excerpts (clearly recognizable although sometimes rephrased) include: II. 2. 180, III. 13–14, III. 73–74, III. 147–48, III. 171–72, III. 183–84, IV. 66–69, IV. 165–66. This list was compiled with the help of the PHOEBUS programme developed by the OBVIL project at the Paris-Sorbonne University, <http://obvil.paris-sorbonne.fr/developpements/phoebus> [accessed 10 July 2016].

264 In particular in Robert Allott's *Englands Parnassus: or the choysest flowers of our moderne poets* (London: For N. L[ing,] C. B[urby] and T. H[ayes], 1600). See below.

sold poorly, at least if one is to believe William Covell's witty remark in his 1595 *Polimanteia* that 'tragick Garnier [should not] have his poor *Cornelia* stand naked on every poste' — by which he probably refers to the early modern habit of using title pages as advertisement posters for printed books, but also perhaps to the unadorned appearance of the title page carrying neither author's name nor printer's mark.[265] The 1595 volume was a reissue of the 1594 text with a new title page, produced for Ling shortly after he ended his formal collaboration with Busby.[266] This new issue may in many ways be read as Ling's attempt to capture a better readership for the text. Kyd's name is advertised on the title page; the new title, focussing on Pompey and on Cornelia's male relatives, seems to target a more masculine audience than the first issue. It is also possible, as Erne has suggested, that Ling was seeking to capitalize on the contemporary *Tragedy of Caesar and Pompey*, a play now lost but which was staged by the Admiral's men in 1594 and 1595.[267]

Despite its modest commercial success, and the fact that it was never performed, *Cornelia* was consistently praised in literary circles. In 1594 it was cited alongside Shakespeare's *Lucrece* in *Epicedium*, an elegy to the memory of Lady Helen Branch, which Boas tentatively attributes to William Herbert.[268] Covell's aforementioned comment on 'naked Cornelia' is actually accompanied by a laudatory marginal note, which also confirms its lack of success: 'a work howsoever not respected yet excellently done by Th. Kid.'[269] Kyd appears in Frances Meres' 1598 *Palladis Tamia* among the list of English 'tragick poets' corresponding to the ancient precedents Sophocles, Euripides and Seneca, although the play is not particularly mentioned. *Cornelia* seems in fact to have been specifically appreciated for its poetical aspects. Thomas Kyd is again listed as one of the 'Moderne and extant Poets' cited in John Bodenham's 1600 anthology of commonplaces, *Bel-vedére*, alongside Jonson, Marlowe

---

[265] Covell, *Polimanteia*, sig. Q3v.

[266] See Johnson, p. 5. Busby and Ling were to continue their collaboration, but in a less systematic way.

[267] As mentioned in Henslowe's *Diary*, ed. by W. W. Greg (London: Bullen, 1908), I, pp. 20–21 and 24.

[268] Boas, pp. lxxv–vi. Potential links between Kyd's *Cornelia* and Shakespeare's *Lucrece* have been suggested by Rolf Soellner, 'Shakespeare's Lucrece and the Sidney/Pembroke Connection', *Shakespeare Studies*, 15 (1982), 1–20.

[269] Covell, *Polimanteia*, sig. Q3v.

and Shakespeare.[270] He is also widely quoted in Robert Allott's poetry miscellany, *England's Parnassus*, also published in 1600. The inclusion of many extracts of *Cornelia* in this volume may of course be explained by the fact that it was produced by Nicholas Ling, who was also responsible for both issues of the play.[271] Yet Kyd's presence here among 'the choysest flowers of our Modern Poets' is meaningful in at least two respects. First, the anthology is organised by commonplaces ('Envy', 'Dissimulation', 'Faith', etc.), many of which are of a didactic kind, thus offering a perfect setting for the moral *sententiae* that abound in *Cornelia*. Some of them are memorable one- or two-liners, such as: 'No feare of death should force us to do ill', or, 'A state divided cannot firmly stand: | Two kings within one realm could never rest.'[272] But longer passages are also taken, for example, from Cicero's condemnation of suicide in Act II, or from the Horatian praise of the golden mean in the chorus of IV. 1.[273] Second, while such excerpts confirm the didactic reading of the play as a source of ready-made material for moral instruction and commonplacing, the miscellany also signals contemporary interest in Kyd's skill as a lyric poet and a versifier. Allot reproduces in particular the eighteen-line nightscape at the beginning of Act III in its entirety, in a section on dawn ('*Gallicinum*', or the cock-crow), which also contains excerpts from Drayton, Spenser, Sidney, Chapman and Marlowe.[274] Many passages otherwise quoted are drawn from the choruses, which, as mentioned above, display a variety of metres and rhyme schemes. Significantly, while translations by Harington, Sylvester or Fairfax

---

[270] Bodenham, *Bel-vedére*, sig. [A5v]. Bodenham does not attribute the excerpts in his anthology to their authors, but some of them have been identified by Charles Crawford in his article, 'Belvedere, or The Garden of the Muses', *Englische Studien*, 43 (1910–11), 198–228. Neil Rhodes also notes that a copy of the 1875 edition of the miscellany at the British Library includes an extensive manuscript list of authors. See *Shakespeare and the Origins of English* (Oxford: Oxford University Press, 2004), p. 172. A search through the PHOEBUS software developed by the Sorbonne's OBVIL project yields about a dozen matches (with minor variants), most of which located in Act II, including: II. 126, 230, 250, 288, 293, 300; but also IV. 2. 127 and V. 227.

[271] Erne notes that Ling was among the first stationers to publish plays with commonplace markers, at the very same time as he was contributing to the dissemination of commonplace books. See Erne, *Shakespeare and the Book Trade* (Cambridge: Cambridge University Press, 2013), p. 173.

[272] Allott, pp. 52 and 66–67, respectively.

[273] Allott, pp. 62 (under 'Despaire') and 39 (under 'Content'), respectively.

[274] Allott, p. 325.

are identified as such by the addition of the abbreviation 'transl.' after the translators' names, passages from *Cornelia* are simply attributed to Kyd. This of course illustrates the process of cultural appropriation that prevailed in contemporary translations of drama; it also confirms Kyd's status as a 'poet' in the developing canon of early modern English literature.

Influence on Early Modern English Drama

As dramatic explorations of Roman history, the influence of both *Antonius* and *Cornelia* can be discerned well into the seventeenth century. Although not all of the numerous plays on the theme of the Roman civil wars published in the late 1590s and 1600s can directly be linked to the Garnier translations,[275] the latter did result in emulation among contemporary playwrights. In 1598 Samuel Brandon composed a *Tragi-comœdie of the Vertuous Octavia*, which, like *Antonius* and *Cornelia*, was apparently not performed. Moving the focus of the action towards Rome and Antony's spurned wife, it emulates both *Antonius* for its topic, and *Cornelia* in offering an edifying portrayal of a virtuous matron. Another intriguing example is a now lost tragedy of *Antony and Cleopatra* by Fulke Greville, which he claims to have destroyed because he was alarmed by its immorality — in itself a fascinating comment on the moral ambiguities inherent in the dramatization of the episode.[276] Sidney Herbert's enduring influence can be traced in Sir William Alexander's *Four Monarchicke Tragedies* (1603–07), Elizabeth Cary's *The Tragedy of Miriam* (1613), and perhaps even Thomas May's *The Tragedy of Cleopatra, Queen of Egypt* (published in 1639, first acted in 1626).

---

[275] The academic tragedy of *Caesar and Pompey, Or Caesar's Revenge* (staged at Trinity College, Oxford, printed in 1606) includes a scene between Pompey and Cornelia, as well as the characters of Brutus and Cassius, but apart from these common themes, the play has little to do with Kyd or Garnier. Cornelia's lament on Pompey's death is quite commonplace, and she commits suicide early in the play (II. 2). Thomas Parrot suggests, however, a possible, but loose influence from Kyd's *Spanish Tragedy* ('The "Academic" Tragedy of "Caesar and Pompey"', *The Modern Language Review*, 5.4 (1910), 435–44).

[276] See Fulke Greville, *A Dedication to Sir Philip Sidney*, in *The Prose Works of Fulke Greville, Lord Brooke*, ed. by John Gouws (Oxford: Clarendon Press, 1986), p. 93. Interestingly, Greville specifically argued that such works were 'no plays for the stage' (p. 134).

Influences of Kyd's *Cornelia* on later plays (apart from Shakespeare's, discussed below) are more difficult to assess. We know through Henslowe's diary of a 1602 collaborative play by Dekker, Drayton, Middleton, Munday and Webster, entitled *Caesar's Fall*, but, like the 1595 *Tragedy of Caesar and Pompey*, it is now lost.[277] George Chapman's *Caesar and Pompey* (published in 1631, but probably written in 1604, and never staged)[278] offers a rather different treatment of the episode. While Chapman shares Garnier's interest in neo-Stoicism, the character of Cornelia plays only a (very) secondary role in the play. Chapman's Pompey is described as a wavering, hesitant character, in sharp contrast with the consistently heroic stature he is given by Garnier and Kyd. More interestingly, perhaps, Richard Ide has highlighted Chapman's subversive refusal of teleological models of history, perhaps a response to the complex outlook on providential history already apparent in Kyd's *Cornelia*.[279] Finally, Thomas May, mostly famous for his translation of Lucan, is also known to have written a tragedy entitled *Julius Caesar* in the 1620s, but the play remained in manuscript and is now lost. Like his *Cleopatra*, however, it should probably be read as an offshoot of his translation of Lucan rather than as a tribute to Sidney Herbert or Kyd.[280]

Finally, both Kyd's and Sidney Herbert's translation of Garnier have long been considered distant sources for Shakespeare's Roman plays, *Julius Caesar* (1599) and *Antony and Cleopatra* (1606–1607). Although there are surprisingly few studies on the relationship between Shakespeare's plays and these precedents, they should clearly be read together as part of the wider series of plays on the civil wars of Rome outlined above.[281] In his edition of Shakespeare's *Antony and Cleopatra* Wilders points out that Shakespeare's tragedy contains 'enough verbal similarities to show that the Countess's

277 *Henslowe's Diary*, II, p. 222.

278 See Cox Jensen, *Reading the Roman Republic*, pp. 133–34.

279 Richard Ide, 'Chapman's "Caesar and Pompey" and the Uses of History', *Modern Philology*, 82.3 (1985), 255–68 (p. 260). Ide also notes the links between Chapman's approach to ancient Stoicism and contemporary commonplacing practices — another element that the play shares with Kyd's translation (but also, arguably, with other examples of neoclassical drama).

280 See Paleit, *War, Liberty, and Caesar*, pp. 215–16. On May's Lucan, see David Norbrook, *Writing the English Republic: Poetry, Rhetoric and Politics, 1627–1660* (Cambridge: Cambridge University Press, 1999), pp. 23–62.

281 For a balanced view of the relationship between Shakespeare's plays and his predecessors, see Cadman, 'Quick Comedians', *passim*.

tragedy lingered in Shakespeare's mind,' but concludes that they are points of detail.[282] Hillman similarly argues that Shakespeare owed more to Jodelle through Daniel than to Sidney Herbert or Garnier.[283] Yet Schanzer, Muir and Spevack have also listed verbal similarities between the two plays, and in his standard study of Shakespeare's sources Bullough interprets such similarities as deriving from Shakespeare's own habit of loosely remembering works he had previously read.[284] As Gillespie has argued, these standard accounts of Shakespeare's relationship to his sources should perhaps be revised in light of his sympathetic treatment of Cleopatra and his questioning of the heroic ideal of masculinity, which he shares with Sidney Herbert (in contrast with Plutarch).[285]

Parallels between Kyd's *Cornelia* and Shakespeare's *Julius Caesar* have also long been noted. Muir, for instance, links Antony's evocation of 'Caesar's Spirit ranging for Revenge' in Act III of *Julius Caesar* to various passages in *Cornelia* where Kyd evokes unburied bodies (sometimes adding to his French source).[286] Similarities have also been found between Shakespeare's characterization of Cassius and Kyd's treatment of the same character in *Cornelia*, IV. 1,[287] and according to Erne, Shakespeare's Brutus 'may well owe something to Kyd's' as well.[288] But these connections have not been teased out,

[282] Wilders in Shakespeare, *Antony and Cleopatra*, ed. by John Wilders (London: Routledge, 1995), p. 62.

[283] Hillman, *French Reflections*, pp. 108 and 140–41.

[284] Ernest Schanzer, '*Antony and Cleopatra* and the Countess of Pembroke's *Antonius*', *Notes & Queries*, 201 (1956), 152–54; Muir, *Sources*, pp. 225–27; Martin Spevack, ed., *A New Variorum Edition of Shakespeare: Antony and Cleopatra* (New York: Modern Language Association, 1990), pp. 475–78; Geoffrey Bullough, *Narrative and Dramatic Sources of Shakespeare: Julius Caesar, Antony and Cleopatra, Coriolanus* (London: Routledge and Kegan Paul, 1957–75), 8 vols, V, p. 231.

[285] See Paleit, *War, Liberty, and Caesar*, pp. 215–16; *CW*, p. 45.

[286] Muir, *Sources*, p. 194. See also Bullough, *Narrative and Dramatic Sources*, p. 30. Stuart Gillespie surprisingly records 'no verbal echoes' of Kyd in Shakespeare's plays; see *Shakespeare's Books. A Dictionary of Shakespeare Sources* (London and New York: Continuum, 2004), p. 183.

[287] Boas, p. lxxxiii and Erne, *Beyond the Spanish Tragedy*, p. 208.

[288] Boas, ibid. and Erne, *Beyond the Spanish Tragedy*, p. 5. Maguin has traced links between Shakespeare's and Kyd's ghosts in *The Spanish Tragedy* back to Garnier through the evocation of Pompey's apparition in Act II of *Cornelia*. See Jean-Marie Maguin, 'Of Ghosts and Spirits Walking by Night – A Joint Examination of the Ghost Scenes in Robert Garnier's *Cornélie*, Thomas Kyd's *Cornelia* and William Shakespeare's *Hamlet*', *Cahiers Elisabéthains*, 1 (1972), 25–40.

and a more systematic study of Shakespeare's debt to the Elizabethan Garnier is clearly overdue.

It is hoped that this edition will sensitize readers to the covert but extremely significant presence of Garnier in England in the period. Far from being effete and marginal productions of an elite for an elite, *Antonius* and *Cornelia* clearly participated in the main linguistic, literary and ideological debates of the late Elizabethan era. They imported a French vernacular model for neo-Senecan drama, which at once converged with an emerging native tradition of Roman plays and contributed to renewing it by an unprecedented focus on character development and pathos, in particular through the use of soliloquies. Besides, they fertilized an already established local vein of politically engaged drama (as emblematized by *Gorboduc*) with a sophisticated dramatic form that enabled playwrights to explore complex political and philosophical issues from a variety of perspectives, ranging from Humanist neo-Stoicism to more radical forms of republicanism.[289]

The two plays also represent eloquent examples of the changing status of early modern translated drama. Anne Lake Prescott notes that Sidney Herbert's translation of *Antonius* is 'a compelling example of how even a close translation can change meaning'[290] — a remark that can also be applied to Kyd's *Cornelia*. But as has become apparent, the plays themselves were re-interpreted and reframed in rapidly evolving contexts, as revealed by the rapid material metamorphosis of *Antonius* into *The Tragedie of Antony*, or that of *Cornelia* into *Pompey the Great*, and their respective inclusion in collections of moral and poetical commonplaces. Such processes demonstrate the variety of cultural uses to which vernacular plays (translated or not) could be put, and give a sense of the changing reading habits that accompanied the explosion of print publication in the period. The material history of both plays is also indicative of the doubly ambivalent status of drama (often sold as ephemera but seeking the more noble status of poetry), and of translations themselves, in a context of increasing commodification of vernacular literature.[291]

---

[289] See Cadman, *Sovereigns and Subjects*, pp. 3 and 7.

[290] Lake Prescott, 'Mary Sidney's "Antonius" and the Ambiguities of French History', p. 233.

[291] On the ambivalent social and literary status of early modern English translators and translations, see Boutcher, 'The Renaissance', in *The Oxford Guide to Literature in English Translation*, ed. by Peter France (Oxford: Oxford University Press, 2000),

But far from representing simple intermediaries in the 'Englishing' of Garnier's drama, both translators clearly intervene as authors in their own right, and in translating his plays they embody an original form of collaborative authorship. This, we hope to have shown, needs to be taken into account in order to reconstruct a more complete view of English drama than is often presented in standard histories of literature. The cases of Mary Sidney Herbert's *Antonius* and Thomas Kyd's *Cornelia* show how translation vitally informed the development of a native English dramatic tradition, and how the history of translation is not separate from but integral to the history of English literature, whose translational (and transnational) roots can no longer be ignored.[292]

pp. 45–55, and Rhodes, 'Status Anxiety and English Renaissance Translation', in *Renaissance Paratexts*, ed. by Smith and Wilson, pp. 107–20. On the place of translations in the early modern English market for print, see Brenda Hosington, 'Commerce, Printing and Patronage', in the *Oxford History of Literary Translation in English, Volume II*, pp. 47–57; and more recently, her collections *Renaissance Cultural Crossroads: Translation, Print and Culture in Britain, 1473–1660* (ed. with Sara Barker, Leiden and Boston: Brill, 2013) and *Translation and Print in Early Modern Europe*, special issue of *Renaissance Studies*, 29.1 (2015).

[292] This point has been made clear by the works of Anne Coldiron, among others. See in particular her 'Translation's Challenges to Critical Categories: Verses from French in the Early English Renaissance', *Yale Journal of Criticism*, 16.2 (2003), 315–44, and, more recently, *Printers Without Borders*.

FURTHER READING

1. ON THE ELIZABETHAN CULTURE OF TRANSLATION

Barker, Sara, and Brenda Hosington, eds, *Renaissance Cultural Crossroads: Translation, Culture and Print in Britain 1476–1640* (Leiden and Boston: Brill, 2013)

Belle, Marie-Alice, ed., *Women's Translations in Early Modern England and France*, special issue of *Renaissance and Reformation*, 35.4 (2012)

Boutcher, Warren, 'The Renaissance', in *The Oxford Guide to Literature in English Translation*, ed. by Peter France (Oxford: Oxford University Press, 2000)

Braden, Gordon, Robert Cummings and Stuart Gillespie, eds, *The Oxford History of Literary Translation in English*, Volume II, 1550–1660 (Oxford: Oxford University Press, 2010)

Burke, Peter, and Ronnie Po-Chia Hsia, eds, *Cultural Translation in Early Modern Europe* (Cambridge: Cambridge University Press, 2007)

Clarke, Danielle, 'Translations', in *The Cambridge Companion to Early Modern Women's Writing*, ed. by Laura Lunger Knoppers (Cambridge: Cambridge University Press, 2009), pp. 167–80

Coldiron, Anne E. B., *Printers Without Borders: Translation and Textuality in the Renaissance* (Cambridge: Cambridge University Press, 2015)

Demetriou, Tania, and Rowan Tomlinson, eds, *The Culture of Translation in Early Modern England and France, 1500–1660* (Basingstoke and New York: Palgrave Macmillan, 2015)

France, Peter, ed., *The Oxford Guide to Literature in English Translation* (Oxford: Oxford University Press, 2000)

Goodrich, Jaime, *Faithful Translators: Authorship, Gender, and Religion in Early Modern England* (Evanston: Northwestern University Press, 2014)

Höfele, Andreas, and Werner von Koppenfels, eds, *Renaissance Go-betweens: Cultural Exchange in Early Modern Europe* (New York: Walter de Gruyter, 2005)

Hosington, Brenda, and Hannah Fournier, 'Translation and Women Translators', in *The Encyclopedia of Women in the Renaissance: Italy, France and England*, ed. by Diana M. Robin, Anne Larsen and Carole Levin (Santa Barbara: University of California Press, 2007), pp. 369–73

Morini, Massimiliano, *Tudor Translation in Theory and Practice* (Farnham: Ashgate, 2006)

Rhodes, Neil, with Gordon Kendal and Louise Wilson, eds, *English Renaissance Translation Theory* (MHRA Tudor & Stuart Series, London: The Modern Humanities Research Association, 2013)

Schmidt, Gabriela, ed., *Elizabethan Translation and Literary Culture* (Berlin and Boston: De Gruyter, 2013)

Schurink, Fred, ed., *Tudor Translation* (London: Palgrave, 2011)

2. ON NEOCLASSICAL DRAMA AND ON SIDNEY HERBERT AND KYD

Bergeron, David M., *Textual Patronage in English Drama, 1570–1640* (Aldershot: Ashgate, 2006)

Braden, Gordon, *Renaissance Tragedy and the Senecan Tradition: Anger's Privilege* (New Haven and London: Yale University Press, 1985)

Brennan, Michael, *Literary Patronage in the English Renaissance: The Pembroke Family* (London: Routledge, 1988)

——, *The Sidneys of Penshurst and the Monarchy, 1500–1700* (Aldershot: Ashgate, 2006)

Bushnell, Rebecca, *Tragedies of Tyrants: Political Thought and Theater in the English Renaissance* (Ithaca: Cornell University Press, 1990)

Cadman, Daniel, *Sovereigns and Subjects in Early Modern Neo-Senecan Drama: Republicanism, Stoicism and Authority* (Farnham: Ashgate, 2015)

Carrère, Felix, *Le Théâtre de Thomas Kyd: contribution à l'étude du théâtre élisabéthain* (Toulouse: Privat, 1951)

Charlton, H. B., *The Senecan Tradition in Renaissance Tragedy* (Manchester: Manchester University Press, 1946)

Clarke, Danielle, 'The Politics of Translation and Gender in the Countess of Pembroke's *Antonie*', *Translation and Literature*, 6 (1997), 149–66

——, *The Politics of Early Modern Women's Writing* (London: Longman, 2001)

Cox Jensen, Freyja, *Reading the Roman Republic in Early Modern England* (Leiden: Brill, 2012)

Demers, Patricia, *Women's Writing in English: Early Modern England* (Toronto: University of Toronto Press, 2005)

Erne, Lukas, *Beyond the Spanish Tragedy: A Study of the Works of Thomas Kyd* (Manchester: Manchester University Press, 2002)

Findlay, Alison, and Stephanie Hodgson-Wright, with Gweno Williams, *Women and Dramatic Production 1550–1700* (London: Longman, 2000)

Freeman, Arthur, *Thomas Kyd, Facts and Problems* (Oxford: Oxford University Press, 1967)

Gillespie, Stuart, *Shakespeare's Books: A Dictionary of Shakespeare Sources* (London and New York: Continuum, 2004 [2001])

Hannay, Margaret P., *Philip's Phoenix: Mary Sidney, Countess of Pembroke* (Oxford: Oxford University Press, 1990)

——, ed., *Ashgate Critical Essays on Women Writers in England*: Mary Sidney, Volume II (London: Ashgate, 2009)

Hannay, Margaret P., Mary Ellen Lamb and Michael G. Brennan, eds, *The Ashgate Research Companion to the Sidneys, 1500–1700* (Farnham and Burlington: Ashgate, 2015), 2 vols

Hillman, Richard, *The French Origins of English Tragedy* (Manchester: Manchester University Press, 2010)

——, *French Reflections in the Shakespearean Tragic* (Manchester: Manchester University Press, 2012)

Holyoake, John, *A Critical Study of the Tragedies of Robert Garnier* (1545–90) (New York: Peter Lang, 1987)

Hosington, Brenda, 'Tudor Englishwomen's Translations of Protestant Texts: The Interplay of Ideology and Political Context', in

Tudor Translation, ed. by Fred Schurink (Basingstoke: Palgrave MacMillan, 2011), pp. 121–42

Jondorf, Gillian, *Robert Garnier and the Themes of Political Tragedy in the Sixteenth Century* (London: Cambridge University Press, 1969)

Ker, James, and Jessica Winston, eds, *Elizabethan Seneca: Three Tragedies* (Tudor and Stuart Translation Series, London: MHRA, 2012)

Kewes, Paulina, '"A Fit Memorial for the Times to Come": Admonition and Topical Application in Mary Sidney's *Antonius* and Samuel Daniel's *Cleopatra*', *The Review of English Studies*, 63.259 (2012), 243–64

Krontiris, Tina, *Oppositional Voices: Women as Writers and Translators of Literature in the English Renaissance* (London: Routledge, 1992)

Lake Prescott, Anne, 'Mary Sidney's "Antonius" and the Ambiguities of French History', *The Yearbook of English Studies*, 38.1 (2008), 216–33

——, 'Mary Sidney's French Sophocles: The Countess of Pembroke reads Robert Garnier', in *Representing France and the French in Early Modern English Drama*, ed. by Jean-Christophe Mayer (Newark: University of Delaware Press, 2008), pp. 68–89

Lamb, Mary Ellen, 'The Myth of the Countess of Pembroke: The Dramatic Circle', *Yearbook of English Studies*, 11 (1981), 194–202

——, 'The Countess of Pembroke and the Art of Dying', in *Women in the Middle Ages and the Renaissance: Literary and Historical Perspectives*, ed. by Mary B. Rose (Syracuse: Syracuse University Press, 1986), pp. 207–26

——, *Gender and Authorship in the Sidney Circle* (Madison: University of Wisconsin Press, 1990)

Lucas, F. L., *Seneca and Elizabethan Tragedy* (New York: Haskell House, 1966)

McDiarmid, Matthew P., 'The Influence of Robert Garnier on Some Elizabethan Tragedies', *Etudes Anglaises*, 11 (1958), 289–302

Murray, Peter, *Thomas Kyd* (New York: Twayne Publishers, 1987)

Muir, Kenneth, *The Sources of Shakespeare's Plays* (London: Methuen, 1977)

Norland, Howard B., *Neoclassical Tragedy in Elizabethan England* (Newark: University of Delaware Press, 2009)

Oberth, Iris, 'Appropriating France in Elizabethan Drama: English Translations of Robert Garnier's Plays', in *Elizabethan Translation and Literary Culture*, ed. by Gabriela Schmidt (Berlin and Boston: De Gruyter, 2013), pp. 275–98

Pender, Patricia, *Early Modern Women's Writing and the Rhetoric of Modesty* (London: Palgrave Macmillan, 2012)

Pentland, Elizabeth A., 'Philippe Mornay, Mary Sidney, and the Politics of Translation', in *Women's Writing / Women's Work in Early Modernity*, *Early Modern Studies Journal*, 6 (Fall 2014), 66–99

Perry, Curtis, 'The Uneasy Republicanism of Thomas Kyd's *Cornelia*', *Criticism*, 48.4 (2008), 535–55

Raber, Karen, ed., *Dramatic Difference: Gender, Class, and Genre in the Early Modern Closet Drama* (Newark: University of Delaware Press, 2001)

Roberts, Josephine A., and James F. Gaines, 'Kyd and Garnier: The Art of Amendment', *Comparative Literature*, 31.2 (1979), 124–33

Sanders, Eve Rachele, *Gender and Literacy on Stage in Early Modern England* (Cambridge: Cambridge University Press, 1998)

Skretkowicz, Victor, 'Mary Sidney Herbert's *Antonius*, English Philhellenism and the Protestant Cause', *Women's Writing*, 6.1 (1999), 7–25

Stillman, Robert E., *Sir Philip Sidney and the Poetics of Renaissance Cosmopolitanism* (Aldershot and Burlington: Ashgate, 2013)

Straznicky, Marta, *Privacy, Playreading, and Women's Closet Drama, 1550–1700* (Cambridge: Cambridge University Press, 2004)

Weller, Barry, 'Mary Sidney Herbert, Countess of Pembroke: *Antonius* (1592)', in *The Ashgate Research Companion to the Sidneys, 1500–1700, Volume II*, ed. by Margaret Hannay, Michael G. Brennan and Mary Ellen Lamb (London: Ashgate, 2009), pp. 199–210

Wilson-Lee, Edward, 'Women's Weapons: Country House Diplomacy in the Countess of Pembroke's French Translations', in *The Culture of Translation in Early Modern England and France, 1500–1660*, ed. by Tania Demetriou and Rowan Tomlinson (Basingstoke: Palgrave Macmillan, 2015), pp. 128–44

Witherspoon, Alexander M., *The Influence of Robert Garnier on Elizabethan Drama* ([Hamden]: Archon Books, 1968 [1924])

Woudhuysen, Henry R., *Sir Philip Sidney and the Circulation of Manuscripts, 1558–1640* (Oxford: Clarendon Press, 1996)

ANTONIUS

Antonius, a Tragedy

The Argument.

After the overthrow of Brutus and Cassius, the liberty of Rome being now utterly oppressed, and the Empire settled in the hands of Octavius Caesar and Marcus Antonius (who for knitting a straighter bond of amity° between them, had taken to wife Octavia, the sister of Caesar), Antonius undertook a journey against the Parthians,[1] *with intent to regain on them the honour won by them from the Romans, at the discomfiture and slaughter of Crassus.*[2] *But coming in his journey into Syria the places renewed in his remembrance the long intermitted love of Cleopatra, Queen of Egypt: who before time had both in Cilicia*[3] *and at Alexandria entertained him with all the exquisite delights and sumptuous pleasures, which a great prince and voluptuous lover could to the uttermost desire. Whereupon omitting his enterprise, he made his return to Alexandria, again falling to his former loves, without any regard of his virtuous wife Octavia, by whom nevertheless he had excellent children. This occasion Octavius took of taking arms against him; and preparing a mighty fleet, encountered him at Actium,*[4] *who also had assembled to that place a great number of galleys of his own, beside which Cleopatra brought with her from Egypt. But at the very beginning of the battle Cleopatra with all her galleys betook her to flight, which Antony seeing could not but follow; by his departure leaving to Octavius the greatest victory which in any sea battle hath been heard. Which he, not negligent to pursue, follows them the next spring, and besiegeth them within Alexandria, where Antony finding all that he trusted to fail him, beginneth to grow jealous and to suspect Cleopatra. She thereupon enclosed herself with two of her women in a monument she had before caused to be built, thence sends him word she was dead; which he believing for truth, gave himself with his sword a deadly wound: but*

[1] A people who originally lived in western Asia (modern-day Iran), home of the Arsacid dynasty, who fought against the Romans.

[2] Marcus Licinius Crassus, a triumvir with Pompey and Julius Caesar, was killed by the Parthians in 53 BC. He was Cornelia's father.

[3] Region in Asia Minor, south of the central Anatolian plateau, which became a Roman province after Pompey subdued it in 67 BC.

[4] A promontory off the west coast of Greece, famous for being the site of the naval battle between Octavius and Antony, which Antony lost.

died not until a messenger came from Cleopatra to have him brought to her to the tomb. Which she not daring to open lest she should be made prisoner to the Romans and carried in Caesar's triumph, cast down a cord from an high window, by the which (her women helping her) she trussed up Antonius half dead, and so got him into the monument. The stage supposed Alexandria; the Chorus first Egyptians, and after Roman soldiers. The history to be read at large in Plutarch[5] *in the life of Antonius.*

[5] Greek historian (AD 46–120) whose *Parallel Lives* were translated by Thomas North in 1579, from the French of Jacques Amyot. Garnier made extensive use of Amyot's version. Garnier adds: 'et au 51. Livre de Dion' ('and in Book 51 of Dio [Cassius]'), but the reference remains untranslated by Sidney Herbert.

The Actors

Antonius
Cleopatra
Eras and Charmion } *Cleopatra's women*
Philostratus, *a Philosopher*
Lucilius
Diomede, *Secretary to Cleopatra*
Octavius Caesar
Agrippa
Euphron, *Teacher of Cleopatra's children*
Children *of Cleopatra*
Dircetus, *the Messenger*
[A Chorus of Egyptians]
[A Chorus of Roman Soldiers]

[ACT I]

[*Enter* ANTONIUS *and* CHORUS OF EGYPTIANS.]

ANTONIUS

Since cruel Heav'ns against me obstinate,[1]
Since all mishaps° of the round engine[2] do
Conspire my harm: since men, since powers divine,
Air, earth, and sea are all injurious;
And that my queen herself, in whom I lived,
The idol of my heart doth me pursue,
It's meet° I die. For her have I forgone
My country, Caesar unto war provoked
(For just revenge of sister's wrong, my wife,[3]
Who moved my queen (ay me!) to jealousy)
For love of her, in her allurements caught
Abandoned life; I honour have despised,
Disdained my friends, and of the stately Rome
Despoiled° the empire of her best attire,
Contemned that power that made me so much feared,
A slave become unto her feeble face.
O cruel traitress, woman most unkind,
Thou dost, forsworn, my love and life betray,
And giv'st me up to rageful enemy,
Which soon (O fool!) will plague thy perjury.
Yielded Pelusium[4] on this country's shore,
Yielded thou hast my ships and men of war,
That nought remains (so destitute am I)
But these same arms which on my back I wear.
Thou shouldst have had them too, and me unarmed
Yielded to Caesar naked of defence.
Which while I bear let Caesar never think

---

[1] The scene opens just after Antony's defeat at Actium in 30 BC.

[2] Commonplace metaphor for the earth. Garnier: 'la ronde machine' ('the round machine', p. 76r).

[3] Antony's marriage with Octavius's sister Octavia was part of the peace treaty negotiated at Brundisium in 40 BC, sealing the second triumvirate between Octavius, Antony and Lepidus. See the Argument above. Cleopatra's jealousy towards Octavia is explicitly mentioned in Plutarch (*Life of Antony*, LVII. 1).

[4] City in Eastern Egypt which, according to Plutarch (*Life of Antony*, LXXIV. 1), Antony thought he had lost because of Cleopatra's betrayal.

Triumph of me shall his proud chariot grace,
Not think with me his glory to adorn,
On me alive to use his victory.
  Thou only Cleopatra triumph hast,
Thou only hast my freedom servile made,
Thou only hast me vanquished; not by force
(For forced I cannot be) but by sweet baits
Of thy eyes' graces, which did gain so fast
Upon my liberty, that nought remained.
None else henceforth, but thou my dearest queen,
Shall glory in commanding Antony.
  Have Caesar fortune and the gods his friends
To him have Jove and fatal sisters[5] given
The sceptre of the earth: he never shall
Subject my life to his obedience.
But when that death, my glad refuge, shall have
Bounded the course of my unsteadfast life,
And frozen corpse under a marble cold
Within tomb's bosom, widow of my soul;
Then at his will let him it subject make,
Then what he will let Caesar do with me,
Make me limb after limb be rent, make me
My burial take in sides of Thracian wolf.[6]
  Poor Antony! Alas, what was the day,
The days of loss that gainèd thee thy love
(Wretch Antony!), since then Megaera[7] pale
With snaky hairs enchained thy misery?
The fire thee burnt was never Cupid's fire
(For Cupid bears not such a mortal brand°)
It was some fury's torch, Orestes' torch,[8]

---

[5] The three Fates of classical mythology, who preside over human destinies.
[6] i.e. feed me to a Thracian wolf. Thrace was a region located on the Black Sea next to Macedonia, renowned for its wild wolves and the ferocity of its inhabitants.
[7] One of the three Erinyes, or Furies, goddesses of revenge in Greek Mythology, who punished wrongdoers that had escaped public justice. They were represented with heads wreathed with serpents.
[8] In Greek mythology, Orestes murdered his mother Clytemnestra and in some versions he was then driven mad by the Furies. See in particular Virgil, *Aeneid*, IV. 471–73: 'aut Agamemnonius scoenis agitatus Orestes, | Armatam facibus matrem et serpentibus atris | Cum fugit' ('as when, on the stage, Orestes, son of Agamemnon, is driven mad, and flees his mother armed with torches and black snakes').

Which sometimes burnt his mother-murdering soul
(When wand'ring mad, rage boiling in his blood,
He fled his fault which followed as he fled)
Kindled within his bones by shadow pale
Of mother slain returned from Stygian lake.[9]
    Antony, poor Antony! Since that day
Thy old good hap° did far from thee retire.
Thy virtue° dead, thy glory made alive
So oft by martial deeds is gone in smoke.
Since then the bays so well thy forehead knew,
To Venus' myrtles[10] yielded have their place;
Trumpets to pipes; field tents to courtly bowers;[11]
Lances and pikes to dances and to feasts.[12]
Since then, O wretch, instead of bloody wars
Thou shouldst have made upon the Parthian kings[13]
For Roman honour filed° by Crassus' foil,[14]
Thou threw'st thy cuirass° off, and fearful° helm,°
With coward courage unto Egypt's queen
In haste to run, about her neck to hang,
Languishing in her arms thy idol made:[15]
In sum, giv'n up to Cleopatra's eyes.
Thou break'st at length from thence, as one encharmed

---

[9] Refers to the river Styx, which in classical mythology marks the boundary of the underworld.

[10] An attribute of Venus, associated with love, whereas the laurel wreath ('the bays') was worn by victorious soldiers. In Canto VI of Ariosto's *Orlando Furioso* (1516), the knight Astolpho is seduced and turned into a myrtle bush by the enchantress Alcina.

[11] Sidney Herbert's addition; probably an allusion to the description of Alcina's gardens in Canto VI of Ariosto's *Orlando Furioso*, famously translated into English by Sir John Harington (1591); or to Spenser's reinterpretation of the passage as Acrasia's 'Bower of Bliss' in Book II of his *Faerie Queene* (1590), dedicated to sensual pleasures.

[12] See Plutarch's extended description of Antony and Cleopatra's excessive feasting in *Life of Antony*, LVI. 4, and North's rendering: 'So that, where in manner all the world in every place was full of lamentations [...] onely in this ile of Samos there was nothing for many dayes space, but singing and pyping, and all the Theatre full of these common players, minstrells, and singing men' (*Lives*, p. 997).

[13] See note 1 to the Argument.

[14] See note 2 to the Argument.

[15] See Plutarch, *Life of Antony*, LXVI. 4, and North's evocative rendering: 'he was so caried away with the vaine love of this woman, as if he had bene glued unto her ...' (*Lives*, p. 1001).

Breaks from th'enchanter that him strongly held.
For thy first reason (spoiling of their force
The poisoned cups of thy fair sorceress)[16]
Recured° thy sprite;° and then on every side
Thou mad'st again the earth with soldiers swarm.
All Asia hid: Euphrates' banks[17] do tremble
To see at once so many Romans there
Breathe horror, rage, and with a threat'ning eye
In mighty squadrons cross his swelling streams.
Nought seen but horse, and fire-sparkling arms;[18]
Nought heard but hideous noise of mutt'ring° troops.
The Parth,° the Mede, abandoning their goods,
Hide them for fear in hills of Hyrcanie,[19]
Redoubting° thee. Then willing to besiege
The great Phraate,[20] head of Medìa,
Thou camped'st at her walls with vain assault,
Thy engines fit (mishap!°) not thither brought,[21]
    So long thou stay'st, so long thou dost thee rest,
So long thy love with such things nourishèd
Reframes, reforms[22] itself and stealingly

---

[16] Garnier: 'les poisons de ta belle sorciere' ('the poisons of thy fair enchantress', p. 77v). See Plutarch, *Life of Antony*, XXXVII. 4 and North's translation: 'being so ravished and enchaunted with the sweete poyson of her love, that he had no other thought but of her …' (*Lives*, p. 987). Probably also an allusion to Ariosto's *Orlando Furioso*, in which Alcina uses magic to seduce Roger. Sidney Herbert's added detail of the 'cups' refers to the enchantress Circe in Book X of the *Odyssey* — on whom Ariosto's character is based — and perhaps also to Spenser's *Faerie Queene*, where Acrasia poisons a knight by having him drink from her 'charmed cup' (II. 1. 55).

[17] River in Mesopotamia (in south-west Asia).

[18] Fire-sparkling] For a similar structure, see for instance Marlowe's 'fire-darting beames', *The Tragedie of Dido, Queene of Carthage* (London, 1594), sig. A3r.

[19] Parthia and Media were mountainous regions south-west of the Caspian sea. Antony was famed for his victorious campaigns in these regions. Hyrcania was one of the adjacent provinces of the Persian empire.

[20] Trisyllabic, like 'Media'. The main city of Media, unsuccessfully besieged by Antony during his war against the Parthians. Several kings of Parthia bear the name of Phraate.

[21] Not thither brought] Plutarch notes that Antony had marched on Phraate in such haste that he had left his war machines behind, which caused the siege to fail (*Life of Antony*, XXXVIII. 2–3).

[22] Reframes, reforms] Frames again (neologism), forms again. Herbert closely paraphrases the French: 'se refait, se reforme, & peu à peu reprend | Sa puissance premiere, & redevient plus grand' ('Replenishes, rekindles itself, and gradually takes up | its initial force, and grows greater again' p. 77v).

Retakes° his force and rebecomes° more great.
For of thy queen the looks, the grace, the words,
Sweetness, allurements, amorous delights,
Entered again thy soul, and day and night,
In watch, in sleep, her image followed thee;
Not dreaming but of her, repenting still
That thou for war hadst such a goddess left.
    Thou car'st no more for Parth,° nor Parthian bow,
Sallies, assaults, encounters, shocks, alarms,
For ditches, rampires,° wards, entrenchèd grounds;
Thy only care is sight of Nilus' streams,[23]
Sight of that face whose guileful semblant° doth
(Wand'ring in thee) infect thy tainted heart.
Her absence thee besots: each hour, each hour
Of stay, to thee impatient seems an age.
Enough of conquest, praise thou deem'st enough,
If soon enough the bristled[24] fields thou see
Of fruitful Egypt, and the stranger flood[25]
Thy queen's fair eyes (another Pharos)[26] lights.
    Returnèd low, dishonourèd, despised,
In wanton love a woman thee misleads,
Sunk in foul sink.° Meanwhile respecting nought
Thy wife Octavia and her tender babes,[27]
Of whom the long contempt against thee whets
The sword of Caesar now thy lord become.
    Lost thy great empire, all those goodly towns
Reverenced thy name[28] as rebels now thee leave;
Rise against thee, and to the ensigns flock
Of conqu'ring Caesar, who enwalls thee round,

---

[23] Garnier has 'les Canopides ondes' ('the waters of Canopus', an Egyptian port near the mouth of the Nile or Nilus, p. 77v). Sidney Herbert replaces this difficult reference with a more evocative one.

[24] Covered with stubble or bristling crop.

[25] i.e. the flooded banks of the river Nile. Garnier: 'sa rive estrangere' ('its foreign shore', p. 78r).

[26] The site of the famous lighthouse, considered one of the seven wonders of the world. Perhaps with a pun on Pharaoh (not in the French, 'Phar').

[27] Compare with Garnier's 'ta géniture' ('your offspring', p. 78r). Octavia already had three children when she was married to Antony. They had two additional daughters together.

[28] i.e. which once revered thy name, etc.

Caged in thy hold, scarce master of thyself,
Late master of so many nations.[29]
  Yet, yet, which is of grief extremest grief,
Which is yet of mischief° highest mischief?
It's Cleopatra, alas! Alas, it's she,
It's she augments the torment of thy pain,
Betrays thy love, thy life (alas!) betrays,
Caesar to please, whose grace she seeks to gain,[30]
With thought her crown to save and fortune make
Only thy foe which common ought have been.[31]
  If her I always loved, and the first flame
Of her heart-killing love shall burn me last,
Justly complain I she disloyal is,
Nor constant is, even as I constant am,
To comfort my mishap,° despising me
No more than when the heavens favoured me.
  But ah, by nature women wav'ring are,
Each moment changing and rechanging minds.[32]
Unwise, who blind in them thinks loyalty
Ever to find in beauty's company.

[*Exit* ANTONIUS.]

CHORUS

The boiling° tempest still
  Makes not sea waters foam,
  Nor still the Northern blast
  Disquiets quiet streams.
  Nor who his chest to fill[33]

[29] The repetition is Sidney Herbert's. Garnier: 'à peine es-tu maistre | De toy, qui le soulois de tant de peuples estre' ('Hardly can you rule | yourself, who over so many peoples used to rule', p. 78r).

[30] Garnier has 'Caesar qu'elle va cherissant' (p. 78r, literally 'Caesar whom she loves increasingly'). Plutarch reports that Cleopatra approached Caesar straight after the defeat at Actium, and that he granted her safety on condition that she cast Antony out, or put him to death (*Life of Antony*, LXXII. 1 and LXXIII. 1).

[31] Turn fortune against you only, when your fate should have been shared.

[32] This is a topos: see Virgil's *Aeneid*, IV. 569–70: 'varium et mutabile semper | Femina' ('an ever-changing, fickle thing is woman'). Also used in *Cornelia*, III. 3. 155.

[33] Garnier here specifically refers to the merchant, who crosses the seas for profit (p. 78v), probably alluding to Horace's *Odes*, I. 1. 15–18: 'Mercator [...] mox reficit rates | quassas, indocilis pauperiem pati' (the merchant [...] soon rebuilds his shattered ships, unwilling to endure poverty'). See also *Cornelia*, III. 3. 181.

Sails to the morning beams,[34]
On waves wind tosseth fast,
Still keeps his ship from home.
Nor Jove still down doth cast
Inflamed with bloody ire°
On man, on tree, on hill,
His darts of thund'ring fire.
Nor still the heat doth last
On face of parchèd plain.
Nor wrinkled cold doth still
On frozen furrows rain.
But still as long as we
In this low world remain,
Mishaps° our daily mates,
Our lives do entertain;
And woes which bear no dates
Still perch upon our heads;
None go, but straight will be
Some greater in their steads.
Nature made us not free,
When first she made us live.[35]
When we began to be,
To be began our woe;[36]
Which growing evermore
As dying life doth grow,
Do more and more us grieve,
And tire us more and more.
No stay in fading states,
For more to height they retch,[37]
Their fellow miseries
The more to height do stretch.
They cling even to the crown,
And threat'ning furious wise

[34] Garnier: 'le Levant', i.e. the Mediterranean countries east of Italy, but also the rising sun.
[35] Contrast with Garnier: 'Nature en naissant nous fait estre | Sugets à les souffrir tousjours' ('Nature subjects us from birth | ever to suffer them'), pp. 78v-79r.
[36] As noted by Ternaux (p. 125), the passage is reminiscent of Lucretius' *De Rerum Natura*, v. 227: 'cui tantum in vita restet transire malorum' ('with so many troubles awaiting [man] through his lifetime').
[37] Archaic variant of 'reach', which must be kept for the rhyme.

From tyrannizing pates[38]
Do often pull it down.
In vain on waves untried
To shun them go we should,
To Scythes and Massagetes[39]
Who near the pole[40] reside;
In vain to boiling° sands
Which Phoebus' battery beats;
For with us still they would
Cut seas and compass lands.
The darkness no more sure
To join with heavy night;
The light which gilds the days
To follow Titan[41] pure;
No more the shadow light
The body to ensue,
Than wretchedness always
Us wretches to pursue.
Oh, blessed who never breathed,
Or whom with pity moved,
Death from his cradle reaved,°
And swaddled in his grave;
And blessèd also he
(As curse may blessing have)
Who low and living free
No prince's charge hath proved.
By stealing sacred fire
Prometheus[42] then unwise,

[38] Heads. The French has 'chef tyrannique des Rois' ('the tyrannical heads of kings', p. 79r). As noted by Ternaux (p. 125), the whole stanza echoes the chorus in Seneca's *Agamemnon*, 57–59: 'O regnorum magnis fallax | Fortuna bonis, | in praecipti dubioque locas | excelsa nimis'. As rendered in John Studley's 1566 translation: 'O Fortune that dost fail the great estate of kings, | On slippery sliding seat thou placest lofty things' (*Elizabethan Seneca*, ed. by Ker and Winston, p. 224).
[39] Warlike nomadic peoples who lived in northern parts of Europe and Asia (and settled around present-day Crimea for the former, and in the Caucasus for the latter), renowned for their horsemanship.
[40] Garnier: 'Loin sur le Boree habiter' ('residing in the remote Borean regions', p. 79r). Boreas was the personification of the northern wind.
[41] The sun god Hyperion was one of the Titans. Garnier only has 'le Soleil' ('the Sun', p. 79r).
[42] A Titan who famously stole fire from the gods to give it to men, and who was eventually punished by Zeus. Garnier here paraphrases Horace's *Odes*, I. 3. 27–33:

Provoking gods to ire,°
The heap of ills did stir,
And sickness pale and cold,
Our end which onward spur
To plague our hands too bold
To filch the wealth of skies.
In heaven's hate since then
Of ill with ill enchained
We, race of mortal men
Full fraught our breasts have borne,
And thousand thousand woes
Our heav'nly souls now thorn,°[43]
Which free before from those
No earthly passion pained.
War and war's[44] bitter cheer°
Now long time with us stay,
And fear of hated foe
Still, still increaseth sore;
Our harms worse daily grow,
Less yesterday they were
Than now, and will be more
Tomorrow than to day.

[*Exit* CHORUS.]

'audax Iapeti genus | ignem fraude mala gentibus intulit; | post ignem aetheria domo | subductum macies et nova febrium | terris incubuit cohors | semotique prius tarda necessitas | leti corripuit gradum' ('By criminal guile, the daring son of Iapetus brought fire to the nations; once fire was stolen from its heavenly home, consumption and a host of new fevers fell upon the earth, and necessary death, until then far and slow, quickened its step').

[43] First use in this sense. Garnier: 'espine [...] | Nostre ame' ('is a thorn in [...] our souls', p. 79v).

[44] The repetition is Sidney Herbert's addition. Garnier: 'Les guerres et leur suite amere' ('Wars and their bitter effects', p. 79v). See also 'still, still', three lines down.

Act II

[Scene 1][1]

[*Enter* Philostratus *and* Chorus of Egyptians.]

Philostratus

What horrible fury,[2] what cruel rage,
O Egypt, so extremely thee torments?
Hast thou the gods so angered by thy fault?
Hast thou against them some such crime conceived,
That their engrainèd° hand lift up in threats
They should desire in thy heart blood to bathe?
And that their burning wrath which nought can quench,
Should pitiless on us still lighten down?[3]
We are not hewn out of the monstrous mass
Of Giants,[4] those, which heavens' wrack° conspired;
Ixion's race, false prater° of his loves;[5]
Nor yet of him who feigned lightnings found;[6]
Nor cruel Tantalus,[7] nor bloody Atreus,
Whose cursèd banquet for Thyestes' plague[8]
Made the beholding sun for horror turn
His back, and backward from his course return,
And hast'ning his wing-footed horses' race[9]
Plunge him in sea for shame to hide his face,

---

[1] Scene breaks added. There are no scene breaks in Garnier either.
[2] Garnier has 'Megere', one of the three Furies (see p. 97, n. 7).
[3] i.e. strike with lightning.
[4] In Classical mythology, the Giants were monstrous creatures, half divine, who fought the gods, and were defeated with the help of Hercules.
[5] In Greek mythology, Ixion, King of Lapithae, tried to seduce Hera, Zeus' wife, and was punished by being tied to a wheel of fire after boasting of his alleged success.
[6] Sidney Herbert omits the name of Salmoneus, which is mentioned in Garnier ('fier Salmoné'). Salmoneus was punished by Jupiter for attempting to imitate thunderbolts with torches. See Virgil's *Aeneid*, VI. 585ff.
[7] Greek mythological figure, half divine, who angered the gods and was famously punished by being made to stand eternally between a pool of water and a tree laden with fruit, without ever being able to satisfy his thirst or his hunger. In some versions, he angered the gods by serving them up his son in a banquet, hence 'cruel'.
[8] Atreus, the mythical king of Mycenae, took revenge on his brother Thyestes, who had seduced his wife, by serving him his own sons in a banquet. See Seneca's tragedy *Thyestes*.
[9] Apollo was believed to drive his horses across the sky to give light to the world.

While sullen night upon the wond'ring world
For midday's light her starry mantle cast.[10]
But what we be, whatever wickedness
By us is done, alas, with what more plagues,
More eager torments could the gods declare
To heav'n and earth that us they hateful hold?
With soldiers, strangers, horrible in arms,
Our land is hid, our people drowned in tears.
But terror here and horror, nought is seen,
And present death prizing° our life each hour.
Hard at our ports and at our porches waits
Our conquering foe; hearts fail us, hopes are dead;
Our queen laments, and this great emperor
Sometime (would now they did!) whom worlds did fear,
Abandonèd, betrayed, now minds no more
But from his evils by hastened death to pass.
Come, you poor people[11] tired with ceaseless plaints°
With tears and sighs make mournful sacrifice
On Isis'[12] altars: not ourselves to save,
But soften Caesar and him piteous° make
To us, his prey, that so his lenity°
May change our death into captivity.
Strange are the evils the fates on us have brought;
Oh, but alas! How far more strange the cause!
Love, love (alas, whoever would have thought?)
Hath lost this realm inflamèd with his fire.
Love, playing love, which men say kindles not

---

[10] The theme of the sun turning back in horror is an epic topos. See in particular Lucan's *Pharsalia*, I. 540–44: 'Ipse caput medio Titan cum ferret Olympo | Condidit ardentes atra caligine currus, | Involvitque orbem tenebris, gentesque coegit | Desperare diem: qualem fugiente per ortus | sole Thyesteae noctem duxere Mycenae'; in Marlowe's translation (published in 1600 but probably composed in the 1580s): 'Titan himselfe throand in the midst of heaven, | His burning chariot plung'd in sable cloudes, | And whelm'd the world in darknesse, making men | Dispaire of day; as did Thiestes towne | (Mycenae), Phoebus flying through the East …' (*Lucans first booke*, sig. D2v).

[11] Garnier: 'nous peuple imbecile' ('we, stupefied people'). Note the change of emphasis on Sidney Herbert's part.

[12] Egyptian goddess identified with the earth and the moon, who was integrated into the Graeco-Roman pantheon. She is sometimes identified with the Greek Demeter or with Aphrodite. Sidney Herbert omits Garnier's adjective, 'Argolique' (from Argos), which emphasizes the Greek connection.

But in soft hearts, hath ashes made our towns.[13]
And his sweet shafts, with whose shot none are killed,
Which ulcer° not, with deaths our lands have filled.
Such was the bloody, murd'ring, hellish love
Possessed thy heart, fair, false guest, Priam's son,[14]
Firing a brand° which after made to burn
The Trojan towers by Grecians ruinate.
By this love, Priam, Hector, Troilus,
Memnon, Deiphobus, Glaucus,[15] thousands more,
Whom red Scamander's armour-cloggèd streams[16]
Rolled into seas, before their dates are dead.
So plaguey° he, so many tempests raiseth,
So murd'ring he, so many cities razeth,
When insolent, blind, lawless, orderless,
With mad delights our sense he entertains.
All-knowing gods our wracks° did us foretell[17]
By signs in earth, by signs in starry spheres,
Which should have moved us, had not destiny
With too strong hand warpèd[18] our misery.
The comets flaming through the scattered clouds
With fiery beams, most like unbroaded° hairs:
The fearful dragon whistling at the banks,
And holy Apis[19] ceaseless bellowing
(As never erst°) and shedding endless tears;
Blood raining down from heav'n in unknown showers:
Our gods' dark faces overcast with woe,

[13] The reference is to Troy, which was burnt to the ground because of Paris's love for Helen.

[14] Paris, the Trojan who abducted the Greek Menelaus's wife, Helen, on a visit to Sparta, which caused the Trojan war (eventually lost by the Trojans). Sidney Herbert paraphrases Garnier's 'Priamide', as 'Priam's son'. Priam was the king of Troy. The episode was considered a notorious *exemplum* of the nefarious power of love.

[15] These are all Trojan heroes who died during the Trojan war, as told in Homer's *Iliad*. Garnier's list is slightly different: 'Priam, Sarpedon, et Troïle, | Glauque, Hector, Deïphobe' (p. 80v).

[16] A river near Troy. The river Garnier mentions is in fact another river close to Troy, 'Simoïs' (p. 80v), which often appears in *The Iliad*.

[17] 61–72] Garnier here closely follows Dio Cassius (*Roman History*, LI. 17. 4–5), who mentions blood showers, a serpent, comets, ghosts, and a weeping and bellowing statue of the Egyptian god Apis.

[18] i.e. cast, brought violently about.

[19] Egyptian bull god.

And dead men's ghosts appearing in the night.
Yea, even this night, while all the city stood
Oppressed with terror, horror, servile fear,
Deep silence over all, the sounds were heard
Of diverse songs, and diverse instruments,
Within the void of air;[20] and howling noise,
Such as mad Bacchus' priests in Bacchus'[21] feasts,
On Nysa[22] make, and (seemed) the company,
Our city lost, went to the enemy.[23]
    So we forsaken both of gods and men,
So are we in the mercy of our foes;
And we henceforth obedient must become
To laws of them who have us overcome.

[*Exit.*]

CHORUS

Lament we our mishaps,°
    Drown we with tears our woe;
    For lamentable haps°
    Lamented easy grow,
    And much less torment bring
    Than when they first did spring.
We want that woeful song,
    Wherewith wood-music's queen[24]
    Doth ease her woes, among
    Fresh spring-time's bushes green,

---

[20] 73–77] See Plutarch, *Life of Antony*, LXXV. 3. Shakespeare dramatizes this detail in *Antony and Cleopatra*, IV. 3.

[21] Roman god of wine and pleasure. Sidney Herbert expands upon Garnier's 'les Edonides', i.e. the Bacchae or Bacchantes, who were the followers of Bacchus on Mount Edon, in ancient Macedonia. Compare with North's version of the passage in Plutarch: 'it is said that sodainly they heard a marvelous sweete harmonie of sundrie sorts of instrumentes of musicke, with the crie of a multitude of people, as they had bene dancing, and had song as they use in Bacchus' feastes' (*Lives*, p. 1003).

[22] The birthplace of Bacchus in India.

[23] Garnier: 'au vaincueur' ('to the victor'), p. 81r.

[24] The nightingale or Philomela, which Garnier mentions by name. The story is told in Ovid's *Metamorphoses*, vi. 459–79. Tereus, king of Thrace, raped his wife Procne's sister, Philomela. Even though Tereus cut off her tongue, Philomela conveyed the identity of the culprit by weaving a tapestry revealing his name. The two sisters fled; Philomela was changed into a nightingale, her sister into a swallow. This and the following mythological *exempla* are taken from the chorus of Seneca's *Agamemnon* (664ff.).

On pleasant branch alone
Renewing ancient moan.
We want that moanful sound,
That prattling Procne makes
On fields of Thracian ground,
Or streams of Thracian lakes,[25]
To empt° her breast of pain,
For Itys[26] by her slain.
Though Halcyons do still,
Bewailing Ceyx's lot,[27]
The seas with plainings fill
Which his dead limbs have got,
Not ever other grave
Than tomb of waves to have.
And though the bird in death
That most Meander[28] loves,
So sweetly sighs his breath
When death his fury proves,°
As almost softs his heart,
And almost blunts his dart.
Yet all the plaints° of those,
Nor all their tearful 'larms,[29]
Cannot content our woes,
Nor serve to wail the harms,
In soul which we, poor we,
To feel enforcèd be.
Nor they of Phoebus bred,[30]
In tears can do so well,

[25] Garnier: 'Sur l'onde Ismarienne | Le jazard Daulien oiseau' ('On the Ismarian shore | the prattling bird from Daulis'), p. 81r. Daulis is the place where Procne was turned into a bird. Ismarus was a mountain in Thrace.

[26] Son of Procne and Tereus, whom Procne killed and served to her husband in revenge for the rape of Philomela.

[27] Kingsfishers, which took their names from Alcyone, Ceyx's wife, who threw herself into the sea after her husband drowned, and was changed by the gods into a kingfisher. See Ovid's *Metamorphoses*, XI. 410–752.

[28] A river in Phrygia, said to have six hundred windings and turnings. It is on its banks that in Greek mythology Cycnus, king of Liguria, was changed into a swan for bewailing the death of Phaëton. Cf. Ovid's *Metamorphoses*, II. 367ff.

[29] Alarms.

[30] Phaëton's sisters wept for his death after he failed to control Apollo's chariot and was thrown into the river Po (see 'Padus' below).

They for their brother shed,
Who into Padus fell,
Rash guide of chariot clear,
Surveyor of the year.
Nor she[31] whom heav'nly powers
To weeping rock did turn,
Whose tears distil in showers,
And show she yet doth mourn,
Wherewith his top to skies
Mount Sipylus doth rise.
Nor weeping drops which flow
From bark of wounded tree,
That Myrrha's shame doth show,[32]
With ours compared may be,
To quench her loving fire
Who durst° embrace her sire.
Nor all the howlings made
On Cybel's sacred hill[33]
By eunuchs of her trade,
Who Atys, Atys[34] still,
With doubled cries resound,
Which Echo[35] makes rebound.
Our plaints° no limits stay,
Nor more than do our woes;
Both infinitely stray
And neither measure knows.
In measure let them plain:°
Who measured griefs sustain.

[*Exit* CHORUS.]

[31] Niobe, who angered the gods by boasting about her numerous children. All her children were slain in revenge, and she was changed by Zeus into a rock or a marble fountain on Mount Sipylus.

[32] Myrrha committed incest with her father and was changed into a myrrh tree. See Ovid's *Metamorphoses*, X. 298–518.

[33] Mount Dindymus or Dindymon in Phrygia, dedicated to the goddess Cybele.

[34] In Ovid, Atys, or Attis, is a shepherd in Phrygia whom the goddess Cybele consecrated to her cult. Because he violated his vow of chastity, she drove him to a frenzy that resulted in Atys castrating himself. He was turned into a pine tree. See Ovid, *Metamorphoses*, X. 104.

[35] A nymph loved by Pan who was turned into a voice that could only repeat what it was told. See Ovid's *Metamorphoses*, III. 338–400.

[Scene 2]

[*Enter*] Cleopatra, Eras, Charmion, Diomede
[*and* Chorus of Egyptians].

Cleopatra

That I have thee betrayed, dear Antony,
My life, my soul, my sun? I had such thought?
That I have thee betrayed, my lord, my king?
That I would break my vowèd faith to thee?
Leave thee? Deceive thee? Yield thee to the rage
Of mighty foe? I ever had that heart?
Rather sharp lightning lighten on my head;
Rather may I to deepest mischief° fall;
Rather the opened earth devour me;
Rather fierce tigers feed them on my flesh;
Rather, O rather let our Nilus send,
To swallow me quick, some weeping crocodile.[1]
And didst thou then suppose my royal heart
Had hatched, thee to ensnare, a faithless love?
And changing mind, as Fortune changèd cheer,°
I would weak thee, to win the stronger, lose?[2]
O wretch! O caitiff!° Oh, too cruel hap!°
And did not I sufficient loss sustain,
Losing my realm, losing my liberty,
My tender offspring, and the joyful light
Of beamy sun, and yet, yet losing more,
Thee, Antony, my care, if I lose not
What yet remained? Thy love, alas! Thy love,
More dear than sceptre, children, freedom, light.
So ready I to row in Charon's barge[3]
Shall lose the joy of dying in thy love;
So the sole comfort of my misery,
To have one tomb with thee is me bereft.

---

[1] According to a widely-held belief, crocodiles could weep to lure their prey.
[2] I would lose you when you are weak, to win the stronger (i.e. Caesar). The antithesis is Sidney Herbert's addition.
[3] Charon conveyed the dead across the river Styx to the underworld in a barge.

So I in shady plains shall plain° alone,[4]
Not, as I hoped, companion of thy moan,
O height of grief!

ERAS

Why with continual cries
Your griefful° harms do you exasperate?
Torment yourself with murdering complaints?
Strain your weak breast so oft, so vehemently?
Water with tears this fair alabaster?
With sorrows sting so many beauties' wound?
Come of so many kings, want you the heart
Bravely, stoutly, this tempest to resist?

CLEOPATRA

My evils[5] are wholly unsupportable,°
No human force can them withstand, but death.

ERAS[6]

To him that strives nought is impossible.

CLEOPATRA

In striving lies no hope of my mishaps.°

ERAS

All things do yield to force of lovely face.[7]

CLEOPATRA

My face too lovely caused my wretched case.
My face hath so entrapped,° so cast us down,
That for his conquest Caesar may it thank,
Causing that Antony one army lost,
The other wholly did to Caesar yield.

---

[4] The polyptoton (plain / [com]plain) is Sidney Herbert's. The 'shady plains' (Garnier: 'l'ombreuse campagne', p. 83r) are the Olympic fields, peopled by the spirits of heroes in classical mythology.

[5] To be pronounced as one syllable (elided as 'eu'lls' in 1592 and 1595).

[6] This stichomythic interruption by Eras, like l. 43, is attributed to Charmion in Garnier (p. 83r). For differences in speech attribution, see Introduction, p. 36.

[7] 41–43 and below] Sequences of single, alternating lines (or stichomythia) are characteristic of Senecan tragedy.

For not enduring (so his amorous sprite°
Was with my beauty fired) my shameful flight,
Soon as he saw from rank wherein he stood
In hottest fight, my galleys making sail,
Forgetful of his charge (as if his soul
Unto his lady's soul had been enchained)
He left his men, who so courageously
Did leave their lives to gain him victory;
And careless both of fame and army's loss,
My oarèd° galleys followed with his ships,
Companion of my flight, by this base part
Blasting his former flourishing renown.[8]

ERAS
Are you therefore cause of his overthrow?

CLEOPATRA
I am sole cause, I did it, only I.

ERAS
Fear of a woman[9] troubled so his sprite?°

CLEOPATRA
Fire of his love was by my fear inflamed.

ERAS
And should he then to war have led a queen?

---

[8] 53–60] See Plutarch, *Life of Antony*, LXVI. 4–5, and North's translation: '(proving that true which an old man spake in myrth, that the soul of a lover lived in another body, and not in his owne) he was so caried away with the vaine love of this woman, as if he had bene glued unto her, and that she could not have removed without moving of him also. For when he saw Cleopatraes shippe under saile, he forgot, forsooke, and betrayed them that fought for him, and imbarked upon a galley with five bankes of o[ars], to follow her that had already begon to overthrow him, and would in the end be his utter destruction' (*Lives*, p. 1001).

[9] Garnier: 'la frayeur d'une femme' ('a woman's fear'). According to Ternaux, Garnier relays Dio's explanation of Cleopatra's flight in terms of feminine weakness: 'true to her nature as a woman and an Egyptian' (*Roman History*, L. 33, Loeb transl.). Sidney's ambiguous rendering seems to obscure the misogynistic slur.

CLEOPATRA

Alas! This was not his offence, but mine.
Antony (ay me, who else so brave a chief!)
Would not I should have taken seas with him;
But would have left me, fearful woman, far
From common hazard of the doubtful war.
 Oh, that I had believed! Now, now of Rome
All the great empire at our beck should bend.
All should obey, the vagabonding Scythes,
The fearèd Germans, back-shooting[10] Parthians,
Wand'ring Numidians, Britons far removed,
And tawny nations scorchèd with the sun.[11]
But I cared not: so was my soul possessed
(To my great harm) with burning jealousy,
Fearing least in my absence Antony
Should, leaving me, retake° Octavia.

CHARMION

Such was the rigour of your destiny.

CLEOPATRA

Such was my error and obstinacy.

CHARMION

But since gods would not, could you do withal?

CLEOPATRA

Always from gods good haps,° not harms, do fall.

CHARMION

And have they not all power on men's affairs?

---

[10] Garnier: 'sagetaires' ('arrow-shooting'). As noted by Hannay (*CW*, I, p. 150), Sidney Herbert here echoes Plutarch's *Life of Crassus* (see North, *Lives*, p. 614: 'the Parthians still drawing back, shotte altogether on every side').

[11] The Scythians, Germans, Parthians, Numidians and Britons all lived at the periphery of the Roman empire and were renowned for their cruelty. The list is an epic / tragic commonplace; see also *Cornelia*, IV. 2. 44–54.

CLEOPATRA

They never bow so low as worldly cares,[12]
But leave to mortal men to be disposed
Freely on earth whatever mortal is.
If we therein sometimes some faults commit,
We may them not to their high majesties,
But to ourselves impute, whose passions
Plunge us each day in all afflictions.
Wherewith when we our souls do thornèd° feel,
Flatt'ring ourselves we say they dest'nies are:
That gods would have it so, and that our care
Could not impeach but that it must be so.

CHARMION

Things here below are in the heav'ns begot,
Before they be in this our world born,
And never can our weakness turn awry
The stayless° course of powerful destiny.
Nought here, force, reason, human providence,
Holy devotion, noble blood, prevails,
And Jove himself whose hand doth heavens rule,
Who both to gods and men as king commands,
Who earth (our firm support) with plenty stores,
Moves air and sea with twinkling of his eye,
Who all can do, yet never can undo
What once hath been by their hard laws decreed.[13]
    When Trojan walls, great Neptune's workmanship,[14]
Environed were with Greeks, and Fortune's wheel
Doubtful ten years now to the camp did turn,
And now again towards the town returned,
How many times did force and fury swell
In Hector's veins, egging him to the spoil

[12] 86–96] This is the traditional Epicurean position, as exposed in Epicurus' *Epistle to Menoeceus*, and in Lucretius's *De Rerum Natura*, II. 646–51.

[13] 97–108] Marked by Garnier as a *sententia*. Charmion here exposes the Stoic doctrine of necessity. Compare with Garnier's more neutral 'Nature en naissant nous fait estre | Sugets à les [les malheurs] souffrir toujours' ('Nature subjects us from birth | ever to suffer them', p. 78v), a couplet already used in the chorus to Act I. 173–75.

[14] According to Ovid, Neptune helped to build the walls of Troy. See *Metamorphoses*, XI. 199–215.

Of conquered foes, which at his blows did fly,
As fearful sheep at fearèd wolves' approach,[15]
To save (in vain, for why? It would not be)
Poor walls of Troy from adversaries' rage,
Who dyed them in blood, and cast to ground,
Heaped them with bloody burning carcasses![16]
    No, madam, think that if the ancient crown
Of your progenitors that Nilus[17] ruled,
Force take from you; the gods have willed it so,
To whom oft-times princes are odious.
They have to everything an end ordained;
All worldly greatness by them bounded is.
Some sooner, later some, as they think best:
None their decree is able to infringe.
But, which is more to us disastered° men,
Which subject are in all things to their will,
Their will is hid; nor while we live, we know
How, or how long we must in life remain.
Yet must we not for that feed on despair,
And make us wretched ere° we wretched be:
But always hope the best, even to the last,
    That from ourselves the mischief° may not grow.
Then, madam, help yourself, leave off in time
Antony's wrack,° lest it your wrack procure.
Retire you from him, save from wrathful rage
Of angry Caesar both your realm and you.
You see him lost, so as your amity°
Unto his evils can yield no more relief.
You see him ruined, so as your support
No more henceforth can him with comfort raise.
Withdraw you from the storm, persist not still

[15] Hector was the main hero of the Trojan camp and was finally killed by Achilles. The comparison of the Trojan warrior to a wolf on the prowl is (ironically) taken from the second book of Virgil's *Aeneid*, which depicts the fall of Troy (*Aeneid*, II. 355–60). See also *Cornelia*, V. 240.

[16] After a siege of ten years, Troy was vanquished, sacked and burnt to the ground by the Greeks.

[17] Sidney here again simplifies Garnier's 'l'onde Canopide' (see above, note 23, p. 100).

To lose yourself: this royal diadem
Regain° of Caesar.[18]

CLEOPATRA

Sooner shining light
Shall leave the day, and darkness leave the night,[19]
Sooner moist currents of tempestuous seas
Shall wave in heaven, and the nightly troops
Of stars shall shine within the foaming waves,
Than I thee, Antony, leave in deep distress.
I am with thee, be it thy worthy soul
Lodge in thy breast, or from that lodging part
Crossing the joyless lake[20] to take her place
In place preparèd for men demi-gods.
Live, if thee please, if life be loathsome die:
Dead and alive, Antony, thou shalt see
Thy princess follow thee, follow, and lament,
Thy wrack,° no less her own than was thy weal.[21]

CHARMION[22]

What helps his wrack° this ever-lasting love?

CLEOPATRA

Help, or help not, such must, such ought I prove.°

CHARMION

Ill done to lose yourself, and to no end.

---

[18] Garnier: 'n'allez de vous mesme | Perdre en vous obstinant ce Royal diadème: | Recourez à César' ('do not risk | losing by yourself, out of obstinacy, this royal diadem: | appeal to Caesar', p. 84v). Sidney seems to have read 'recouvrez' (do retrieve) instead of 'recourez' (do appeal).

[19] Compare with Garnier: 'Plustost le jour qui luit | Obscur se couvrira du voile de la nuict' ('sooner will the shining day | turn dark and be dimmed with the veil of night', p. 84v).

[20] The lake formed by the river Styx, the main river of the underworld. Garnier has simply 'l'Acheron' (a branch of the Styx).

[21] i.e. welfare, possibly also common weal (i.e. commonwealth, *OED* 'weal' n.1, 3 b, for *res publica*). Garnier: 'ton empire' (p. 85r).

[22] Lines 161, 163 and 171 are attributed to Eras in Garnier (p. 85r). For changes in speech attributions, see p. 112, n. 6 and p. 173, n. 13, and Introduction, p. 36.

CLEOPATRA
How ill think you to follow such a friend?

CHARMION
But this your love nought mitigates his pain.

CLEOPATRA
Without this love I should be inhumane.

CHARMION
Inhumane he, who his own death pursues.

CLEOPATRA
Not inhumane who miseries eschews.°

CHARMION
Live for your sons.

CLEOPATRA
Nay, for their father die.

CHARMION
Hard-hearted mother!

CLEOPATRA
Wife[23] kind-hearted I.

CHARMION
Then will you them deprive of royal right?

CLEOPATRA
Do I deprive them? No, it's dest'ny's might.

CHARMION[24]
Do you not them deprive of heritage,
That give them up to adversary's hands;

---

[23] According to Dio Cassius, Antony had actually married Cleopatra. See Introduction, pp. 29–30.
[24] 173–78] This speech is attributed to Eras in Garnier (p. 85r).

A man forsaken fearing to forsake,
Whom such huge numbers hold environèd,
T'abandon one 'gainst whom the frowning world
Banded with Caesar makes conspiring war.

CLEOPATRA

The less ought I to leave him left of all.
A friend in most distress should most assist.[25]
If that, when Antony great and glorious,
His legions led to drink Euphrates' streams,[26]
So many kings in train redoubting° him,
In triumph raised as high as highest heav'n,
Lord-like disposing as him pleasèd best,
The wealth of Greece, the wealth of Asia,[27]
In that fair fortune had I him exchanged
For Caesar, then, men would have counted me
Faithless, inconstant, light: but now the storm
And blust'ring tempest driving on his face,
Ready to drown, alas, what would they say?
What would himself in Pluto's mansion[28] say?
If I, whom always more than life he loved,
If I, who am his heart, who was his hope,
Leave him, forsake him (and perhaps in vain)
Weakly to please who him hath overthrown?
Not light, inconstant, faithless should I be,
But vile, forsworn, of treach'rous cruelty.

CHARMION

Cruelty to shun, you self-cruel are.[29]

CLEOPATRA

Self-cruel° him from cruelty to spare.

---

[25] Not marked as a *sententia* in Garnier.

[26] The allusion is to Antony's campaign in Parthia, a region expanding East of the Euphrates river.

[27] Through his successful campaigns, Antony secured both Greece and the East as his share in the triumvirate with Octavius and Lepidus in 40 BC.

[28] i.e. Hades, the underworld.

[29] Compare with Garnier: 'Fuyant la cruauté vous l'exercez sur vous' ('Fleeing others' cruelty, you are still cruel to yourself', p. 85v).

CHARMION

Our first affection to ourself is due.

CLEOPATRA

He is myself.[30]

CHARMION

Next it extends unto
Our children, friends, and to our country soil.
And you for some respect of wively love,
(Albeit scarce wifely) lose your native land,
Your children, friends, and (which is more) your life;
With so strong charms doth love bewitch our wits:
So fast in us this fire once kindled flames.
Yet if his harm by yours redress might have!

CLEOPATRA

With mine it may be closed in darksome grave.

CHARMION

And that, as Alcest[31] to herself unkind,
You might exempt him from the laws of death!
But he is sure to die; and now his sword
Already moisted is in his warm blood,
Helpless for any succour° you can bring
Against death's sting, which he must shortly feel.
Then let your love be like the love of old
Which Carian queen[32] did nourish in her heart
Of her Mausolus: build for him a tomb
Whose stateliness a wonder new may make.
Let him, let him have sumptuous funerals,
Let grave° thereon the horror of his fights;
Let earth be buried with unburied heaps.

---

[30] Garnier: 'Mon espous est moymesme' ('My husband is myself', p. 85v).

[31] Alcestis, a model of wifely love in Greek mythology, became the heroine of a play by Euripides. She agreed to die in lieu of her husband so he could live longer.

[32] Queen Artemisia, of Caria, another example of wifely love. She built a monument for her dead husband Mausoleus at Halicarnassus (in 353 BC), which became one of the seven wonders of the world.

Frame[33] their Pharsaly,[34] and discoloured streams
Of deep Enipeus;[35] frame the grassy plain,
Which lodged his camp at siege of Mutina;[36]
Make all his combats, and courageous acts,
And yearly plays to his praise institute;
Honour his memory, with doubled care
Breed and bring up the children of you both
In Caesar's grace, who as a noble prince
Will leave them lords of this most glorious realm.

CLEOPATRA

What shame were that? Ah, gods! What infamy?
With Antony in his good haps° to share,
And overlive° him dead; deeming enough
To shed some tears upon a widow tomb?
The after-livers[37] justly might report
That I him only for his empire loved,
And high estate; and that in hard estate
I for another did him lewdly leave.
Like to those birds[38] wafted with wand'ring wings
From foreign lands in spring-time here arrive,
And live with us so long as summer's heat,
And their food lasts, then seek another soil;
And as we see with ceaseless fluttering
Flocking of seely° flies a brownish cloud
To vintaged wine yet working in the tun,[39]
Not parting thence while they sweet liquor taste,

---

[33] Here represent (on the tomb). Garnier: 'Pharsale y soit pourtrait' ('let Pharsalia be there portrayed', p. 86r). The representation (or *ekphrasis*) of famous battles on a wall, monument or shield is an epic commonplace; see Homer's *Iliad*, XVIII, or Virgil's *Aeneid*, I and VIII.

[34] Pharsalus, or Pharsalia, in Thessaly, the site of the famous battle in which Antony and Caesar fought and defeated Pompey.

[35] The river flowing near Pharsalus.

[36] i.e. Modena, which was besieged by Antony in 43 BC.

[37] Later ages, posterity. Garnier: 'Les races à venir' ('generations to come', p. 86r).

[38] 241–44] The simile is taken from Virgil's *Aeneid*, VI. 310–12: '… ad terram gurgite ab alto | quam multae glomerantur aves, ubi frigidus annus | trans pontum fugat et terris immittit apricis' ('as many as the birds that flock from the deep onto the land, when the cold season chases them across the sea and pushes them towards warmer grounds').

[39] i.e. maturing in the barrel.

After, as smoke, all vanish in the air,
And of the swarm not one so much appear.

ERAS

By this sharp death what profit can you win?

CLEOPATRA

I neither gain nor profit seek therein.

ERAS

What praise shall you of after-ages get?

CLEOPATRA

Nor praise, nor glory in my cares are set.

ERAS

What other end ought you respect, than this?

CLEOPATRA

My only end, my only duty is.

ERAS

Your duty must upon some good be founded!

CLEOPATRA

On virtue it, the only good, is grounded.

ERAS

What is that virtue?

CLEOPATRA

That which us beseems.[40]

ERAS

Outrage ourselves? Who that beseeming deems?

---

[40] i.e. seems fit or right. As noted by Ternaux (p. 139), Garnier here paraphrases Cicero, *De Finibus*, IV. 54: 'summum bonum posuisset in ingenii praestantia, quam virtutem vocamus, nec quicquam aliud bonum esse dixisset, nisi quod esset honestum' ('[Zeno] established the supreme good as that excellence of mind, which we call virtue, and he declared that good to be nothing else but what is proper').

CLEOPATRA

Finish I will my sorrows, dying thus.[41]

ERAS

Minish° you will your glories doing thus.[42]

CLEOPATRA

Good friends I pray you seek not to revoke
My fixed intent of following Antony.[43]
I will die. I will die: must not his life,
His life and death by mine be followèd?
Meanwhile, dear sisters, live: and while you live,
Do often honour to our lovèd tombs.
Strew them with flowers, and sometimes happily
The tender thought of Antony your lord
And me, poor soul, to tears shall you invite,
And our true loves[44] your doleful° voice commend.

CHARMION

And think you, madam, we from you will part?
Think you alone to feel death's ugly[45] dart?
Think you to leave us? And that the same sun
Shall see at once you dead, and us alive?
We'll die with you, and Clotho,[46] pitiless
Shall us with you in hellish boat[47] embark.

CLEOPATRA

Ah, live, I pray you. This disastered° woe
Which racks my heart, alone to me belongs;

---

[41] Sidney Herbert omits the adjective 'genereuse' in Garnier: 'J'esteindray mes ennuis d'une mort genereuse' ('I will extinguish my sorrows with a generous [i.e. noble] death', p. 86v).

[42] Garnier's nuance qualifying Cleopatra's death is omitted here: 'vous teindrez vostre los d'une mort furieuse' ('you will taint your glory with a furious death', p. 86v). The line is originally spoken by Charmion (p. 86v). See ll. 161, 163, 173–78 above.

[43] Compare with Garnier: 'suivre mon Antoine aux Enfers palissans' ('follow my Antony to the paling underworld', p. 86v).

[44] Garnier has: 'saintes amours' ('sacred love', p. 86v).

[45] This adjective is not in Garnier.

[46] One of the three Fates, or Parcae, who holds the distaff. Garnier is more generic: 'l'impiteuse Parque' (p. 87r).

[47] Charon's barge conveying the souls of the dead to the underworld.

My lot longs° not to you; servants to be
No shame, no harm to you, as is to me.
  Live, sisters, live, and seeing his suspect°
Hath causeless me in sea of sorrows drowned,
And that I cannot live, if so I would,
Nor yet would leave this life, if so I could,
Without his love, procure me, Diomed,
That 'gainst poor me he be no more incensed.
Wrest out of his conceit that harmful doubt,
That since his wrack° he hath of me conceived —
Though wrong conceived, witness you reverent gods,
Barking Anubis, Apis bellowing[48] —
Tell him, my soul burning, impatient,
Forlorn with love of him, for certain seal
Of her true loyalty my corpse hath left,
T'increase of dead the number numberless.[49]
  Go then, and if as yet he me bewail,
If yet for me his heart one sigh forth breathe,
Blessed shall I be, and far with more content
Depart this world, where so I me torment.
Mean season,[50] us let this sad tomb enclose,
Attending° here till death conclude our woes.

DIOMED

I will obey your will.

CLEOPATRA

So the desert°
The gods repay of thy true faithful heart.

[*Exeunt all but* DIOMED *and* CHORUS.]

---

[48] Anubis was the Egyptian jackal-headed god of the dead. Apis was an Egyptian bull deity, one of the most worshipped gods of Egypt as a fertility god. See above, p. 107, n. 19.

[49] 293–296] See Plutarch, *Life of Antony*, LXXVI. 2, and North's translation: 'Then she, being affraied of his fury, fled into the tombe which she had caused to be made, and there she locked the dores unto her, and shut all the springes of the lockes with great boltes, and in the mean time sent unto Antonius to tell him that she was dead' (*Lives*, p. 1006).

[50] i.e. in the meantime.

DIOMED

And is't not pity, gods, ah, gods of heav'n,
To see from love such hateful fruits to spring?
And is't not pity that this firebrand so
Lays waste the trophies of Philippi[51] fields?
Where are those sweet allurements, those sweet looks,
Which gods themselves right heart-sick would have made?
What doth that beauty, rarest gift of heav'n,
Wonder of earth? Alas, what do those eyes?
And that sweet voice all Asia understood,
And sunburnt Afrique[52] wide in deserts spread?
Is their force dead? Have they no further power?
Cannot by them Octavius be surprised?
Alas! If Jove in midst of all his ire,°
With thunderbolt in hand some land to plague,
Had cast his eyes on my queen, out of hand[53]
His plaguing bolt had fall'n out of his hand;
Fire of his wrath into vain smoke should turn,
And other fire within his breast should burn.
 Nought lives so fair. Nature by such a work
Herself, should seem, in workmanship hath passed.
She is all heav'nly: never any man
But seeing her was ravished with her sight.
The alabaster covering of her face,[54]
The coral colour her two lips engrains,°
Her beamy[55] eyes two suns of this our world,
Of her fair hair the fine and flaming gold,
Her brave straight stature, and her winning parts,
Are nothing else but fires, fetters, darts.

---

[51] A city founded by Philip of Macedonia, and famous for the battle in which Antony and Octavius defeated Brutus and Cassius in 42 BC. Garnier: 'l'honneur Macedon' ('the Macedonian glory', p. 87v).

[52] Pronounced as two syllables. Garnier: 'Afrique noire' ('black Africa', p. 87v).

[53] In the sense of immediately, suddenly (French 'soudain', Garnier, p. 87v). Pun (with 'out of his hand') added by Sidney Herbert.

[54] Sidney Herbert omits Garnier's mention of her 'saintly' face (Garnier: 'son visage saint', p. 87v). The portrait that follows is typical of the neo-Petrarchan vogue in early modern poetry. It also follows Plutarch's description of Cleopatra in *Life of Antony*, XXVII. 2.

[55] i.e. emitting beams of light, radiant. According to the ancient theory of extramission still current in the Renaissance, visual perception was made possible by rays of light emitted by the eyes. The whole passage (324–32) echoes the neo-Petrarchan rhetoric of the blazon.

Yet this is nothing the enchanting skills
Of her celestial sprite,° her training° speech,
Her grace, her majesty, and forcing° voice,
Whether she it with fingers' speech consort,
Or hearing sceptered kings' ambassadors
Answer to each in his own language make.
Yet now, at need, it aids her not at all
With all these beauties,[56] so her sorrow stings.
Darkened with woe, her only study is
To weep, to sigh, to seek for loneliness.
Careless of all, her hair disordered hangs;
Her charming eyes whence murd'ring looks did fly,
Now rivers grown, whose wellspring anguish is,
Do trickling wash the marble of her face.
Her fair discovered breast with sobbing swoll'n
Self-cruel she[57] still martyreth with blows.
Alas! It's our ill hap,° for if her tears
She would convert into her loving charms
To make a conquest of the conqueror,[58]
(As well she might, would she her force employ)
She should us safety from these ills procure,
Her crown to her, and to her race assure.
Unhappy he, in whom self-succour° lies,
Yet self-forsaken wanting succour° dies.

[*Exit* Diomed.]

CHORUS

O sweet fertile land, wherein
Phoebus[59] did with breath inspire
Man who men did first begin,[60]

---

[56] All these beauties are no use to her.

[57] Garnier: 'inhumaine à soy mesme' ('inhuman to herself', p. 88r).

[58] Garnier: 'Pour se rendre Caesar serf de ses volontez' ('to make Caesar a slave to her desires', p. 88r).

[59] Garnier simply has: 'le Soleil' ('the Sun', p. 88r).

[60] Garnier has only: 'Le premier homme d'argile' ('the first man made of clay', p. 88r). While Garnier seems to allude to the Egyptian myths of the origins of mankind, according to which Osiris, god of the Nile, taught men how to till the land, Sidney Herbert refers instead to the Greek and Roman versions in which Prometheus first made men of clay, but they were senseless until Phoebus brought life down to them from the ethereal spheres. Humanist commentators usually saw this myth as an allegory of the civilizing power of the arts.

Formèd first of Nilus' mire,
Whence of arts the eldest kinds,
Earth's most heavenly ornament
Were as from their fountain sent
To enlight° our misty minds,
Whose gross sprite° from endless time
As in darkened prison pent,
Never did to knowledge clime.
Where the Nile, our father good,
Father-like[61] doth never miss
Yearly us to bring such food,
As to life requirèd is;
Visiting each year this plain,
And with fat slime cov'ring it,
Which his seven mouths do spit,
As the season comes again,
Making thereby greatest grow
Busy reapers' joyful pain,
When his floods do highest flow.
Wand'ring prince of rivers thou,
Honour of the Ethiop's land,
Of a lord and master now
Thou as slave in awe must stand.
Now of Tiber[62] which is spread
Less in force, and less in fame,
Reverence thou must the name,
Whom all other rivers dread,
For his children swoll'n in pride,
Who by conquest seek to tread
Round this earth on every side.
Now thou must begin to send
Tribute of thy wat'ry store,
As sea paths thy steps shall bend,
Yearly presents more and more.
Thy fat scum, our fruitful corn,
Pilled° from hence with thievish hands,
All unclothed shall leave our lands
Into foreign country born,

[61] A repetition not in Garnier, who has 'debonnaire' ('kind-hearted', p. 88v).
[62] The famous river that flows through Rome.

Which puffed up with such a prey
Shall thereby the praise adorn
Of that sceptre Rome doth sway.
Nought thee helps thy horns to hide[63]
Far from hence in unknown grounds,
That thy waters wander wide,
Yearly breaking banks and bounds;°
And that thy sky-coloured brooks
Through a hundred peoples pass,
Drawing plots for trees and grass
With a thousand turns and crooks,
Whom all weary of their way,
Thy throats[64] which in wideness pass
Pour into their mother[65] sea.
Nought so happy hapless° life
In this world as freedom finds:
Nought wherein more sparks are rife
To inflame courageous minds;
But if force must us enforce,
Needs a yoke to undergo,
Under foreign yoke to go
Still it proves a bondage worse,
And doublèd subjectiòn
See we shall, and feel, and know,
Subject to a stranger grown.[66]
From hence forward for a king,
Whose first being from this place
Should his breast by nature bring
Care of country to embrace;
We at surly face must quake

[63] The Egyptian goddess Hathor, usually associated with the yearly floods of the Nile, was represented as a cow-headed figure. It was also believed that the sources of the Nile were hidden, see Ovid, *Metamorphoses*, II. 254–55.
[64] Garnier: 'sept larges gosiers' ('seven wide mouths', p. 89r) — an allusion to the seven mouths of the Nile; see Ovid's *Metamorphoses*, I. 422–23.
[65] Sidney Herbert's addition. Garnier: 'les flots mariniers' ('the maritime floods,' p. 89r).
[66] 420–23] All this speech is in trochaic tetrameters. Garnier: 'Et double sugection | Sentons en nostre courage | D'une estrange nation' ('our hearts consider it | a double subjection | to be subjected to a foreign nation', p. 89r) All this speech is in trochaic tetrametres. On the fear of being under the yoke of a foreign nation, see Introduction, p. 43.

Of some Roman madly bent,
Who our terror to augment,
His proconsul's axe[67] will shake,
Driving with our kings from hence
Our established government,
Justice sword, and law's defence.[68]
Nothing worldly of such might
But more mighty destiny,
By swift time's unbridled flight[69]
Makes in end his end to see.
Everything time overthrows,
Nought to end doth steadfast stay.
His great scythe mows all away,
As the stalk of tender rose.
Only immortality
Of the heavens[70] doth it oppose
'Gainst his powerful deity.[71]
One day there will come a day
Which shall quail° thy fortune's flower,[72]
And thee ruinèd low shall lay
In some barb'rous prince's power;
When the pity-wanting fire
Shall, O Rome, thy beauties burn,
And to humble ashes turn

---

[67] A proconsul was the governor or military commander of a Roman province. His symbol of office was the *fasces*, a bound bundle of wooden rods sometimes including an axe.
[68] Compare with Garnier: 'L'observance salutaire | De nos politiques lois' ('The salutary observance | of our city's laws', p. 89r).
[69] 436–40] A common tragic topos. The 'tempus edax' (greedy time) theme is to be found in Seneca's tragedies (see for example *Troas*, and Jasper Heywood's 1566 translation: 'For greedy time it doth devour us all | The world it sways to Chaos' heap to fall' (*Elizabethan Seneca*, p. 100). This passage is also reminiscent of du Bellay's *Antiquités de Rome* (as noted by Ternaux, p. 142), which was translated by Spenser as *The Ruines of Rome*, in his 1591 volume of *Complaints* (dedicated to Mary Sidney Herbert). See in particular Sonnet 3, and Spenser's translation: 'The pr[e]y of time, which all things doth devowre | [...] O worlds inconstancie | That which is firme doth flitte and fall away ...' (*Complaints*, sig. R1r).
[70] Garnier: 'ciel estoilé' ('starry heavens', p. 89v).
[71] 435–44] Marked as *sententiae* in Garnier.
[72] The repetition (day ... day) in l. 445, and the topos of 'Fortune's flower' in l. 447 are Sidney Herbert's. Garnier: 'Il viendra quelque journee | Pernicieuse à ton heur' ('Some day will come | that will be woeful to your life', p. 89v).

Thy proud wealth and rich attire,
Those gilt roofs which turret-wise,
Justly making envy mourn,
Threaten now to pierce[73] skies.[74]
As thy forces fill each land,
Harvests making here and there,
Reaping all with ravening hand
They find growing anywhere;
From each land so to thy fall
Multitudes repair shall make,
From the common spoil to take
What to each man's share may fall.
Fingered° all thou shalt behold:
No jot left for token's sake,
That thou wert so great of old.
Like unto the ancient Troy,
Whence derived thy founders be,
Conqu'ring foe shall thee enjoy,
And a burning prey in thee.
For within this turning ball
This we see, and see each day:
All things fixèd ends do stay,[75]
Ends to first beginnings fall;
And that nought, how strong or strange
Changeless doth endure always,
But endureth fatal change.

[*Exit* CHORUS.]

---

[73] Pronounced as having two syllables for metric reasons.

[74] 459–55] Garnier: '… O Rome, ira saccageant | Tes richesses orgueilleuses, | Et tes bastimens dorez, | Dont les pointes envieuses | Percent les cieux etherez' (' O Rome, shall destroy | your proud riches and your gilt buildings, | whose envious spires | pierce the ethereal heavens', p. 89v). The fall of great cities is a tragic commonplace. See also du Bellay's *Antiquités de Rome*, sonnet 7 (as noted by Ternaux, p. 142), and Spenser's rendering: 'Triumphant arcks, spyres neighbours to the skie, | That you to see doth th'heaven itself appal | Alas, by little ye to nothing flie | The peoples fable, and the spoyle of all' (*Complaints*, sig. R2v). See *Cornelia*, II. 267–74.

[75] All things find finite ends ('to stay' as 'wait for, await', *OED* 19). Garnier: 'Nous voyons journellement | Qu'au premier commencement | Toute chose en fin retourne' ('We daily see | that in the end, everything returns | to its first beginnings', p. 90r). The topoi of mutability and eternal recurrence are also exploited in *Cornelia* (II. 2. 349–50).

[ACT III][1]

[*Enter*] ANTONIUS, LUCILIUS [*and* CHORUS OF EGYPTIANS].

ANTONIUS

Lucil,[2] sole comfort of my bitter case,
The only trust, the only hope I have,
In last despair: ah, is not this the day
That death should me of life and love bereave?
What wait I for, that have no refuge left,
But am sole remnant of my fortune left?
All leave me, fly me; none, no, not of them
Which of my greatness greatest good received,
Stands with my fall: they see me as now ashamed
That heretofore° they did me ought regard;
They draw them back, showing they followed me,
Not to partake my harms, but cozen° me.

LUCILIUS

In this our world nothing is steadfast found,
In vain he hopes, who here his hopes doth ground.

ANTONIUS

Yet nought afflicts me, nothing kills me so,
As that I so my Cleopatra see
Practise° with Caesar,[3] and to him transport
My flame, her love, more dear than life to me.

LUCILIUS

Believe it not: too high a heart she bears,
Too princely thoughts.

ANTONIUS

Too wise a head she wears,
Too much inflamed with greatness, evermore
Gaping° for our great empire's government.

---

[1] Act break is missing in both 1592 and 1595, but present in Garnier.

[2] Short for Lucilius. The character is called 'Lucile' in Garnier. See Plutarch, *Life of Antony*, LXIX. 1.

[3] On Cleopatra's negotiations with Caesar, see above, note 30, p. 101.

LUCILIUS
So long time you her constant love have tried.

ANTONIUS
But still with me good fortune did abide.

LUCILIUS
Her changèd love what token makes you know?

ANTONIUS
Pelusium lost, and Actium overthrown,[4]
Both by her fraud; my well-appointed fleet,
And trusty soldiers in my quarrel armed,
Whom she, false she, instead of my defence,
Came to persuade to yield them to my foe.
Such honour Thyre[5] done, such welcome given,
Their long close talks I neither knew, nor would,
And treacherous wrong Alexas[6] hath me done,
Witness too well her perjured love to me.
But you, O gods (if any faith regard),
With sharp revenge her faithless change reward.[7]

LUCILIUS
The dole° she made upon our overthrow,
Her realm given up for refuge to our men,
Her poor attire when she devoutly kept
The solemn day of her nativity,
Again the cost and prodigal expense

---

[4] Pelusium was a city across the Nile delta from Alexandria, lost by Antony after the battle of Actium in 31 BC (see p. 96, n. 4). 'Overthrow' in 1592 and 1595, because of the rhyme.

[5] The handsome Thyrsus or Thyreus, appointed by Octavius to negotiate with Cleopatra, aroused Antony's jealousy during his embassy. Garnier is following Plutarch's *Life of Antony*, LXXIII. 2.

[6] According to Plutarch, Alexas the Laodicean betrayed Antony to King Herod, and was put to death on Octavius's orders (*Life of Antony*, LXXII. 2–3).

[7] The wordplay on faith/faithless is not in Garnier: 'si quelque Dieux ont soin des amitiez, | Ses trompeurs changemens seront d'eux chatiez' ('if there be gods that care about [broken] friendships, | they will punish her deceitful changes', pp. 90v–91r). Garnier here echoes Dido's invectives against unfaithful Aeneas (Virgil's *Aeneid*, v. 519–20), but Sidney Herbert retains her ironic play on the notion of 'pietas' (faith / faithfulness); see in particular *Aeneid*, IV. 382: 'si quid pia numina possunt …'.

Showed when she did your birthday celebrate,[8]
Do plain enough her heart unfeignèd prove,
Equally touched, you loving, as you love.

ANTONIUS

Well, be her love to me or false, or true,
Once in my soul a cureless wound I feel
I love, nay, burn in fire of her love:
Each day, each night her image[9] haunts my mind,
Herself my dreams; and still I tired am,
And still I am with burning pincers nipped.
Extreme my harm; yet sweeter to my sense
Than boiling° torch of jealous torments' fire,
This grief, nay, rage, in me such stir doth keep,
And thorns° me still, both when I wake and sleep.
  Take Caesar conquest, take my goods, take he
Th'honour to be lord of the earth alone,
My sons, my life bent headlong to mishaps,°
No force, so not my Cleopatra take.
So foolish I, I cannot her forget,
Though better were I banished her my thought,
Like to the sick, whose throat the fever's fire
Hath vehemently with thirsty drought inflamed,
Drinks still, albeit the drink he still desires
Be nothing else but fuel[10] to his flame.
He cannot rule himself: his health's respect
Yieldeth to his distempered stomack's heat.

LUCILIUS

Leave off this love that thus renews your woe.

ANTONIUS

I do my best, but ah, cannot do so.

LUCILIUS

Think how you have so brave a captain been,
And now are by this vain affection fall'n.

---

[8] 38–42] Garnier closely follows Plutarch here, *Life of Antony*, LXXIII. 3.
[9] Garnier: 'son idole faux' ('her false image', p. 91r).
[10] 'Fuel' here pronounced as two syllables for metric reasons.

ANTONIUS

The ceaseless thought of my felicity
Plunges me more in this adversity.
For nothing so a man in ill torments,
As who to him his good state represents.[11]
This makes my rack, my anguish, and my woe
Equal unto the hellish passions grow,
When I to mind my happy puissance° call,
Which erst° I had by warlike conquest won,
And that good fortune which me never left,
Which hard disaster now hath me bereft.
With terror tremble all the world I made
At my sole word, as rushes in the streams
At water's will: I conquered Italy,
I conquered Rome, that nations so redoubt.°
I bore (meanwhile besieging Mutina)[12]
Two consuls'[13] armies for my ruin brought,
Bathed in their blood, by their deaths witnessing
My force and skill in matters martìal.
To wreak° thy uncle,[14] unkind Caesar, I
With blood of enemies the banks imbrued°
Of stained Enipeus,[15] hindering his course,
Stopped with heaps of pilèd carcasses;
When Cassius and Brutus,[16] ill betide,[17]
Marched against us, by us twice put to flight,
But by my sole conduct; for all the time
Caesar, heart-sick with fear and fever lay.
Who knows it not? And how by every one
Fame of the fact was giv'n to me alone.
There sprang the love, the never changing love,

---

[11] This is a tragic topos, to be found for example in Euripides, *Troades*, 635–40.
[12] See p. 121, n. 36.
[13] That is, Pansa and Hirtius, who fought Antony at the battle of Mutina.
[14] Julius Caesar was Octavius's great uncle.
[15] The mention of a river 'stained' with blood is an epic topos; see in particular, as noted by Ternaux (p. 145), Lucan's *Pharsalia*, VII. 116: 'Sanguine Romano quam turbidus ibit Enipeus' ('how troubled with Roman blood will the Enipeus flow').
[16] Defeated by Antony and Octavius at Philippi in 42 BC, Cassius and Brutus committed suicide. They played important roles in the conspiracy against Julius Caesar.
[17] i.e. unhappy event.

Wherein my heart hath since to yours been bound.
There was it, my Lucil, you Brutus saved,
And for your Brutus Antony you found.[18]
Better my hap° in gaining such a friend,
Than in subduing such an enemy.
Now former virtue dead doth me forsake,
Fortune engulfs me in extreme distress;
She turns from me her smiling countenance,
Casting on me mishap upon mishap;°
Left and betrayed of thousand thousand friends
Once of my suit, but you, Lucil, are left,
Remaining to me steadfast as a tower
In holy love, in spite of Fortune's blasts.
But if of any god my voice be heard,
And be not vainly scattered in the heav'ns,
Such goodness shall not gloriless be lost,
But coming ages still thereof shall boast.

LUCILIUS

Men in their friendship ever should be one,
And never ought with fickle Fortune shake,°
Which still removes,° nor will, nor knows the way,
Her rolling bowl[19] in one sure state to stay.
Wherefore we ought as borrowed things receive
The goods' light she lends us to pay again;
Not hold them sure, nor on them build our hopes
As on such goods as cannot fail, and fall;
But think again, nothing is durable,
Virtue except, our never failing host:
So bearing sail when favouring winds do blow,
As frowning tempests may us least dismay
When they on us do fall, not over-glad
With good estate, nor over-grieved° with bad,[20]
Resist mishap.°

---

[18] Lucilius surrendered himself to Antony in order to spare Brutus, which impressed Antony, and determined their friendship. See Plutarch, *Life of Antony*, LXIX. 1.
[19] i.e. rotating sphere. Fortune was often represented as a woman standing on a sphere or on a wheel, to suggest her inconstancy.
[20] 117–31] Marked in Garnier as *sententiae*.

ANTONIUS

Alas! It is too strong.
Mishaps° oft times are by some comfort born:
But these (ay me!), whose weights oppress my heart,
Too heavy lie, no hope can them relieve.
There rests no more, but that with cruel blade
For ling'ring death a hasty way be made.

LUCILIUS

Caesar, as heir unto his father's state,[21]
So will his father's goodness imitate,
To you-ward,[22] whom he knows allied in blood,
Allied in marriage,[23] ruling equally
Th'empire with him, and with him making war,
Have purged the earth of Caesar's murderers.
You into portions parted have the world
Even like co-heirs their heritages part;
And now with one accord so many years
In quiet peace both have your charges ruled.

ANTONIUS

Blood and alliance nothing do prevail
To cool the thirst of hot ambitious breasts:
The son his father hardly can endure,
Brother his brother, in one common realm.[24]
So fervent this desire to command,
Such jealousy it kindleth in our hearts,

---

[21] Octavius was Julius Caesar's adopted son.

[22] i.e. towards you. Julius Caesar was famous for his clemency ('his father's goodness') towards his former enemies.

[23] Allied in marriage] Garnier: 'Qui estes son beau frere' ('since you are his brother-in-law', p. 92v). According to Plutarch (*Life of Antony*, II. 1), Antony's mother was related to Julius Caesar, and hence to Octavius (who was Caesar's grand-nephew and his adopted son). This is also a reference to Antony's marriage to Octavia, Octavius's sister (see the allusion to 'sister' / 'wife', I. 9), which led to the second triumvirate (43–33 BC), and subsequent sharing of the empire between Octavius, Lepidus and Antony (hence 'ruling equally | Th'empire with him').

[24] As noted by Ternaux (p. 145), Garnier paraphrases Lucan's *Pharsalia*, II. 149–51: '... nati maduere paterno | Sanguine: certatem est cui cervix parentis | Cederet: in fratrim ceciderunt praemia fratres' ('children bathed in the blood of their fathers; there were fights over who would take one's father's head; brothers murdered their brothers for a prize').

Sooner will men permit another should
Love her they love, than wear the crown they wear.
All laws it breaks, turns all things upside down:
Amity,° kindred, nought so holy is
But it defiles. A monarchy to gain
None cares which way, so he may it obtain.[25]

LUCILIUS

Suppose he monarch be and that this world
No more acknowledge sundry emperors,
That Rome him only fear, and that he join
The east with west, and both at once do rule:[26]
Why should he not permit you, peaceably
Discharged of charge and empire's dignity,
Private to live reading philosophy,
In learned Greece, Spain, Asia, any land?[27]

ANTONIUS

Never will he his empire think assured
While in this world Mark Antony shall live.
Sleepless suspicion, pale distrust, cold fear
Always to princes company do bear
Bred of reports, reports which night and day
Perpetual guests from court go not away.

LUCILIUS

He hath not slain your brother Lucius,[28]
Nor shortened hath the age of Lepidus,[29]
Albeit both into his hands were fall'n,
And he with wrath against them both inflamed.
Yet one, as lord in quiet rest doth bear

---

[25] 151–58] Marked as *sententiae* in Garnier.
[26] The Roman empire was traditionally divided between the eastern and western provinces, each attributed to one of the two consuls.
[27] Antony did actually make this request to Octavius, who denied it to him.
[28] Lucius Antonius rebelled against Octavius, together with Antony's third wife Fulvia, but he had to surrender at Perusia (Perugia) in 40 BC. He then became governor of Spain.
[29] The third triumvir with Antony and Octavius, who was deposed in 36 BC. Antony obtained for him the title of *pontifex maximus* ('highest priest').

The greatest sway in great Iberia;[30]
The other with his gentle prince retains
Of highest priest the sacred dignity.

ANTONIUS
He fears not them, their feeble force he knows.

LUCILIUS
He fears no vanquished overfilled with woes.

ANTONIUS
Fortune may change again.

LUCILIUS
A downcast foe
Can hardly rise, which once is brought so low.

ANTONIUS
All that I can is done; for last assay
(When all means failed) I to entreaty fell,
(Ah, coward creature!) whence again repulsed,
Of combat I unto him proffer made;[31]
Though he in prime, and I by feeble age
Mightily weakened both in force and skill.
Yet could not he his coward heart advance,
Basely afraid to try so praiseful chance.
This makes me plain,° makes me myself accuse;
Fortune in this her spiteful force doth use
'Gainst my grey hairs; in this, unhappy, I
Repine° at heav'ns in my haps° pitiless.
A man, a woman both in might and mind,[32]
In Mars's school who never lesson learned,
Should me repulse, chase, overthrow, destroy,
Me of such fame, bring to so low an ebb?

---

[30] Present-day Spain and Portugal.

[31] According to Plutarch (*Life of Antony*, LXII. 3), Antony offered to fight Octavius in single combat, which the latter ignored. Plutarch comments on the age difference (hence 'feeble age'). Antony was about 53 at the time.

[32] Garnier: 'un homme effeminé de corps & de courage' ('an effeminate man, both in his body and his heart', p. 93v).

Alcides' blood,[33] who from my infancy
With happy prowess crownèd have my praise,
Witness thou, Gaul unused to servile yoke,
Thou, valiant Spain, you, fields of Thessaly,
With millions of mourning cries bewailed,
Twice watered now with blood of Italy.[34]

LUCILIUS
Witness may Afrique, and of conquered world
All four[35] quarters witnesses may be.
For in what part of earth inhabited,
Hungry of praise have you not ensigns spread?

ANTONIUS
Thou know'st, rich Egypt (Egypt of my deeds
Fair and foul subject), Egypt ah, thou know'st
How I behaved me fighting for thy king,[36]
When I regained° him his rebellious realm:
Against his foes in battle showing force,
And after fight in victory remorse.
 Yet if to bring my glory to the ground,
Fortune had made me overthrown by one
Of greater force, of better skill than I,
One of those captains[37] fearèd so of old,
Camill, Marcellus, worthy Scipio,
This late great Caesar, honour of our state,
Or that great Pompey[38] agèd grown in arms,

---

[33] The blood, i.e. bloodline, of Hercules (Alcides; Garnier: 'le sang d'Hercule', p. 93v), from whom Antony was allegedly descended.

[34] An allusion to the battles of Pharsalus, or Pharsalia, (48 BC) and Philippi (42 BC), both in Thessaly.

[35] four] Pronounced as two syllables for metric reasons (originally spelled 'fower').

[36] Ptolemy XII, Cleopatra's father, whom Antony helped reinstate after he had been deposed. See Plutarch, *Life of Antony*, III. 4–5. Plutarch makes particular note of Antony's clemency against his Egyptian opponents, whom Ptolemy would have massacred (hence l. 216: 'after fight in victory remorse').

[37] Garnier: 'Empereurs' (p. 93v). Sidney Herbert reads the title 'imperator' with its original meaning of 'victorious general', hence 'captains'.

[38] 221–23] All heroes of Roman history. Marcus Furius Camillus was a Roman general who conquered the Gauls; Marcellus, consul and general, conquered Syracusa; Scipio Africanus, consul and general, destroyed Carthage in 146 BC. Julius Caesar ruled Rome and extended Roman rule in Gaul and Britain. Pompey, the

That after harvest of a world of men[39]
Made in a hundred battles, fights, assaults,
My body thorough-pierced° with push of pike
Had vomited my blood, in blood my life,
In midst of millions, fellows in my fall,
The less her wrong, the less should be my woe;
Nor she should pain, nor I complain me so.[40]
No, no, whereas I should have died in arms,
And vanquished oft new armies should have armed,
New battles giv'n, and rather lost with me
All this whole world submitted unto me:
A man who never saw enlacèd° pikes
With bristled points against his stomach bent,
Who fears the field, and hides him cowardly,
Dead at the very noise the soldiers make.
His virtue: fraud, deceit, malicious guile;
His arms, the arts that false Ulysses[41] used,
Known at Modena,[42] where the consuls both
Death-wounded were, and wounded by his men
To get their army, war with it to make
Against his faith, against his country soil.
Of Lepidus,[43] which to his succours° came,
To honour whom he was by duty bound,
The empire he usurped, corrupting first
With baits and bribes the most part of his men.
Yet me hath overcome, and made his prey,
And state of Rome with me hath overcome.

---

famous Roman general, one of the triumvirs with Caesar and Crassus, became Caesar's opponent in the civil war, and was murdered in Egypt. The list of victorious generals is an epic / tragic topos.

[39] Garnier: 'la moisson d'un monde de soudars' ('the harvest of a world of soldiers', p. 94r). The depiction of the battlefield in terms of a harvest is a favourite metaphor of Garnier's, also to be found throughout *Cornélie* (see pp. 43v, 46v and 69r, and Kyd's translation in I. 216–17, II. 187, and V. 246–82, respectively).

[40] 229–30] These two lines are an addition of Sidney Herbert's.

[41] Homer's hero was considered by the Trojans to be cunning and traitorous.

[42] Called by its Latin name of Mutina further up. A battle won by Antony against the consuls Pansa and Hirtius in 43 BC. See p. 121, n. 36.

[43] See p. 96, n. 3 and p. 136, n. 23. Although Lepidus supported him, Caesar stripped him of his power. Garnier calls him 'triumvir Lepide' ('the triumvir, Lepidus', p. 94v).

Strange! One disordered act at Actium
The earth subdued, my glory hath obscured.
For since, as one whom heaven's wrath attaints,°
With fury caught, and more than furious
Vexed with my evils, I never more had care
My armies lost, or lost name to repair:
I did no more resist

LUCILIUS

All war's affairs,
But battles most, daily have their success,
Now good, now ill; and though that Fortune have
Great force and power in every worldly thing,
Rule all, do all, have all things fast enchained
Unto the circle of her turning wheel,[44]
Yet seems it more than any practice else
She doth frequent Bellona's[45] bloody trade;
And that her favour, wav'ring as the wind,
Her greatest power therein doth oft'nest show.
Whence grows[46] we daily see, who in their youth
Got honour there, do lose it in their age,
Vanquished by some less warlike than themselves,
Whom yet a meaner man shall overthrow.
Her use is not to lend us still her hand,
But sometimes headlong back again to throw,
Whereby her favour she hath us extolled
Unto the top of highest happiness.[47]

ANTONIUS

Well ought I curse within my grievèd soul,
Lamenting day and night, this senseless love,
Whereby my fair enticing foe entrapped°
My heedless reason, could no more escape.
It was not Fortune's ever changing face,

[44] Garnier: 'autour de son roüet' ('around her spinning wheel', p. 94v).
[45] The Roman goddess of war.
[46] i.e. comes to pass, follows (*OED* 12c). This predates the first recorded use of this word in this sense.
[47] 257–74] Marked as *sententiae* in Garnier. A similar development on the fickleness of fortune, and the unexpected turns of war, is to be found in the chorus of *Cornelia*, II. 338–53.

It was not Dest'ny's changeless violence
Forged my mishap.° Alas, who doth not know
They make, nor mar, nor anything can do.[48]
Fortune which men so fear, adore, detest,
Is but a chance whose cause unknown doth rest.
Although oft-times the cause is well perceived,
But not th'effect the same that was conceived.
Pleasure, nought else, the plague of this our life,
Our life which still a thousand plagues pursue,
Alone hath me this strange disaster spun,
Fall'n from a soldier to a chamberer,[49]
Careless of virtue, careless of all praise.
Nay, as the fatted swine in filthy mire
With glutted heart I wallowed in delights,
All thoughts of honour[50] trodden under foot.
So I me lost; for finding this sweet cup
Pleasing my taste, unwise I drank my fill,[51]
And through the sweetness of that poison's power
By steps I drove my former wits astray.
I made my friends, offended, me forsake,
I holp° my foes against myself to rise.
I robbed my subjects, and for followers
I saw myself beset with flatterers.
Mine idle arms fair wrought with spiders' work,
My scattered men without their ensigns strayed.
Caesar meanwhile, who never would have dared
To cope with me, me suddenly despised,

[48] 279–81] This passage is not marked as *sententiae* in Garnier.

[49] A bedchamber attendant, a servant. Slightly different from Garnier's 'casanier' (homebound, domestic). The term, however, seems to have acquired a pejorative sense in French at the time, as later endorsed by Furetière (1690) — 'poltron, fainéant' ('coward, sluggard') — and the dictionary of the Académie Française (1694) — 'ne se dit que d'un fainéant' ('only as pertaining to a sluggard').

[50] Garnier: 'honnestes desirs' ('honest desires', p. 95r).

[51] The cup suggests a parallel between Cleopatra and the enchantress Circe (see above, p. 99, n. 16) as represented in mythology and in Homer's *Odyssey*, X. Those who drank from her cup were turned into swine, and, as Alciato's famous *Book of Emblems* (first published 1531) specifies, they 'los[t] all reason in their mind' ('rationem animi perdere', Emblem LXXVI, 'Cavendum meretricibus' ('Beware of prostitutes'). See also Geoffrey Whitney's English edition, *A Choice of Emblems* (first published 1580), Emblem LXXXII: 'Like brutish beasts they spend their time, and have no sense at all'.

Took heart to fight, and hoped for victory
On one so gone, who glory had forgone.

LUCILIUS

Enchanting pleasure, Venus' sweet delights,[52]
Weaken our bodies, over-cloud our sprites,°
Trouble our reason, from our hearts out chase
All holy virtues lodging in their place;
Like as the cunning fisher takes the fish
By traitor bait whereby the hook is hid,[53]
So pleasure serves to vice instead of food
To bait our souls thereon too lickerish.°[54]
This poison deadly is alike to all,
But on great kings doth greatest outrage work.
Taking the royal sceptres from their hands,
Thence forward to be by some stranger borne.
While that their people charged with heavy loads
Their flatt'rers pill,° and suck their marrow[55] dry,
Not ruled but left to great men as a prey,
While this fond° prince himself in pleasures drowns
Who hears nought, sees nought, doth nought of a king,
Seeming himself against himself conspired.
Then equal Justice wand'reth banishèd,
And in her seat sits greedy[56] Tyranny.
Confused disorder troubleth all estates,
Crimes without fear and outrages are done.
Then mutinous Rebellion shows her face,
Now hid with this, and now with that pretence,
Provoking enemies, which on each side
Enter at ease, and make them lords of all.
The hurtful works of pleasure here behold.[57]

---

[52] Garnier: 'delices de Cypris' ('Cypris' delights', p. 95r). Cypris was another name for Venus.

[53] See Alciato's Emblem LXXV, 'In amatores meretricum' ('Against the lovers of prostitutes'), which represents a cunning fisherman armed with a hook.

[54] Fond of delicate fare, but could also mean lecherous. Garnier: 'Pour nostre ame amorcer, qui en est trop friande' ('To bait our over-greedy souls', p. 95r).

[55] Sidney Herbert has 'mary', probably archaic for 'marrow'.

[56] Garnier: 'avare' ('miserly, p. 95v).

[57] 309–35] This whole passage is marked as *sententiae* in Garnier.

ANTONIUS

The wolf is not so hurtful to the fold,
Frost to the grapes, to ripened fruits the rain,
As pleasure is to princes full of pain.

LUCILIUS

There needs no proof, but by th'Assyrian king,[58]
On whom that monster woeful wrack° did bring.

ANTONIUS

There needs no proof, but by unhappy I,
Who lost my empire, honour, life thereby.

LUCILIUS

Yet hath this ill so much the greater force,
As scarcely any do against it stand:
No, not the demi-gods the old world knew,
Who all subdued, could pleasure's power subdue.
  Great Hercules,[59] Hercules once that was
Wonder of earth and heav'n, matchless in might,
Who Antaeus, Lycus, Geryon overcame,
Who drew from hell the triple-headed dog,
Who Hydra killed, vanquished Achelous,
Who heavens' weight on his strong shoulders bore,
Did he not under pleasure's burden bow?
Did he not captive to this passion yield,
When by his captive[60] so he was inflamed,

---

[58] Sardanapalus, king of Assyria, who is supposed to have lived in the seventh century BC, was renowned for his decadence and cruelty.

[59] Some of the Hercules' twelve famed labours are mentioned below: he killed the giant Antaeus, killed Lycus who threatened his wife Megara, stole the cattle of the monster Geryon, descended into the underworld to bring the dog Cerberus back, killed the many-headed monster Hydra from Lerna, defeated the river god Achelous, and held the world on his shoulders for Atlas. But like Antony, he fell under a woman's spell. The parallel is suggested in Plutarch (*A Comparison of Demetrius and Antony*, III. 3) and alluded to in Shakespeare's *Antony and Cleopatra*, IV. 3.

[60] The repetition of 'captive' is Sidney Herbert's. Garnier: 'Omphale [...] Meonienne Royne' ('Omphale [...] the Meonian queen', p. 96r). Omphale was queen of Maeonia in Lydia. Hercules fell in love with her and she famously set him to spin for her, and made him exchange clothes with her (see for example Ovid's *Ars Amatoria*, II. 217–20). Sidney Herbert, however, seems to merge two different legends, for Omphale had Hercules captive as her slave, but was not his captive. In Ovid's *Heroides*, IX, as

As now yourself in Cleopatra burn?
Slept in her lap, her bosom kissed and kissed,
With base unseemly service bought her love,
Spinning at distaff, and with sinewy hand
Winding on spindles' thread, in maid's attire?
His conqu'ring club at rest on wall did hang;
His bow unstringed he bent not as he used:
Upon his shafts the weaving spiders spun;
And his hard cloak the fretting° moths did pierce.
The monsters, free and fearless all the time,
Throughout the world the people did torment,
And more and more increasing day by day,
Scorned his weak heart become a mistress' play.[61]

ANTONIUS

In only this like Hercules am I,
In this I prove me of his lineage right;
In this himself, his deeds I show in this,
In this, nought else, my ancestor he is.
   But go we. Die I must, and with brave end
Conclusion make of all foregoing harms.
Die, die I must: I must a noble death,
A glorious death unto my succour° call.
I must deface the shame of time abused,
I must adorn the wanton loves I used,
With some courageous act; that my last day
By mine own hand my spots may wash away.
   Come, dear Lucil. Alas! Why weep you thus?
This mortal lot is common to us all.
We must all die, each doth in homage owe
Unto that god that shared the realms below.[62]
Ah, sigh no more. Alas! Appease your woes,
For by your grief my grief more eager grows.

[*Exeunt.*]

---

well as in Seneca's *Hercules Oetaeus*, Hercules falls in love with a captive princess, Iole, who causes his death by fuelling Dejanirah's jealousy. Both plays lay a similar emphasis on the effeminization of the hero.

[61] i.e. a plaything.

[62] 385–386] Marked as *sententiae* in Garnier.

CHORUS[63]

Alas, with what tormenting fire
Us martyreth this blind desire
To stay our life from flying!
How ceaselessly our minds doth rack,
How heavy lies upon our back
This dastard° fear of dying!
Death[64] rather healthful succour° gives,
Death rather all mishaps° relieves,
That life upon us throweth;
And ever to us death unclose
The door whereby from cureless woes
Our weary soul out goeth.
What goddess else more mild than she
To bury all our pain can be,
What remedy more pleasing?
Our painèd hearts when dolour stings,
And nothing rest, or respite brings,
What help have we more easing?
Hope which to us doth comfort give,
And doth our fainting hearts revive,
Hath not such force in anguish;
For promising a vain relief,
She oft us fails in midst of grief,
And helpless lets us languish.
But Death, who call on her at need,
Doth never with vain semblant° feed,
But when them sorrow paineth,
So rids their souls of all distress,
Whose heavy weight did them oppress,
That not one grief remaineth.
Who fearless and with courage bold
Can Acheron's[65] black face behold,

---

[63] 387–470] Marked as *sententiae* in Garnier.

[64] Garnier: 'La mortelle Parque' ('The lethal Parcae', p. 96v). The repetition of 'death' is Sidney Herbert's.

[65] A river of the underworld. As noted by Ternaux (p. 149), the passage is reminiscent of Seneca's *Agamemnon*, 589–600: 'perrumpet omne | Servitium contemptor levium deorum | Qui vultus Acherontis atri | Qui Styga tristem non tristis videt' ('he will break all bounds, he who, scorning the fickle gods, can look without fear on the dark face of Acheron, and on fearsome Styx').

Which muddy water beareth;
And crossing over in the way
Is not amazed at peruke° grey
Old rusty Charon weareth?
Who void of dread can look upon
The dreadful shades that roam alone,[66]
On banks where sound no voices;
Whom with her fire-brands and her snakes
No whit afraid Alecto[67] makes,
Nor triple-barking noises.[68]
Who freely can himself dispose
Of that last hour which all must close,
And leave this life at pleasure;
This noble freedom more esteems,
And in his heart more precious deems,
Than crown and kingly treasure.
The waves which Boreas'[69] blasts turmoil
And cause with foaming fury boil,
Make not his heart to tremble;
Nor brutish broil,° when with strong head
A rebel people madly led
Against their lords assemble;
Nor fearful face of tyrant wood,[70]
Who breathes but threats, and drinks but blood,
No, nor the hand which thunder,
The hand of Jove which thunder bears,
And ribs of rock in sunder tears,
Tears mountains' sides in sunder;[71]

---

[66] The souls of the dead, wandering in the underworld.

[67] One of the Furies.

[68] The barking of three-headed Cerberus, the monstrous dog which guarded the entrance into Hell.

[69] Northern wind. See p. 103, n. 40.

[70] i.e. mad, lunatic. The theme of the Stoic hero unshaken by the crowds or menacing tyrants is taken from Horace, *Odes*, III. 3. 1–4: 'Iustum et tenace propositi virum | non civium ardor prava iubentium | non voltus instantis tyranni | mente quatit solida ...' ('For just men of steadfast purpose, neither the raging crowds urging them to do wrong, nor the menacing frown of a tyrant is enough to shake their strong minds ...'). See also *Cornelia*, II. 306–09.

[71] 442–446] Sidney Herbert redistributes Garnier's text slightly, for metrical reasons: the initial couplet of the stanza is turned into a sense unit, like the quatrain that follows. This results in l. 442 being compressed (one line for two lines in Garnier),

Nor bloody Mars's butchering hands,[72]
Whose lightnings desert lay[73] the lands,
  Whom dusty clouds do cover,
From off whose armour sun-beams fly,[74]
And under them make quaking lie
  The plains whereon they hover;
Nor yet the cruel murd'ring blade
Warm in the moisty° bowels made
Of people pell-mell° dying
In some great city put to sack
By savage tyrant brought to wrack,°
  At his cold mercy lying.
How abject him, how base, think I,[75]
Who wanting courage cannot die,
  When need him thereto calleth!
From whom the dagger drawn to kill
The cureless griefs that vex him still
  For fear and faintness falleth!
O Antony, with thy dear mate,[76]
Both in misfortunes fortunate,
  Whose thoughts to death aspiring
Shall you protect from victor's rage,
Who on each side doth you encage,
  To triumph much desiring.
That Caesar may you not offend,

---

and one more line for the quatrain — Sidney Herbert turns three lines of Garnier into four. She also adds repetitive effects. Compare with Garnier: 'la dextre tonnante | De Jupiter qui accravante | D'un rocher l'indomtable flanc' ('the booming right hand | of Jupiter, that shatters | the indomitable flank of rocks', p. 97v). See (as noted by Ternaux, p. 151) Seneca's *Agamemnon*, 594–95: 'aut iniqui | Flamma Tonantis' ('nor the fire of the cruel Thunderer').

[72] The reference to Mars and the butchering metaphor are Sidney Herbert's. Garnier has: 'la carnagere guerre' ('slaughtering war', p. 97v).

[73] Garnier: 'les foudres desertans la terre.' Garnier uses a usually intransitive verb in a resultative sense ('lightning-bolts that turn the earth into a desert', p. 97v).

[74] Sidney Herbert does not translate Garnier's 'bataillons' and 'soudars' responsible for the dust and the scintillating steel, which makes for a poetical vision in French: 'les bataillons poudroyans | De soudars ardans en leurs armes, | Et les gros scadrons de gendarmes' ('the dust-raising battalions | of soldiers in their shimmering armours | and large squadrons of armed men', p. 97v). This is an epic topos; see also *Cornelia*, v. 151–59.

[75] think I] Not in Garnier.

[76] Compare with Garnier: 'bien heureuse nostre Royne' ('our happy queen', p. 97v).

Nought else but death can you defend,
   Which his weak force derideth.
And all in this round earth contained,
Powerless on them whom once enchained,
   Avernus' prison[77] hideth;
Where great Psammetich's[78] ghost doth rest,
Not with infernal pain possessed,
   But in sweet fields[79] detained;
And old Amasis'[80] soul likewise,
And all our famous Ptolemies
   That whilom° on us reigned.

[*Exit* CHORUS.]

---

[77] The caves next to Lake Arvernus were thought to mark the entry into the underworld (see Virgil's *Aeneid*, VI). Here synonymous with Hades.
[78] Psammetichus, King of Egypt in the Ptolemaic line.
[79] i.e. the Elysian fields; Garnier: 'les Elysiennes plaines' (p. 98r).
[80] The Greek name for Ahmès II, a pharaoh of the sixth century BC. This line was three lines up in Garnier.

ACT IV

[*Enter*] CAESAR, AGRIPPA [*and* CHORUS OF ROMAN SOLDIERS].

CAESAR

You ever-living gods which all things hold
Within the power of your celestial hands,
By whom heat, cold, the thunder, and the wind,
The properties of interchanging months,
Their course and being have; which do set down
Of empires[1] by your destined decree,
The force, age, time, and subject to no change
Change all, reserving° nothing in one state.
You have advanced, as high as thund'ring heav'n[2]
The Romans' greatness by Bellona's[3] might,
Mast'ring the world with fearful violence,
Making the world widow of liberty.
Yet at this day this proud exalted Rome
Despoiled,° captived, at one man's will doth bend:
Her empire mine, her life is in my hand,
As monarch I both world and Rome command;
Do all, can all; forth my commandment cast
Like thund'ring fire from one to other pole,
Equal to Jove; bestowing by my word
Haps and mishaps°, as Fortune's king and lord.
    No town there is, but up my image sets,[4]
But sacrifice to me doth daily make;
Whither where Phoebus join his morning steeds,
Or where the night them weary entertains,

[1] Three syllables.
[2] Caesar's speech is reminiscent of Atraeus' hubristic challenge to the gods in Seneca's *Thyestes* (885–89): 'Aequalis astris gradior et cunctus super | altum superbo vertice attingens polum | Nunc decora regni teneo, nunc solium patris | Dimitto superos: summa votorum attigi …' In Jasper Heywood's 1560 translation: 'Now equal with the stars I walk, beyond each other wight, | With haughty head the heavens above and highest pole I smite […] | I now let go the gods, for all my will I have obtained' (*Elizabethan Seneca*, p. 192).
[3] See p. 141, n. 45.
[4] Erects a statue.

Or where the heat the Garamants[5] doth scorch,
Or where the cold from Boreas' breast is blown,
All Caesar do both awe and honour bear,
And crownèd kings his very name do fear.
Antony knows it well, for whom not one
Of all the princes all this earth do rule
Arms against me, for all redoubt° the power
Which heav'nly powers on earth have made me bear.
Antony, he poor man with fire inflamed,
A woman's beauties kindled in his heart,
Rose against me, who longer could not bear
My sister's wrong he did so ill entreat.
Seeing her left while that his lewd delights
Her husband with his Cleopatra took
In Alexandria, where both nights and days
Their time they passed in nought but loves and plays.[6]
All Asia's forces into one he drew,
And forth he set upon the azured waves
A thousand and a thousand ships, which filled
With soldiers, pikes, with targets,° arrows, darts,
Made Neptune quake, and all the wat'ry troops
Of glaucs and tritons[7] lodged at Actium.
But mighty gods, who still the force withstand
Of him, who causeless doth another wrong,
In less than moment's space reduced to nought
All that proud power by sea or land he brought.

AGRIPPA

Presumptuous pride of high and haughty sprite,°
Voluptuous care of fond° and foolish love,
Have justly wrought his wrack,° who thought he held,

[5] The Garamantes (spelt here Garamants for metric reasons), a people of Africa, living south of Cyrene, in southern Libya, at the extreme limit of Ptolemy's map of 'terra cognita'.

[6] Garnier: 'aux delices d'Amour' ('in Love's delights', p. 98v). See Plutarch, *Life of Antony*, XXIX. 1 and above, p. 98, n. 12.

[7] Mythological sea-creatures (see also *Cornelia*, I. 91). Tritons are mermen usually following the sea-god Triton. Glaucus was also a sea-god, half-man, half-fish (see Ovid's *Metamorphoses*, VIII. 917–59). Although common in Renaissance French poetry, the generic use of 'glauques' to designate Glaucus-like mermen is rare in English.

By overweening,° Fortune in his hand.
Of us he made no count, but as to play,
So fearless came our forces to assay.
So sometimes fell[8] to sons of mother earth,
Which crawled to heav'n war on the gods to make,
Olymp on Pelion, Ossa on Olymp,
Pindus on Ossa, loading by degrees,
That at hand-strokes with mighty clubs they might
On mossy rocks the gods make tumble down.[9]
When mighty Jove with burning anger chafed,[10]
Disbrained with him Gyges and Briareus,[11]
Blunting his darts upon their bruisèd bones.
For no one thing the gods can less abide,
In deeds of men, than arrogance and pride;
And still the proud, which too much takes in hand,
Shall foulest fall, where best he thinks to stand.

CAESAR

Right as some palace, or some stately tower,
Which overlooks the neighbour buildings round
In scorning wise,[12] and to the stars up grows,
Which in short time his own weight overthrows.[13]
What monstrous pride, nay, what impiety
Incensed him onward to the gods' disgrace?
When his two children, Cleopatra's brats,[14]
To Phoebe and her brother[15] he compared,

---

[8] i.e. it thus happened.

[9] The Giants sought to attack the gods by piling Mount Pelion on top of Mount Ossa in order to climb Mount Olympus, but were killed by Apollo. See Ovid's *Metamorphoses*, I. 152–57. As Ternaux notes (p. 153), the myth offers a commonplace example of disordered ambition in early modern poetry.

[10] One line missing following this one, probably dropped by the printer, which should have been l. 64: 'Maint trait de foudre aigy desserra sur Typhé' ('with many a sharp lightning-bolt [he] struck Typhon', p. 99r).

[11] Garnier places them by mistake among the rebellious giants. In fact, they helped overthrow the Titans and helped Jove fight the rebelled giants. They are mentioned in Hesiod.

[12] In a scorning manner.

[13] A topos already used in II. 2. 467–74.

[14] Garnier: 'deux jumeaux d'adultere' ('adultery's twins', p. 99v). Sidney Herbert omits the reference to adultery.

[15] In classical mythology Phoebe is the moon goddess and sister to Phoebus (Apollo), the sun god. According to Plutarch (*Life of Antony*, XXXVI. 3) and Dio (*Roman*

Latona's race, causing them to be called
The sun and moon? Is not this folly right
And is not this the gods to make his foes?
And is not this himself to work his woes?

AGRIPPA

In like proud sort he caused his head to lose
The Jewish king Antigonus,[16] to have
His realm for balm,[17] that Cleopatra loved,
As though on him he had some treason proved.

CAESAR

Lydia to her, and Syria, he gave,
Cyprus of gold, Arabia rich of smells,[18]
And to his children more, Cilicia,
Parths,° Medes, Armenia, Phoenicia,
The kings of kings proclaiming them to be,
By his own word, as by a sound decree.

AGRIPPA

What? Robbing his own country of her due?
Triumphed he not in Alexandria,
Of Artabasus the Armenian King,[19]
Who yielded on his perjured word to him?

History, XXI. 8), Antony named his children by Cleopatra Helios (the sun in Greek) and Selene (the moon). Garnier has: 'comparant à Diane & et Phebus son frere | Race Latonienne' ('comparing [them] to Diana and Phebus her brother | both of Leto', p. 99v).

[16] King of Judea whom, according to Plutarch (*Life of Antony*, XXXVI. 2), Antony ordered to be beheaded, although no other king had ever been so punished.

[17] The province of Judea was well-known for its production of scented oils. See again Plutarch (ibid.) and North's translation: 'that country of J[ew]rie where the true balme is' (*Lives*, p. 986).

[18] Countries given to Cleopatra by Antony, according to Plutarch (ibid.). Garnier: 'Cypre aux veines d'or' ('Cyprus with her veins of gold', p. 99v).

[19] Artabasus or Artavasdes was an Armenian King conquered by Antony. According to Plutarch (*Life of Antony*, L. 4), Antony organized an unauthorized triumph in Alexandria, which angered Rome. Simply mentioned as 'prince Armenien' in Garnier ('Armenian prince', p. 99v).

CAESAR

Nay, never Rome more injuries received,
Since thou, O Romulus,[20] by flight of birds
With happy hand the Roman walls[21] didst build,
Than Antony's fond loves to it hath done.
Nor ever war more holy, nor more just,
Nor undertaken with more hard constraint,
Than is this war; which were it not, our state
Within small time all dignity should lose.
Though I lament (thou, sun, my witness art,
And thou, great Jove) that it so deadly proves,
That Roman blood should in such plenty flow,
Wat'ring the fields and pastures where we go.
What Carthage in old hatred obstinate,
What Gaul still barking at our rising state,
What rebel Samnite, what fierce Pyrrhus' power,
What cruel Mithridates, what Parth° hath wrought
Such woe to Rome?[22] Whose commonwealth he had,
Had he been victor, into Egypt brought.[23]

AGRIPPA

Surely the gods, which have this city built
Steadfast to stand as long as time endures,

---

[20] The legendary founder of Rome chose the site at the prompting of an augury (hence 'flight of birds'). Garnier only has: 'toy Quirin' ('you, Quirinus'); Quirinus was the name frequently given to divinized Romulus).

[21] Garnier: 'Romulides tours' ('Romulidean towers', p. 99v). The Romulides are the descendants of Romulus, and by extension the Romans.

[22] Octavius mentions Rome's great enemies: Carthage, vanquished *c.* 149 BC by Scipio; Gaul by Julius Caesar in 52 BC. The formidable Samnites were a people of the Abruzzi mountains who fought the Romans, but eventually lost in 290 BC. Pyrrhus (319–270 BC), cousin to Alexander the Great, king of Epirus, courageously fought the Romans at great cost in the third century BC. During his campaigns against the Romans, the Greek king of Pontus, Mithridates VII (111–63 BC), was vanquished by Pompey, but according to Plutarch he was renowned for his cruelty against inhabitants of the Roman dominions in Asia. The Parthians possessed an empire that stretched from the Euphrates to the Indus and resisted the progress of Rome for three centuries, from 53 BC on.

[23] i.e. he would have given it to Egypt. Sidney Herbert here again simplifies Garnier's circumlocution for Egypt: 'il eust sa république, | S'il eust ésté vainqueur, fait en brief Canopique' ('had he been successful, | he would have founded his republic in Canopic land', p. 100r).

Which keep the Capitol,[24] of us take care,
And care will take of those shall after come,
Have made you victor, that you might redress
Their honour grown by passèd mischiefs° less.

CAESAR

The seely°[25] man when all the Greekish sea[26]
His fleet had hid, in hope me sure to drown,[27]
Me battle gave; where fortune in my stead,
Repulsing him his forces disarrayed.
Himself took flight, soon as his love he saw
All wan through fear with full sails fly away.
His men, though lost, whom none did now direct,
With courage fought, fast grappled ship with ship,
Charging, resisting, as their oars would serve,
With darts, with swords, with pikes, with fiery flames.[28]
So that the darkened night her starry veil
Upon the bloody sea had over-spread,
Whilst yet they held; and hardly, hardly then,
They fell to flying on the wavy plain.
All full of soldiers overwhelmed with waves,
The air throughout with cries and groans did sound;
The sea did blush with blood; the neighbour shores
Groaned, so they with shipwrecks pestered were,
And floating bodies left for pleasing food

---

[24] Rome's main hill, and the seat of political and religious power.
[25] The French is ambiguous: 'le miserable' (p. 100r), which could mean either 'unhappy man' or 'villain'.
[26] Garnier: 'l'onde Ionie' ('the Ionic waves', p. 100r). The battle of Actium was fought on the Ionian Sea.
[27] i.e. when he had covered all the sea with his fleet. Garnier is probably referring to the way Antony lined up all his ships across the gulf at Actium, first in order to dissuade Octavius from a direct attack and cut him off from fresh water sources (Plutarch, *Life of Antony*, LXIII. 1), and second to create the equivalent of a battle on land (LXV. 2–3).
[28] See Plutarch, *Life of Antony*, LXVI. 2 and North's translation: 'the souldiers fought with their pykes, halberds, and darts, and threw pots and darts with fire' (*Lives*, p. 1001).

To birds, and beasts, and fishes of the sea.[29]
You know it well, Agrippa.[30]

AGRIPPA

Meet° it was
The Roman empire so should rulèd be
As heav'n is ruled; which turning over us,
All under-things by his example turns.
Now as of heav'n, one only Lord we know,
One only lord should rule this earth below.
When one self° power is common made to two,
Their duties they nor suffer will, nor do.[31]
In quarrel still, in doubt, in hate, in fear;
Meanwhile the people all the smart do bear.

CAESAR[32]

Then to the end none, while my days endure,
Seeking to raise himself may succours° find,
We must with blood mark this our victory,
For just example to all memory.
Murder we must, until not one we leave,
Which may hereafter us of rest bereave.

AGRIPPA

Mark it with murders? Who of that can like?[33]

---

[29] 138–39] Compare with *Cornélie* (p. 52v): 'pasture des oiseaux, | Pasture des poissons qui rament sous les eaux' ('food for birds, | food for the fish that row under the sea'), and Kyd's translation in II. 2. 19.

[30] Agrippa had been in command of part of the fleet at Actium.

[31] See Lucan, *Pharsalia*, I. 92–93 (as noted by Ternaux, p. 155): 'Nulla fides regni sociis, omnisque potestas | Impatiens consortis erit', and Marlowe's translation: 'Shall never faith be found in fellow kings. | Dominion cannot suffer partnership' (*Lucans first booke*, sig. B2v). See also *Cornelia*, I. 34–35.

[32] The following debate between magnanimity and punishment is loosely based on the dialogue between Seneca and Nero in Seneca's *Octavia* (440–61). It is a commonplace theme in neoclassical Humanist drama. See *Cornelia*, IV. 2. 125–28, for a similar debate, where Julius Caesar defends instead the advantages of mercy over revenge.

[33] In Garnier, Agrippa is more assertive: 'De meurtres il ne faut remarquer vostre empire' ('With murders your empire should not be tainted', p. 100v). The passage between ll. 156 and 179 is marked as *sententiae* in Garnier.

CAESAR
Murders must use, who doth assurance seek.

AGRIPPA
Assurance call you enemies to make?[34]

CAESAR
I make no such, but such away I take.

AGRIPPA
Nothing so much as rigour doth displease.

CAESAR
Nothing so much doth make me live at ease.

AGRIPPA
What ease to him that fearèd is of all?

CAESAR
Feared to be, and see his foes to fall.

AGRIPPA
Commonly fear doth breed and nourish hate.

CAESAR
Hate without power comes commonly too late.

AGRIPPA
A fearèd prince hath oft his death desired.

CAESAR
A prince not feared hath oft his wrong conspired.

AGRIPPA
No guard so sure, no fort so strong doth prove.
No such defence, as is the people's love.

---

[34] Garnier: 'On ne s'asseure point, des ennemis faisant' ('One does not assure one's realm by making enemies', p. 100v).

CAESAR

Nought more unsure, more weak, more like the wind,
Than people's favour still to change enclined.

AGRIPPA

Good gods! What love to gracious prince men bear!

CAESAR

What honour to the prince that is severe!

AGRIPPA

Nought more divine than is benignity.

CAESAR

Nought likes the gods as doth severity.

AGRIPPA

Gods all forgive.

CAESAR

On faults they pains do lay.

AGRIPPA

And give their goods.

CAESAR

Oft times they take away.

AGRIPPA

They wreak° them not, O Caesar, at each time
That by our sins they are to wrath provoked.
Neither must you (believe, I humbly pray)
Your victory with cruelty defile.
The gods it gave, it must not be abused,
But to the good of all men mildly used,
And they be thanked, that having giv'n you grace
To reign alone, and rule this earthly mass,
They may hence forward° hold it still in rest,
All scattered power united in one breast.

CAESAR

But what is he that breathless comes so fast,
Approaching us, and going in such haste?

AGRIPPA

He seems afraid, and under his arm I
(But much I err[35]) a bloody sword espy.

CAESAR

I long to understand what it may be.
[*Enter* DIRCETUS, *the Messenger.*]

AGRIPPA

He hither comes: it's best we stay and see.

DIRCETUS

What good god now my voice will reinforce,
That tell I may to rocks, and hills, and woods,
To waves of sea, which dash upon the shore,
To earth, to heav'n, the woeful news I bring?

AGRIPPA

What sudden chance thee towards us hath brought?

DIRCETUS

A lamentable chance. O wrath of heav'ns!
O gods too pitiless!

CAESAR

What monstrous hap°
Wilt thou recount?

DIRCETUS

Alas too hard mishap°!
When I but dream of what mine eyes beheld,
My heart doth freeze, my limbs do quivering quake,
I senseless stand, my breast with tempest tossed
Kills in my throat my words, ere° fully born.

---

[35] i.e. 'if I am not mistaken'.

Dead, dead he is: be sure of what I say,
This murdering sword[36] hath made the man away.

CAESAR

Alas, my heart doth cleave, pity me racks,
My breast doth pant to hear this doleful° tale.
Is Antony then dead? To death, alas!
I am the cause despair him so compelled.
But soldier, of his death the manner show,[37]
And how he did this living light forgo.

DIRCETUS

When Antony no hope remaining saw[38]
How war he might, or how agreement make;
Saw him betrayed by all his men of war
In every fight as well by sea, as land;
That not content to yield them to their foes,
They also came against himself to fight;
Alone in court he gan° himself torment,
Accuse the queen, himself of her lament,
Called her untrue and traitress, as who sought
To yield him up she could no more defend;
That in the harms which for her sake he bore,
As in his blissful state, she might not share.
  But she again, who much his fury feared,
Got to the tombs, dark horror's dwelling place;
Made lock the doors, and pull the herses° down.
Then fell she wretchèd, with herself to fight:
A thousand plaints,° a thousand sobs she cast
From her weak breast which to the bones was torn.
Of women, her, the most unhappy called,
Who by her love, her woeful love, had lost
Her realm, her life, and more, the love of him,
Who while he was, was all her woe's support.
But that she faultless was, she did invoke

---

[36] According to Plutarch (*Life of Antony*, LXXVIII. 1), Dircetus, a member of Antony's guard, announced the news of his death to Octavius, and showed him Antony's bloodied sword as evidence.
[37] i.e. tell about.
[38] 214–18] Garnier closely follows Plutarch, *Life of Antony*, LXXVI. 2.

For witness heav'n, and air, and earth, and sea.
Then sent him word she was no more alive,
But lay enclosèd dead within her tomb.
This he believed, and fell to sigh and groan,
And crossed his arms, then thus began to moan.

CAESAR

Poor hopeless man!

DIRCETUS

'What dost thou more attend°?
Ah, Antony! Why dost thou death defer,
Since Fortune thy professèd enemy,
Hath made to die, who only made thee live?'
Soon as with sighs he had these words up closed,[39]
His armour he unlaced and cast it off,
Then all disarmed he thus again did say:
My queen, my heart, the grief that now I feel,
Is not that I your eyes, my sun, do lose,
For soon again one tomb shall us conjoin;[40]
I grieve, whom men so valorous did deem
Should now than you of lesser valour seem.
So said, forthwith he Eros to him called,
Eros, his man, summoned him on his faith
To kill him at his need. He[41] took the sword,
And at that instant stabbed therewith his breast,
And ending life[42] fell dead before his feet.
'O Eros, thanks' (quoth Antony) 'for this
Most noble act, who powerless me to kill,
On thee hast done what I on me should do.'
Of speaking thus he scarce had made an end,
And taken up the bloody sword from ground,
But he his body pierced; and of red blood
A gushing fountain all the chamber filled.

---

[39] 246–65] See again Plutarch, *Life of Antony*, LXXVI. 3–4.
[40] Garnier: 'bien tost nous serons ensemble en un cercueil' ('soon we will be joined in one coffin', p. 102r).
[41] i.e., Eros (repeated in the French).
[42] Compare with Garnier: 'Il vomit sang & ame' ('He spewed out [his] blood and soul', p. 102r). See also Sidney Herbert's soberer description of Cleopatra's agony below.

He staggered at the blow, his face grew pale,
And on a couch all feeble down he fell,
Swooning with anguish; deadly cold him took,
As if his soul had then his lodging left.
But he revived, and marking all our eyes
Bathed in tears, and how our breasts we beat
For pity, anguish, and for bitter grief,
To see him plunged in extreme wretchedness,
He prayed us all to haste his ling'ring death:
But no man willing, each himself withdrew.
Then fell he new to cry and vex himself,
Until a man from Cleopatra came,[43]
Who said from her he had commandement[44]
To bring him to her to the monument.
The poor soul at these words even rapt with joy,
Knowing she lived, prayed us him to convey
Unto his lady. Then upon our arms
We bore him to the tomb, but entered not.
For she who fearèd captive to be made,
And that she should to Rome in triumph go,
Kept close the gate; but from a window high
Cast down a cord,° wherein he was impacked.°[45]
Then by her women's help the corpse[46] she raised,
And by strong arms into her window drew.
So pitiful a sight was never seen.[47]
Little and little Antony was pulled,
Now breathing death; his beard was all unkempt,
His face and breast all bathèd in his blood.
So hideous yet, and dying as he was,
His eyes half-closed upon the queen he cast,
Held up his hands, and holp° himself to raise,
But still with weakness back his body fell.
The miserable lady with moist eyes,
With hair which careless on her forehead hung,

---

[43] 277–313] Garnier follows and expands Plutarch, *Life of Antony*, LXXVII. 1–2.
[44] Spelled as in French, for metric reasons (4 syllables).
[45] Garnier: 'empaqueta' (p. 102v). Compare with North: 'trussed' (*Lives*, p. 1006).
[46] i.e. body (alive or dead). Added by Sidney Herbert (Garnier only has the personal pronoun 'le').
[47] The phrase echoes North's Plutarch: 'they never sawe so pittiful a sight' (*Lives*, p. 1006).

With breast which blows had bloodily benumbed,
With stooping head, and body downward bent,
Enlaced° her in the cord,[48] and with all force
This life-dead[49] man courageously upraised.
The blood with pain into her face did flow,
Her sinews stiff, herself did breathless grow.
The people which beneath in flocks beheld,
Assisted her with gesture, speech, desire;[50]
Cried and encouraged her, and in their souls
Did sweat, and labour, no whit less than she,
Who never tired in labour, held so long
Helped by her women, and her constant heart,
That Antony was drawn into the tomb,[51]
And there (I think) of dead augments the sum.
The city all to tears and sighs is turned,
To plaints° and outcries horrible to hear:[52]
Men, women, children, hoary-headed age
Do all pell-mell° in house and street lament,
Scratching their faces, tearing of their hair,
Wringing their hands, and martyring their breasts.
Extreme their dole,° and greater misery
In sackèd towns can hardly ever be.
Not if the fire had scaled the highest towers;
That all things were of force and murder full,
That in the streets the blood in rivers streamed,
The son his sire saw in his bosom slain,
The sire his son; the husband reft° of breath
In his wife's arms, who furious runs to death.
Now my breast wounded with their piteous plaints°
I left their town, and took with me this sword,

---

[48] i.e. entwined herself in the rope.

[49] i.e. half-dead. Garnier: 'demy mort' (p. 103r).

[50] Sidney Herbert seems to read Garnier's 'à l'envy' (i.e. with all their strength) literally (p. 103r).

[51] Garnier: 'le sepulchre sombre' ('the dark sepulchre', p. 103r).

[52] 314–21] See Virgil's *Aeneid*, IV. 666–70: 'Lamentis gemituque et femineo ululatu | Tecta fremunt; resonat magnis plangoribus aether, | Non aliter, quam si immissis ruat hostibus omnis | Karthago aut antiqua Tyros, flammaeque furentes | Culmina perque hominum uoluantur perque deorum' ('The roofs tremble with lamentations, cries, and women's howls, the air resounds with a great complaint; not otherwise, than if the invading enemy were destroying all Carthage or the ancient Tyr, and the rooftops of houses and temples were engulfed in raging flames').

Which I took up at what time Antony
Was from his chamber carried to the tomb,
And brought it you, to make his death more plain,
And that thereby my words may credit gain.

CAESAR

Ah, gods, what cruel hap!° Poor Antony,
Alas, hast thou this sword so long time borne
Against thy foe, that in the end it should
Of thee his lord the cursèd murd'rer be?[53]
O Death, how I bewail thee! We (alas!)
So many wars have ended, brothers, friends,
Companions, cousins, equals in estate;
And must it now to kill thee be my fate?

AGRIPPA

Why trouble you yourself with bootless° grief?
For Antony, why spend you tears in vain?
Why darken you with dole° your victory?
Meseems° yourself your glory do envy.
Enter the town, give thanks unto the gods.

CAESAR

I cannot but his tearful chance lament,
Although not I, but his own pride the cause,
And unchaste love of this Egyptìan.

AGRIPPA

But best we sought into the tomb to get,
Lest she consume in this amazèd case
So much rich treasure, with which happily
Despair in death may make her feed the fire;
Suff'ring the flames her jewels to deface,
You to defraud, her funeral to grace.
Send then to her, and let some mean be used

---

[53] 334–37] See Plutarch, *Life of Antony*, LXXVIII. 2 (North: 'Caesar hearing this newes, straight withdrewe him selfe into a secret place of his tent, and there burst out with teares, lamenting his hard and miserable fortune, that had bene his friende and brother in law, his equal in the Empire, and companion with him in sundry great exploytes and battells.' *Lives*, p. 1007).

With some devise so hold her still alive,
Some fair large promises: and let them mark
Whither they may by some fine cunning sleight
Enter the tombs.

CAESAR

Let Proculeius[54] go,
And feed with hope her soul disconsolate.
Assure her so, that we may wholly get
Into our hands her treasure and herself.
For this of all things most I do desire,
To keep her safe until our going hence:
That by her presence beautified may be
The glorious triumph Rome prepares for me.[55]

[*Exeunt.*]

CHORUS OF ROMAN SOLDIERS[56]

Shall ever civil bate°
    Gnaw and devour our state?
    Shall never we this blade
    Our blood hath bloody made[57]
    Lay down? These arms down lay
    As robes we wear alway?[58]
    But as from age to age
So pass from rage to rage?[59]
Our hands shall we not rest
    To bathe in our own breast?
    And shall thick in each land
    Our wretched trophies stand,
    To tell posterity,

---

[54] Proculeius was Octavius's envoy in Plutarch (*Life of Antony*, LXXVIII. 3) and in Jodelle's *Cleopâtre captive* (Paris, 1553).

[55] The phrase echoes North's *Lives* (p. 1007): '[Caesar] thought that if he could take Cleopatra, and bring her alive to Rome, she would marvellously beautifie and sette out his triumph' (see Hannay et al., *Works*, I. p. 150).

[56] Garnier: 'soldats césariens' ('Cesarian soldiers', p. 104r).

[57] The polyptoton is Sidney Herbert's addition. Garnier: 'Des glaives dans nostre sang teints' ('swords tainted with our blood', p. 104r).

[58] always, spelled 'alway' here because of the rhyme.

[59] The repetition of 'rage' is not in Garnier: 'Nous irons-nous de race en race | Massacrer eternellement?' ('Will we keep slaughtering one another | from age to age?', p. 104r).

What mad impiety
Our stony stomachs[60] led
Against the place us bred?
Then still must heaven view
The plagues that us pursue,
And everywhere descry
Heaps of us scattered lie,
Making the stranger plains
Fat with our bleeding rains
Proud that on them their grave
So many legions have.
And with our fleshes still
Neptune his fishes fill,[61]
And drunk with blood from blue
The sea take blushing hue;
As juice of Tyrian shell,[62]
When clarified well
To wool[63] of finest fields
A purple gloss it yields.
But since the rule of Rome,
To one man's hand is come,
Who governs without a mate
Her now united state,
Late jointly ruled by three
Envying mutually,
Whose triple yoke much woe
On Latins' necks did throw,
I hope the cause of jar,°
And of this bloody war,
And deadly discord, gone
By what we last have done;

[60] Garnier: 'nos ames trop dures' ('our over-hardened souls', p. 104r). See *Cornélie* ('d'un coeur endurci', 'with a hardened heart', p. 69r) and Kyd's translation ('our stony hearts',v. 272).

[61] 393–96] Garnier: 'Que Neptune en remplisse és ondes | Le sein des Phoques vagabondes, | Et que la Mer peinte de bleu | Rougisse du sang qu'elle a beu' ('Let Neptune fill [with blood] among the waves | the flanks of the wandering seals | and let the blue-painted sea | blush from drinking so much blood', p. 104v).

[62] Tyrian purple was made from shells found in the eastern Mediterranean. A purple toga was usually worn by victorious generals at their triumph.

[63] Garnier has: 'laine Canusienne' ('Canusian wool', p. 104v). The city of Canusium was supposed to produce the finest wool, and was also renowned for its purple dye.

Our banks shall cherish now
The branchy pale-hewed bow
Of Olive, Pallas' praise,[64]
Instead of barren bays.
And that his temple door,
Which bloody Mars before
Held open, now at last
Old Janus shall make fast,[65]
And rust the sword consume,
And spoiled of waving plume,
The useless morion[66] shall
On crook° hang by the wall.
At least if war return,
It shall not here sojourn,
To kill us with those arms
Were forged for others' harms;
But have their points addressed,
Against the Germans' breast,
The Parthians' feignèd flight,
The Biscay'ns' martial might.[67]
Old memory doth there,
Painted on forehead wear
Our fathers'[68] praise, thence torn
Our triumphs' bays have worn;
Thereby our matchless Rome
Whilom° of shepherds come
Raised to this greatness stands,
The queen of foreign lands.

---

[64] The olive tree was associated with peace and fertility, and was an emblem of Pallas, the goddess of wisdom. It is usually opposed to the laurel crown of victorious warriors.

[65] The doors of the temple of Janus (god of doors and gates, and of beginnings and ends) were open in time of war and closed in time of peace.

[66] Morions were helmets without a visor worn in the sixteenth and seventeenth centuries. The anachronism is Garnier's.

[67] All traditional (and future) enemies of Rome. Instead of Biscayans, Garnier has 'Cantabres inhumains' (inhabitants of Cantabria, a Spanish region on the Bay of Biscay). As noted by Ternaux (p. 161), the idea that war against the traditional enemies of Rome is preferable to civil war is taken from Lucan's *Pharsalia*, I. 21–23 (in Marlowe's translation: 'Roome if thou take delight in impious warre, | First conquer all the earth, then turne thy force | Against thy selfe: as yet thou wants not foes.' *Lucans first booke*, sig. B1r).

[68] Compare with Garnier: 'Nos Empereurs' (p. 105r).

Which now even seems to face
The heav'ns, her glory's place;
Nought resting under skies[69]
That dares affront her eyes.
So that she needs but fear
The weapons Jove doth bear,
Who angry at one blow
May her[70] quite overthrow.

[*Exit* CHORUS.]

---

[69] Garnier: 'en ce rond' ('on this globe', p. 105r).
[70] Garnier: 'l'Empire Romain' (p. 105v). Sidney Herbert cancels two references to the empire, here and in II. 2. 160 and III. 220 (see p. 139, n. 37)

ACT V

[*Enter*] CLEOPATRA, EUPHRON, CHILDREN OF CLEOPATRA, CHARMION, ERAS.

CLEOPATRA

O cruel fortune! O accursèd lot!
O plaguey° love! O most detested brand!°
O wretched joys! O beauties miserable!
O deadly state! O deadly royalty!
O hateful life! O queen most lamentable!
O Antony by my fault buriable!°[1]
O hellish work of heav'n! Alas! The wrath
Of all the gods at once on us is fall'n.
Unhappy queen! Oh, would I in this world
The wand'ring light of day had never seen!
Alas! Of mine the plague and poison I[2]
The crown have lost my ancestors me left,
This realm I have to strangers subject made,
And robbed my children of their heritage.
Yet this is nought (alas!) unto the price
Of you dear husband, whom my snares entrapped;°
Of you, whom I have plagued, whom I have made
With bloody hand a guest of mouldy tomb;
Of you, whom I destroyed, of you, dear lord,
Whom I of empire, honour, life, have spoiled.
O hurtful woman! And can I yet live,
Yet longer live in this ghost-haunted tomb?
Can I yet breathe? Can yet in such annoy,°
Yet can my soul within this body dwell?
O sisters,[3] you that spin the threads of death!
O Styx! O Phlegethon![4] You brooks of hell!
O imps of night!

[1] Garnier also uses a neologism, 'sepulturable' (p. 105v).

[2] The choice to have 'I' at the end of a line is Sidney Herbert's. A similar self-characterization of Cornelia as a 'plague' to her husband can also be found in *Cornelia*, II. 58.

[3] The three Fates, or Parcae, that give death by cutting the threads of life. Garnier names two of them, Atropos and Clotho.

[4] Like the more familiar Styx, Phlegethon is a river of the classical underworld, mentioned in Virgil's *Aeneid*, VI.

EUPHRON

Live for your children's sake:
Let not your death of kingdom them deprive.
Alas, what shall they do? Who will have care?
Who will preserve this royal race of yours?
Who pity take? Even now meseems° I see
These little souls to servile bondage fall'n,
And borne in triumph.

CLEOPATRA

Ah, most miserable!

EUPHRON

Their tender arms with cursèd cord° fast bound
At their weak backs.

CLEOPATRA

Ah gods, what pity more!

EUPHRON

Their seely° necks to ground with weakness bend —

CLEOPATRA

Never on us, good gods, such mischief° send.

EUPHRON

And pointed at with fingers as they go.[5]

CLEOPATRA

Rather a thousand deaths!

EUPHRON

Lastly, his knife
Some cruel caitiff°[6] in their blood imbrue.°

---

[5] Garnier includes a reference to the people: 'Et au doigt les monstrer la tourbe citoyenne' ('the muddy populace [will] point their fingers at them', p. 106r).

[6] Garnier: 'l'infame bourreau' ('the reviled executioner', p. 106r).

CLEOPATRA

Ah, my heart breaks. By shady banks of hell,
By fields whereon the lonely ghosts do tread,
By my soul, and the soul[7] of Antony,
I you beseech, Euphron, of them have care.
Be their good Father, let your wisdom let
That they fall not into this tyrant's hands.
Rather conduct them where their frizzèd° locks
Black Ethiops to neighbour sun do show,
On wavy ocean at the water's will,
On barren cliffs of snowy Caucasus,
To tigers swift, to lions, and to bears;[8]
And rather, rather unto every coast,
To ev'ry land and sea: for nought I fear
As rage of him, whose thirst no blood can quench.
  Adieu, dear children, children dear adieu;
Good Isis[9] you to place of safety guide,
Far from our foes, where you your lives may lead
In free estate devoid of servile dread.
  Remember not, my children, you were born
Of such a princely race;[10] remember not
So many brave kings which have Egypt ruled
In right descent your ancestors have been;
That this great Antony your father was,
Hercules' blood,[11] and more than he in praise.
For your high courage such remembrance will,
Seeing your fall with burning rages fill.
  Who knows if that your hands, false Destiny,
The sceptres promised of imperious Rome,
Instead of them shall crooked sheephooks bear,
Needles or forks, or guide the cart, or plough?

---

[7] Compare with Garnier: 'les Manes d'Antoine' (p. 106r). The Manes were the spirits of the dead.

[8] The association of these animals with Caucasus (as a metaphor for cruelty) is a commonplace, see for example *Aeneid*, IV. 366–67.

[9] Main Egyptian divinity. Garnier calls her 'sainte Isis' (p. 106v).

[10] See Seneca, *Troades*, 712 (as noted by Ternaux, p. 161): 'Pone ex animo reges atavos' ('put out of your mind your royal ancestors'). The whole passage is reminiscent of Andromache's farewell to her son in Seneca's play, and perhaps even more of Seneca's own Greek source, Euripides' *Troades*.

[11] On Hercules' blood, see p. 139, n. 33.

Ah, learn t'endure: your birth and high estate
Forget, my babes, and bend to force of fate.
Farewell, my babes, farewell, my heart is closed
With pity and pain, myself with death enclosed,
My breath doth fail. Farewell for evermore,
Your sire and me you shall see never more.
Farewell sweet care,[12] farewell.

CHILDREN
Madam, adieu.

CLEOPATRA
Ah, this voice kills me. Ah, good gods! I swoon.
I can no more, I die.

ERAS
Madam, alas!
And will you yield to woe? Ah, speak to us.

EUPHRON
Come, children.

CHILDREN
We come.

EUPHRON
Follow we our chance.
The gods shall guide us.

[*Exeunt* EUPHRON *and* CHILDREN.]

CHARMION
Oh, too cruel lot!
Oh, too hard chance! Sister, what shall we do,
What shall we do, alas, if murdering dart
Of death arrive while that in slumb'ring swoon
Half-dead she lie with anguish overgone?

---

[12] Compare with Garnier's oxymoron: 'douce cure' ('sweet burden', 'cure' being derived from the Latin, *cura*: worry, charge).

ERAS

Her face is frozen.

CHARMION

Madam, for god's love
Leave us not thus: bid us yet first farewell.
Alas! Weep over Antony: let not
His body be without due rites entombed.

CLEOPATRA

Ah, ah.

CHARMION

Madam.

CLEOPATRA

Ay me!

CHARMION[13]

How faint she is!

CLEOPATRA

My sisters, hold me up. How wretchèd I,
How cursèd am; and was there ever one
By Fortune's hate into more dolours thrown?
Ah, weeping Niobe,[14] although thy heart
Beholds itself enwrapped in causeful woe
For thy dead children, that a senseless rock
With grief become, on Sipylus thou stand'st
In endless tears; yet didst thou never feel
The weights of grief that on my heart do lie.
Thy children thou, mine I, poor soul, have lost,
And lost their father, more than them I wail,
Lost this fair realm; yet me the heavens' wrath
Into a stone not yet transformèd hath.
Phaëton's sisters,[15] daughters of the sun,

[13] Garnier attributes this speech to Eras. For the changes in speech attributions in this scene, see Introduction, p. 36.
[14] On Niobe, see p. 110, n. 31.
[15] See p. 109, n. 30. Garnier has: 'vierges Phaëtontides' ('virgins', p. 107r).

Which wail your brother fall'n into the streams
Of stately Po,[16] the gods upon the banks
Your bodies to bank-loving alders turned.
For me, I sigh, I ceaseless weep, and wail,
And heaven pitiless laughs at my woe,
Revives, renews it still: and in the end
(Oh, cruelty!) doth death[17] for comfort lend.
    Die Cleopatra then, no longer stay
From Antony, who thee at Styx[18] attends:°
Go join thy ghost with his, and sob no more
Without his love within these tombs enclosed.

ERAS

Alas! Yet let us weep, lest sudden death
From him our tears, and those last duties take,
Unto his tomb we owe.

CHARMION

Ah, let us weep,
While moisture lasts, then die before his feet.

CLEOPATRA

Who furnish will mine eyes with streaming tears,
My boiling° anguish worthily to wail,
Wail thee Antony, Antony my heart?
Alas, how much I weeping liquor want!
Yet have mine eyes quite drawn their conduits° dry[19]
By long beweeping my disastered° harms.
Now reason is that from my side they suck
First vital moisture, then the vital blood.
Then let the blood from my sad eyes[20] outflow,

---

[16] Garnier mentions the mythological river of Hades associated with the river Po: 'du superbe Eridan' ('the proud Eridanos', p. 107r). According to Ovid (*Metamorphoses*, II. 345–66), Phaëton's sisters were turned into alder trees as they wept for his death.
[17] Garnier: 'la violente mort' ('violent death', p. 107r).
[18] Garnier does not name the river Styx: 'aux rives palissantes' ('on the pale shores', p. 107r).
[19] Literally rendered from Garnier: 'mes yeux ont espuisé leurs veines' ('my eyes have drained their channels', p. 107v).
[20] Compare with Garnier's conceit: 'ma lampe jumelle' ('twin lamp', p. 107v).

And smoking° yet with thine in mixture grow.
Moist it, and heat it new, and never stop,
All wat'ring thee, while yet remains one drop.

CHARMION

Antony, take our tears: this is the last
Of all the duties we to thee can yield,
Before we die.

ERAS

These sacred obsequies,°
Take Antony, and take them in good part.

CLEOPATRA

O goddess, thou whom Cyprus doth adore,[21]
Venus of Paphos, bent to work us harm
For old Iulus' brood,[22] if thou take care
Of Caesar, why of us tak'st thou no care?
Antony did descend as well as he
From thine own son[23] by long enchainèd line;
And might have ruled by one and selfsame fate,
True Trojan blood,[24] the stately Roman state.
Antony, poor Antony, my dear soul,
Now but a block, the booty of a tomb,
Thy life thy heat is lost, thy colour gone,
And hideous paleness on thy face hath seized.
Thy eyes, two suns, the lodging place of love,
Which yet for tents to warlike Mars did serve,
Locked up in lids (as fair day's cheerful light
Which darkness flies) do winking° hide in night.

---

[21] Garnier: 'O Deesse adoree en Cypre & Amathonte, | Paphienne Venus' ('O goddess revered in Cyprus and Amathus, | Venus of Paphos', p. 107v). See Horace, *Odes*, I. 30. 1: 'O Venus regina Cnidi Paphique …' ('O Venus, queen of Cnidus and Paphos').

[22] Aeneas's son, also sometimes called Ascanius, supposed to be an ancestor of the founders of Rome, Romulus and Remus, and of the *gens Julia*, to which Julius Caesar belonged. Venus was Aeneas's mother and was thus believed to favour the line of Caesar.

[23] Aeneas, whose name is actually mentioned in Garnier (p. 107v).

[24] Garnier has: 'vray sang Dardanien' ('true Dardanian blood', p. 107v). Dardanus, the mythical founder of Troy, was an ancestor of Aeneas.

Antony, by our true loves I thee beseech,[25]
And by our hearts sweet sparks have set on fire,
Our holy marriage, and the tender ruth°
Of our dear babes, knot of our amity,°
My doleful° voice thy ear let entertain,
And take me with thee to the hellish plain,
Thy wife, thy friend. Hear, Antony, oh hear
My sobbing sighs, if here thou be, or there.
I lived thus long,[26] the wingèd race of years
Ended I have as destiny decreed,
Flourished and reigned, and taken just revenge
Of him who me both hated and despised.
Happy, alas, too happy! If of Rome
Only the fleet had hither never come.
And now of me an image great shall go
Under the earth to bury there my woe.[27]
What say I? Where am I? O Cleopatra,
Poor Cleopatra, grief thy reason reaves.°
No, no, most happy in this hapless° case,
To die with thee, and dying thee embrace:
My body joined with thine, my mouth with thine,
My mouth, whose moisture-burning sighs have dried
To be in one self° tomb, and one self chest,
And wrapped with thee in one self sheet to rest.

---

[25] 153–57] The passage is reminiscent of Dido's plea in Virgil's *Aeneid*, IV. 314–16: 'per ego has lacrimas dextramque tuam te | […] Per conubia nostra, per inceptos hymenaeos, | […] Oro' ('by my tears and the right hand you gave me, […] by our union, and by our marriage just begun, […] I implore you').

[26] In 1592 and 1595 the personal pronoun 'I' does not appear. This edition adopts this emendation for two reasons. First, the syntax and metrical pattern both require the insertion of 'I'; second, the first person does appear in Garnier, in this passage, which Sidney Herbert otherwise closely follows. Garnier: 'I'ay vescy jusqu'ici, j'ay la course empennee | De mes ans …' ('I have lived so far, and run the feathery course | of my years', p. 108r).

[27] 161–68] This is a close rendering of Dido's final words in Virgil's *Aeneid*, IV. 653–58: 'Vixi et quem dederat cursum Fortuna peregi, | Et nunc magna mei sub terras ibit imago. | Urbem praeclaram statui, mea moenia vidi, | Ulta virum poenas inimico a fratre recepi, | Felix, heu nimium felix, si litora tantum | Numquam Dardaniae tetigissent nostra carinae' ('I lived, and ran the course Fortune had allotted me, and now a great image of me will go under the ground. I founded a brilliant city, I saw my own walls, I avenged my husband and punished my hostile brother; happy, alas! too happy, had the Trojan ships never touched upon our shores'). Garnier keeps the original mention of a 'hostile brother' ('frere ennemy'), which Sidney Herbert only renders as 'him'.

The sharpest torment in my heart I feel
Is that I stay from thee, my heart, this while.
Die will I straight now, now straight will I die,
And straight with thee a wand'ring shade will be,
Under the cypress trees thou haunt'st alone,
Where brooks of hell do falling seem to moan.[28]
But yet I stay, and yet thee overlive,°
That ere° I die due rites I may thee give.
A thousand sobs I from my breast[29] will tear,
With thousand plaints° thy funerals adorn;
My hair shall serve for thy oblatìons,
My boiling° tears for thy effusìons,
Mine eyes thy fire: for out of them the flame
(Which burnt thy heart on me enamoured[30]) came.
Weep, my companions, weep, and from your eyes
Rain down on him of tears a brinish stream.[31]
Mine can no more, consumèd by the coals
Which from my breast, as from a furnace, rise.[32]
Martyr your breasts with multiplièd blows,
With violent hands tear off your hanging hair,
Outrage your face! Alas, why should we seek
(Since now we die) our beauties more to keep?
I, spent in tears, not able more to spend,
But kiss him now, what rests me more to do?

---

[28] Garnier: 'Au lamentable bruit des eaux Acherontees' ('to the sorrowful sound of Acheron's waters', p. 108v). The allusion is to the *lugentes campi* (fields of sorrow) of the classical underworld, which held the souls of those who died unhappily (usually, for love). In Virgil's *Aeneid*, VI. 649–74, Aeneas meets there the spirit of Dido, then reunited with her husband Sichaeus.

[29] Compare with Garnier: 'de mes entrailles' ('my entrails'), rhyming with 'funerailles' ('funerals'), p. 108v.

[30] Garnier has: 'le cœur amoureux de ta Dame' ('your heart enamoured with your lady', p. 108v). The image of the eyes shooting out fire and enflaming the beloved's heart is a Petrarchan commonplace; see p. 125, n. 54.

[31] See Garnier: 'un torrent larmoyeux' ('a torrent of tears'). Compare with Sidney Herbert's translation of Petrarch's *Triumph of Death* (*c.* 1590), I. 118–20: 'How manie dropps did flowe from brynie spring | In who there sawe those sightfull fountaines drye, | For whom this heart so long did burne and sing' (*Works*, I, p. 276); and *The Countess of Pembroke's Arcadia* (1593), IV, p. 206: 'With that worde there flowed out two rivers of tears out of her fayre eyes, [...] love only according to the temper of it melting it selfe into those briny tokens of passion'.

[32] Garnier: 'la braise | Que vomist ma poitrine ainsi qu'une fournaise' ('the embers | that my breast spews out like a furnace', p. 108v).

Then let me kiss you, you fair eyes, my light,
Front seat of honour, face most fierce, most fair!
O neck, O arms, O hands, O breast where death
(O mischief°) comes to choke up vital breath![33]
A thousand kisses, thousand thousand more
Let you my mouth for honours farewell give,
That in this office weak my limbs may grow,
Fainting on you, and forth my soul may flow.[34]

[*She dies. Exeunt.*]

At Ramsbury, 26. of November, 1590.

[33] Compare with Garnier: 'vient de faire [...] son parricide effort' ('[death] has dealt [...] its parricidal blow', p. 108v).
[34] Garnier: 'Et qu'en un tel devoir mon corps affoiblissant | Defaille dessus vous, mon ame vomissant' ('And let my body thus growing weak | faint over you, spewing forth my soul', p. 108v).

CORNELIA

To the virtuously noble, and rightly honoured Lady,
the *Countess of Sussex.*

Having no leisure, most noble Lady, but such as evermore is travailed° with the afflictions of the mind — than which the world affords no greater misery — it may be wondered at by some, how I durst° undertake a matter of this moment,° which both requireth cunning, rest and opportunity; but chiefly, that I would attempt the dedication of so rough unpolished a work,[1] *to the survey of your so worthy self.*

But being well instructed in your noble and heroic dispositions, and perfectly assured of your honourable favours past[2] *— though neither making needless glosses of the one, nor spoiling paper with the other's Pharisaical*[3] *embroidery — I have presumed upon your true conceit and entertainment of these small endeavours, that thus I purposed to make known, my memory of you and them to be immortal.*

A fitter present for a patroness so well accomplished I could not find, than this fair precedent° of honour, magnanimity, and love. Wherein, what grace that excellent Garnier hath lost by my default, I shall beseech your Honour to repair, with the regard of those so bitter times, and privy broken passions that I endured in the writing it.[4]

And so vouchsafing° but the passing of a winter's week with desolate Cornelia, I will assure your Ladyship my next summer's better travail° with the tragedy of Portia.[5] *And ever spend one hour of the day in some kind service to your Honour, and another of the night in wishing you all happiness, perpetually thus devoting my poor self,*

Your Honour's, in all humbleness,

T[*homas*] *K*[*yd*].

---

[1] An example of the modesty topos usual in translation prefaces (see also below, 'these small endeavours'), which should not necessarily be read as an indication of Kyd's hasty composition of the translation.

[2] According to Freeman (p. 34), Kyd had probably met the Countess when (presumably) employed by her father-in-law, Henry Radcliffe, 4th Earl of Sussex. See Introduction, p. 51.

[3] Boastful; in reference to the figure of the arrogant Pharisee in Luke 18. 9–14.

[4] A possible allusion to the deaths of Henry Radcliffe, Earl of Sussex, and his wife in the last months of 1593. Kyd is also probably referring to his imprisonment in 1593, and his subsequent difficulties in finding patronage.

[5] Garnier's *Porcie*, the prequel to *Cornélie* and *Marc Antoine* in his trilogy of Roman plays. The three plays were published together in Garnier's 1585 edition of his *Tragédies*, which Kyd probably used to translate *Cornelia*.

The Argument.

Cornelia, the daughter of Metellus Scipio,[1] *a young Roman lady, as much accomplished with the graces of the body and the virtues of the mind as ever any was, was first married to young Crassus,*[2] *who died with his father in the discomfiture of the Romans against the Parthians. Afterward she took to second husband Pompey the Great,*[3] *who, three years after, upon the first fires of the civil wars betwixt him and Caesar, sent her from thence to Mytilene,*[4] *there to attend the uncertain success of those affairs. And when he saw that he was vanquished at Pharsalia,*[5] *returned to find her out, and carry her with him into Egypt, where his purpose was to have reinforced a new army, and give a second assault to Caesar.*

In this voyage, he was murdered by Achillas and Septimius the Roman[6] *before her eyes, and in the presence of his young son Sextus, and some other senators his friends. After which, she retired herself to Rome. But Scipio her father, being made General of those that survived after the battle, assembled new forces, and occupied the greater part of Africa, allying himself to Juba King of Numidia.*[7] *Against all whom, Caesar, after he had ordered the affairs of Egypt*

---

[1] Quintus Metellus Scipio, a senator, military leader and staunch opponent of Caesar. He was Roman consul together with Pompey in 52 BC; he convinced the Senate to go to war with Caesar in 49 BC and subsequently led the Roman troops against him in Greece and Asia Minor.

[2] Publius Crassus served in Gaul under Caesar and became a prominent political figure of the late republic. He married Cornelia in 55 or 54 BC. He was the son of Marcus Crassus, the third man in the so-called 'first triumvirate' allying Caesar and Pompey between 60 and 53 BC. He was killed, along with his father, at the battle of Carrhae (in modern-day eastern Turkey) against the Parthians in 53 BC.

[3] Pompey was Caesar's main opponent in the civil war. He was called 'the great' due to his many military successes. He shared the consulate with Caesar in the so-called 'first triumvirate' in 60 BC, and married Caesar's daughter Julia, but the alliance fell through with her death in 53 BC, leading to the civil war. He married Cornelia in 52 BC.

[4] A town on the east coast of Greece.

[5] In central Greece, where the decisive battle of the civil war was held (48 BC), and Pompey's party was defeated.

[6] As related in Plutarch's *Life of Pompey* (LXXIX. 3). Achillas was the counsellor to young king of Egypt, Ptolemy XIII, who advised him to have Pompey murdered on his arrival in Egypt. Septimius was a leader of the Roman troops in Egypt.

[7] Juba was Pompey's main ally in North Africa. He had defeated Caesar's troops in 49 BC.

and the state of Rome, in the end of winter marched. And there, after many light encounters, was a fierce and furious battle given amongst them near the walls of Thapsus.[8] *Where Scipio seeing himself subdued, and his army scattered, he betook himself with some small troop to certain ships, which he had caused to stay for him.*

Thence he sailed toward Spain, where Pompey's faction[9] *commanded, and where a sudden tempest took him on the sea, that drove him back to Hippon,*[10] *a town in Africa at the devotion of Caesar, where, lying at anchor, he was assailed, beaten and assaulted by the adverse fleet. And for he would not fall alive into the hands of his so mighty enemy, he stabbed himself, and suddenly leapt over board into the sea, and there died.*

Caesar, having finished these wars, and quietly reduced the towns and places thereabout to his obedience, returned to Rome in triumph for his victories. Where this most fair and miserable lady,[11] *having overmourned° the death of her dear husband, and understanding of*[12] *these cross events and hapless° news of Africa, together with the piteous manner of her father's end, she took — as she had cause — occasion to redouble both her tears and lamentations; wherewith she closeth the catastrophe*[13] *of this their tragedy.*[14]

---

[8] In modern-day Tunisia. The battle of Thapsus was held in 46 BC.

[9] Garnier: 'les enfans de Pompée' ('Pompey's children', p. 39r).

[10] In modern-day Algeria, a major North-African city at the time.

[11] Compare with Garnier: 'la miserable Cornelie' ('miserable Cornelia', p. 39v).

[12] i.e. hearing of.

[13] Technically, the catastrophe is the final resolution of a tragedy.

[14] Kyd leaves out Garnier's mention of his literary sources: 'Vous verrez ce discours amplement traité en Plutarque ès vies de Pompée, de Cesar, et de Caton d'Utique; en Hirtius, cinquième livre des guerres civiles d'Appian, et quarante-troisième de Dion' ('You will find this treated at length in Plutarch's lives of Pompey, Caesar and Cato; in Hirtius, in the fifth book of Appian's *Civil Wars*, and in the forty-third book of Dio['s *Roman History*]', p. 39v). Note however that Appian treats of the civil war in Book II of his *Civil Wars*, and that Garnier omits Lucan's *Pharsalia*, a major source throughout the play.

Interlocutores[15]

M[arcus Tullius] Cicero
Philip
Deci[mus] Brutus[16]
M[ark] Antony
Cornelia
C[aius] Cassius
Julius Caesar
The Messenger
Chorus[17]
[A Chorus of Caesar's friends]

[15] Kyd uses the Latin for speakers, after Garnier's 'Interlocuteurs' (p. 39v).
[16] The first name of Caesar's famous adoptive son and murderer was actually Marcus Junius Brutus. He was at first a partisan of Pompey and fought in the latter's camp at Pharsalia, but Caesar forgave him and made him governor of Cisalpine Gaul. Decimus Brutus Albinus, a relative of Marcus, fought on Caesar's side, and is described by ancient sources as very close to him. Both are presented in historical sources as the main instigators, alongside Cassius, of the conspiracy against Caesar. Although Garnier probably had Marcus Brutus in mind, elements pertaining to both historical figures are ascribed to his 'Decimus' throughout the play. On Garnier's confusion over the two characters see Ternaux, p. 39.
[17] Of Roman citizens and ladies, friends of Cicero and Cornelia.

ACT I

[*Enter* CICERO *and* CHORUS.]

CICERO

Vouchsafe° immortals, and, above the rest,
Great Jupiter, our city's sole protector,[1]
That if, provoked against us by our evils,
You needs will plague us with your ceaseless wrath,
At least to choose those forth that are in fault,
And save the rest in these tempestuous broils:°
Else let the mischief° that should them befall,
Be poured on me, that one may die for all.[2]
  Oft hath such sacrifice appeased your ires,°
And oft ye have your heavy hands withheld
From this poor people, when, with one man's loss,
Your pity hath preserved the rest untouched;
But we, disloyal to our own defence,
Faint-hearted do those liberties enthral,°
Which to preserve unto our after-good,[3]
Our fathers hazarded their dearest blood.
  Yet Brutus, Manlius, hardy Scevola,
And stout Camilius are returned from Styx,[4]

---

[1] Rome was under the chief tutelage of Jupiter, the father and ruler of all Roman gods.

[2] An echo of John 11. 50: 'that one man die for the people, and that the whole nation perish not' (Geneva Bible). The reference to Scripture is not as clear in Garnier: 'Et le malheur de tous versez dessus mon chef' ('and the misfortune of all [be] heaped upon my head', p. 40r), which, according to Ternaux (p. 41), echoes instead Lucan's *Pharsalia*, II. 306–08: 'O utinam caelique deis Erebique liceret | Hoc caput in cunctas damnatum exponere poenas' ('If only the gods of heaven and Erebus could take my head in expiation for all [these] evils').

[3] i.e. for our future welfare.

[4] All mythical defenders of Rome: Lucius Junius Brutus was the founder and first consul of the Roman republic (509 BC) after overthrowing the tyrant Tarquin the Elder; Marcus Manlius saved the republic at the time of the invasion of Rome by the Gauls in 390 BC; Gaius Mucius Scevola famously thrust his hand into the fire to demonstrate the courage of Roman soldiers at the time of the war against the Etruscans (508 BC); Marcus Furius Camilius presided over Rome's second foundation after the invasion by the Gauls, and was hailed as Rome's 'second father'. Unlike Kyd, Garnier names them in chronological order. In Greek and Roman mythology, the river Styx separated the world of the living from the underworld.

Desiring arms to aid our Capitol.[5]
Yea, come they are, and fiery as before,
Under a tyrant see our bastard hearts
Lie idly sighing, while our shameful souls
Endure a millìon[6] of base controls.°
    Poisoned Ambition, rooted in high minds,
'Tis thou that train'st° us into all these errors:
Thy mortal covetise° perverts our laws,
And tears our freedom from our franchised° hearts.
Our fathers found thee at their former walls,
And humbled,[7] to their offspring left thee dying.
Yet thou, reviving, soiledst our infant town
With guiltless blood by brothers' hands outlaunched,
And hang'st (O hell!),[8] upon a fort half-finished,
Thy monstrous murder for a thing to mark.[9]
But faith continues not where men command:
Equals are ever bandying for the best;
A state divided cannot firmly stand;
Two kings within one realm could never rest.[10]
This day, we see, the father and the son[11]
Have fought like foes Pharsalia's misery;
And with their blood made marsh the parchèd plains,
While th'earth that groaned to bear their carcasses,
Bewailed th'insatiate° humours[12] of them both,
That as much blood in wilful folly spent,
As were to tame the world sufficìent.

---

[5] One of Rome's seven hills, on which stood the temple of Jupiter, which constituted the religious and political heart of the ancient city.

[6] Three syllables, for metrical reasons.

[7] Refers to 'thee', i.e. 'Ambition'.

[8] Garnier: 'ô crime' (p. 40v). On Kyd's frequent insertion of references to heaven and hell, see Introduction, pp. 56–58.

[9] i.e. as a spectacle to behold.

[10] 34–37] See Lucan, *Pharsalia*, I. 92–93: 'Nulla fides regni sociis, omnisque potestas | Impatiens consortis erit', and Marlowe's translation: 'Shall never faith be found in fellow kings. | Dominion cannot suffer partnership' (*Lucans first booke*, sig. B2v). See also *Antonius*, IV. 146–47.

[11] Although much older, Pompey had been Caesar's son-in-law at the time of the 'first triumvirate' (see above, p. 182, n. 3). Garnier: 'le fils et le beau-père' ('son and father-in-law', p. 40v).

[12] Garnier: 'cette faim gloutonne' ('such a gluttonous hunger' p. 40v).

Now, Parthia, fear no more, for Crassus' death[13]
That we will come thy borders to besiege,
Nor fear the darts of our courageous troops.
For those brave soldiers, that were sometime wont°
To terrify thee with their names,[14] are dead.
And civil fury, fiercer than thine hosts,°
Hath in a manner this great town o'erturned,
That whilom° was the terror of the world,
Of whom so many nations stood in fear,
To whom so many nations prostrate stooped,
O'er whom, save heaven, nought could signorize,°
And whom, save heaven, nothing could affright:
Impregnable, immortal, and whose power
Could never have been curbed, but by itself.[15]
For neither could the flaxen-haired high Dutch,
A martial people madding° after arms,
Nor yet the fierce and fiery-humoured French,[16]
The Moor that travels to the Lybian sands,
The Greek, th'Arabian, Macedons or Medes,[17]
Once dare t'assault it, or attempt to lift
Their humbled heads in presence of proud Rome,
But by our laws from liberty restrained,
Like captives lived eternally enchained.[18]
But Rome (alas!), what helps it that thou tied'st
The former world to thee in vassalage?°
What helps thee now t'have tamed both land and sea?
What helps it thee that under thy control,
The morn and midday both by east and west,[19]

---

[13] In revenge for Crassus's death. Cornelia's first husband, Crassus, had been killed in the Roman war against Parthia (see above, p. 182, n. 2).

[14] i.e. 'that used to terrify thee …'

[15] 54–58] As noted by Ternaux (p. 45), this passage in Garnier is adapted from Horace's *Epodes*, 16. 1–8. See also *Pharsalia*, I. 71–72, and Marlowe's translation: 'Rome was so great it could not beare itself' (*Lucans first booke*, sig. B2r).

[16] Kyd's expansion of Garnier ('le Gaulois ardant', 'the fiery Gauls', p. 41r), probably for the sake of assonance.

[17] Macedonia is a region to the north of Greece; the ancient Mede kingdom covered parts of modern-day Iran and Turkey.

[18] Garnier is more specific: 'servilement croisant | Les bras bouclez au dos d'un gros carcas pesant' ('like captives, with their arms crossed | behind their backs and locked in strong, heavy chains', p. 41r).

[19] Garnier: 'Que te sert d'enfermer sous le pouvoir Latin | L'Aquilon, le Midi, le

And that the golden Sun where'er he drive
His glitt'ring chariot,[20] finds our ensigns spread,
Sith° it contents not thy posterity,
But, as a bait for pride — which spoils us all —
Embarks us in so perilous a way,
As menaceth our death, and thy decay?
For, Rome, thou now resemblest a ship,
At random wand'ring in a boist'rous sea,[21]
When foaming billows feel the northern blasts:
Thou toil'st in peril, and the windy storm
Doth topsy-turvy toss thee as thou floatest.
Thy mast is shivered,° and thy main sail torn,
Thy sides sore beaten, and thy hatches broke.°
Thou want'st thy tackling, and a ship unrigged
Can make no shift° to combat with the sea.
See how the rocks do heave their heads at thee,
Which, if thou shouldst but touch, thou straight becom'st
A spoil° to Neptune, and a sportful prey
To th'glaucs and tritons,[22] pleased with thy decay.
Thou vaunt'st° not of thine ancestors in vain,[23]
But vainly count'st thine own victorious deeds.
What helpeth us the things that they did then,
Now we are hated both of gods and men?
Hatred accompanies prosperity,
For one man grieveth at another's good,
And so much more we think our misery,
The more that Fortune hath with others stood:
So that we seld° are seen, as wisdom would,

Couchant, le Matin' (p. 41r) — i.e. 'what do you gain by submitting the north [the Aquilon is the north wind], the south ['le Midi'], the west ['le Couchant'] and the east ['le Matin'] under Latin rule …'

[20] In Roman mythology, the sun, or Phoebus, ran his chariot through the sky from east to west.

[21] The metaphor of the ship of state is an ancient commonplace, but, as Ternaux notes (p. 47), Garnier seems to follow more specifically Horace's *Odes*, I. 14.

[22] Mythological sea-creatures (Garnier: 'glauques et tritons'; also in *Antonius*, IV. 46. Glaucus was also a sea-god, half-man, half-fish; although common in Renaissance French poetry, the generic use of 'glauques' to designate Glaucus-like mermen is rare in English.

[23] The antithesis is Kyd's addition; see Garnier: 'Tu te vantes en vain de tes nobles ayeux, | Tu racontes en vain tes faicts victorieux' ('You boast of your noble ancestors in vain, | you proclaim your victorious feats in vain', p. 41v).

To bridle time with reason, as we should.[24]
For we are proud when Fortune favours us,
As if inconstant Chance were always one,
Or standing now, she would continue thus.
O fools, look back, and see the rolling stone,
Whereon she, blindly lighting,° sets her foot,
And slightly° sows[25] *that seldom taketh root.*
  Heav'n, heretofore° inclined to do us good,
Did favour us with conquering our foes,
When jealous Italy, exasperate°
With our uprising, sought our city's fall.
But we, soon tickled with such flatt'ring hopes,
Waged further war with an insatiate° heart,
And tired our neighbour countries so with charge,
As with their loss, we did our bounds° enlarge.
  Carthage and Sicily we have subdued,[26]
And almost yokèd all the world beside;
And solely through desire of public rule,[27]
Rome and the earth are waxen° all as one.
Yet now we live despoiled° and robbed by one
Of th'ancient freedom wherein we were born;[28]
And ev'n that yoke that wont° to tame all others,
Is heavily returned upon ourselves.
A note of Chance that may the proud control,[29]
And show God's wrath against a cruel soul.
For heav'n delights not in us, when we do
That to another, which ourselves disdain:
Judge others as thou wouldst be judged again;

---

[24] Compare with Garnier: 'peu souvent en temps calme nous chaut | De tenir la raison pour bride comme il faut' ('in peaceful times, we rarely care | to use our reason as a bridle [of our passions], as we should', p. 41v).
[25] Kyd elaborates on Garnier's commonplace depiction of Fortune as a woman standing on a rolling bowl ('les piez … sur le haut d'une boule roulez', p. 41v). The sowing metaphor is his addition, perhaps reminiscent of the parable of the sower in Matthew 13.
[26] A reference to the Punic wars and the destruction of Carthage, which ensured Rome's control over the Mediterranean.
[27] Garnier: 'le seul appétit de commander par tout' ('the sole desire of ruling over all', p. 41v).
[28] Compare with Garnier: 'la liberté franche' ('unbridled freedom', p. 41v).
[29] i.e. 'see how Chance may control the proud'; 124–25 not marked as *sententiae* in Garnier.

And do but as thou wouldst be done unto.
For sooth to say, in reason, we deserve
To have the selfsame measure that we serve.[30]
What right had our ambitious ancestors,
Ignobly issued from the cart and plough,[31]
To enter Asia? What, were they the heirs
To Persia or the Medes, first monarchies?[32]
What interest had they to Aferique?[33]
To Gaul or Spain? Or what did Neptune owe us
Within the bounds° of further Brittany?[34]
Are we not thieves and robbers of those realms
That owed us nothing but revenge for wrongs?[35]
What toucheth° us the treasure or the hopes,
The lives or liberties of all those nations
Whom we by force have held in servitude?
Whose mournful cries and shrieks to heav'n ascend,
Importuning[36] both vengeance and defence
Against this city, rich of violence.
'Tis not enough (alas!) our power t'extend,
Or overrun the world from east to west,
Or that our hands the earth can comprehend,
Or that we proudly do what like us best.[37]

---

[30] An echo of Matthew 7. 2: 'For with what judgment ye judge, ye shall be judged, and with what measure ye mete, it shall be measured unto you again' and 7. 12: 'Therefore whatsoever ye would that men should do to you: even so do ye to them' (Geneva Bible). Garnier has: '[les Dieux] veulent que l'on juge l'autre par soymesme | Et comme nous ferons qu'on nous face de mesme' ('[the Gods] want us to judge others as we would ourselves, | and, as we will treat others, so to be treated in our turn', p. 42r).

[31] A possible allusion to Romulus, Rome's mythical founder, who famously drew the sacred boundaries of the city with a plough. Compare with Garnier: 'Ignoblement issus de grands-peres champestres' ('lowly descended from country-born ancestors', p. 42r). The expression is also found in Kyd's *Housholders Philosophie* ('called from the Plough and Carte', see Boas, *Works*, p. lxiii).

[32] Garnier: 'les monarques premiers' ('first monarchs', p. 42r). Persia and the ancient kingdom of Media were usually considered as the cradles of ancient civilisation.

[33] Africa; three syllables, for metrical reasons.

[34] Great Britain — hence the mention of Neptune, the god of the sea. Garnier: 'Que nous devait Neptune en l'extrême Bretagne?' ('What owed us Neptune in remote Britain?', p. 42r).

[35] 'but revenge for wrongs' is Kyd's addition.

[36] Calling, pressing for vengeance.

[37] i.e. what pleases us best. The whole line is Kyd's addition. Garnier has instead: 'Et

He lives more quietly whose rest is made,[38]
And can with reason chasten his desire,
Than he that blindly toileth for a shade,[39]
And is with others' empire set on fire.
Our bliss consists not in possessiòns,
But in commanding our affectiòns
In virtue's choice, and vice's needful chase[40]
Far from our hearts, for staining of our face.[41]

[*Exit.*]

CHORUS

Upon thy back, where misery doth sit,
O Rome, the heavens with their wrathful hand
Revenge the crimes thy fathers did commit.
But if their further fury to withstand,
Which o'er thy walls thy wrack° sets menacing,
Thou dost not seek to calm heav'n's ireful° king,
A further plague will pester all the land.
The wrath of heav'n, though urged, we see is slow
In punishing the evils we have done;[42]
For what the father hath deserved, we know,
Is spared in him, and punished in the son.[43]
But to forgive the apter that they be,
They are the more displeasèd when they see
That we continue our offence begun.
Then from her loathsome cave doth Plague repair,°

voir sous mesme joug l'Ethiope et le Gete' ('and to see the Ethiopians and the Getae joined under the same yoke', p. 42r).

[38] Kyd reworks the following passage in order to include a main tenet of Stoicism, the attainment of *ataraxia*, or detached inner-peace. Garnier: 'Celuy commande plus, qui vit du sien contant' ('He has more power, who can be content with his possessions', p. 42r).

[39] i.e. strives after vain things. Garnier: 'après l'or ne soupire' ('[he who] does not strive after gold', p. 42v).

[40] i.e. in choosing virtue, and chasing vice.

[41] i.e. for fear it should stain our faces (with shame).

[42] Garnier: 'L'ire des bons Dieux excitée | Est paresseuse à nous punir' ('The wrath of the good gods, once stirred, is slow [lit. 'lazy'] in punishing us', p. 42v). Kyd's version brings out the Christian undertones of the passage.

[43] An echo of 1 Kings 11. 11–12 and 1 Kings 21. 29, where God spares Solomon and Ahab (respectively), but brings his punishment on their sons. Garnier is less specific: 'Souvent la peine méritée | Se garde aux races à venir' ('often, a punishment we deserve | is carried over the next generations', p. 42v).

That breathes her heavy poisons down to hell,[44]
Which with their noisome fall corrupt the air;
Or meagre° famine, which the weak foretell,[45]
Or bloody war (of other woes the worst)
Which, where it lights,° doth show the land accursed,[46]
And ne'er did good wherever it befell.
War, that hath sought th'Ausonian fame to rear,
In warlike Emony[47] — now grown so great[48]
With soldiers' bodies that were buried there —
Which yet to sack us, toils in bloody sweat
T'enlarge the bounds° of conqu'ring Thessaly,[49]
Through murder, discord, wrath, and enmity,
Ev'n to the peaceful Indians' pearlèd seat;[50]
Whose entrails[51] fired with rancour, wrath and rage,
The former petty combats did displace,°
And camp to camp did endless battles wage,
Which, on the mountain tops of warlike Thrace,[52]
Made thund'ring Mars, dissention's common friend,
Amongst the forward soldiers first descend,
Armed with his blood-besmeared keen coutelas.[53]

---

[44] Garnier: 'l'Averne', that is, Mount Avernus, the supposed entrance to the underworld.

[45] Probably, because the weak are first to die. Not in Garnier: 'La Famine chagrineuse | Aux membres faibles de maigreur' ('sad-faced Famine, | so thin her limbs grow weak', p. 42v).

[46] i.e. reveals that the land is accursed. The last two lines of the stanza are Kyd's addition.

[47] Aemonia, in central Greece, where the battle of Pharsalia took place.

[48] Compare with Garnier: 'grosse', i.e. pregnant (with corpses), p. 43r.

[49] The region in central Greece where Pharsalia was located.

[50] The association of India with pearls was commonplace at the time. Kyd significantly widens the scope of the Roman civil war; compare with Garnier (more accurately): 'Jusques dans la campagne More' ('as far as the Moorish plains', p. 43r).

[51] Kyd interprets this stanza as a development of the previous two ('War, […] whose entrails …'), while Garnier introduces another subject: 'celuy […] qui fit […] Herisser un camp' ('The man … who first … established a bristling camp', p. 43r). The actions and punishment depicted in the following stanzas originally refer to this 'man'. Kyd instead continues to address the figure of war. ('O war, if thou were subject but to death …').

[52] A region in southeastern Europe covering parts of modern-day Greece, Bulgaria and western Turkey. Thracians had a reputation for being a ferocious and bloodthirsty people.

[53] Cutlass, or short sabre. The older spelling was retained here for metrical reasons.

Who[54] first attempted to excite to arms
   The troops enragèd with the trumpets' sound,
Head-long to run and wreak no after-harms,[55]
   Where in the flowered meads dead men were found;
Falling as thick, through warlike cruelty,
   As ears of corn for want of husbandry,
   That, wasteful, shed their grain upon the ground.[56]
O war,[57] if thou were subject but to death,
   And by desert° mightst fall to Phlegethon,[58]
The torment that Ixion suffereth,[59]
   Or his whose soul the vulture seizeth on,[60]
Were all too little to reward thy wrath;
   Nor all the plagues that fiery Pluto[61] hath
   The most outrageous sinners laid upon.
Accursèd caitives,° wretches that we are,
   Perceive we not that for the fatal doom,
The Fates[62] make haste enough: but we, by war,
   Must seek in hell[63] to have a hapless° room?
Or fast enough do foolish men not die,
   But they, by murder of themselves, must hie°
   Hopeless to hide them in a hapless° tomb?

---

[54] 'Who' could either refer back to 'War', or to 'thund'ring Mars'.

[55] i.e. cause no further harm. The evocation of retreating troops no longer fighting is Kyd's addition. Garnier simply has: 'pour les precipiter au fer' — which could either mean 'pushing them to take arms', or 'causing them to fall by the sword' (p. 43r).

[56] The theme of waste is Kyd's addition. Garnier: 'Comme quand les bleds moissonnez | Tombent en javelles barbues' ('As the cropped corn | falling into bristling sheaves', p. 43r).

[57] 'O war' is Kyd's addition. See above, n. 51.

[58] One of the rivers of the underworld.

[59] In classical mythology, Ixion, King of Lapithae, tried to seduce Jupiter's wife, and was punished by being tied to a wheel of fire after boasting of his alleged success.

[60] Prometheus, who was condemned to have his liver eaten daily by a vulture for stealing fire from the gods.

[61] God ruling over the classical underworld. Kyd's characterization of Pluto as 'fiery' is an addition, as is the mention of 'the most outrageous sinners'. See Garnier: 'Pluton y devroit employer | Tous les tourmens de son abysme' ('Pluto should apply to him | every torment in his gaping hell', p. 43v).

[62] In classical mythology, Fate was represented by three sisters, the Parcae. Garnier: 'la Parque' (p. 43v).

[63] Compare with Garnier: 'dans le ventre obscur des tombeaux' ('in the dark entrails of our tombs', p. 43v). The metaphor is partly conveyed in the closing line of the stanza.

All sad and desolate our city lies,
  And for fair corn-ground[64] are our fields surcloyed°
With worthless gorse, that yearly fruitless dies,
  And chokes the good, which else we had enjoyed.[65]
Death dwells within us, and if gentle peace
  Descend not soon, our sorrows to surcease,°
  Latium,[66] already quailed,° will be destroyed.

[*Exit* CHORUS.]

[64] i.e. instead of fair corn fields.
[65] Again, the themes of waste and barrenness are Kyd's addition, with a possible echo of the parable of the sower in Matthew 13 (see above, p. 189, n. 25).
[66] i.e. Rome.

ACT II

[*Enter*] CORNELIA, CICERO [*and* CHORUS].

[CORNELIA]
And will ye needs bedew° my dead-grown joys,
And nourish sorrow with eternal tears,
O eyes, and will ye ('cause I cannot dry
Your ceaseless springs), not suffer me to die?
Then make the blood from forth my branch-like veins,
Like weeping rivers, trickle by your vaults;
And sponge° my body's heat of moisture so,
As my displeasèd soul may shun my heart.
Heav'ns let me die, and let the Destinies
Admit me passage to th'infernal lake;[1]
That my poor ghost may rest where pow'rful Fate,
In Death's sad kingdom, hath my husband lodged.
Fain would I die, but darksome ugly Death
Withholds his dart, and in disdain doth fly me,
Maliciously knowing that hell's horror
Is milder than mine endless discontent.
And that if Death upon my life should seize,
The pain supposèd would procure mine ease.
But ye sad powers, that rule the silent deeps
Of dead-sad night, where sins do mask unseen;[2]
You that amongst the darksome mansìons
Of pining ghosts, 'twixt sighs, and sobs, and tears,
Do exercise your mirthless empery;°
Ye gods, at whose arbitrament° all stand,
Dislodge[3] my soul, and keep it with yourselves,
For I am more than half your prisoner:
My noble husbands' (more than noble) souls[4]
Already wander under your commands.

---

[1] Passage to the underworld was granted by the three Parcae, also named Fates or Destinies. The lake mentioned here is the Stygian lake, formed by the waters of the river Styx.
[2] A departure from Garnier: 'où les trespasses vont' ('where the deceased walk about', p. 44r). Compare with *Spanish Tragedy*, II. 1. 24: 'O heavens, why made you night to cover sinne?' (see Roberts and Gaines, p. 127).
[3] Literally; see Garnier: 'démaisonnez mon âme' ('un-house my soul', p. 44r).
[4] i.e. the souls of Crassus and of Pompey.

Oh, then, shall wretched I — that am but one,
Yet once both theirs[5] — survive, now they are gone?
    Alas! Thou shouldst, thou shouldst, Cornelìa,
Have broke[6] the sacred thread that tied thee here,
When as thy husband Crassus, in his flower,
Did first bear arms, and bare away thy love![7]
And not, as thou hast done, go break the bands°
By calling Hymen once more back again.[8]
Less hapless,° and more worthily, thou mightst
Have made thine ancestors and thee renowned:[9]
If, like a royal dame,[10] with faith fast kept,
Thou with thy former husband's death hadst slept.[11]
    But partial Fortune, and the pow'rful Fates,
That at their pleasures wield our purposes,
Bewitched my life, and did beguile my love.
Pompey, the fame that ran of thy frail honours
Made me thy wife, thy love, and, like a thief,
From my first husband stole my faithless grief.
    But if (as some believe) in heav'n or hell
Be heav'nly powers, or infernal spirits,
That care to be avenged of lovers' oaths —[12]
Oaths made in marrìage, and after broke —

---

[5] An expansion of Garnier: 'et moy l'amour des deux' ('and I who was loved by both', p. 44r).

[6] In ancient mythology, one died when the thread of life was cut by one of the Parcae, or fatal sisters. See Garnier: 'le fil sacré dont la Parque te lie' ('the sacred thread with which the Parcae bind you', p. 44r).

[7] The archaic form 'bare' (for 'bore') was kept here for the sake of assonance. Compare with Garnier: 'emporté de Bellone, emporta tes amours' ('[was] borne away by Bellona, and bore away your love', p. 44r). Bellona is the goddess of war.

[8] Hymen is the god of marriage. In ancient Rome, it was sometimes considered a fault for a widow to marry again. See for example Virgil's *Aeneid*, IV, of which this passage is reminiscent.

[9] A slight variation from Garnier: 'et plus digne du nom | De tes braves ayeux' ('worthier of the name | of your brave ancestors', p. 44r).

[10] Garnier: 'en femme magnanime' ('as a magnanimous [in the sense of noble] woman', p. 44r).

[11] Kyd removes a mythological allusion in Garnier: 'qui sa foi loyale | Veut rendre à son époux en l'onde stygiale' ('[a wife] who will pledge her loyal faith | to her husband even in the waters of Styx', p. 44r).

[12] See *Aeneid*, IV. 520–21: 'si quod non aequo foedere amantes | Curae numen habet iustumque memorque' ('if there be an equitable divinity that cares for and remembers lovers unequally bound').

Those powers, those spirits, moved with my light faith,
Are now displeased with Pompey and myself,
And do with civil discord, furthering it,
Untie the bands° that sacred Hymen knit.
Else only I am cause of both their wraths,[13]
And of the sin[14] that sealeth up thine eyes,
O deplorable Pompey! I am she,
I am that plague, that sacks thy house and thee.
For 'tis not heav'n, nor Crassus ('cause he sees
That I am thine) in jealousy pursues us.
No, 'tis a secret cross, an unknown thing
That I received from heaven at my birth,
That I should heap misfortunes on their head,
Whom once I had received in marriage bed.[15]
    Then ye, the noble Romulists[16] that rest,°
Henceforth forbear to seek my murd'ring love,
And let their double loss, that held me dear,[17]
Bid you beware, for fear you be beguiled.
Ye may be rich and great in Fortune's grace,
And all your hopes with hap° may be effected,
But if ye once be wedded to my love,
Clouds of adversity will cover you.
So pestilently[18] fraught with change of plagues
Is mine infected bosom from my youth.
Like poison that, once lighting° in the body,
No sooner toucheth than it taints the blood,
One while the heart, another while[19] the liver,
According to th'encountering passages;
Nor spareth it what purely feeds the heart
More than the most infected filthiest part.

---

[13] i.e. against Pompey and Cornelia (see above: 'displeased with Pompey and myself').
[14] Compare with Garnier: 'du trépas cruel' ('of cruel death', p. 44v).
[15] See Lucan's *Pharsalia*, III. 21–22: 'semperque potentes | Detrahere in cladem fato damnata maritos' (the fates have cursed her always to cause the downfall of her powerful husbands').
[16] Descendants of Romulus, Romans.
[17] i.e. 'the loss of both men (Crassus and Pompey) who held me dear'.
[18] Garnier: 'tant je suis pestilente' ('so pestilent am I', p. 45r).
[19] i.e. now … now.

Pompey, what holp° it thee[20] (say, dearest life)
Tell me, what holp° thy warlike valiant mind
T'encounter with[21] the least of my mishaps?°
What holp° it thee that under thy command
Thou saw'st the trembling earth with horror 'mazed?
Or where the Sun forsakes th'Ocèan[22] sea,
Or watereth his coursers in the west,[23]
T'have made thy name be far more famed and feared
Than summer's thunder to the silly herd?[24]
What holp° it that thou saw'st, when thou wert young,
Thy helmet decked with coronets° of bays?[25]
So many enemies in battle ranged
Beat back like flies[26] before a storm of hail?
T'have looked askance and seen so many kings
To lay their crowns and sceptres at thy feet;
T'embrace thy knees, and humbled by their fate,
T'attend° thy mercy in this mournful state?[27]
Alas! And herewithal,° what holp° it thee
That ev'n in all the corners of the earth,
Thy wand'ring glory[28] was so greatly known?
And that Rome saw thee while thou triumphedst thrice
O'er three parts of the world that thou hadst yoked?[29]
That Neptune welt'ring° on the windy plains

---

[20] i.e. 'what availed' ('holp' is an archaic form of 'helped').

[21] Here in the sense of 'fight', meaning: what availed your valiant mind against the ill-fortune I brought you, etc.

[22] Here Ocean is used as an adjective, derived from the Latin, Oceanus (hence the diaeresis 'Ocèan', also found below at III. 2. 2). Oceanus was the river-god encircling the earth for the Ancients: Phoebus was believed to rise from its waters in the East. See also p. 244, n. 6.

[23] Phoebus, the mythological god of the sun, rose from the ocean in the east and drove his chariot across the sky during the day, diving again into the sea in the evening.

[24] Shepherd (Garnier: 'paisans', i.e. swains, p. 45r).

[25] It was customary for victorious generals to wear crowns of laurel, or bay, when parading in triumph through the streets of Rome. Pompey celebrated three triumphs.

[26] Instead of 'flies', Garnier has 'espics', i.e. ears of corn (p. 45r), in keeping with his extended metaphor for the battlefield.

[27] An important part of the traditional ceremony of triumph consisted in having one's defeated enemies lay down their arms and humble themselves in public.

[28] Pompey led many military operations across the empire.

[29] Pompey was victorious in Africa, in western Europe, and in the East — the three traditional sections of the Roman empire. See Plutarch, *Life of Pompey*, XLV. 5, and North's 1579 translation: 'But the greatest honour that ever he w[on …] was this: that he made his third triumphe of the three partes of the world' (*Lives*, p. 701).

Escaped not free from thy victorious hands,[30]
Since thy hard hap,° since thy fierce destiny,
Envious of all thine honours, gave thee me!
By whom the former course of thy fair deeds,
Might with a biting bridle be restrained;
By whom the glory of thy conquests got,
Might die disgraced with mine unhappiness.
O hapless° wife, thus ominous° to all,
Worse than Megaera,[31] worse than any plague!
What foul infernal,[32] or what stranger hell,
Henceforth wilt thou inhabit, where thy hap°
None other's hopes with mischief may entrap?[33]

CICERO

What end, O race of Scipio,[34] will the Fates
Afford your tears? Will that day never come
That your disastrous griefs shall turn to joy,
And we have time to bury our annoy?°

CORNELIA

Ne'er shall I see that day, for heav'n and time
Have failed in power to calm my passiòn.
Nor can they, should they pity my complaints,
Once ease my life, but with the pangs of death.

CICERO

The wide world's accidents are apt to change.
And tickle° Fortune stays not in a place,
But like the clouds, continually doth range,
Or like the sun that hath the night in chase.[35]
Then as the heav'ns — by whom our hopes are guided —
Do coast the earth with an eternal course,[36]

---

[30] An allusion to Pompey's campaign against pirates across the Mediterranean. The 'windy plains' was a commonplace metaphor for the sea.
[31] One of the three Furies.
[32] i.e. infernal region (usually in the plural).
[33] i.e. 'where your ill-fortune will deceive no one else in their hopes'.
[34] Cornelia's father was Quintus Metellus Scipio.
[35] These two lines added by Kyd.
[36] According to the ancient, Ptolemaic cosmology, the heavens comprised various spheres rotating around the earth.

We must not think a misery betided°
Will never cease, but still grow worse and worse.
When icy winter's past, then comes the spring,
Whom summer's pride with sultry heat pursues;
To whom mild autumn doth earth's treasure bring,
The sweetest season that the wise can choose.[37]
Heav'n's influence was ne'er so constant yet,
In good or bad as to continue it.
When I was young, I saw against poor Sylla,[38]
Proud Cinna, Marius, and Carbo fleshed°
So long, till they gan° tyrannize the town,
And spilt such store of blood in every street,
As there were none but dead men to be seen.
Within a while, I saw how Fortune played,
And wound those tyrants underneath her wheel,[39]
Who lost their lives and power at once, by one,
That to revenge himself did with his blade
Commit more murder than Rome ever made.[40]
Yet Sylla, shaking tyranny aside,
Returned due honours to our commonwealth,[41]
Which peaceably retained her ancient state,
Grown great without the strife of citizens;
Till this ambitious tyrant's time,[42] that toiled

---

[37] 132–35] A significant expansion of Garnier. According to Boas, Kyd's praise of autumn as the 'sweetest season' can be traced to Tasso's *Padre di Famiglia*, which Kyd translated as *The Housholder's Philosophy* in 1588: 'Therefore I conclude that Autumn is the most noble and best season of the yeere, and that which is indeed most acceptable to the Housekeeper' (*Works*, p. 249).

[38] Cicero refers to the civil wars between Marius and Sulla (87–82 BC). At the end of the first civil war, Cornelius Sulla, with the help of Pompey, had defeated and exiled Gaius Marius; yet he was forced to leave after Marius's faction won the consular elections (87 BC). Lucius Cinna, one of the consuls, argued for the return of Marius, thus causing the Senate to revoke his consulship. Marius however returned from his exile and established himself and Cinna as consuls for the year 86 BC. After Marius's death, Cinna shared the consulship with Gnaeus Carbo, without election, for the next four years.

[39] According to the commonplace representation of Fortune with a turning wheel.

[40] Sulla returned to Rome in 83 BC, and won the second civil war in 82 after an exceptionally bloody battle at the gates of Rome. Carbo was captured and executed by Pompey, and Caesar, a partisan of Marius, was forced into exile.

[41] Sulla achieved significant reforms of the Senate in order to maintain the aristocratic republican regime.

[42] i.e. Caesar.

To stoop the world and Rome to his desires.
But flatt'ring Chance, that trained° his first designs,
May change her looks, and give the tyrant over,
Leaving our city, where so long ago
Heav'ns did their favours lavishly bestow.

CORNELIA

'Tis true, the heav'ns — at least wise° if they please —
May give poor Rome her former liberty.
But though they would, I know they cannot give
A second life to Pompey, that is slain.

CICERO

Mourn not for Pompey, Pompey could not die
A better death than for his country's weal.
For oft he searched amongst the fierce alarms,
But, wishing, could not find so fair an end;
Till fraught with years and honour both at once,
He gave his body as a barricade
For Rome's defence, by tyrants overlaid.
Bravely he died,[43] and haply° takes it ill,
That envious we repine° at heaven's will.

CORNELIA

Alas, my sorrow would be so much less,
If he had died his falchion° in his fist;
Had he amidst huge troops of armèd men
Been wounded by another any way:
It would have calmèd many of my sighs.
For why, t'have seen his noble Roman blood
Mixed with his enemies, had done him good.
  But he is dead (O heav'ns!), not dead in fight,
With pike in hand, upon a fort besieged,
Defending of a breach, but basely slain,
Slain traitorously, without assault in war.[44]
Yea, slain he is, and bitter Chance decreed
To have me there, to see this bloody deed!

---

[43] Compare with Garnier: 'il est mort bien-heureux' ('he died a happy man', p. 46r).
[44] Pompey was murdered upon his arrival in Egypt (see p. 182, n. 6).

I saw him, I was there, and in mine arms
He almost felt the poniard° when he fell.
Whereat, my blood stopped in my straggling veins,
Mine hair grew bristled, like a thorny grove;[45]
My voice lay hid half-dead within my throat;
My frightful° heart, stunned in my stone-cold breast,
Faintly redoubled every feeble stroke.
My spirit, chainèd with impatient rage,
Did raving strive to break the prison ope,°
Enlarged, to drown the pain it did abide
In solitary Lethe's sleepy tide.[46]
Thrice, to absent me from this hateful light,
I would have plunged my body in the sea.
And thrice detained,[47] with doleful° shrieks and cries,
With arms to heav'n upreared,[48] I gan° exclaim
And bellow forth against the gods themselves
A bead-roll° of outrageous blasphemies.
Till (grief to hear, and hell for me to speak[49])
My woes waxed° stronger, and my self grew weak.
Thus day and night I toil in discontent,
And sleeping wake, when sleep itself that rides
Upon the mists, scarce moisteneth mine eyes.
Sorrow consumes me, and instead of rest,
With folded arms I sadly sit and weep.
And if I wink,° it is for fear to see
The fearful° dream's effects that trouble me.[50]

---

[45] Garnier: 'comme espics dans les plaines' ('like ears of wheat in the plains', p. 46v). The whole passage is an epic / tragic topos; see for example Virgil's *Aeneid*, II. 774: 'obstipui, steteruntque comae et uox faucibus haesit' ('I was struck silent, my hair stood on end and my voice stuck in my throat').

[46] i.e. 'and once free, to drown the pain [my spirit] endured in the sleepy waters of Lethe'. Lethe was one of the rivers of the classical underworld; the deceased forgot their past lives as soon as they drank from its waters.

[47] i.e. stopped (by friends, etc.). See Garnier: 'Et trois fois retenue … avec force de bras' ('Three times stopped … by strong hands', p. 46v).

[48] Not in Garnier. See however Kyd's *Spanish Tragedy*, III. 13. 68: 'With mournefull eyes and hands to heaven uprear'd', and below, V. 1. 130: 'with blubbered eyes and hands to heav'n upreared' (as noted by Robert and Gaines, p. 127).

[49] 'grief … to speak' is Kyd's addition. An epic / tragic commonplace; see for example *Aeneid*, II. 204: 'horresco referens' ('I shudder at the words').

[50] i.e. 'the frightful essence [or reality] of the dreams that trouble me'.

O heavens, what shall I do? Alas, must I,
Must I myself be murd'rer of myself?
Must I myself be forced to ope° the way
Whereat my soul in wounds may sally forth?

CICERO

Madam, you must not thus transpose° yourself.
We see your sorrow, but who sorrows not?
The grief is common. And I muse, besides
The servitude that causeth all our cares,
Besides the baseness wherein we are yoked,
Besides the loss of good men dead and gone,
What one he is that in this broil° hath been
And mourneth not for some man of his kin?

CORNELIA

If all the world were in the like distress,
My sorrow yet would never seem the less.

CICERO

Oh, but men bear misfortunes with more ease,
The more indifferèntly that they fall,
And nothing more, in uproars, men can please,
Than when they see their woes not worst of all.[51]

CORNELIA

Our friends' misfortune doth increase our own.

CICERO

But ours of others will not be acknown.°

CORNELIA

Yet one man's sorrow will another touch.

CICERO

Ay, when himself will entertain none such.

---

[51] See the chorus in Seneca's *Troas*, 1009–10: 'Dulce maerenti populus dolentum | Dulce lamentis resonare gentes' ('It is sweet for those who mourn to see the whole people grieve, it is sweet to hear nations echo one's lament').

CORNELIA

Another's tears draw tears from forth our eyes.

CICERO

And choice of streams the greatest river dries.

CORNELIA

When sand within a whirlpool lies unwet,[52]
My tears shall dry, and I my grief forget.

CICERO

What boot your tears, or what avails your sorrow
Against th'inevitable dart of death?
Think you to move with lamentable plaints°
Persephone,[53] or Pluto's ghastly spirits,
To make him live that's lockèd in his tomb,
And wand'reth in the centre of the earth?
No, no, Cornelia, Charon takes not pain
To ferry those that must be fetched again.[54]

CORNELIA

Proserpina[55] indeed neglects my plaints,°
And hell itself is deaf to my laments.
Unprofitably should I waste my tears,
If over Pompey I should weep to death,
With hope to have him be revived by them.
Weeping avails not, therefore do I weep:
Great losses greatly are to be deplored,
The loss is great that cannot be restored.

---

[52] The conceit is Kyd's. Garnier: 'Les miennes tariront, quand cendre en un cercueil | Je ne sentirai plus ny tristesse ny dueil' ('Mine [tears] will be dried when, turned to ashes in a coffin, | I shall no longer grieve or mourn', p. 47v).

[53] Pronounced as having three syllables. Goddess of the classical underworld, wife of Pluto, who abducted her from the world of the living. She was only allowed her to come back to earth once a year: her arrival was associated with spring, and her return to the underworld, with winter.

[54] Charon ferried the souls of the deceased across the rivers Styx and Acheron.

[55] Latin name for Persephone.

CICERO

Nought is immortal underneath the sun,[56]
All things are subject to death's tyranny:
Both clowns and kings one selfsame course must run,[57]
And whatsoever lives, is sure to die.
Then wherefore mourn you for your husband's death
Sith° being a man, he was ordained to die?
Sith° Jove's own sons,[58] retaining human shape,
No more than wretched we their death could 'scape.
Brave Scipio, your famous ancestor,[59]
That Rome's high worth to Afrique did extend;
And those two Scipios,[60] that in person fought
Before the fearful° Carthaginian walls,
Both brothers, and both war's fierce lightning fires,
Are they not dead? Yes, and their death (our dearth)
Hath hid them both emboweled in the earth.
And those great cities, whose foundations reached
From deepest hell, and with their tops touched heaven;
Whose lofty towers, like thorny-pointed spears,
Whose temples, palaces, and walls embossed,
In power and force, and fierceness, seemed to threat
The tired world, that trembled with their weight;
In one day's space, to our eternal moans,
Have we not seen them turned to heaps of stones?[61]

---

[56] A reminiscence of Ecclesiastes. Garnier has 'sur la terre globeuse' ('on the earth's globe', p. 47v).

[57] See Horace's *Odes*, I. 4. 13–14 (as noted by Ternaux, p. 66): 'Pallida mors aequo pulsat pede pauperum tabernas | regumque turris' ('Pale death strikes with equal foot the huts of paupers and the towers of kings').

[58] Jupiter had many children with various women: being half-human, they shared their mothers' mortal condition.

[59] Publius Cornelius Scipio, also called Scipio Africanus the Elder, famous for defeating Hannibal in the second Punic war against Carthage (202 BC).

[60] Scipio Aemilianus, and his brother Quintus Aemilianus, who had both been adopted into the family of Scipio the Elder, and fought in the third Punic war against Carthage. Scipio was hailed as Scipio Africanus the Younger after the final capitulation and utter destruction of Carthage (146 BC).

[61] The fall of great cities is a tragic commonplace, which is also used in *Marc Antoine* (p. 89v and Sidney Herbert's translation in II. 2. 445ff). This passage is reminiscent of du Bellay's *Antiquités de Rome* (see Ternaux, p. 66), which was translated by Spenser as *The Ruines of Rome* in his 1591 volume of *Complaints*, dedicated to Mary Sidney Herbert. See for instance Spenser's rendering of Sonnet 7, 5–6: 'Triumphant arks, spyres neighbours to the skie, | That you to see doth th'heaven itself appall …' (*Complaints*, sig. R2v).

Carthage can witness,[62] and thou, heaven's handwork,
Fair Ilium,[63] razèd by the conqu'ring Greeks;
Whose ancient beauty, worth and weapons, seemed
Sufficient to have tamed the Myrmidons.[64]
But whatsoe'er hath been begun, must end.
Death, haply° that our willingness doth see,
With brandished dart, doth make the passage free,
And timeless doth our souls to Pluto send.

CORNELIA

Would Death had steeped his dart in Lerna's blood,[65]
That I were drowned in the Tartarean deeps.[66]
I am an offering fit for Acheron.[67]
A match more equal never could be made,
Than I, and Pompey, in th'Elysian shade.[68]

CICERO

Death's always ready, and our time is known
To be at heav'n's dispose, and not our own.

CORNELIA

Can we be over-hasty to good hap?°

CICERO

What good expect we in a fiery gap?[69]

CORNELIA

To 'scape the fears that follow Fortune's glances.

---

[62] See above, p. 189, n. 26.
[63] Troy, which was sacked by the Greeks.
[64] The troops of Greek warrior Neoptolemus, or Pyrrhus, who savagely destroyed Troy.
[65] The many-headed hydra of Lerna was killed by Hercules, who dipped his weapons in its poisoned blood.
[66] The Stygian lake (see p. 195, n. 1 above).
[67] One of the rivers of the underworld (see above)
[68] Another periphrasis for the underworld. The souls of heroes rested in the Elysian fields. Garnier has in fact 'la triste campagne' (p. 48r), which designates the fields of sorrow ('lugentes campi') where those who died an unhappy death (typically, deserted heroines) were sent.
[69] Compare with Garnier, 'fosse ombreuse', i.e. the pit inhabited by the shades of the deceased.

CICERO

A noble mind doth never fear mischances.

CORNELIA

A noble mind disdaineth servitude.

CICERO

Can bondage true nobility exclude?

CORNELIA

How if I do, or suffer that I would not?

CICERO

True noblesse never doth the thing it should not.

CORNELIA

Then must I die.

CICERO

Yet dying think this still;
No fear of death should force us to do ill.

CORNELIA

If death be such, why is your fear so rife?

CICERO

My works will show I never feared my life.

CORNELIA

And yet you will not that in our distress
We ask death's aid to end life's wretchedness.

CICERO

We neither ought to urge, nor ask a thing
Wherein we see so much assurance lies.
But if perhaps some fierce offended king,
To fright us, set pale death before our eyes,
To force us do that goes against our heart;
T'were more than base in us to dread his dart.[70]

[70] As noted by Ternaux (p. 70), Garnier follows the depiction of Stoic constancy as

But when, for fear of an ensuing ill,
We seek to shorten our appointed race,
Then 'tis for fear that we ourselves do kill,
So fond we are to fear the world's disgrace.

CORNELIA

'Tis not for frailty or faint cowardice
That men, to shun mischances, seek for death.
But rather he that seeks it, shows himself
Of certain courage 'gainst uncertain chance.
He that retires not at the threats of death,
Is not, as are the vulgar, slightly fayed,[71]
For heav'n itself, nor hell's infectious breath,[72]
The resolute at any time have stayed.
And, sooth to say, why fear we when we see
The thing we fear, less than the fear to be.[73]
Then let me die my liberty to save,
For 'tis a death to live a tyrant's slave.[74]

CICERO

Daughter, beware how you provoke the heav'ns,
Which in our bodies, as a tower of strength,[75]
Have placed our souls, and fortified the same,
As discreet princes set their garrisons
In strongest places of their provinces.
Now, as it is not lawful for a man,

---

evoked in Horace's *Odes*, III. 3, 1–4: 'Iustum et tenace propositi virum | Non civium ardor prava iubentium | Non voltus instantis tyranni | Mente quatit solida ...' ('For just men of steadfast purpose, neither the raging crowds urging them to do wrong, nor the menacing frown of a tyrant is enough to shake their strong minds' ...). The topos is also to be found in *Antonius*, III. 438–42.

[71] i.e. of slight build or composition.

[72] Lake Avernus, by the supposed entrance to the underworld, was reputed to emit deadly vapours.

[73] Cornelia answers with arguments derived from Cicero's own writings: see for example *De Senectute*, XX, where Cicero exposes the vanity of fearing one's death by citing the example of fearless warriors.

[74] The focus on 'liberty' is Kyd's. Garnier: 'il faut d'une mort brave | Frauder notre Tyran pour ne luy estre esclave' ('we must, by a brave death, | defraud our tyrant and not be his slave', p. 48v).

[75] The metaphor of the soul as an inner citadel is a Stoic commonplace.

At such a king's departure or decease,[76]
To leave the place, and falsify his faith,
So in this case, we ought not to surrender
That dearer part, till heav'n itself command it.[77]
For as they lent us life to do us pleasure,
So look they for return of such a treasure.

[*Exeunt.*]

CHORUS

Whate'er the massy earth hath freight°
Or on her nurse-like back sustains,
Upon the will of heav'n doth wait,
And doth no more than it ordains.
All fortunes, all felicities,
Upon their motion[78] *do depend,*
And from the stars doth still arise
Both their beginning and their end.
The monarchies that cover all
This earthly round° *with majesty,*
Have both their rising and their fall,
From heav'n and heaven's variety.[79]
Frail men, or man's more frail defence,
Had never power to practise stays°
Of this celestial influence,
That governeth and guides our days.
No cloud but will be overcast;
And what now flourisheth, must fade;
And that that fades, revive at last,
To flourish as it first was made.
The forms of things do never die,
Because the matter that remains

[76] Garnier: 'au desceu' (p. 49r), i.e. without the knowledge of (see note below). Kyd probably read 'au décès' (i.e. at the death of').

[77] See Cicero, *De Senectute*, XX. 73: 'Vetat Pythagoras inussu imperatoris, id est Dei, de praesidio et statione vitae decedere' ('Pythagoras forbids that we should leave our post and station in life without orders from our general, that is God'). See also Ternaux, p. 70. Conforming one's mind to the divine will is one of the major tenets of ancient Stoicism.

[78] The motion of the heavens.

[79] 342–49] Garnier here evokes the Stoic doctrine of eternal recurrence, which associated the circular motion of the stars with the cyclical nature of human history. See also *Antonius*, II. 2. 470–77.

Reforms° another thing thereby,
That still the former shape retains.
The roundness of two bowls cross-cast,[80]
So they with equal pace be aimed,
Shows their beginning by their last,
Which by old nature is new-framed.
So peopled cities that of yore
Were desert fields where none would bide,
Become forsaken as before,
Yet after are re-edified.
Perceive we not a petty vein,°
Cut from a spring by chance or art,
Engend'reth fountains, whence again
Those fountains do to floods convert?
Those floods to waves, those waves to seas,
That oft exceed their wonted° bounds:°
And yet those seas, as heavens please,
Return to springs by undergrounds.
Ev'n so our city, in her prime,[81]
Prescribing princes everything,
Is now subdued by conqu'ring time,
And liveth subject to a king.[82]
And yet, perhaps, the sun-bright crown
That now the tyrant's head doth deck
May turn to Rome with true renown,
If Fortune chance but once to check.°

---

[80] i.e. if one casts two bowls in opposite directions, and at an equal pace, they will end up each where the other started. A reference to the game of bowls, popular in Tudor England. Garnier's mention of the 'boules mouvantes' (p. 49v) refers instead to the circular movement of the planets around the earth, according to Ptolemaic cosmology.

[81] 385–92] Kyd departs from Garnier here, who suggests that Rome will again be subjected to kings, as she has already been: 'Comme notre ville maistresse | Des princes a senty les lois | La suite des temps vainqueresse | L'assujetira sous les Rois', etc. ('As our city, once a ruler, | did experience the yoke of princes, | so the conquering times to come | will submit her again to kings', p. 49v). Kyd reverts the perspective, evoking instead the return of Rome's past grandeur. Note here again the parallel with du Bellay's *Antiquités de Rome*, Sonnet 3, and Spenser's rendering: 'And how that she [Rome], which with her mightie powre | Tam'd all the world, hath tam'd herselfe at last, | The pr[e]y of time, which all things doth devowre' (*Complaints*, sig. R1v).

[82] i.e. a tyrant. Assuming the name of king was a political taboo and a capital offence at the time of the Roman republic.

The stately walls that once were reared,
And by a shepherd's hands erect
(With hapless° brothers' blood besmeared)[83]
Shall show by whom they were infect;°
And once more unjust Tarquin's frown,[84]
With arrogance and rage enflamed,
Shall keep the Roman valour down,
And Rome itself a while be tamed;
And chastest Lucrece[85] once again,
Because her name dishonoured stood,
Shall by herself be careless° slain,
And make a river of her blood,
Scorning her soul a seat should build
Within a body, basely seen
By shameless rape to be defiled,
That erst° was clear as heaven's Queen.[86]
But, heav'ns, as tyranny shall yoke
Our bastard hearts with servile thrall,°
So grant your plagues — which they provoke —
May light° upon them once for all.
And let another Brutus rise,[87]
Bravely to fight in Rome's defence,
To free our town from tyranny,
And tyrannous proud insolence.

[*Exit* CHORUS.]

[83] Romulus, the founder of Rome (see p. 190, n. 31), killed his twin brother Remus by the walls of the new city.
[84] Tarquin the Elder, also known as Tarquinius Superbius (i.e. the arrogant — hence 'with arrogance and rage enflamed') was Rome's last king before the establishment of the republic.
[85] Lucrece committed suicide despite the pleas of her family after being raped by Sextus Tarquinius, Tarquin the Elder's son.
[86] Diana, the virgin goddess of the moon, whose name means 'heavenly' — although the expression also refers to the Virgin Mary. This line is not in the original.
[87] Who overthrew Tarquin the Elder (see p. 185, n. 4). Also an allusion, of course, to the younger Brutus who conspired against Caesar, and is to appear in Act IV.

ACT III

[SCENE 1]

[*Enter*] CORNELIA [*and*] CHORUS.

[CORNELIA]
The cheerful cock, the sad night's comforter,[1]
Waiting upon the rising of the sun,
Doth sing to see how Cynthia[2] shrinks her horn,
While Clitie[3] takes her progress to the east,
    Where, wringing wet with drops of silver dew,
    Her wonted° tears of love she doth renew.
The wand'ring swallow, with her broken song,
The country wench unto her work awakes;
While Cytherea,[4] sighing, walks to seek
Her murdered love transformed into a rose,[5]
    Whom, though she see, to crop she kindly fears,
    But, kissing, sighs, and dews him with her tears,
Sweet tears of love, remembrancers[6] to time;
Time past with me that am to tears converted,
Whose mournful passions dull the morning's joys,
Whose sweeter sleeps are turned to fearful° dreams,
    And whose first fortunes, filled with all distress,
    Afford no hope of future happiness.
But what disastrous or hard accident,
Hath bathed your blubbered eyes in bitter tears,

---

[1] The passage from lines 1–18 is an addition of Kyd's. Garnier's Act III begins at line 19.

[2] Another name for Diana, goddess of the moon (her 'horn' represents the moon's crescent).

[3] Or Clitia, a nymph who was abandoned by the sun god Phoebus and was turned into a heliotrope, forever following the sun's course from east to west (see Ovid's *Metamorphoses*, IV. 256ff.).

[4] Another name for Venus.

[5] Adonis, who was killed by a wild boar at the command of Diana. According to Ovid (*Metamorphoses*, X. 731–39), the blood from his wounds turned into an anemone. As noted by Erne (*Beyond the Spanish Tragedy*, p. 208), lines 10–13 are reminiscent of Hieronymo's speech in *The Spanish Tragedy*, II. 5. 47–49: 'Sweet lovely rose, ill pluckt before thy time, […] Ile kisse thee now, for words with teares are staide' (*Works*, p. 34).

[6] Reminders, or markers of time. Remembrancers were officers of the Exchequer, whose role was to compile tax records.

That thus consort me in my misery?
Why do you beat your breasts? Why mourn you so?
 Say, gentle sisters, tell me, and believe
 It grieves me that I know not why you grieve.

CHORUS

O poor Cornelia, have not we good cause,
For former wrongs to furnish us with tears?[7]

CORNELIA

Oh, but I fear that Fortune seeks new flaws,
And, still unsatisfied, more hatred bears.

CHORUS

Wherein can Fortune further injure us,
Now we have lost our conquered liberty,[8]
Our commonwealth, our empire, and our honours,
Under this cruel Tarquin's tyranny?[9]
Under his outrage now are all our goods,[10]
Where scatterèd they run by land and sea,
Like exiled us, from fertile Italy,
To proudest Spain, or poorest Getulie.[11]

CORNELIA

And will the heav'ns, that have so oft defended
Our Roman walls from fury of fierce kings,
Not once again return our senators,
That, from the Lybic plains and Spanish fields,
With fearless hearts do guard our Roman hopes?
Will they not once again encourage them
To fill our fields with blood of enemies,
And bring from Afrique, to our Capitol,
Upon their helms° the empire that is stole?°

[7] Garnier: 'n'avons nous assez | De quoi fournir de pleurs' ('have we not enough to furnish all with tears', p. 50v).
[8] Garnier only writes 'liberté'.
[9] See above, p. 211, n. 84.
[10] i.e. our good men, our worthies (Garnier: 'presque tous les bons', i.e. 'almost all our worthies', p. 50v).
[11] Pompey's troops had retreated to Northern Africa, or Getulia, and Spain (see the Argument).

Then home-born household gods,[12] and ye good spirits,
To whom in doubtful things we seek access,
By whom our family hath been adorned,
And gracèd with the name of African,[13]
Do ye vouchsafe° that this victorious title,
Be not expired in Cornelia's blood;
And that my father now, in th'Afric° wars,
The selfsame style° by conquest may continue.
But wretched that I am, alas! I fear.

CHORUS

What fear you Madam?

CORNELIA

That the frowning heavens
Oppose themselves against us in their wrath.

CHORUS

Our loss, I hope, hath satisfied their ire.°

CORNELIA

Oh no, our loss lifts Caesar's fortunes higher.

CHORUS

Fortune is fickle.

CORNELIA

But hath failed him never.

CHORUS

The more unlike she should continue ever.

CORNELIA

My fearful° dreams do my despairs redouble.

---

[12] Garnier: 'Penates saincts, Lares' (p. 50v). The Penates and Lares were domestic deities who protected the family and the Roman state.

[13] The spirits of the ancestors, or Manae, were also believed to watch over the family. In this case, Cornelia refers to Scipio Africanus the Elder and the Younger (see above, p. 205, nn. 59 and 60).

CHORUS

Why suffer you vain dreams your head to trouble?

CORNELIA

Who is not troubled with strange visìons?

CHORUS

That of our spirit are but illusìons.

CORNELIA

God grant these dreams to good effect be brought.

CHORUS

We dream by night what we by day have thought.[14]

CORNELIA

The silent night that long had sojournèd,
Now gan° to cast her sable mantle off,
And now the sleepy Wainman[15] softly drove
His slow-paced team, that long had travellèd.
When, like a slumber, if you term it so,
A dullness, that disposeth us to rest,
Gan° close the windows of my watchful eyes,
Already tired and laden with my tears.
And lo! Methought, came gliding by my bed
The ghost of Pompey, with a ghastly look:[16]
All pale and brawn-fall'n,° not in triumph borne
Amongst the conquering Romans as he used,
When he, enthronized, at his feet beheld
Great emperors fast bound in chains of brass;
But all amazed, with fearful° hollow eyes,
His hair and beard deformed[17] with blood and sweat,

[14] The Chorus here presents the Epicurean approach to dreams as laid out in Lucretius' *De Rerum Natura*, IV, against the usual belief in their prophetic value.
[15] The constellation of Bootes, or the Herdsman, driving his oxen ('slow-paced team') across the sky.
[16] The apparition of a ghost is an epic and tragic commonplace. This passage in Garnier is particularly modelled on Aeneas' encounter with Hector's ghost in Virgil's *Aeneid*, II. 268–79.
[17] i.e. disfigured, tainted. See *Aeneid*, II. 277: 'squalentem barbam et concretos sanguine crines' ('his beard filthy and his hair matted with blood').

Casting a thin coarse linsel° o'er his shoulders,
That, torn in pieces, trailed upon the ground.
And gnashing of his teeth, unlocked his jaws,
Which slightly covered[18] with a scarce-seen skin,
This solemn tale he sadly did begin:
'Sleep'st thou, Cornelia? Sleep'st thou, gentle wife,
And seest thy father's misery and mine?[19]
Wake, dearest sweet, and, o'er our sepulchres,
In pity show thy latest love to us!
Such hap° as ours attendeth° on my sons,
The selfsame foe and fortune following them:
Send Sextus[20] over to some foreign nation,
Far from the common hazard of the wars;
That, being yet saved, he may attempt no more
To venge° the valour that is tried before.'[21]
He said. And suddenly a trembling horror,
A chill-cold shivering, settled in my veins,
Brake up my slumber; when I oped° my lips
Three times to cry, but could nor cry, nor speak.
I moved mine head, and flung abroad mine arms
To entertain° him, but his airy spirit
Beguilèd mine embracements, and, unkind,
Left me embracing nothing but the wind.[22]
O valiant soul, when shall this soul of mine
Come visit thee in the Elysian shades?[23]

---

[18] The verb seems to be implied: 'the which being slightly covered', etc.

[19] Kyd simplifies Garnier: 'et vostre pere et moy | Vous devrions esmouvoir de prendre tant d'émoy' ('your father and myself | should move you [with shame] for being so moved', p. 51r).

[20] Sextus Pompeius, who was present at his father's death, fled to Spain, where he joined his elder brother Gnaeius Pompeus who had gathered troops against Caesar. Gnaeius was defeated and killed at the battle of Munda (45 BC). Sextus came back to Rome and was briefly allied to Octavius and Antony, but the peace was short-lived and he eventually died as Antony's prisoner in 35 BC.

[21] Kyd seems to refer to Pompey's valour. Compare with Garnier: 'qu'il ne retente plus … | Pour me cuider venger, un Mars trop éprouvé' ('Let him not, in an attempt to avenge me, call on Mars again, who proved his worth too many times', p. 51v).

[22] 101–05] See *Aeneid*, II. 792–793: 'Ter conatus ibi collo dare bracchia circum; | Ter frustra comprensa manus effugit imago | Par levibus ventis volucrique simillima somno' ('Three times I sought to fold my arms around her neck; three times my hands embraced her image in vain as she vanished, much like a light breeze and a fleeting dream').

[23] See p. 206, n. 68.

O dearest life! Or when shall sweetest death
Dissolve the fatal trouble[24] of my days,
And bless me with my Pompey's company?
But may my father (O extreme mishap!°)
And such a number of brave regiments
Made of so many expert soldìers,
That loved our liberty and followed him,
Be so discomfited?[25] Oh, would it were
But an illusion!

CHORUS

Madam, never fear,
Nor let a senseless idol[26] of the night
Increase a more than needful fear in you.

CORNELIA

My fear proceeds not of an idle dream,
For 'tis a truth that hath astonished me.
I saw great Pompey, and I heard him speak;
And thinking to embrace him, oped° mine arms,
When drowsy sleep, that waked me at unwares,
Did with his flight unclose my fearful eyes
So suddenly that yet methinks I see him.[27]
Howbeit, I cannot touch him, for he slides
More swiftly from me than the ocean glides.

CHORUS

These are vain thoughts, or melancholy shows,
That wont° to haunt and trace° by cloistered tombs,
Which eaths° appear in sad and strange disguises.
To pensive minds deceivèd with their shadows,
They counterfeit the dead in voice and figure,
Divining of our future miseries.

---

[24] Kyd omits Garnier's allusion to Clotho, one of the three Parcae, who wove the thread of life: 'quand viendra la sevère Clothon | Despecer de mes jours le fatal peloton' ('when will severe Clotho | undo the fatal skein of my days', p. 51v).
[25] Defeated, routed (Garnier: 'desfaict'). Kyd omits Garnier's implication that Scipio is dead, 'tombé dans la barque légère' ('fallen into the light boat [of Charon]', p. 51v).
[26] A vain image (Garnier: 'un idole faux', p. 51v). The pun with 'idle' ('an idle dream', 119) is Kyd's.
[27] The shift into the present tense is not in the original.

For when our soul the body hath disgaged,°
It seeks the common passage of the dead,
Down by the fearful° gates of Acheron;
Where, when it is by Aeacus adjudged,
It either turneth to the Stygian lake,
Or stays forever in th'Elysian fields;[28]
And ne'er returneth to the corpse interred,
To walk by night, or make the wise afeared.
None but inevitable, conquering Death[29]
Descends to hell, with hope to rise again;
For ghosts of men are locked in fiery gates,
Fast guarded by a fell remorseless monster.[30]
And therefore think not it was Pompey's sprite,°
But some false demon that beguiled your sight.

[*Exeunt.*]

---

[28] Aeacus was one of the judges of the underworld. This journey is similarly evoked by the ghost of Andrea in the Induction to the *Spanish Tragedy*.

[29] Garnier writes instead: 'Personne que la Mort inevitable domte | En ce monde laissé des Enfers ne remonte' ('nobody, once conquered by death, | can come back to this world', etc., p. 52r).

[30] Cerberus, the three-headed dog that watched the gates of the underworld. Garnier: 'ils ont Cerbere' ('they have Cerberus', p. 52r).

[Scene 2]

[*Enter* Cicero.]

Cicero

Then, O world's Queen, O town that didst extend
Thy conquering arms beyond the Ocèan,[1]
And throng'dst° thy conquests from the Lybian shores
Down to the Scythian swift-foot° fearless porters,[2]
Thou art embased,° and at this instant[3] yield'st
Thy proud neck to a miserable yoke!
Rome thou art tamed, and th'earth dewed with thy blood
Doth laugh to see how thou art signorized.°
The force of heav'n exceeds thy former strength,
For thou that wont'st° to tame and conquer all,
Art conquered now with an eternal fall.
Now shalt thou march, thy hands fast bound behind thee,
Thy head hung down, thy cheeks with tears besprent,°
Before the victor, while thy rebel son,
With crownèd front, triumphing follows thee.
Thy bravest captains, whose courageous hearts,
Joined with the right, did re-enforce° our hopes,
Now murdered lie for fowl to feed upon:[4]
Petraeus, Cato, and Scipio are slain,
And Juba, that amongst the Moors did reign.[5]
Now, you whom both the gods and Fortune's grace
Hath saved from danger in these furious broils,°
Forbear to tempt the enemy again,
For fear you feel a third calamity.
Caesar is like a brightly flaming blaze

---

[1] Kyd omits Garnier's personification of the Ocean: 'jusqu'aux sillons flotans | Du vieillard Ocean' ('unto the wavy furrows of old man Ocean', p. 52r).

[2] The Scythians were a nomadic people living in the area of the Caucasus mountains and the Black Sea.

[3] i.e. after Caesar's victory at the battle of Thapsus (46 BC).

[4] Kyd omits the second line of the couplet: '… pasture des oiseaux, | Pasture des poissons qui rament sous les eaux' ('now food for birds, | food for the fish that swim [lit. row] under the sea', p. 52v).

[5] Marcus Petraeus (or Petreius), Marcus Cato of Utica (or the Younger) and Quintus Metellus Scipio, all three major generals of Pompey's faction who were defeated at Thapsus. Juba, King of Numidia, gave his support to them (see the Argument). They all committed suicide after the defeat.

That fiercely burns a house already fired;
And ceaseless launching out on every side,
Consumes the more, the more you seek to quench it,
Still darting sparkles, till it find a train[6]
To seize upon, and then it flames amain.[7]
The men, the ships, wherewith poor Rome affronts him,
All pow'rless, give proud Caesar's wrath free passage.
Nought can resist him: all the power we raise
Turns but to our misfortune, and his praise.
'Tis thou, O Rome, that nursed his insolence.
'Tis thou, O Rome, that gav'st him first the sword
Which, murder-like, against thyself he draws,
And violates both God and Nature's laws;
Like moral Aesop's misled country swain,°[8]
That found a serpent pining in the snow,
And full of foolish pity took it up,
And kindly laid it by his household fire,
Till, waxen° warm, it nimbly gan° to stir,
And stung to death the fool that fostered her.
O gods that once had care of these our walls,
And fearless kept us from th'assault of foes;
Great Jupiter, to whom our Capitol
So many oxen yearly sacrificed;[9]
Minerva, Stator,[10] and stout Thracian Mars,[11]

---

[6] Either a shoot (of a tree), or a trail (typically, of gunpowder).

[7] i.e. with full force. A significant departure from Garnier, who notes instead that the fire comes to a sudden end: 'et puis il tombe mort' ('and then it dies out', p. 52v). Kyd's rendering is reminiscent of Lucan's comparison of Caesar to a lightning bolt in *Pharsalia*, I. 151–57; see in particular Marlowe's translation of I. 153–57: 'Filling the world, leaps out and throws forth fire, | Affrights poor fearful men, and blasts their eyes | With overthwarting flames, and raging shoots | Amongst the air and nought resisting it | Falls, and returns, and shivers where it lights' (*Lucans first booke*, sig. B3r).

[8] See Aesop's fable of the farmer and the snake, well known to the Elizabethan public as it constituted typical grammar-school reading material. Garnier tells instead the fable of a shepherd who takes a wolf cub in his care, an adapted version of the chorus in Aeschylus's *Agamemnon* (see Ternaux, p. 84).

[9] Jupiter's temple was one of the major buildings on Rome's Capitol.

[10] Minerva was the goddess of war, daughter of Jupiter, here designed by his attribute 'Stator', i.e. 'the Stayer'. Garnier only refers to Jupiter ('grand Jupiter') by his two attributes: 'Feretrien [Witness], Stateur' (p. 53r). The temples of Jupiter Stator and Jupiter Feretrius were located in Rome's forum.

[11] On the association of Thrace with war, see above, p. 192, n. 52.

Father to good Quirinus, our first founder;[12]
To what intent have ye preserved our town,
This stately town, so often hazarded,
Against the Samnites, Sabins, and fierce Latins?[13]
Why from once footing in our fortresses,
Have ye repelled the lusty warlike Gauls?[14]
Why from Molossus[15] and false Hannibal,
Have ye reserved° the noble Romulists?°
Or why from Cat'line's lewd conspiracies[16]
Preserved ye Rome by my prevention?
  To cast so soon a state so long defended,
Into the bondage where, enthralled,° we pine?
To serve — no stranger, but amongst us — one
That with blind frenzy buildeth up his throne?
  But if in us be any vigour resting,°
If yet our hearts retain one drop of blood,
Caesar, thou shalt not vaunt° thy conquest long,
Nor longer hold us in this servitude,[17]
Nor shalt thou bathe thee longer in our blood:
For I divine that thou must vomit it,
Like to a cur that carrion hath devoured,
And cannot rest until his maw° be scoured.
  Think'st thou to signorize,° or be the king
Of such a number, nobler than thyself?[18]
Or think'st thou Romans bear such bastard hearts,
To let thy tyranny be unrevenged?
No, for methinks I see the shame, the grief,

[12] Romulus, founder of Rome, who received the title of Quirinus (Quirinus being an ancient deity of war) after his death. Romulus and Remus were sons of Mars.

[13] Here Garnier alludes to the mythical, early days of Rome, which were marked by various wars against neighbouring peoples. The Samnites and the Latins were tribes situated south of Rome; the Sabine wars were famously launched by the Romans' rape of Sabine women.

[14] On the sack of Rome by the Gauls (390 BC), see above, p. 185, n. 4.

[15] Pyrrhus, king of Epirus and Macedon, who repeatedly defeated Rome before losing the battle of Beneventum (275 BC).

[16] Lucius Catilina, or Catiline, a Roman senator who conspired to overthrow the Roman republic (63 BC). Cicero famously denounced him in his *Catiline Orations*, forcing him into exile.

[17] Compare with Garnier: 'Tu ne tiendras long temps le joug dessur nos testes' ('you shall not keep this yoke over our heads for long', p. 53v).

[18] Compare with Garnier: 'aussi nobles que toi' ('as noble as yourself', p. 53v).

The rage, the hatred that they have conceived:
And many a Roman sword already drawn,
T'enlarge the liberty that thou usurp'st;
And thy dismembered body, stabbed and torn,[19]
Dragged through the streets, disdainèd to be borne.[20]

[*Exit.*]

[19] Cicero predicts Caesar's famous assassination in 44 BC.
[20] This line is Kyd's addition.

[SCENE 3]

[*Enter*] PHILIP, CORNELIA [*and* CHORUS].

[PHILIP]
Amongst the rest of mine extreme mishaps,°
I find my fortune not the least in this,
That I have kept my master company,
Both in his life and at his latest hour:[1]
Pompey the Great, whom I have honourèd
With true devotion, both alive and dead.
One selfsame ship contained us when I saw
The murd'ring Egyptians bereave his life;
And when the man that had affright the earth
Did homage to it[2] with his dearest blood;
O'er whom I shed full many a bitter tear,
And did perform his obsequies° with sighs:
And on the strand upon the riverside,
Where to my sighs the waters seemed to turn,
I wove a coffin for his corpse of segs,[3]
That with the wind did wave like bannerets,
And laid his body to be burned thereon.
Which when it was consumed I kindly took,
And sadly closed within an earthen urn
The ashy relics of his hapless° bones:
Which having 'scaped the rage of wind and sea,
I bring to fair Cornelia to inter[4]
Within his elder's tomb that honoured her.

CORNELIA
Ay me, what see I?

PHILIP
Pompey's tender bones,
Which, in extremes,[5] an earthen urn containeth.

---

[1] 1–5] Here Garnier paraphrases Plutarch, *Life of Pompey*, LXXX. 3.
[2] i.e. to the earth. Not in the original.
[3] Sedges, a flag-like plant (hence 'bannerets', or small banners, below) growing in wet places.
[4] As detailed in Plutarch, *Life of Pompey*, LXXX. 3 and LXXX. 6.
[5] At last, in the very end (from the Latin, *in extremis*).

CORNELIA

O sweet, dear, deplorable cinders!
O miserable woman, living dying!
O poor Cornelia, born to be distressed,
Why liv'st thou toiled, that, dead, might'st lie at rest?[6]
O faithless hands that, under cloak of love,
Did entertain him, to torment him so![7]
O barbarous, inhuman, hateful traitors,
This your disloyal dealing hath defamed
Your king,[8] and his inhospitable seat,
Of the extremest and most odious crime
That 'gainst the heavens might be imagined!
For ye have basely broke the law of arms,[9]
And outraged over[10] an afflicted soul;
Murdered a man that did submit himself,
And injured him that ever used you kindly![11]
For which misdeed, be Egypt pesterèd,
With battle, famine, and perpetual plagues:
Let aspics, serpents, snakes, and Lybian bears,
Tigers, and lions, breed with you forever,
And let fair Nilus, wont° to nurse your corn,
Cover your land with toads and crocodiles,
That may infect, devour and murder you!
Else earth make way, and hell receive them quick:
A hateful race, 'mongst whom there doth abide
All treason, luxury, and homicide.

---

[6] The paradox is Kyd's. Garnier: 'hé n'aura jamais fin | Le cours de cette vie où me tient le destin? | […] N'est-il temps qu'on me fasse au sepulchre descendre?' ('Alas, will there never be an end | to this life, to which Fate keeps me bound? | […] Is it not time I should be brought down to my grave?', p. 54r).

[7] According to Plutarch, it looked at first as if Pompey would be welcomed into Egypt, but he was stabbed as he disembarked onto the shore (*Life of Pompey*, LXXIX. 3).

[8] Ptolemy XIII, king of Egypt. See above, p. 182, n. 6.

[9] Compare with Garnier: 'le devoir d'hostelage' ('hospitality's duty', p. 54r). Hospitality was deemed a sacred duty in ancient Rome.

[10] i.e. behaved outrageously against.

[11] Ptolemy XII (father to Ptolemy XIII, who ordered Pompey's death) had turned to Pompey for help when his throne was threatened, and had obtained Rome's official recognition of his position as king of Egypt and ally of Rome in 63 BC.

PHILIP

Cease these laments.

CORNELIA

I do but what I ought
To mourn his death.

PHILIP

Alas, that profits nought.

CORNELIA

Will heaven let treason be unpunished?

PHILIP

Heavens will perform what they have promised.

CORNELIA

I fear the heavens will not hear our prayer.

PHILIP

The plaints° of men oppressed do pierce the air.[12]

CORNELIA

Yet Caesar liveth still.

PHILIP

Due punishment
Succeeds° not always after an offence.
For oftentimes, 'tis for our chastisement
That heaven doth with wicked men dispense,[13]
That when they[14] *list, they may, with usury,*
For all misdeeds pay home the penalty.

---

[12] Kyd omits the following lines: 'C.: Nos suppliantes voix leurs courages n'émeuvent? | P.: De nulles passions emouvoir ne se peuvent. | C.: Ne font-ils pas justice à ceux qui la vont demandant? | P.: Or qu'on ne la demande, ils nous la vont rendant.' ('C.: Do our supplications not move their hearts? | P.: They cannot be moved by any passion. | C.: But do they not grant justice to those who request it? | P.: Even when it is not requested, they will still render it', p. 54v).

[13] i.e. that heaven spares wicked men.

[14] i.e. heavens, or the gods (Garnier: 'les grands Dieux', 'the great gods', p. 54v).

CORNELIA

This is the hope that feeds my hapless° days,
Else had my life been long ago expired.
I trust the gods, that see our hourly wrongs,
Will fire his shameful body with their flames.
Except some man, resolvèd, shall conclude,
With Caesar's death to end our servitude.
Else, God tofore,[15] my self may live to see
His tired corpse lie toiling in his blood,
Gored with a thousand stabs, and round about,
The wrongèd people leap for inward joy.
And then, come murder, then, come ugly death,
Then, Lethe, open thine infernal lake,
I'll down with joy, because before I died,
Mine eyes have seen what I in heart desired.[16]
Pompey may not revive, and, Pompey dead,
Let me but see the murd'rer murderèd.

PHILIP

Caesar bewailed his death.

CORNELIA

His death he mourned,
Whom while he lived, to live like him he scorned.

PHILIP

He punishèd his murd'rers.

CORNELIA

Who murdered him
But he that followed Pompey with the sword?
He murdered Pompey that pursued his death,
And cast the plot to catch him in the trap;
He that of his departure took the spoil,

[15] God assisting.

[16] An echo of Luke, 2. 29–30: 'Lord, now lettest thou thy servant depart in peace […] For mine eyes have seen thy salvation' (Geneva Bible). Not in Garnier: 'Je descendrai joyeuse, ayant ains que mourir | Obtenu le seul bien que je peux requerir' ('I will go down with joy, having obtained, before I died, | the only thing I could request', p. 55r).

Whose fell ambition, founded first in blood,[17]
By nought but Pompey's life could be withstood.

PHILIP

Photis and false Achillas he beheaded.[18]

CORNELIA

That was, because that Pompey being their friend,[19]
They had determined once of Caesar's end.

PHILIP

What got he by his death?

CORNELIA

Supremacy.

PHILIP

Yet Caesar speaks of Pompey honourably.

CORNELIA

Words are but wind, nor meant he what he spoke.

PHILIP

He will not let his statuès[20] be broke.°

CORNELIA

By which disguise — whate'er he doth pretend —
His own from being broke° he doth defend.[21]
And by the trains° wherewith he us allures,[22]
His own estate more firmly he assures.

---

[17] Not in Garnier: 'la gloutte envie | De commander' ('[Caesar's] gluttonous appetite | for power', p. 55r).

[18] According to Plutarch, Achillas ordered Pompey's murder, and Photinus, a eunuch at the court of Ptolemy, performed it. Both were put to death by Caesar (*Life of Pompey*, LXXX. 5).

[19] As advisors to Ptolemy XIII, who was at first Pompey's ally. See above, n. 7 and 11.

[20] The trisyllabic pronunciation preserves the metre, as in IV. 2. 190. Also in Shakespeare, *Julius Caesar*, II. 2. 76 and III. 2. 193.

[21] An allusion to Cicero's comment, as reported by Plutarch (*Life of Caesar*, LVII. 4), that 'Caesar setting up Pompeys images againe, he made his owne to stand the surer' (North, *Lives*, p. 790).

[22] i.e. and alluring us by these guiles.

PHILIP

He took no pleasure in his death, you see.

CORNELIA.

Because himself of life did not bereave him.[23]

PHILIP

Nay, he was moved with former amity.°

CORNELIA

He never trusted him but to deceive him;
But, had he loved him with a love unfeigned,
Yet had it been a vain and trustless league;
For there is nothing in the soul of man
So firmly grounded, as can qualify
Th'inextinguible thirst of signory.°
Not heaven's fear, nor country's sacred love,
Not ancient laws, nor nuptial chaste desire,
Respect of blood, or — that which most should move —
The inward zeal that Nature doth require:[24]
All these, nor anything we can devise
Can stoop the heart resolved to tyrannize.[25]

PHILIP

I fear your griefs increase with this discourse.[26]

CORNELIA

My griefs are such, as hardly can be worse.

---

[23] Not in the original. Garnier's Cornélie argues instead that Caesar sought Pompey's death because the latter tried to defend of Rome's freedom: 'puis qu'il vouloit la liberté défendre' (p. 55r).

[24] Garnier is more specific: 'non l'amour ordinaire | Du pere à ses enfans, des enfans à leur pere' ('the natural love of father | to child, and of child to father', p. 55v).

[25] Compare with Garnier: 'un cœur, que le soin furieux | De maistriser chacun, maistrise ambitieux' ('his heart, ambitiously ruled | by the furious desire to rule over all', p. 55v).

[26] Two lines omitted here. 'P.: Laissez cela, Madame. C.: Il faut que je le laisse, | Attendant des grands Dieux la faveur vengeresse' ('P.: Madam, leave this. C.: So I must, | and wait for the great gods' avenging favours', p. 55v).

PHILIP

Time calmeth all things.

CORNELIA

No time qualifies
My doleful° spirit's endless miseries.[27]
My grief is like a rock, whence, ceaseless, strain°
Fresh springs of water at my weeping eyes,
Still fed by thoughts, like floods with winter's rain.
For when to ease th'oppression of my heart,
I breathe an autumn[28] forth of fiery sighs,
Yet herewithal° my passion neither dies,
Nor dries the heat the moisture of mine eyes.

PHILIP

Can nothing then recure° these endless tears?

CORNELIA

Yes, news of Caesar's death that med'cine bears.

PHILIP

Madam, beware, for should he hear of this,
His wrath against you 'twill exasperate.

CORNELIA

I neither stand in fear of him nor his.

PHILIP

'Tis policy° to fear a pow'rful hate.

CORNELIA

What can he do?

---

[27] Four lines omitted after this: 'Plustot dedans la mer les animaux paistront, | Et les poissons flottans sur la terre naistront: | Plustost le clair soleil ne luira plus au monde, | Que mon mal se relâche, et ma peine feconde'. ('Sooner will beasts graze upon the sea, | sooner will fish be born floating on land, | sooner will the sun cease to shine upon the earth, | than will my pain and my fertile sorrow find relief', p. 55v).
[28] Garnier: 'un Auton de soupirs' ('an Auton of sighs', p. 55v). The Auton (or Autan) is a hot, southern wind.

PHILIP

Madam, what cannot men
That have the power to do what pleaseth them?

CORNELIA

He can do me no mischief° that I dread.

PHILIP

Yes, cause your death.

CORNELIA

Thrice happy were I dead.

PHILIP

With rigorous torments.

CORNELIA

Let him torture me,
Pull me in pieces, famish, fire me up,
Fling me alive into a lion's den:[29]
There is no death so hard torments me so,
As his extreme triumphing in our woe.
But if he will torment me, let him then
Deprive me wholly of the hope of death:
For I had died before the fall of Rome,
And slept with Pompey in the peaceful deeps,[30]
Save that I live in hope to see ere° long,
That Caesar's death shall satisfy his wrong.

[*Exeunt* PHILIP *and* CORNELIA.]

CHORUS

Fortune in pow'r imperious,
Used o'er the world and worldlings[31] *thus*
To tyrannize,

---

[29] An echo of Seneca, *Troas*, 582–83: 'Propone flammas, vulnera, et diras mali | Doloris artes et famem et saevam sitim' ('Threaten me with fire, wounds, and the dire arts of torture, and hunger, and cruel thirst'). See Ternaux, p. 94.

[30] Garnier is more expressive here: 'Je mourrois, je mourrois, et le tombeau chery | M'auroit desjà rendue au sein de mon mari' ('I had died, I had died, and the blissful tomb | had already sent me back to my husband's side', p. 56r).

[31] Garnier only has 'ceste rondeur' ('this round orb', a paraphrase for the earth,

When she hath heaped her gifts on us,
Away she flies.
Her feet, more swift than is the wind,
Are more inconstant in their kind
Than autumn blasts,
A woman's shape, a woman's mind,
That seldom lasts.[32]
One while she bends her angry brow,
And of no labour will allow.
Another while,
She fleers° again, I know not how,
Still to beguile.
Fickle in our adversities,
And fickle when our fortunes rise,
She scoffs at us:
That, blind herself, can blear our eyes,[33]
To trust her thus.
The sun that lends the earth his light,
Beheld her never overnight
Lie calmly down,
But in the morrow following, might
Perceive her frown.
She hath not only power and will,
T'abuse the vulgar wanting skill,
But when she list,
To kings and clowns doth equal ill
Without resist.[34]

---

p. 56r). Perhaps an allusion to Jan van der Noot's *Theatre for Voluptuous Worldlings* (1569), which contained many illustrated poems on the decay of Rome, and more generally, on the inconstancy of fortune (including an elaborate engraving on the 'ship of state' theme). The poems in the English *Theatre* are translations of Petrarch's *Visions*, and of du Bellay's *Songe*, by Edmund Spenser.

[32] These two lines are Kyd's addition. The association of fickleness with women is a commonplace, most famously formulated in *Aeneid*, IV. 569–670: 'varium et mutabile semper | Femina' ('an ever-changing, fickle thing is woman'). See also *Antonius*, I. 145–46.

[33] According to the usual representation of Fortune as a blindfolded woman. Garnier evokes instead her no less traditional wheel: 'De nous elle se joue | Qui tournons sans cesse agitez | Au branle de sa roue' ('She mocks us | as we endlessly roll and turn | with the motion of her wheel', p. 56v).

[34] A slight variation from Garnier: 'un grand empire [...] | Comme un simple ménage' ('a great empire [...] | as well as a humble household', p. 56v). Kyd's version echoes the evocation of death in II. 2. 254–55.

Mischance that every man abhors,
And cares for crownèd emperors
She doth reserve,
As for the poorest labourers
That work or starve.
The merchant that for private gain
Doth send his ships to pass the main,
Upon the shore,
In hope he shall his wish obtain,
Doth thee adore.[35]
Upon the sea, or on the land,
Where health or wealth,[36] *or vines do stand,*
Thou canst do much,
And often help'st the helpless hand,[37]
Thy power is such.
And many times, disposed to jest,
'Gainst one whose power and cause is best,
Thy power to try,
To him that ne'er put spear in rest
Giv'st victory.[38]
For so the Lybian monarchy,
That with Ausonian[39] *blood did dye*
Our warlike field,
To one that ne'er got victory,
Was urged° *to yield.*[40]
So noble Marius, Arpin's friend,
That did the Latin state defend
From Cymbrian rage,[41]

---

[35] This is a commonplace, taken from Horace's *Odes*, I. 1. 15–18, also to be found in *Antonius*, I. 153–54.

[36] Compare with Garnier: 'tous les métiers | Qui s'exercent aux villes' ('all trades | that are held in cities' p. 57r).

[37] These two lines are Kyd's addition.

[38] The notion that Fortune favours the wrong cause against the just is Kyd's. For Garnier, Fortune can cause the stronger party to lose against inexperienced warriors: 'Qui au fort de sa gloire | Perd contre un jeune belliqueur | La vie et la victoire' ('who in the apex of his glory | still loses both life and victory | to the hands of a young enemy', p. 57r).

[39] i.e. Italian.

[40] 196–200] The allusion is to Hannibal, king of Libya, who lost the battle of Zama (202 BC), near Carthage, to Scipio Africanus, then only aged 33.

[41] Gaius Marius took command of the war against the Germanic tribe of the Cimbri

Did prove° thy fury in the end
Which nought could swage.°
And Pompey whose days haply° led,
So long thou seemedst t'have favourèd,
In vain, 'tis said,
When the Pharsalian field he led
Implored thine aid.
Now Caesar, swoll'n with honour's heat,
Sits signorizing° in her seat,[42]
And will not see
That Fortune can her hopes defeat
What e'er they be.
From Chance is nothing franchisèd,
And till the time that they are dead,
Is no man blessed.[43]
He only, that no death doth dread,
Doth live at rest.

[*Exit* CHORUS.]

---

as Rome was losing ground, and managed to defeat them in 101 BC. Kyd seems to have misunderstood Garnier's epithet for Marius, 'l'honneur d'Arpin' ('the pride of Arpinium', p. 57r): Arpinium was Marius's birthplace.

[42] Fortune's seat. See also below: 'her hopes', as Kyd expands on Garnier's paradox: 'Ne prevoyant de son bon-heur | La constante inconstance' ('Without foreseeing his good fortune's | constant inconstancy', p. 57v).

[43] An echo of the final chorus in Sophocles' *Oedipus Rex*.

ACT IV

[SCENE 1]

[*Enter*] CASSIUS, DECIMUS BRUTUS[1] [*and* CHORUS].

[CASSIUS]
Accursèd Rome, that arm'st against thyself
A tyrant's rage, and mak'st a wretch thy king!
For one man's pleasure,[2] O injurious Rome,
Thy children 'gainst thy children thou hast armed,
And thinkst not of the rivers of their blood,
That erst° was shed to save thy liberty,
Because thou ever hatedst monarchy.[3]
Now o'er our bodies tumbled up on heaps
Like cocks of hay when July shears the field,
Thou build'st thy kingdom, and thou seat'st thy king,
And to be servile (which torments me most)
Employ'st our lives, and lavishest our blood!
O Rome, accursèd Rome, thou murd'rest us,
And massacrest thyself in yielding thus!
Yet are there gods, yet is there heav'n and earth,
That seem to fear a certain Thunderer![4]
No, no, there are no gods, or if there be,
They leave to see[5] into the world's affairs;
They care not for us, nor account of men,
For what we see is done, is done by chance.[6]

---

[1] See above, p. 184, n. 16.

[2] The definition of tyranny as 'one man's pleasure' is a theme of major importance, both in Garnier and in Kyd. See above, III. 3. 132, and below, 102–03.

[3] Cassius' republican discourse is fiercer here than in Garnier: 'Pour n'estre point esclave et ne porter flechie | Au service d'un seul le joug de Monarchie' ('To avoid being a slave, bending your neck | and serving one man under the yoke of monarchy', p. 57v).

[4] Jove, whose attribute is thunder.

[5] i.e. do not see into, fail to take interest in the world's affairs.

[6] Cassius here echoes the Epicurean approach to providence and the gods. See also Lucan's *Pharsalia*, VII. 445–55 (as noted by Ternaux, p. 99): 'Sunt nobis nulla profecto | Numina; cum caeco rapiantur saecula casu | Mentimur regnare Iovem. Spectabit ab alto | Aethere Thassalicas, teneat cum fulmina, caedes […] Mortalia nulli | Sunt curata deo' ('We have no gods indeed; for the ages are swept along by blind chance, and falsely we say that Jove reigns. As if he were to look from the high

'Tis Fortune rules, for equity and right
Have neither help nor grace in heaven's sight.
Scipio hath wrenched° a sword into his breast,
And lanced[7] his bleeding wound into the sea;
Undaunted Cato tore his entrails out;[8]
Afranius and Faustus murdered died;[9]
Juba and Petreus, fiercely combating,
Have each done other equal violence.[10]
Our army's broken, and the Lybian bears
Devour the bodies of our citizens;
The conqu'ring tyrant, high in Fortune's grace,
Doth ride triumphing o'er our commonwealth,[11]
And, mournful, we behold him bravely mounted,
With stern looks, in his chariot, where he leads
The conquered honour of the people yoked.
So Rome to Caesar yields both pow'r and pelf,°
And o'er Rome Caesar reigns in Rome itself.
But Brutus, shall we dissolutely° sit,
And see the tyrant live to tyrannize?
Or shall their ghosts that died[12] to do us good
Plain° in their tombs of our base cowardice?
Shall lamèd soldiers and grave grey-haired men[13]
Point at us in their bitter tears, and say,
'See where they go, that have their race forgot,

---

heaven, his lightning in hand, down to the Thessalian massacres! [...] No god cares for mortal affairs').

[7] Probably to be understood as 'launched', see Garnier: 'Scipion s'est [...] sanglant eslancé dedans la mer voisine' ('Scipio [...] bleeding threw himself into the nearby sea', p. 58r); but also the medical sense of 'lancing' a wound, i.e. bleeding it.

[8] Scipio and Cato were both generals of Pompey's army (see above, p. 219, n. 5). The details of their deaths are taken from Appian's *Civil Wars*, II. 99–100 (see Ternaux, p. 100).

[9] According to Hirtius (*De Bello Africo*, XCV) Lucius Afranius and Faustus Cornelius Sulla, son of Lucius Sulla, sought to escape to Spain, but were taken captive with their families, and later killed by Caesar's troops.

[10] Juba and Petreius were emprisoned together. In order to die honourably, Juba arranged for a duel, in which he killed Petreius before committing suicide. See Appian's *Civil Wars*, II. 100.

[11] Compare with Garnier: 'trionfer de la perte commune' ('triumphing over our common loss', p. 58r).

[12] i.e. the ghosts of those who died.

[13] Kyd's expansion of 'les Peres vieux' ('our ancient fathers').

And rather choose unarmed to serve with shame,
Than armed to save their freedom and their fame!'

BRUTUS

I swear by heav'n, th'immortals' highest throne,
Their temples, altars, and their images,
To see — for one — that Brutus suffer not
His ancient liberty[14] to be repressed.
I freely marched with Caesar in his wars,[15]
Not to be subject, but to aid his right.
But if, envenomed with ambitious thoughts,
He lift his hand imperiously o'er us,
If he determine but to reign in Rome,
Or followed Pompey but to this effect;
Or if, these civil discords now dissolved,
He render not the empire back to Rome,
Then shall he see that Brutus, this day, bears
The selfsame arms to be avenged on him,
And that this hand — though Caesar blood abhor[16] —
Shall toil in his, which I am sorry for.
  I love, I love him dearly. *But the love*
That men their country and their birth-right bear
Exceeds all loves, and dearer is by far
Our country's love, than friends or children are.

CASSIUS

If this brave care be nourished in your blood,
Or if so frank a will your soul possess,
Why haste we not, ev'n while these words are uttered,
To sheathe our new-ground swords in Caesar's throat?
Why spend we daylight, and why dies he not,

---

[14] Garnier simply has 'notre liberté' ('our freedom', p. 58r).

[15] Decimus Brutus served under Caesar in the Gallic wars and in the civil war against Pompey; Marcus Brutus, who had originally fought on Pompey's side (see above, p. 184, n. 16), was made governor of Cisalpine Gaul by Caesar in 47 BC.

[16] 'though Caesar blood abhor' is Kyd's addition. This is a recurring theme (see below, l. 199), originally derived from Plutarch, who notes that Caesar was popular among Romans because he won victories without bloodshed, and showed mercy to his enemies (*Life of Caesar*, LVII. 3). The formula, however, has a Christian connotation, as it echoes the ancient maxim, 'Ecclesia abhorret a sanguine' ('the Church abhors blood').

That, by his death, we wretches may revive?
We stay too long, I burn till I be there
To see this massacre, and send his ghost
To theirs, whom subtly he for monarchy
Made fight to death with show of liberty.[17]

BRUTUS

Yet haply° he, as Sulla whilom° did,
When he hath rooted civil war from Rome,
Will therewithal discharge the power he hath.[18]

CASSIUS

Caesar and Sulla, Brutus, be not like.
Sulla, assaulted by the enemy,
Did arm himself, but in his own defence,
Against both Cinna's host° and Marius.[19]
Whom when he had discomfited and chased,
And of his safety throughly° was assured,
He laid apart the power that he had got,
And gave up rule, for he desired it not.
    Where° Caesar that in silence might have slept,
Nor urged by ought but his ambition,[20]
Did break into the heart of Italy;
And like rude Brennus[21] brought his men to field,
Traversed the seas; and shortly after, backed
With wintered° soldiers used to conquering,
He aimed at us, bent to exterminate
Whoever sought to intercept° his state.
    Now, having got what he hath gapèd° for,
Dear Brutus, think you Caesar such a child,
Slightly° to part with so great signory?°

---

[17] i.e. to join the ghosts of those whom, by ruse, he made fight to death for monarchy, under the appearance of fighting for liberty. Garnier evokes instead the dead, whom cruel Caesar deprived of life as defenders of freedom: 'que pour la liberté | Le méchant a privez de la douce clairté' (p. 58v).

[18] On Lucius Sulla, see above, p. 200, n. 38. At the issue of the civil wars with Marius, Sulla took the office of dictator, i.e. supreme ruler, for four years, after which he restored the republican regime (81 BC).

[19] On the wars between Marius and Sulla, see above, p. 200, n. 38.

[20] Kyd's expansion of Garnier's 'sans avoir ennemy' ('even without enemy', p. 59r).

[21] The leader of the Gallic armies that sacked Rome in 390 BC.

Believe it not, he bought it dear, you know,
And travellèd too far[22] to leave it so.

BRUTUS
But Cassius, Caesar is not yet a king.

CASSIUS
No, but dictator, in effect as much.[23]
He doth what pleaseth him (a princely thing)
And wherein differ they whose power is such?

BRUTUS
He is not bloody.

CASSIUS
But by bloody jars°
He hath unpeopled most part of the earth.
Both Gaul and Afrique perished by his wars.
Egypt, Emathia,[24] Italy and Spain
Are full of dead men's bones, by Caesar slain.
Th'infectious plague, and famine's bitterness,
Or th'ocean whom no pity can assuage,
Though they contain dead bodies numberless,
Are yet inferìor to Caesar's rage,
Who, monster-like, with his ambitìon,
Hath left more tombs than ground to lay them on.

BRUTUS
Soldiers with such reproach should not be blamed.

CASSIUS
He with his soldiers hath himself defamed.

---

[22] Garnier: 'trop y a travaillé' ('toiled too hard for this', p. 59r). Travelled has three syllables for metrical reasons.
[23] An echo of Plutarch, *Life of Caesar*, LVII. 1. North: 'This was a plaine tyranny' (*Lives*, p. 789).
[24] A poetic name for central Greece — with a reference to Lucan's *Pharsalia*, I. 1: 'Bella per Emathios plus quam civilia campos | Canimus' ('Of wars worse than civil over the fields of Emathia I sing').

BRUTUS

Why then, you think there is no praise in war?

CASSIUS

Yes, where the causes reasonable are.

BRUTUS

He hath enriched the empire with new states.

CASSIUS

Which with ambition now he ruinates.

BRUTUS

He hath revenged the Gauls' old injury,[25]
And made them subject to our Roman laws.

CASSIUS

The restful Almains, with his cruelty,
He rashly stirred against us without cause,[26]
And hazarded our city and ourselves
Against a harmless nation, kindly given,[27]
To whom we should do well, for some amends,
To render him, and reconcile old friends.
These nations did he purposely provoke
To make an army for his after-aid
Against the Romans, whom in policy°
He trained in war to steal their signory,°
Like them that, striving at th'Olympian sports
To grace themselves with honour of the game,
Anoint their sinews[28] *fit for wrestling,*
And ere° they enter, use some exercise;[29]
The Gauls were but a fore-game,° fetched about

---

[25] i.e. the sack of Rome.

[26] The allusion is to Caesar's punitive expedition against German settlers in Gaul, in which many civilians were massacred (55 BC).

[27] i.e. genial, benign. Not in Garnier: 'un peuple innocent' ('an innocent people', p. 59) refers to Caesar's unwarranted attack of German tribes.

[28] Trisyllabic for metrical reasons.

[29] 134–37] Garnier expands upon Plutarch here (*Life of Caesar*, XXVIII. 2–3). North: 'like a wrestler that studieth for trickes to overthrowe his adversary, he went farre from Rome, to exercise himselfe in the warres of Gaule, where he did trayne his armie' (*Lives*, p. 777). Not marked as *sententiae* in Garnier.

For civil discord, wrought by Caesar's sleights,
Whom to be king himself he soon removed,
Teaching a people hating servitude
To fight for that that did their deaths conclude.

BRUTUS

The wars once ended, we shall quickly know
Whether he will restore the state or no.

CASSIUS

No Brutus, never look to see that day,
For Caesar holdeth signory° too dear;
But know, while Cassius hath one drop of blood
To feed this worthless body that you see —
What reck I death[30] to do so many good? —
In spite of Caesar, Cassius will be free.

BRUTUS

A generous or true ennobled spirit,
Detests to learn what tastes of servitude.

CASSIUS

Brutus, I cannot serve nor see Rome yoked,
No, let me rather die a thousand deaths!
The stiff-necked horses champ not on the bit,
Nor meekly bear the rider but by force;
The sturdy oxen toil not at the plough,
Nor yield unto the yoke but by constraint:[31]
Shall we then that are men, and Romans born,
Submit us to unurgèd° slavery?
Shall Rome, that hath so many overthrown
Now make herself a subject to her own?[32]
    O base indignity! A beardless youth,
Whom King Nicomedes could overreach,[33]

---

[30] i.e., 'what does death matter to me'. Kyd's addition.

[31] 155–58] Not marked as *sententiae* in Garnier.

[32] Compare with Garnier: 'Rome sera sujette, elle qui les provinces | Souloit assujettir, assujettir les Princes?' ('Will Rome serve, that used to make provinces | serve her, and also princes?', p. 60r).

[33] Kyd omits the sexual allusion and pun in Garnier: 'un home effeminé, | Que le Roi Nicomede a jeune butiné' ('an effeminate man, | whom King Nicomedes once tasted

Commands the world, and bridleth all the earth,
And like a prince controls the Romulists,°
Brave Roman soldiers, stern-born sons of Mars!
And none, not one, that dares to undertake
The intercepting° of his tyranny!
O Brutus, speak! Oh, say, Servilius![34]
Why, cry you aim,[35] and see us usèd thus?
 But Brutus lives, and sees, and knows, and feels
That there is one that curbs their country's weal.°
Yet as he were the semblance, not the son,
Of noble Brutus, his great grandfather,[36]
As if he wanted hands, sense, sight, or heart,
He doth, deviseth, sees nor dareth ought,
That may extirp° or raze these tyrannies!
Nor ought doth Brutus that to Brute belongs,
But still increaseth, by his negligence,
His own disgrace, and Caesar's violence.
 The wrong is great, and over-long endured:
We should have practisèd, conspired, conjured
A thousand ways and weapons, to repress,
Or kill outright this cause of our distress.

[*Exeunt.*]

CHORUS

Who prodigally spends his blood
 Bravely to do his country good,
 And liveth to no other end,
 But resolutely to attempt
 What may the innocent defend,
 And bloody tyrant's rage prevent;
And he, that in his soul assured,
 Hath water's force, and fire endured,

in his youth', p. 60r). Nicomedes IV was King of Bithynia. During his first campaign in Asia, Caesar spent such a long time at his court that, according to Suetonius (*Life of Caesar*, XLIX), the rumour developed of an affair between them and Caesar was nicknamed 'Queen of Bithynia'.

[34] Servilia was Caesar's mistress, and Marcus Brutus's mother.

[35] To cry aim (an expression probably originating in archery) is to encourage from afar, without becoming involved.

[36] The allusion is to Brutus, who caused the fall of Tarquinius Superbus and proclaimed the republic. See above, p. 185, n. 4.

And passed the pikes of thousand hosts,°
To free the truth from tyranny,
And fearless scours in danger° *coasts,*
T'enlarge his country's liberty,
Were all the world his foes before,
Now shall they love him evermore:[37]
His glory spread abroad by fame,
On wings of his posterity,
From obscure death shall free his name,
To live in endless memory.
All after-ages shall adore
And honour him with hymns therefore.
Yearly the youth for joy shall bring
The fairest flowers that grow in Rome.
And yearly in the summer[38] *sing*
O'er his heroic kingly tomb.
For so the two Athenians,[39]
That from their fellow citizens
Did freely chase vile servitude,
Shall live for valiant prowess blessed.
No sepulchre shall e'er exclude
Their glory equal with the best.[40]
But when the vulgar, mad and rude,
Repay good with ingratitude,
Hardly then they them reward,[41]
That to free them from the hands
Of a tyrant, ne'er regard
In what plight their person stands.
For high Jove that guideth all,
When he lets his just wrath fall,
To revenge proud diadems,
With huge cares doth cross kings' lives,

---

[37] Compare with Garnier: 'Comme un Peuple, ne tombe pas | De la mort gloute le repas' ('As a nation cannot perish, | devoured by gluttonous death', p. 60v).
[38] Garnier has: 'au beau jour retourné', that is, at the anniversary date (p. 60v).
[39] Harmodios and Aristogiton, who plotted to overthrow the Greek tyrants Hippias and Hipparchus in 514 BC, and who were subsequently executed.
[40] i.e. no monument will fail to record their glory. Compare with Garnier: 'Et jamais au sépulchre creux | Ne sera leur gloire cachée' ('And never will the deep grave | hide away their glory', p. 60v).
[41] i.e. hardly do they reward those who, to free them from the hands, etc.

Raising treasons in their realms,
By their children, friends or wives.
Therefore he whom all men fear,
Feareth all men everywhere.
Fear, that doth engender hate —
Hate enforcing them thereto —
Maketh many undertake
Many things they would not do.
Oh, how many mighty kings
Live in fear of petty things![42]
For when kings have sought, by wars,
Stranger towns to have o'erthrown,
They have caught deservèd scars,[43]
Seeking that was not their own.
For no tyrant, commonly,
Living ill, can kindly° *die.*
But either trait'rously surprised[44]
Doth coward poison quail° *their breath,*
Or their people have devised,
Or their guard, to seek their death.
He only lives most happily,
That free and far from majesty,
Can live content, although unknown:[45]
He fearing none, none fearing him;
Meddling with nothing but his own,
While gazing eyes at crowns grow dim.

[*Exit* CHORUS.]

---

[42] A slight departure from Garnier, whose emphasis is on the turns of fortune: 'O combien les Rois sont couverts | Tous les jours de hazards divers! | Qu'au sort est sujette leur vie!' ('O see how kings | are every day subjected to various perils! | How their lives are ruled by chance!', p. 61r).

[43] Kyd's addition.

[44] Refers back to 'no tyrant' (hence below, 'their breath').

[45] Garnier is more specific: 'caché dessous un toict de chaume …' ('hidden away under a thatch roof', p. 61v) — a paraphrase of Seneca, *Phaedra*, 1126–27: 'Servat placidos obscura quies | Prebet somnos casa securos' ('An obscure, quiet life keeps one at peace, one sleeps safely in a humble cottage').

[SCENE 2]

[*Enter*] CAESAR, MARK ANTONY
[*and* A CHORUS OF CAESAR'S FRIENDS].

CAESAR

O Rome, that with thy pride dost overpeer°
The worthiest cities of the conquered world!
Whose honour, got by famous victories,
Hath filled heav'n's fiery vaults with frightful horror!
O lofty towers! O stately battlements!
O glorious temples! O proud palaces!
And you brave walls, bright heaven's masonry,
Graced with a thousand kingly diadems,
Are ye not stirrèd with a strange[1] delight,
To see your Caesar's matchless victories?
And how your empire and your praise begins[2]
Through fame, which he of stranger nations wins?
    O beauteous Tiber,[3] with thine easy streams,
That glide as smoothly as a Parthian shaft,
Turn not thy crispy° tides like silver curl,
Back to thy grass-green banks to welcome us,[4]
And with a gentle murmur haste to tell
The foaming seas the honour of our fight?
Trudge° not thy streams to Triton's mariners[5]
To bruit° the praises of our conquests past?
And make their vaunts° to old Oceanus,[6]
That henceforth Tiber shall salute the seas,
More famed than Tiger or fair Euphrates?[7]

---

[1] i.e. uncommon, extraordinary.
[2] Garnier has: 'accroître vostre empire' ('increase your empire', p. 61v).
[3] The river running through Rome, often personified as a man with long, wavy hair and beard.
[4] An expansion of the original: 'ne doublent-ils leur crespe à tes verdureux flancs' ('do they not fold their curly waves along your green banks', p. 61v).
[5] Triton is the messenger god of the sea. He is often represented accompanied with mermen, or tritons, surrounding him. Garnier: 'aux Tritons mariniers' ('to the sea-born tritons', p. 61v).
[6] Oceanus is the god personifying the enormous river which, in ancient Rome, was believed to circle the world. Being the father of all rivers and streams, he is traditionally depicted as an old man. See Garnier: 'au père Océan' (p. 61v).
[7] The Tigris and the Euphrates are the two rivers in Mesopotamia that defined the fertile crescent long known as the cradle of ancient civilisation.

Now all the world well-nigh doth stoop to Rome.
The sea, the earth, and all is almost ours.
Be it where the bright Sun with his neighbour beams,
Doth early light the pearlèd Indians,
Or where his chariot stays to stop the day,[8]
Till heav'n unlock the darkness of the night;
Be it where the sea is wrapped in crystal ice,
Or where the summer doth but warm the earth;[9]
Or here, or there, where is not Rome renowned?
There lives no king, how great so e'er he be,
But trembleth if he once but hear of me.
Caesar is now earth's fame, and Fortune's terror,
And Caesar's worth hath stained[10] old soldiers' praises.
Rome, speak no more of either Scipio,[11]
Nor of the Fabii, or Fabricians,[12]
Here let the Decii[13] and their glory die.
Caesar hath tamed more nations, ta'en more towns,
And fought more battles than the best of them.
Caesar doth triumph over all the world,
And all they scarcely conquerèd a nook.
The Gauls, that came to Tiber to carouse,
Did live to see my soldiers drink at Loire;[14]
And those brave Germans, true-born martialists,[15]
Beheld the swift Rhine under-run° mine ensigns;
The Britons,[16] locked within a watery realm,

[8] On the Sun and his chariot, see above, p. 188, n. 20. Compare with Garnier: 'où son char lassé de la course du jour | Le ciel quitte à la nuict' ('where, his chariot tired from the day's course, | [the sun] leaves the sky to the night', p. 62r).
[9] Garnier mentions countries where the earth is scorched to the core: 'où le chaud rostist l'estomach de la terre' (p. 62r).
[10] i.e. obscured.
[11] The first had defeated Hannibal, the second had razed Carthage. See above, p. 205, nn. 59 and 60.
[12] Ancient families of Rome. Quintus Fabius Maximus was famous for his victories in the Latin wars, and his descendant, Quintus Fabius 'Cunctator' had stopped Hannibal's troops during the second Punic war. Gaius Fabricius Luscinus distinguished himself in the war against Pyrrhus.
[13] Another ancient Roman family. Publius Decius and his son were famous for sacrificing their lives to ensure Rome's victory in the Latin wars.
[14] The Loire river was the site of an important Roman victory in the Gallic wars.
[15] Men of war (Mars was the god of war). See Garnier: 'nés au métier de Mars' ('born to the trade of Mars', p. 62r). The allusion is to Caesar's German campaign in 57 BC.
[16] Caesar first established a Roman colony in Britain in 55 BC.

And walled by Neptune, stooped to me at last.
The faithless Moor, the fierce Numidian,[17]
Th'earth that the Euxine sea makes sometimes marsh,[18]
The stony-hearted people that inhabit
Where sev'nfold Nilus doth disgorge itself,
Have all been urged° to yield to my command.[19]
Yea, ev'n this city that hath almost made
An universal conquest of the world,
And that brave warrior my brother-in-law,[20]
That, ill-advised, repinèd at my glory:
Pompey, that second Mars, whose haught° renown
And noble deeds were greater than his fortunes,
Proved° to his loss, but e'en in one assault,
My hand, my hap,° my heart exceeded his,
When the Thessalian fields were purpled o'er
With either army's murdered soldiers' gore;
When he, to conquering accustomèd,
Did conquered fly, his troops discomforted.°
Now Scipio, that longed to show himself
Descent of African,[21] so famed for arms,
He durst° affront me and my warlike bands
Upon the coasts of Libya, till he lost
His scattered army; and to shun the scorn
Of being taken captive, killed himself.
Now therefore let us triumph, Antony,
And rend'ring thanks to heaven as we go
For bridling those that did malign° our glory,
Let's to the Capitol.[22]

ANTONY

Come on, brave Caesar,
And crown thy head, and mount thy chariot.

---

[17] Kyd omits 'les Iberes lointains' (i.e. the Spaniards, p. 62r).

[18] The marshlands of the province of Pontus, on the southern shore of the Black Sea (or Euxine). Originally an ally of Pompey, the province was finally subdued by Caesar in 47 BC.

[19] An allusion to the battle of the Nile (47 BC), where Caesar's troops defeated Ptolemy's army and established Cleopatra as queen of Egypt.

[20] Pompey had in fact been Caesar's son in law. Garnier: 'mon gendre' (p. 62r).

[21] See above, p. 205, nn. 59 and 60.

[22] Where the celebration of triumphs usually ended.

Th'impatient people run along the streets,
And in a rout against thy gates, they rush
To see their Caesar, after dangers past,
Made conqueror and emperor at last.

CAESAR

I call to witness heav'n's great Thunderer,
That 'gainst my will I have maintained this war,
Nor thirsted I for conquests bought with blood.
I joy not in the death of citizens:
But through my self-willed enemies' despite
And Romans' wrong was I constrained to fight.

ANTONY

They sought t'eclipse thy fame, but destiny
Reversed th'effect of their ambitìon,
And Caesar's praise increased by their disgrace
That recked not of his virtuous deeds.[23] But thus
We see it fareth with the envìous.[24]

CAESAR

I never had the thought to injure them.
Howbeit, I never meant my greatness should
By any other's greatness be o'erruled.
For as I am inferior to none,
So can I suffer no superiors.[25]

ANTONY

Well, Caesar, now they are discomfited,
And crows are feasted with their carcasses;
And yet I fear you have too kindly saved
Those that your kindness hardly will requite.[26]

---

[23] i.e. Caesar's glory was increased by the disgrace of those who did not recognize his virtuous deeds.

[24] In Garnier, the sentence is formulated as a wish: 'Ainsi tousjours advienne aux hommes envieux!' ('May such always be the fate of envious men!', p. 63r).

[25] See Lucan, *Pharsalia*, I. 125: 'Nec quisquam iam ferre potest Caesarve priorem' (as noted by Ternaux, p. 114), and Marlowe's translation: 'Pompey could bide no equal, nor Caesar no superior' (*Lucans first booke*, sig. B3r).

[26] i.e. those that will hardly return your kindness. Caesar famously graced many of his former enemies, in particular Marcus Brutus.

CAESAR

Why Antony, what would you wish me do?
Now shall you see that they will pack to Spain,
And joinèd with the exiles, there encamp,
Until th'ill spirit that doth them defend[27]
Do bring their treasons to a bloody end.

ANTONY

I fear not those that to their weapons fly,
And keep their state in Spain, in Spain to die.

CAESAR

Whom fear'st thou then, Mark Antony?

ANTONY

The hateful crew,
That wanting power in field to conquer you,
Have in their coward souls devisèd snares
To murder thee, and take thee at unwares.°

CAESAR

Will those conspire my death that live by me?

ANTONY

In conquered foes what credit can there be?[28]

CAESAR

Besides their lives, I did their goods restore.

ANTONY

Oh, but their country's good concerns them more.

CAESAR

What, think they me to be their country's foe?

---

[27] The phrase 'doth them defend' is not in the original. Garnier: 'les va guidant' ('leading them', p. 63r). Kyd perhaps read 'cuidant' (taking care of them).

[28] This line marked as a *sententia* in Garnier: 'Aux ennemis domtez il n'y a point de foi' ('conquered enemies have no faith', p. 63r).

ANTONY
No, but that thou usurp'st the right they owe.°

CAESAR
To Rome have I submitted mighty things.

ANTONY
Yet Rome endures not the command of kings.

CAESAR
Who dares to contradict our empery?°

ANTONY
Those whom thy rule hath robbed of liberty.

CAESAR
I fear them not whose death is but deferred.

ANTONY
I fear my foe until he be interred.

CAESAR
A man may make his foe his friend, you know.

ANTONY
A man may easier make his friend his foe.

CAESAR
Good deeds the cruellest heart to kindness bring.

ANTONY
But resolution is a deadly thing.[29]

CAESAR
If citizens my kindness have forgot,
Whom shall I then not fear?

[29] 125–28] These lines marked as *sententiae* in Garnier (p. 63v). A similar debate between mercy and revenge is to be found in *Marc Antoine* (*Antonius*, IV. 150–87), with Octavius defending instead the advantages of suppressing one's enemies.

ANTONY
Those that are not.

CAESAR
What, shall I slay them all that I suspect?

ANTONY
Else cannot Caesar's empery° endure.

CAESAR
Rather I will my life and all neglect!
Nor labour I my vain life to assure,
But so to die, as dying I may live,
And leaving off this earthly tomb of mine,
Ascend to heav'n upon my wingèd deeds.
And shall I not have livèd long enough,
That in so short a time am so much famed?
Can I too soon go taste Cocytus' flood?[30]
No, Antony, death cannot injure us,[31]
For he lives long that dies victorious.

ANTONY
Thy praises show thy life is long enough,
But for thy friends and country, all too short.
Should Caesar live as long as Nestor[32] did,
Yet Rome may wish his life eternizèd.

CAESAR
Heav'n sets our time, with heav'n may nought dispense.

ANTONY
But we may shorten time with negligence.

CAESAR
But Fortune and the heav'ns have care of us.

---

[30] Cocytus was one of the rivers of the classical underworld.
[31] A simplification of Garnier: 'Hastive ores ne peut la mort siller mes yeux' ('Death could not be hasty that now would close my eyes', p. 63v).
[32] Mythical king of Pylus (see Garnier: 'Pylien Nestor'), appearing in Homer as the figure of the wise and experienced old man.

ANTONY

Fortune is fickle, heaven imperious.

CAESAR

What shall I then do?

ANTONY

As befits your state,
Maintain a watchful guard about your gate.

CAESAR

What more assurance may our state defend
Than love of those that do on us attend?

ANTONY

There is no hatred more, if it be moved,
Than theirs whom we offend and once beloved.[33]

CAESAR

Better it is to die than be suspicious.[34]

ANTONY

'Tis wisdom yet not to be credulous.

CAESAR

The quiet life that carelessly is led,
Is not alonely happy in this world,
But death itself doth sometime pleasure us.
That death that comes unsent for or unseen,
And suddenly doth take us at unware,
Methinks is sweetest. And if heav'n were pleased,
I could desire that I might die so well.
The fear of evil doth afflict us more,
Than th'evil itself, though it be ne'er so sore.

[*Exeunt* CAESAR *and* ANTONY.]

---

[33] An expansion of Garnier: 'il n'est telle rancueur qu'elle est de citoyens' ('there is no worse hatred than that of citizens', p. 64r).

[34] See Plutarch, *Life of Caesar*, LVII. 4 and North's translation: '[Caesar] said, it was better to dye once, th[a]n alwayes to be affrayed of death' (*Lives*, p. 790).

A CHORUS OF CAESAR'S FRIENDS

O fair sun, that gently smiles
From the orient-pearlèd isles,[35]
Gilding these our gladsome days
With the beauty of thy rays:
Free from rage of civil strife,
Long preserve our Caesar's life
That from sable Afrique brings
Conquests whereof Europe rings.
And fair Venus, thou of whom
The Eneades are come,[36]
Henceforth vary not thy grace
From Iulus' happy race.[37]
Rather cause thy dearest son,
By his triumphs new begun,
To expel from forth the land
Fierce war's quenchless fire-brand;
That of care acquitting us,
Who at last adore him thus,
He a peaceful star appear,
From our walls all woes to clear.
And so let his warlike brows
Still be decked with laurel boughs,
And his statuès new set
With many a fresh-flow'red coronet.°[38]
So in every place let be
Feasts and masques, and mirthful glee,[39]
Strewing roses in the street,
When their emperor they meet.
He his foes hath conquerèd,
Never leaving till they fled,
And abhorring blood,[40] at last

[35] Garnier: 'Des bords perleux de l'Orient' ('from Orient's pearly shores', p. 64r).
[36] The descendants of Aeneas. According to Virgil, Venus was the mother of Aeneas, the mythical founder of the *gens Iulia*, and therefore Caesar's ancestor.
[37] See note above. Iulus was the son of Aeneas.
[38] Garnier: 'De lauriers revestues' ('bedecked with laurels', p. 64v).
[39] An expansion of Garnier: 'on n'aperçoive que festons' ('let there be wreathes everywhere', p. 64v).
[40] Compare with Garnier: 'sans meurtrir personne' ('without harming anyone', p. 64v). See above, p. 236, n. 16.

Pardoned all offences past.
For high Jove the heavens among —
Their support that suffer wrong —[41]
Doth oppose himself again
Bloody-minded cruel men.
For he shorteneth their days,
Or prolongs them with dispraise;[42]
Or, his greater wrath to show,
Gives them over to their foe.
Caesar, a citizen so wronged
Of the honour him belonged,[43]
To defend himself from harms
Was enforced to take up arms.
For he saw that Envy's dart,
Pricking still their poisoned heart
For his sudden glory got,
Made his envious foe so hot.
Wicked Envy, feeding still,
Foolish those that do thy will!
For thy poisons in them pour
Sundry passions every hour,
And to choler[44] doth convert
Purest blood about the heart;
Which, o'erflowing of their breast,
Suff'reth nothing to digest.
Other men's prosperity
Is their infelicity,
And their choler then is raised,
When they hear another praised.
Neither Phoebus' fairest eye,
Feasts, nor friendly company,
Mirth, or whatsoe'er it be,
With their humour can agree.
Day or night they never rest,
Spiteful Hate so pecks their breast,

[41] 'Their support …' refers to 'high Jove'.
[42] This line added by Kyd.
[43] i.e. that is due to him.
[44] i.e. bile. According to Galen's theory of humours, envy was related to an excess of bile in the body.

Pinching their perplexèd° lungs
With her fiery poisoned tongues;
Fire-brands in their breasts they bear,
As if Tisiphon[45] *were there;*
And their souls are pierced as sore
As Prometheus' ghost, and more.
Wretches, they are woe-begone,
For their wound is always o'en,[46]
Nor hath Chiron[47] *power or skill*
To recure° them of their ill.

[*Exit* CHORUS.]

[45] Tisiphone, one of the Furies, who pursued murderers with firebrands.
[46] i.e. open. Garnier: 'la playe ne se ferme point' ('their wound never heals', p. 65r).
[47] The eldest and wisest of Centaurs. These half-man, half-horse, mythological creatures were credited with curing skills.

ACT V

[*Enter*] MESSENGER, CORNELIA [*and*] CHORUS.

MESSENGER [*aside*]

Unhappy man, amongst so many wracks°[1]
As I have suffered both by land and sea,
That scornful destiny[2] denies my death!
Oft have I seen the ends of mightier men,
Whose coats of steel base death hath stol'n into;
And in this direful war, before mine eyes,
Beheld their corpses scattered on the plains,
And endless numbers killing by my side,
Nor those ignoble, but the noblest lords;
'Mongst whom, above the rest that moves me most,
Scipio, my dearest master, is deceased.
And death, that sees the nobles' blood so rife,
Full-gorgèd triumphs,[3] and disdains my life!

CORNELIA

We are undone!

CHORUS

Scipio hath lost the day,
But hope the best, and harken to his news.

CORNELIA

O cruel Fortune!

MESSENGER [*aside*]

These misfortunes yet
Must I report to sad Cornelìa;
Whose ceaseless grief, which I am sorry for,
Will aggravate my former misery.

---

[1] Kyd omits two lines here: '… entre mille dangers | De fer, de feu, de sang, et de flots estrangers, | Entre mille trespas, entre mille traverses | Que j'ay souffert …' ('… among a thousand dangers | by the sword, by fire, by blood and by foreign seas, | among a thousand deaths and obstacles …', p. 65v).

[2] Garnier: 'la Parque me dédaigne' ('the Parcae ignore me', p. 65v).

[3] An expansion of: 'la mort assouvie | De tant de noble sang' ('Death [has been] sated | with so much noble blood', p. 65v).

CORNELIA

Wretch that I am, why leave I not the world?
Or wherefore am I not already dead?
O world! O wretch!

CHORUS

Is this th'undaunted heart
That is required in extremities?
Be more confirmed!° And Madam, let not grief
Abuse your wisdom like a vulgar wit.
Haply° the news is better than the noise:[4]
Let's hear him speak.

CORNELIA

Oh no, for all is lost!
Farewell dear father!

CHORUS

He is saved perhaps.

MESSENGER

[*Aside*] Methinks I hear my master's daughter speak.
— What sighs, what sobs, what plaints,° what passiòns
Have we endured, Cornelia, for your sake![5]

CORNELIA

Where is thine emperor?[6]

MESSENGER

Where our captains are.[7]
Where are our legions? Where our men at arms?
Or where so many of our Roman souls?
The earth, the sea, the vultures and the crows,
Lions and bears are their best sepulchres.

---

[4] Compare with Garnier: 'Peut-être la route est moindre que le bruit' ('our loss may be lesser than the rumour', p. 65v).

[5] Garnier has: '… quelles pleurs | Suffiront, Cornelie, a plaindre vos malheurs' ('… will be enough, Cornelia, to mourn your misfortunes', p. 65v).

[6] The title of *imperator* was originally granted to successful military commanders.

[7] Garnier has a question: 'Où sont nos Capitaines?' ('Where are our captains?', p. 65v).

CORNELIA

Oh, miserable!

CHORUS

Now I see the heavens
Are heaped with rage and horror 'gainst this house.

CORNELIA

O earth, why op'st° thou not?[8]

CHORUS

Why wail you so?
Assure yourself that Scipio bravely died,
And such a death excels a servile life.[9]

[CORNELIA]

Say, Messenger.

[CHORUS][10]

The manner of his end
Will haply° comfort this your discontent.

CORNELIA

Discourse the manner of his hard mishap,
And what disastrous accident did break
So many people bent so much to fight.

MESSENGER[11]

Caesar, that wisely knew his soldiers' hearts,
And their desire to be approved° in arms,

---

[8] Garnier invokes instead the Parcae sisters: 'Venez me prendre, ô Parque' ('Come and fetch me, Parcae', p. 66r).

[9] An expansion of the original: 'Il est mort vaillament, n'est-il pas mieux que nous?' ('He bravely died, is he not more fortunate than we are?', p. 66r).

[10] We follow Garnier here in attributing the cue, 'Say Messenger' ('Or conte Messager', p. 66r) to Cornelia. The 1594 edition omits this change, but includes a line-break after the cue, which usually indicates a change of speaker, although Cornelia is not named.

[11] The Messenger's report of the battle, or of the death of key characters represents a set speech, a *passage obligé* of neoclassical tragedy. According to Ternaux (p. 126), this is the longest in Garnier's entire œuvre. Boas notes many parallels between this speech and that of the General in *The Spanish Tragedy*, I. 2.

Sought nothing more than to encounter us.
And therefore faintly skirmishing in craft,[12]
Lamely they fought, to draw us further on.
Oft to provoke our wary well-taught troops,
He would attempt the entrance on our bars,°
Nay, ev'n our trenches, to our great disgrace,
And call our soldiers cowards to their face.
    But when he saw his wiles,[13] nor bitter words
Could draw our captains to endanger us,
Coasting along and following by the foot,
He thought to tire and weary us from thence;
And got his willing hosts°[14] to march by night,
With heavy armour on their hardened backs,[15]
Down to the seaside. Where before fair Thapsus,[16]
He made his pioneers (poor weary souls![17])
The selfsame day to dig and cast new trenches
And plant strong barricades. Where he, encamped,
Resolved by force to hold us hard at work.
Scipio no sooner heard of his designs,
But being afeared to lose so fit a place,
Marched on the sudden to the self-same city,
Where few men might do much,[18] which made him see
Of what importance such a town would be.
    The fields are spread, and as a household camp
Of creeping emmets in a country farm,[19]
That come to forage when the cold begins,
Leaving their crannies to go search about,
Cover the earth so thick, as scarce we tread
But we shall see a thousand of them dead;
    Ev'n so our battles° scattered on the sands

[12] The phrase 'in craft' is Kyd's addition.

[13] i.e. his guiles, his stratagems. Kyd's addition.

[14] Garnier simply has: 'fait marcher son armee' ('marches his troops', p. 66r).

[15] Here again, Kyd intensifies Caesar's soldiers' efforts; see Garnier: 'les armes sur le dos' ('carrying ther arms on their backs', p. 66r).

[16] See above, p. 183, n. 8.

[17] Compare with Garnier: 'ses gens lassez' ('his weary men', p. 66r).

[18] Garnier writes instead, following Hirtius, that the city was defended by a commander named Virgil, with few soldiers: 'avec peu de gens y commandait Virgile' (p. 66v).

[19] The comparison of troops to ants ('emmets') is an epic commonplace; see for example *Aeneid*, IV. 402–07.

Did scour the plains in pursuit of the foe.
One while at Thapsus we begin t'entrench,
To ease our army if it should retire;
Another while we softly sally forth,
And wakeful Caesar that doth watch our being,
When he perceives us marching o'er the plain,
Doth leap for gladness; and, to murder vowed,
Runs to the tent for fear we should be gone,
And quickly claps his rusty armour on.
For true it is, that Caesar brought at first
An host° of men to Afrique, meanly armed,[20]
But such as had brave spirits, and combating,
Had power and wit to make a wretch a king.[21]
Well, forth to field they marchèd all at once,
Except some few that stayed to guard the trench.
Them Caesar soon and subtly[22] sets in rank;
And every regiment, warned with a word
Bravely to fight for honour of the day.
He shows that ancient soldiers need not fear
Them that they had so oft disorderèd,
Them that already dreamed of death or flight,
That, tired, would ne'er hold out, if once they see
That they o'erlaid them[23] in the first assault.
Meanwhile, our emperor,[24] at all points armed,
Whose silver hairs and honourable front
Were warlike locked within a plumèd cask,°
In one hand held his targe° of steel embossed,
And in the other grasped his coutelas;
And with a cheerful look surveyed the camp,
Exhorting them to charge and fight like men,
And to endure whate'er betided° them.
'For now, quoth he, is come that happy day,

[20] Garnier: 'qui n'avoyent rien que la targue et la pique, | Le fer dessur le dos' ('who had nothing but shields and spears, | and their plates on their backs', p. 66v). According to Hirtius, Scipio's troops were not only more numerous than Caesar's, but they also had war elephants.
[21] Compare with Garnier: 'sçavoient faire un Colonel vaincueur' ('knew how make their colonel victorious', p. 66v).
[22] The word 'subtly' is Kyd's addition.
[23] i.e. if they [Scipio's soldiers] see that Caesar's troops overpower them.
[24] i.e. our leader. Scipio gained the title of *imperator* for his victorious campaign in Turkey.

Wherein our country shall approve° our love.
Brave Romans, know, this is the day and hour
That we must all live free, or friendly die.
For my part, being an ancient senator,
An emperor and consul,[25] I disdain
The world should see me to become a slave.[26]
I'll either conquer, or this sword you see —
Which brightly shone — shall make an end of me.
  We fight not, we, like thieves, for others' wealth.
We fight not, we, t'enlarge our scant confines;
To purchase fame to our posterities,
By stuffing of our trophies in their houses;
But 'tis for public freedom that we fight,
For Rome we fight, and those that fled for fear!
Nay more, we fight for safety of our lives,
Our goods, our honours, and our ancient laws.[27]
As for the Empire, and the Roman state,
Due to the victor, thereon ruminate:°
  Think how this day the honourable dames,
With blubbered eyes, and hands to heav'n upreared,[28]
Sit invocating for us to the gods,
That they will bless our holy purposes.
Methinks I see poor Rome in horror clad,[29]
And agèd senators, in sad discourse,
Mourn for our sorrows and their servitude.
Methinks I see them, while lamenting thus,[30]
Their hearts and eyes lie hov'ring over us.
  On, then, brave men, my fellows and Rome's friends,
To show us worthy of our ancestors!
And let us fight with courage and conceit,

---

[25] Scipio was consul with Pompey for the year 52 BC.

[26] See Lucan, *Pharsalia*, VII. 382: 'ne discam servire senex' ('so that I should not be taught to serve in my old age'), as noted by Ternaux (p. 128).

[27] Compare with Garnier: 'les loix' ('our laws', p. 67r).

[28] Kyd's addition, see above, p. 202, n. 48.

[29] Garnier: 'en horreur' (p. 67r). The clothing metaphor is probably motivated by the Latin use of 'horrens' in reference to mourning attire (see below, 'mourn for our sorrows').

[30] Refers to 'them', i.e. 'aged senators'; see Garnier: 'tous larmoyeux' ('all teary-eyed', p. 67r).

That we may rest the masters of the field;
That this brave tyrant valiantly beset
May perish in the press before our faces;
And that his troops, as touched with lightning flames,
May by our horse° in heaps be overthrown,
And he, blood-thirsting, wallow in his own.'[31]
  This said.[32] His army, crying all at once,
With joyful tokens[33] did applaud his speeches;
Whose swift shrill noise did pierce into the clouds,
Like northern winds that beat the hornèd Alps.[34]
The clatt'ring armour buskling° as they paced
Rang through the forests with a frightful noise,[35]
And every echo took the trumpets' clang;
When, like a tempest raised with whirlwind's rage,
They ran at ever'each other hand and foot,
Wherewith the dust, as with a darksome cloud
Arose, and overshadowed horse and man.
The darts and arrows on their armour glanced
And with their fall the trembling earth was shaken.
The air, that thickened with their thund'ring cries,
With pale wan clouds discolourèd the sun.
The fire in sparks from forth their armour flew
And with a duskish yellow choked the heavens.
The battles° locked,[36] with bristle-pointed spears
Do at the half-pike° freely charge each other
And dash together like two lusty bulls[37]

---

[31] The specific mention of Caesar's death is not in the original: 'Et que ses bataillons [...] ensanglantent la poudre' ('let his bataillons [...] soak the dust with blood', p. 67v).

[32] i.e., so he spoke. Garnier: 'Ainsi dit' (p. 67v). Garnier follows the usual framing of battle speeches in epic poetry.

[33] i.e., signs of joy.

[34] Garnier: 'aux Alpes cornues' ('the horned Alps', p. 67v), a commonplace epithet in French Renaissance poetry.

[35] A slight departure from the original, in which the army's shouts resound through the woods.

[36] In military terms, to lock the lines (here, 'battles'), is to set them as close together as possible. Garnier: 'les bataillons serrez' (p. 67v).

[37] This epic simile is taken from *Aeneid*, XII. 715–22: 'velut [...] | Cum duo conversis inimica in proelia tauri | Frontibus incurrunt', etc. ('As [...] when two bulls, competing in fierce battle, run head to head', etc.). Kyd is actually closer to Virgil than Garnier.

That, jealous of the heifer in the herd,
Run head to head, and sullen will not yield,
Till, dead or fled, the one forsake the field.
   The shivered° lances, rattling in the air,
Fly forth as thick as motes about the sun;[38]
When with their sword, fleshed° with the former fight,
They hew their armour, and they cleave their casks,°
Till streams of blood like rivers fill the downs;°
That being infected with the stench thereof
Surcloys[39] the ground, and of a champant° land
Makes a quagmire, where knee-deep they stand.
   Blood-thirsty Discord,[40] with her snaky hair,
A fearful° hag with fire-darting eyes,
Runs 'cross the squadrons with a smoky brand;°
And with her murd'ring whip encourageth
The over-forward° hands to blood and death.
   Bellona[41] fired with a quenchless rage
Runs up and down, and in the thickest throng,
Cuts, casts the ground, and madding° makes a pool
Which in her rage, free passage doth afford,
That with our blood she may anoint her sword.
   Now we, of our side, urge° them to retreat,
And now before them we retire as fast.
As on the Alps, the sharp north-northeast wind
Shaking a pine tree with their greatest power,
One while the top doth almost touch the earth,
And then it riseth with a counterbuff;°[42]

---

[38] Garnier: 'comme fétus' ('like chaff', p. 67v). Compare with *Spanish Tragedy*, I. 2. 54: 'And shivered Launces darke the troubled aire' (see Erne, *Beyond the Spanish Tragedy*, p. 55).

[39] i.e. gorges the ground. Refers back to 'blood'.

[40] The goddess Discordia, as depicted in Virgil's *Aeneid*, VI. 280–81: 'Discordia demens | Vipereum crinem vittis innexa cruentis' ('raging Discord, her snaky hair coiled in bloody knots'). Garnier: 'La discorde sanglante, à longs serpens crineuse' ('Bloody discord, with her long curls of snakes', p. 68r).

[41] Ancient goddess of war. Her presence on the battlefield, together with Discord, is an epic commonplace. See for example Virgil's *Aeneid*, VIII. 703–04; 'Et scissa gaudens vadit Discordia palla | Qua cum sanguineo sequitur Bellona flagello' ('And Discord in her torn robes joyously treads, followed by Bellona with her bloody whip'). See also *Spanish Tragedy*, I. 2. 52: 'Now while Bellona rageth heere and there' (as noted by Erne, *Beyond the Spanish Tragedy*, p. 55).

[42] The epic simile of the tree shaken by the winds originates in *Aeneid*, IV. 441–43:

So did the armies press and charge at each other,
With selfsame courage, worth, and weapons too;
And prodigal of life for liberty,[43]
With burning hate let each at other fly.
Thrice did the cornets of the soldiers, cleared,
Turn to the standard to be new supplied;[44]
And thrice the best of both was fain to breathe;
And thrice recomforted, they bravely ran
And fought as freshly as they first began;
Like two fierce lions fighting in a desert[45]
To win the love of some fair lioness,
When they have vomited their long-grown rage,
And proved° each other's force sufficìent,
Passant regardant[46] softly their retire,
Their jawbones dyed with foaming froth and blood,
Their lungs, like sponges, rammed within their sides,
Their tongues discovered, and their tails long trailing,
Till jealous rage, engenderèd with rest,
Returns them sharper set than at the first,
And makes them couple when they see their prize,
With bristled backs, and fire-sparkling eyes,
Till tired or conquered, one submits or flies.[47]
Caesar, whose kinglike looks like day-bright stars
Both comfort and encourage his to fight,

'Ac velut [...] quercum | Alpini Boreae nunc hinc nunc flatibus illinc | Erruere inter se certant' ('Like [...] an oak, which the northern winds of the Alps blow here and there as they strive to uproot it'). Garnier: 'quand la Bize et le Nort | Contre-soufflent un Pin' ('when the North and North-east winds | toss a pine tree back and forth', p. 68r).

[43] The phrase 'for liberty' is Kyd's addition. Garnier: 'Couroient à la victoire, et prodigues de vie' ('They ran to victory, prodigal with their lives', p. 68r).

[44] i.e. the lines of soldiers, thinned out (by the battle), turn back to their standards. 'Cornets' is here used in the military sense, designating the wing of an army. Garnier: 'les bataillons esclaircis de soldars | S'allèrent rallier dessous les estendars' ('the thinned out battalions | gathered under their standards', p. 68r).

[45] See Lucan's *Pharsalia*, I. 205–10, and Marlowe's translation: 'Like a lion of scorched desert Afric, | Who seeing hunters pauseth till fell wrath | And kingly rage increase, then having whisked | His tail athwart his back, and crest heav'd up, | With jaws wide open ghastly roaring out' (*Lucans first booke*, sig. [B4v]).

[46] A term of heraldry, indicating that a beast is walking with its front paw raised, while looking back over its shoulder. Kyd's addition; see Garnier: 'à trois pas se retirent' ('take three steps back', p. 68v).

[47] Garnier: 'tant que l'un des deux meure' ('until one of them dies', p. 68v).

Marched through the battle° laying still about him[48]
And subtly marked whose hand was happiest;
Who nicely did but dip his spear in blood,
And who more roughly smeared it to his fist;
Who, staggering, fell with every feeble wound,
And who, more strongly, paced it through the thickest:[49]
Him he enflamed, and spurred, and filled with horror;
As when Alecto[50] in the lowest hell
Doth breathe new heat within Orestes' breast,
Till outward rage with inward grief begins,
A fresh remembrance of our former sins.[51]
For then, as if provoked with pricking goads,
Their warlike armies, fast locked foot to foot,[52]
Stooping their heads, low bent to toss their staves,
They fiercely open both battalions,[53]
Cleave, break, and raging tempest-like o'erturn,
Whate'er makes head to meet them in this humour.
Our men at arms, in brief, begin to fly;
And neither prayers, entreaty, nor example
Of any of their leaders left alive
Had power to stay them in this strange career:
Straggling, as in the fair Calabrian fields,[54]
When wolves for hunger ranging from the wood
Make forth amongst the stock, that scattered flies
Before the shepherd, that resistless lies.[55]

---

[48] i.e. marched among his troops, who stood silent around him. This and the following five lines echo Lucan's *Pharsalia*, VII. 558–65.

[49] Garnier mentions instead 'those who fall and die in the fray': 'ceux qui trespassoyent estendus dans la presse' (p. 68v). Kyd's version is perhaps motivated by *Pharsalia*, VII. 564: 'Quem pugnare juvet' ('who fights with joy').

[50] One of the Furies, who pursued Orestes and drove him to madness for the murder of his mother, Clytemnestra.

[51] Kyd's addition, echoing the 1559 *Book of Common Prayer*: 'the remembrance of them [our sins] is grievous unto us; the burden of them is intolerable' (from the 'General Confession' in the Order of the Holy Communion).

[52] See above, p. 261, n. 36.

[53] Garnier has: 'ouvrent [...] les phalanges Libyques' ('break the Lybian phalanxes', i.e. Scipio's, p. 68v).

[54] Calabria is the region lying at the extreme south of Italy. The wolf simile echoes Virgil's *Aeneid*, IX. 59–68. See also *Antonius*, II. 2. 116.

[55] Garnier writes, on the contrary: 'Aux yeux de leurs bergers, qui hardis les desfendent' ('before the eyes of the shepherds, who valiantly defend them', p. 68v).

CORNELIA

O cruel fortune!

MESSENGER

None resisting now,
The field was filled with all confusìon
Of murder, death, and direful massacres.
The feeble bands that yet were left entire
Had more desire to sleep than seek for spoil.[56]
No place was free from sorrow, everywhere
Lay armèd men, o'ertrodden with their horses.
Dismembered bodies, drowning in their blood,
And wretched heaps, lie mourning of their maims;
Whose blood, as from a sponge, or bunch of grapes
Crushed in a wine-press,[57] gusheth out so fast,
As with the sight doth make the sound aghast.
Some should you see that had their heads half-cloven,[58]
And on the earth their brains lie trembling.
Here one new wounded helps another dying;[59]
Here lay an arm, and there a leg lay shivered;°
Here horse and man, o'erturned, for mercy cried,
With hands extended to the merciless,
That stopped their ears, and would not hear a word,
But put them all, remorseless, to the sword.
He that had hap° to 'scape doth help afresh
To reinforce the side whereon he served.
But seeing that there, the murd'ring enemy
Pell-mell° pursued them like a storm of hail,
They gan° retire where Juba was encamped;

[56] These two lines are not in the original. Garnier, according to his usual metaphor, evokes whole companies falling down in heaps like sheaves of wheat: 'les bandes entieres | Trebuchoyent plus espois que javelles blatieres' ('whole companies of men | fell to the ground more thickly than harvested wheat', p. 69r).

[57] Garnier: 'ou l'amas raisineux | Qu'un pesant fust escache en un pressouer vineux' ('the mass of grapes | crushed under a heavy plank in the winepress', p. 69r). Kyd's succint rendering is reminiscent of Revelation 14. 20: 'And the winepress was trodden without the city, and blood came out of the winepress' (Geneva Bible).

[58] The graphic description of mutilated bodies is an epic commonplace. Compare also with *Spanish Tragedy*, I. 2. 57–62 (as noted by Boas, pp. 433–34).

[59] Not in the original; Garnier evokes soldiers holding their slippery entrails as they die: 'soustenoyent | De leurs mourantes mains leurs boyaux qui trainoyent' (p. 69r).

But there had Caesar eftsoons° tyrannized,[60]
So that, despairing to defend themselves,
They lay aside their armour, and at last,
Offered to yield unto the enemy,
Whose stony heart,[61] that ne'er did Roman good
Would melt with nothing but their dearest blood.

[CORNELIA][62]

And Scipio, my father?

[MESSENGER]

When he beheld
His people so discomfited and scorned;
When he perceived the labour profitless,
To seek by new encouraging his men,
To come upon them with a fresh alarm;
And when he saw the enemy's pursuit
To beat them down as fierce as thund'ring flints,
And lay them level with the chargèd earth,
Like ears of corn[63] with rage of windy show'rs,
Their battles° scattered, and their ensigns taken;
And to conclude, his men dismayed to see
The passage choked with bodies of the dead;
Incessantly lamenting th'extreme loss
And souspirable° death of so brave soldiers,
He spurs his horse,[64] and breaking through the press,
Trots to the haven, where his ships he finds,
And hopeless trusteth to the trustless winds.
Now had he thought to have arrived in Spain
To raise new forces and return to field;
But as one mischief° draws another on,

---

[60] The expression is Kyd's. Garnier has: 'de malheur l'occupait' ('unfortunately occupied it', p. 69r).

[61] Garnier: 'd'un cœur endurci' ('with a hardened heart', p. 69r). As noted by Lovascio, Kyd here echoes Caesar's 'Complaint' in the 1587 edition of the *Mirror for Magistrates* (405–06): 'my stony heart and breast | Received so many wounds for just revenge ...'. The phrase may also be traced to Ezekiel 36. 26: 'I will take away the stony heart out of your body' (Geneva Bible).

[62] The cue is obviously Cornelia's ('my father'). The copy-text omits her name, although the cue is followed by a line-break, which usually indicates a change of speaker.

[63] Kyd's addition, probably to compensate for the omitted metaphor at l. 246–47.

[64] Not mentioned in Garnier, who has Scipio simply 'make his way' to the haven ('chemina vers le port', p. 69v).

A sudden tempest takes him by the way,
And casts him up near the coasts of Hippon,[65]
Where th'adverse navy, sent to scour the seas,
Did hourly keep their ordinary course;
Wherein, seeing himself at anchor, slightly° shipped,[66]
Besieged, betrayed by wind, by land, by sea —
All raging mad to rig his better vessels,
The little while this naval conflict lasted —
Behold! His own[67] was fiercely set upon:
Which being sore beaten, till it brake again
Ended the lives of his best fighting men.
  There did the remnant of our Roman nobles,
Before the foe, and in their captain's presence,
Die bravely, with their falchions° in their fists.
Then Scipio, that saw his ships through-galled,°
And by the foe fulfilled[68] with fire and blood,
His people put to sword, sea, earth and hell,
And heav'n itself conjured to injure him,
Stepped to the poop, and with a princely visage[69]
Looking upon his weapon dyed with blood,
Sighing, he set it to his breast, and said:
'Since all our hopes are by the gods beguiled,
What refuge now remains for my distress,
But thee, my dearest, ne'er-deceiving sword?
Yea, thee, my latest fortunes' firmest hope:
By whom I am assured this hap° to have,
That being free born, I shall not die a slave.'
  Scarce had he said, but cruelly resolved
He wrenched° it to the pommel through his sides,

---

[65] In Northern Africa, see the Argument and p. 183, n. 10.

[66] Equipped with less ships. Lines 298–304 are a significant departure from the original, where Caesar's navy see Scipio in a disadvantageous posture, and attack his ships, causing the death of Scipio's best soldiers: 'Qui le voyant à l'ancre avec peu de vaisseaux, | Assiegé de la terre, et du vent, et des eaux | L'investit de furie, enfonçant en peu d'heures | Que dura le combat, ses navires meilleures: | Le sien fut assailli, qui debatu long temps | Fist terminer la vie aux meilleurs combatans' ('seeing his few ships at anchor, | besieged at once by [the troops on] land, by the winds, and the waters, | [Caesar] furiously attacked him, and in a few hours | of battle sunk his best ships. | [Scipio']s own ship was assailed, and the long ensuing fight | put an end to the lives of his best soldiers', p. 69v).

[67] i.e. his own ship.

[68] An intensive form of 'filled', obviously for the sake of alliteration.

[69] Garnier: 'd'un visage franc' (p. 69v), i.e. calm, even.

That from the wound the smoky° blood[70] ran bubbling:
Wherewith he staggered, and I stepped to him
To have embraced him. But he, being afraid
T'attend° the mercy of his murd'ring foe,
That still pursued him and oppressed his ships,
Crawled to the deck, and life with death to ease,[71]
Headlong he threw himself into the seas.

CORNELIA

O cruel Gods! O heav'n! O direful Fates!
O radiant sun that slightly° gild'st our days!
O night stars, full of infelicities!
O triple-titled Hecat,[72] queen and goddess,
Bereave my life, or living strangle me!
Confound me quick, or let me sink to hell!
Thrust me from forth the world, that 'mongst the spirits
Th'infernal lakes[73] may ring with my laments.
O miserable, desolate, distressful wretch,
Worn with mishaps, yet in mishaps abounding!
What shall I do, or whither shall I fly
To venge° this outrage, or revenge my wrongs?
    Come, wrathful Furies with your ebon locks,[74]
And feed yourselves with mine enflamèd blood!
Ixion's torment, Sysiph's rolling stone,
And th'eagle tiring on Prometheus,[75]
Be my eternal tasks, that th'extreme fire
Within my heart may from my heart retire.
    I suffer more, more sorrows I endure
Than all the captives in th'infernal court.[76]
O troubled Fate! O fatal misery,

[70] A literal rendition of Garnier: 'le sang chaud et fumeux sortit en bouillonnant' ('his hot, smoking blood flowed out in bubbling streams', p. 70r).

[71] Kyd's addition. Garnier has: 'roidissant les bras' ('his arms stiffening', p. 70r).

[72] Hecate, goddess of the night, often associated with the moon, and usually represented in three forms.

[73] On the lakes of Hades, see above, p. 195, n. 1.

[74] On the Furies, see above, p. 97, n. 7.

[75] On Ixion and Prometheus, see above, p. 105, n. 5 and p. 103, n. 42, respectively. Sisyphus had been condemned by Jupiter to endlessly push a boulder up a hill, only to see it roll back down every time.

[76] Garnier has 'aux infernaux palus' ('the infernal marshes', p. 70v), in reference to the lakes of the underworld.

That unprovokèd deal'st so partially!
Say, fretful heav'ns, what fault have I committed
Or wherein could mine innocence offend you,
When, being but young, I lost my first love, Crassus?
Oh, wherein did I merit so much wrong
To see my second husband Pompey slain?
But 'mongst the rest, what horrible offence,
What hateful thing unthought of have I done,[77]
That, in the midst of this my mournful state,
Nought by my father's death could expiate?
Thy death, dear Scipio, Rome's eternal loss,[78]
Whose hopeful life preserved our happiness;
Whose silver hairs encouragèd the weak;
Whose resolutions did confirm° the rest;
Whose end, sith° it hath ended all my joys,
O heav'ns at least permit, of all these plagues
That I may finish the catastrophe,
Sith° in this widowhood of all my hopes
I cannot look for further happiness!
For, both my husbands and my father gone,
What have I else to wreak your wrath upon?[79]
Now, as for happy thee, to whom sweet death
Hath given blessed rest for life's bereaving,
O envious Julia,[80] in thy jealous heart
Venge° not thy wrong upon Cornelia:
But, sacred ghost, appease thine ire,° and see
My hard mishap in marrying after thee.
Oh, see mine anguish! Haply° seeing it,
'Twill move compassion in thee of my pains,
And urge thee, if thy heart be not of flint,[81]

---

[77] An expansion of Garnier's 'qu'ay-je commis' ('what have I done', p. 70v).
[78] This and the following three lines added by Kyd, probably as an encomium of Henry Radcliffe, 4th Earl of Sussex, father-in-law to Kyd's dedicatee, who had presumably employed Kyd in the late 1580s, and who died in December 1593. See Introduction, pp. 51–52.
[79] i.e. for you to wreak, etc.
[80] Pompey's fourth wife, Caesar's daughter, who died in 53 BC. In Lucan's *Pharsalia*, III. 9–35, her jealous ghost appears to Pompey, tormenting him for marrying Cornelia, and predicting his death.
[81] Garnier uses instead the usual classical comparison to a tiger: 'le cœur | Plus que d'une Tigresse enyvré de rigueur' ('a heart | more drunk with cruelty than that of a tigress', p. 70v).

Or drunk with rigor, to repent thyself
That thou enflamedst so cruel a revenge
In Caesar's heart, upon so slight a cause;
And mad'st him raise so many mournful tombs,
Because thy husband did revive the lights[82]
Of thy forsaken bed; unworthily
Opposing of thy fretful jealousy,
'Gainst this mishap, as it my help had been,
Or as if second marriage were a sin![83]
    Was never city where calamity[84]
Hath sojourned with such sorrow as in this?
Was never state wherein the people stood
So careless of their conquered liberty,[85]
And careful of another's tyranny?
    O gods, that erst° of Carthage took some care,
Which by our fathers pitiless was spoiled;[86]
When thwarting destiny, at Afric° walls[87]
Did topside-turvy turn their commonwealth;
When forceful weapons fiercely took away
Their soldiers, sent to nourish up those wars;
When, fired, their golden palaces fell down;
    When through the slaughter th'Afric° seas were dyed,
And sacred temples quenchlessly enflamed;
Now is our hapless° time of hopes expired;
Then satisfy yourselves with this revenge,
Content to count the ghosts of those great captains,
Which, conquered, perished by the Roman swords!
The Hannons, the Hamilcars, Asdrubals,
Especially that proudest Hannibal,[88]

---

[82] In ancient Rome, wedding ceremonies involved the lighting of torches.
[83] This line added by Kyd.
[84] This and the following four lines are spoken by the Chorus in Garnier. We have not re-instated Garnier's speakers here because, contrary to the previous case (see p. 266, n. 61), the copy-text does not seem to indicate a missing cue.
[85] Garnier simply has 'la Liberté' ('liberty', p. 71r).
[86] On the Punic wars against Carthage, see above, p. 205, nn. 59 and 60.
[87] i.e. at the walls of Africa, a metonymy for Carthage. A slight departure from Garnier, who evokes fate fighting against Carthage's troops: 'le destin contraire aux phalanges d'Afrique' (p. 71r).
[88] All famous leaders of ancient Carthage. There were several famous warriors named Hanno (here spelled Hannon), but Garnier probably has in mind the general who caused the defeat of Carthage in the first Punic war. Hamilcar Barca fought against

That made the fair Thrasimene so desert.[89]
For e'en those fields that mourned to bear their bodies
Now laden groan to feel the Roman corpses.
Their earth we purple o'er, and on their tombs
We heap our bodies, equalling their ruin.
And as a Scipio did reverse their power,[90]
They have a Scipio to revenge them on.
   Weep therefore, Roman dames,[91] and from henceforth
Vailing° your crystal eyes to your fair bosoms,
Rain showers of grief upon your rose-like cheeks,
And dew yourselves with springtides of your tears.
Weep, ladies, weep, and with your reeking sighs
Thicken the passage of the purest clouds,
And press the air with your continual plaints.°
Beat at your ivory breasts, and let your robes,
Defaced and rent, be witness of your sorrows!
And let your hair, that wont° be wreathed in tresses,
Now hang neglect'ly,° dangling down your shoulders,
Careless of art, or rich accoutrements;
That with the gold and pearl we used before,
Our mournful habits may be decked no more.
   Alas, what shall I do? O dear companions,[92]
Shall I, oh, shall I live in these laments,
Widowed of all my hopes, my haps, my husbands,
And last, not least, bereft of my best father,
And of the joys mine ancestors enjoyed
When they enjoyed their lives and liberty?[93]
And must I live to see great Pompey's house,
A house of honour and antiquity,

---

the Romans in Sicily during the second Punic war; he had two sons, Hasdrubal, and the better-known Hannibal, who famously crossed the Alps with his elephants to fight Rome.

89 Garnier has: 'si roux' ('so red', p. 71r). The allusion is to the battle of Lake Thrasimene where the Roman troops were ambushed and massacred by Hannibal's army (217 BC).

90 Scipio Africanus, Cornelia's ancestor. See p. 205, n. 59.

91 417–30] In Garnier, this passage is spoken by the Chorus, not by Cornelia: 'Pleurons, ô troupe aimée', etc. ('Let us weep, beloved company …', pp. 71r–v).

92 Cornelia's final speech starts here in Garnier (p. 71v).

93 A punning expansion of Garnier's 'et du bien | Qu'avait en liberté mon lignage ancien' ('and of the possessions | that my ancient family freely enjoyed', p. 71v).

Usurped in wrong by lawless Antony?[94]
Shall I behold the sumptuous ornaments,
Which both the world and Fortune heaped on him,
Adorn and grace his graceless enemy?
Or see the wealth that Pompey gained in war,
Sold at a pike,° and borne away by strangers?
Die, rather die, Cornelia! And to spare
Thy worthless life that yet must one day perish,
Let not those captains vainly lie interred,
Or Caesar triumph in thine infamy,
That wer't the wife of th'one, and th'other's daughter!
But if I die before I have entombed
My drownèd father in some sepulchre,
Who will perform that care in kindness for me?
Shall his poor wand'ring limbs lie still tormented,
Tossed with the salt waves of the wasteful seas?[95]
No, lovely father, and my dearest husband,
Cornelia must live — though life she hateth —
To make your tombs, and mourn upon your hearses:
Where, languishing, my fumous[96] faithful tears
May trickling bathe your generous sweet cinders;
And afterward, both wanting strength and moisture,
Fulfilling° with my latest sighs and gasps
The happy vessels that enclose your bones,
I will surrender my surchargèd life,
And when my soul earth's prison shall forgo,[97]
Increase the number of the ghosts below.

[*Exeunt.*]

Non prosunt Domino quae prosunt omnibus | Artes.[98]

Tho[mas] Kyd.

[94] According to Plutarch, Mark Antony purchased Pompey's house (*Life of Antony*, x. 2).
[95] An expansion of 'les meurtieres vagues' ('the murderous waves', p. 71v).
[96] i.e. hot. A literal rendition of Garnier: 'mes pleurs fumeuses' (p. 71v).
[97] Kyd's metaphor, see *Spanish Tragedy*, I. 1. 1–2 (as noted by Boas, p. 436): 'When this eternall substance of my soule | Did live imprison'd in my wanton flesh …'. Garnier has: 'tombant legere Ombre' ('as I go down, a weightless shadow', p. 71v).
[98] Kyd's colophon. From Ovid's *Metamorphoses*, I. 524 ('the arts that help all others are of no use to their master').

TEXTUAL NOTES

Both Mary Sidney's *Antonius* and Thomas Kyd's *Cornelia* were issued twice. First published as *Antonius, a tragoedie* in 1592, Mary Sidney Herbert's translation was reprinted three years later under the title *The Tragedie of Antonie*. The copy-text for this edition is the first edition, as the second printing is derived from the first, with very few variants and a new title. The two editions have been collated, and the main variants are recorded below. Kyd's play was first published as *Cornelia* in 1594, then one year later as *Pompey the Great, his faire Corneliaes tragedie*. The 1595 edition is in fact a reissue of the 1594 edition with a new title page (and a new title). This edition has retained the first titles for both plays, because they seemed closer to the authors' intentions, although the variant titles are significant (see Introduction).

We have silently expanded and regularized speech tags and punctuation. Spelling has been fully modernized. The verb suffix -ed has been marked as -èd when sounded for reasons of versification. Elisions have also been indicated wherever they appeared necessary for metrical reasons — on the grounds that most of them were marked in the copy-text, which reflects an authorial or editorial concern for issues of versification.

Capitalization has not been retained, except in obvious cases of personifications, and neither has italicization, which was used mostly for proper names. Passages that were isolated typographically in the originals, either by inverted commas or italics (or Roman type for texts printed in italics, as in the case of *Antonius*), are printed here in italics. These lines represent *sententiae*, that is, passages usually bearing general didactic value (see Introduction on this practice, which is derived from classical drama). In the few instances where the translators do not visually isolate the *sententiae* (where Garnier had done so), a footnote has been added to indicate this.

Minimal stage directions have been added in square brackets where necessary to satisfy modern usage, because it is our belief that these plays were meant to be recited or performed. There are no stage directions as such in the original texts (nor in Garnier's texts for that matter, although they were indeed performed), which is in keeping with the conventions of neoclassical drama at the time. The names of the speakers are usually mentioned in a group at the beginning of each scene. Group entries have been split when needed, for clarity's sake, and, where missing, speech attributions have been inserted in square brackets. In classical tragedy the Chorus enters only once and remains on stage to comment on the action, but because in both plays Garnier resorts to a different Chorus in the course of the play, it has seemed justified to treat the Chorus as characters, i.e. to make them enter and exit, so the second Chorus could enter. In *Cornelia* the Chorus is in fact mentioned in the *dramatis personae* and treated as a character, even interacting with the characters in III. 1 and V.

All act numbers are indicated in the original texts in their Latin forms (except in *Antonius* where one act break is missing). The occasional missing act number has been reinstated in square brackets. There are no scene breaks in either of the plays (in French or English), and each act is usually composed of one long scene. In *Antonius*, however, Act II has been divided into two scenes, because Philostratus clears the stage before Cleopatra and her followers appear; and in *Cornelia*, Acts III and IV have been divided into three and two scenes, respectively, to comply with the entrances of new groups of characters.

MARY SIDNEY HERBERT, COUNTESS OF PEMBROKE: *ANTONIUS*

Antonius exists in two editions; no manuscript is extant. It was entered in the Stationers' Register on 3 May 1592, and was first published with a discourse by Philippe de Mornay also translated by Mary Sidney Herbert in a small unpaginated quarto (13 × 17.5 cm):

> A | Discourse of Life | *and Death.* | Written in French by *Ph.* | *Mornay.* | Antonius, | *A Tragœdie written also in French* | by *Ro. Garnier.* | Both done in English by the | *Countesse of Pembroke.* | AT LONDON, | Printed for *William Ponsonby.* | 1592.

The printer is identified by ESTC as John Windet. The text was reprinted separately three years later as a small unpaginated octavo (7 × 12.5 cm):

> THE | TRAGEDIE OF | Antonie. | *Doone into English by the* | Countesse of | *Pembroke* | [device] | Imprinted at London for *William* | *Ponsonby* 1595.

Both editions have the same running title: ANTONIUS. They are here identified as:

1592] STC 18138, *A discourse of life and death*
1595] STC 11623

Only five copies of the 1592 quarto of the play are extant; they are preserved in the British Library (BL C.57.d.16), the Library of Emmanuel College (Cambridge University), the Bodleian Library (Tanner 234(5), which lacks *A Discourse*), the Folger Library (STC 18138) and the Huntington Library (46000, which is the copy digitized for EEBO as STC 18138). The copy at the Beinecke Library at Yale is indicated in ESTC as missing *Antonius*.

Our copy text is 1592 STC 18138, the copy from the Huntington Library (which is a partially corrected version), and designated below as 1592. It is collated with the London copy of 1592 C.57.d.16 (BL 1592 below) and three 1595 copies, STC 11623 from the Huntington, and British Library C.57 aa.18 and G.11159. The copy shelf-marked BL C.57.d.16 is the only copy that includes duplicate versions of sig. F1, one the uncorrected state, the other the corrected F1: this BL copy also includes the corresponding uncorrected sig. F4, and an uncorrected state of G4. The pages in this copy are mounted on larger leaves, and sig. I1 is bound erroneously with the verso first. Only significant differences between the two 1592 copies have been listed below, however, as most changes affect spacing and spelling; the corrected 1592 occasionally introduces new mistakes.

The 1595 edition is derived from the 1592 corrected version, as indicated by several typographical mistakes that are introduced (errors of capitalization in the Choruses, for instance, or occasional missing letters or words), although some typographical errors of the 1592 edition were also corrected in 1595. However, the 1592 edition is relatively authoritative (see variants below).[1] It is believed that the printing might have been supervised by the Countess of Pembroke, who was a careful reader of her own work, as evidenced by one of her working copies of the *Psalms* singled out by the editors of the *Collected Works*; the relative imperfection of 1595 points to a lesser likelihood that she supervised that edition.[2] Printed, according to STC, by John Windet for William Ponsonby, 1592 is a quarto of thirteen quires of four leaves and one of two: A-N^4 O^2 (-E4). E4 is missing in all extant copies.[3] The play proper is: F-N^4 O^2. There are a few press variants which are listed in the *Collected Works*.[4] The list

[1] For a full history of the text, see *Collected Works*, I, p. 305–10. This edition lists some of the mistakes introduced by the 1595 edition (306).

[2] *Collected Works*, I, p. 307.

[3] E3, F3, I2, K3, L3, M3, O2 not signed, H3 signed H5, L2 signed L3.

[4] *Collected Works*, I, pp. 306–10.

of variants below mainly includes corrections to the copy text of 1592. Corrections in spelling and punctuation have not been recorded.

Ten copies of the octavo 1595 edition are preserved, in the British Library (C.57.aa.18 and G.11159), the Edinburgh University Library (De.2/1.52), the Bodleian Library (8° A 129 Linc.), the Victoria and Albert Museum National Art Library (Dyce 3944), the Newberry Library (VAULT Case 3A 546), the Folger Library (STC 11623), the Huntington Library (59871, which provides the electronic copy of STC 11623), the University of Texas at Austin Library (Pforz 398), Yale Beinecke Library (Hfb9 139q), and Williams College Chapin Library (STC 11623). The name of the printer, P[eter] S[hort], is derived from STC. The 1595 edition is an octavo of 7 quires of 8 leaves (A–G^8).

There are no major differences to report between the three 1595 copies (BL C.57.aa.18, BL G 11159, and Huntington 59871) collated for this edition, and they are all designated as 1595 in the list of variants.

Mary Sidney Herbert's translation is based on the 1585 edition of Robert Garnier's *Marc Antoine* in *Les Tragédies de Robert Garnier* (Paris: Mamert Patisson, 1585), which was the last to be revised by the author before his death. The play was first published in French in 1578 (*Marc Antoine, Tragedie*, Paris: Mamert Patisson, 1578), but we can be sure that Mary Sidney used the 1585 volume because her translation includes the numerous corrections specific to that edition, but none of the subsequent (non-authorial) changes.[5] We have also made use of the recent edition by Jean-Claude Ternaux (Paris: Classiques Garnier, 2010), which documents the variants in each edition.

The text was edited twice in the nineteenth century (see the list of editions in the bibliography) and seven times in the twentieth century. In 1865, Barnwell offered a modernized version of the 1595 text with no critical apparatus, while Luce produced the first scholarly, old-spelling edition in 1897, for which she chose the 1592 text as copy text (unfortunately this edition is erroneous in many instances). In the twentieth century, Sidney's *Antonius* has attracted a great deal of attention, first for its possible influence on Shakespeare's *Antony and Cleopatra*: an old-spelling version of the 1595 text was thus published by Geoffrey Bullough in *Narrative and Dramatic Sources*

[5] *Collected Works*, I, p. 307.

of Shakespeare in 1966, and Marvin Spevack also published a diplomatic edition of the 1592 text in *A New Variorum Edition of Shakespeare: Antony and Cleopatra* in 1990. From the 1980s onwards, however, *Antonius* was published three times in collections or anthologies of works by early modern women: first in a 1987 anthology edited by Katharina Wilson (which includes a slightly abridged, modernized version of the 1595 text, edited by Coburn Freer); then in two collections designed for students, a modern-spelling edition of the 1595 text edited by S. P. Cerasano and M. Wynne-Davies in 1996 (and still in print), and an old-spelling version of the 1595 text by Diane Purkiss for Penguin in 1998 (currently out of print). In 1998, Margaret Hannay, Noel J. Kinnamon and Michael G. Brennan published the first volume of the Clarendon *Collected Works* of Sidney, with an old-spelling edition of the 1592 text. They subsequently published a fully modernized version of this text in *Selected Works of Mary Sidney Herbert*, in 2005 in the *Medieval and Renaissance Texts and Studies* series in Arizona (also still in print).

While all the previous editions are valuable in their own right, this one differs from them by offering a fully modernized version of the 1592 text, collated with the 1595 text and checked against the French original, with a full critical apparatus.

Variants

Antonius, a Tragedy] no intermediate title-page in 1592 (in the general title of the work: Antonius, *A Tragœdie*); the Tragedie of Antonie 1595.

The Argument
1. liberty] 1592, 1595; libertin BL 1592 (cancelled F1)
7. Crassus] 1592, 1595; Cassius BL 1592 (cancelled F1); in his] 1592, 1595; into BL 1592 (cancelled F1)
11. pleasures] 1592, 1595; pleasure BL 1592 (cancelled F1)
17. Actium] 1592, 1595; Actin BL 1592 (cancelled F1)

Act I.
ANTONIUS] Speech heading as title in 1592; as running title 1595
21. Pelusium] 1595; Pelusuim 1592
34. forced] forste 1592, 1595
74. Cuirass] Curiace 1592, 1595
79. break'st] breakest 1592, 1595

86. Romans] Romanes 1595; Komanes 1592
89. fire-sparkling] fier sparkling 1592, 1595
119. low] loe 1592, BL 1592, 1595
123. thee] 1592, 1595; the BL 1592
124. sword] 1592, 1595; swoord BL 1592
129. caged] 1592, 1595, cag'de BL 1592
131. grief] 1592, 1595; gricf BL 1592
135. (alas!)] BL 1592; alas!) 1592, 1595
138. common] 1592, 1595; comon BL 1592
140. heart-killing] 1592, 1595; killing BL 1592
154. Sails] sayles 1592, 1595; Soules BL 1592
156. keeps] BL 1592; kepes 1592, 1595
164. rain] raine BL 1592; raigne 1592, 1595

Act II. Scene 1] No scene division in 1592, 1595
51. Firing] 1595; Fi'ring 1592
58. razeth] raiseth 1592, 1595
104. Ceyx's] Ceyx 1592, 1596
135. Myrrha's] Myrrhas 1592 (Mirrahs BL 1592); Mirrhas 1595. / doth] 1595; do 1592, BL 1592).
Scene 2] No scene division in 1592, 1595.
2. sun] Sunne 1592; sunne BL 1592, 1595
14. hatched] hatcht 1592, 1595; hatche BL 1592
16. stronger, lose] stronger, loose 1592, 1595; stronger loose BL 1592
26. lose] leese 1592, 1595 (archaic for lose)
171. deprive] 1595; deprive not 1592
179. left] 1595; lest 1592
205. albeit] albee 1592, 1595
239. estate] 1595; high st ate: 1592
261. dying] dieng 1592, 1595
333. enchanting] enchaunting 1595; e'nchaunting 1592
339. it aids] 1595; she aides 1592

Act III] Not in 1592, 1595
0. ANTONIUS] M. ANTONIUS] 1592, 1595
1. ANTONIUS] *M. Ant.* 1592, 1595
20. wears] wear 1592, 1595
23. LUCILIUS] 1595; Li. 1592
26. Actium overthrown] Actian overthrow 1592, 1595 (grammatical liberty for the rhyme)

63. Albeit] albee 1592, 1595
64. fuel] fewell 1592, 1595
67. Off] of 1592, 1595
85. bore] bare 1592, 1595
124. on such] 1595; one such 1592
198. Mars's] Marses 1592; Mars his 1595
208. four] fower 1592, 1595
229. should be] Oxford; should 1592, 1595
264. Bellona's] Bellonas 1595; Ballonas 1592
268. got] gatt 1592, 1595
272. again] a gaine 1592, 1595
296. drank] drunke 1592, 1595
298. drove] drave 1592, 1595
316. lickerish] licourishe 1592; liquorishe 1595
322. marrow] mary 1592, 1595
352. bore] bare 1592, 1595
389. flying] flieng 1592, 1595
392. dying] dieng 1592, 1595
406. our fainting] 1595; or fainting 1592
442. breathes] breaths 1592, 1595
447. Mars's] Marses 1592, 1595
455. dying] dieng 1592, 1595
458. lying] lieng 1592, 1595

Act IV.
0. AGRIPPA] *Agrippa. Dircetus*. the Messenger. 1592, 1595 (the group entry has been dissociated)
27. do] 1592; doth 1595
39. Alexandria] 1595; Alexandrie 1592
46. glaucs] Glauques 1592, 1595
82. Lose] leese 1592, 1595
133. flying] flieng 1592, 1595
193. Enter DIRCETUS, the Messenger] M (after 1592, 1595, where Dircetus was made to enter with the other characters above)
224. bore] bare 1592, 1595
268. Swooning] Swounding 1592; Sounding 1595
283. bore] bare 1592, 1595
288. help] 1595; helpt 1592
294. dying] dieng 1592, 1595
299. hung] hong 1592, 1595
309. whit] 1595; white 1592

359. cunning sleight] conning slight 1592, cunning slight 1595.
394. drunk] dronk 1592, 1595

Act V.
36. EUPHRON] Eph. 1592
47. frizzed] freezed 1592, 1595
78. swoon] swounde 1592, swound 1595
85. swoon] swound 1592, 1595
91. CHARMION. How faint] 1595 (Ch.); Cl. How faint 1592
161. I lived] Lived 1592, 1595
172. dying] dieng 1592, 1595

THOMAS KYD: *CORNELIA*

Kyd's translation was entered in the Stationers' Register on 26 January 1594 and first published in 1594 as a quarto (13 × 17.4 cm).

> [device] | CORNELIA. | AT LONDON, | Printed by *James Roberts*, for N.[icholas] L.[ing] | and *John Busbie.* | 1594.

It was issued again in 1595, with a different title page bearing the translator's name:

> Pompey the Great, | his faire | *Corneliaes Tragedie:* | Effected by her Father and Hus- | bandes downe-cast, death | and fortune. | *Written in French, by that excellent* | *Poet Ro: Garnier; and tran-* | *slated into English by Thomas* | *Kid.* | [device] | AT LONDON | Printed for Nicholas Ling. | 1595

ESTC identifies the printer as James Roberts. Apart from the title-page (and reset a4), the 1595 text is identical to 1594. The two issues of Q are here identified as:

Qa] STC 11622
Qb] STC 11622a

Copies of Qa are preserved as British Library C.34.e.47, C.34.d.6 and C.12.f.5.(1.); National Library of Scotland Bute.311; Bodleian Library Mal.219 (5); Folger STC 11622; Huntington 59877 (digitized for EEBO as STC 11622); and University of Texas at Austin Library Pforz 396. According to ESTC, a copy is also held at the Victoria and Albert Museum. It consists of a quarto of 13 quires (a^4, A–L^3), the last leaf blank, with ornamented title-page and the running title *CORNELIA*; the name of the bookseller, Nicholas Ling, is derived from STC. There are no page numbers. The last lines of the play are followed by the words: '*Non prosunt Domino quae prosunt omnibus; Artes*. Tho: Kyd.', on the verso of sig. L3.

Copies of Qb can be found in the British Library (C.34.e.27), in the Bodleian Library (Mal. 177), and in Worcester College Library, Oxford; in the Folger Library (PR1400 11622A), the Huntington Library (12102, digitized for EEBO as STC 11622A), at Cornell University, Ithaca, and the University of Texas at Austin Library (Pforz 397). It is a reissue of 1594, with the outer fold of the preliminary sheet (a1 and a4) replaced by a cancel, containing the new title page (verso blank) and a reprint of the end of the Argument with the *dramatis personae* on the verso on [a4].

Our copy-text is Huntington 59877 (STC 11622), a copy of Qa with very few misprints (see below). As first suggested by Markscheffel (and confirmed by an examination of the variants in all four sixteenth-century editions of Garnier's *Cornélie*),[6] Kyd's translation is based on the 1585 *Tragedies de Robert Garnier*. The 1585 edition has been used as our reference text, together with Jean-Claude Ternaux's critical edition of *Cornélie* (in *Théâtre Complet*, III, Paris: Classiques Garnier, 2002), which documents the variants in all editions of the text.

There has been no new critical edition of Kyd's *Cornelia* since the beginning of the twentieth century. There were many reissues of Robert Dodsley's *Select Collection of English Old Plays*, originally published in 1744, with *Cornelia* in vol. 11. The collection was re-edited by Isaac Reed in 1780, with *Cornelia* included in vol. 2. A new edition in twelve volumes by Isaac Reed, Octavius Gilchrist and John Payne Collier was published in 1825 (London: Septimus Prowett), with *Cornelia* again in the second volume. A fourth, enlarged fifteen-volume edition was published by William C. Hazlitt in 1874 (London: Reeves and Turner). *Cornelia* was then included in vol. 5, together with Kyd's *Spanish Tragedy* and *Soliman and Perseida*. The last edition of the nineteenth century was Heinrich Gassner's *Cornelia von Thomas Kyd. Nach dem Drucke von Jahre 1594* (Munich: Wolf, 1894). An original-spelling edition of the text was finally included with a full critical apparatus in Frederick Boas's *The Works of Thomas Kyd* (Oxford: Clarendon Press, 1901, second edition 1955, reprinted 1967).

[6] Thomas Markscheffel, *Thomas Kyds Tragödien* (Weimar: Drück der Hof-Buchdruckerei, 1885), p. 4. See also Gassner, p. vi.

This edition differs from all former ones by offering a fully modernized version of the 1594 text, collated with the 1595 text, together with a full critical apparatus (see Introduction for more details on our editorial approach).

Variants

Cornelia] Qa; Pompey the Great, his faire *Corneliaes Tragedie:* Effected by her Father and Husbandes downe-cast, death and fortune. *Written in French, by that excellent Poet Ro: Garnier; and translated into English by Thomas Kid.*, Qb.

The Argument
15. precedent] president Q[7]
17. Africa] Afrique Q
34. Overmourned] Ouer-mour'd Q
26, 35. Africa] Affrique Q

Act I] Actus Primus Q
30. soiledst] foil'dst Q [Most probably a misprint. Garnier: 'tu souillas', p. 40v]
83. topsy-turvy] topside-turuey Q
140. owed] ought Q
202. mightst] mighst Q
218. chokes] choake Q

Act II] Actus Secundus
34. thy] my [Garnier: 'emporta tes amours', p. 44r] Q
57. O deplorable Pompey] Thyne eyes (O deplorable Pompey) Q
94. seen] see Q
196. plunged] plund'd Q
198. upreared] uprea'd Q
250. deplored] depror'd Q
292. follow] followes Q

Act III. Scene 1] Actus Tertius. (No scene division in Q)
1. CORNELIA] No speech heading in Q
78. he] we Q [Garnier: 'tel qu'il souloist être' ('as he used to be'), p. 51r]
130. eaths] eath's Q

---

[7] No additional variants between Qa and Qb.

Scene 3. 43. aspics] aspies Q
80. scorned] scorne

Act IV. Scene 1] Actus Quartus. (No scene division in Q)
Scene 2. 64. gore] goe Q
66. discomfited] discomforted Q
104. encamp] encampt Q

Act V] Actus Quintus Q
16. misfortunes] misfortues Q
42. CORNELIA] Not in Q; CHORUS] Not in Q
154. whirlwind] whire-wind Q
274. CORNELIA] Not in Q; [MESSENGER] Not in Q
312. Stepped] Stepts Q
458. fumous] famous Q [cf. Garnier: 'mes pleurs fumeuses' ('my smoking tears', p. 71v)]

GLOSSARY

NB: This is a context-based glossary only. For fuller definitions, see *OED*.

A

acknown	acknowledged, recognized
Afrique, Afric	Africa, African
amain	again
amity	goodwill, friendship, love
annoy	distress
approve	put to the test, experience
arbitrament	judgment
at least wise	at least
attaint	accuse
attend	wait (from the French, *attendre*)

B

band	bond, pledge
bar	barricade
bate	strife, contention
battles	battalions
bead-roll	list, litany
bedew	to wet (with dew)
besprent	besprinkled
betide	happcn
boiling	hot; raging
bootless	useless, unnecessary
bounds	boundaries
brand	fire, conflagration
brawn-fallen	shrunken, thin
broil	trouble; strife
broke	broken
bruit	proclaim
buriable	ready to be buried
buskle	shake

C

caitiff (1)	villain.
caitiff (2)	miserable, wretched
careless	unflinching, unfeeling
cask	helmet
champant, champaign	level ground, field
cheer	face, countenance
check	stop suddenly, halt
conduit	fountain, channel
confirm	settle, make firm
control	check, means of restraint
cord	rope
coronet	crown
counterbuff	shock of recoil
covetise	covetousness, envy
cozen	cheat, deceive
crispy	rippled, wavy (from the French, *crespé*)
crook	hook
cuirass	breastplate

D

danger	dangerous, perilous
dastard	cowardly
desert	merit, reward
despoiled	plundered, stripped of possessions
disastered	hapless, ill-starred
discomforted	discomfited, defeated
disgage	release, disengage
displace	replace
dissolutely	weakly
dole	grief, weeping, lament
doleful	sorrowful
downs	fields
durst	dared

E

eaths	easily
eftsoons	again
embased	abased, defeated

empery	emporium, power
empt	empty
engrain	dye crimson or scarlet
enlaced	entangled, entwined
enlight	illuminate, enlighten
entertain	hold, retain
enthral	restrain, enslave
entrap	ensnare, catch in a trap
ere	before
erst	at first, before
eschew	avoid, escape, dodge
exasperate	incensed
extirp	uproot

F

falchion	short, curved sword
fearful	frightening
filed	defiled, sullied
finger	pilfer, plunder
fleer	smile in an enticing manner
fleshed (against)	bent against (from the French, *acharné*)
fond	foolish, doting
forcing	powerful
fore-game	preliminary game
franchised	made free
freight	freighted, trans: carried as freight
fretting	devouring, gnawing
frightful	fearful
frizzed	curly (from the French, *frisé*)
fulfil	fill up

G

gan	began to
gape for	long for
grave	engrave
griefful	painful, lamentable
grow	come to pass, follow

H

half-pike	a short, barbed spear
hap	fortune, fate, event (happy or unhappy)
hapless	miserable, unhappy
haply	perhaps
haught	high
helm	helmet
hence forward	henceforth
heretofore	formerly
herewithal	besides
herse	portcullis
hie	hasten
holp	helped (archaic preterite)
horse	cavalry
host	troop, company

I

imbrue	stain, dye (in blood)
impacked	tied up (from the French, *empaqueté*)
infect	tainted
insatiate	never satisfied, insatiable
intercept	stop, check
ire	wrath
ireful	wrathful

J

jar	discord, strife.

K

kindly	naturally (according to kind)

L

lenity	mercifulness, mercy
let	prevent
lickerish	fond of delicate fare; greedy; lecherous
light	alight, descend
linsel	shroud (from the French, *linceuil*)
long	belong

M

mad	yearn, become infatuated
madding	maddened
malign	begrudge
maw	stomach (of an animal)
meagre	thin, gaunt
meet	appropriate
meseems	it seems to me
minish	diminish
mischief	ill-fortune, distress
mishap	misfortune; unfortunate event
moisty	wet
moment	importance
mutter	murmur, whisper

N

neglectly	negligently

O

oared	having oars
obsequies	funeral rites, funerals
ominous	disastrous
ope	open
outlaunched	spilled out, shed
overforward	over-eager
overgrieve	grieve excessively
over-grieved	overwhelmed
overlive	survive, outlive
overmourn	mourn excessively
overpeer	tower over, surpass
overween	be presumptuous, overestimate
owe	own

P

Parth	Parthian
pell-mell	in disorder, in confusion
pelf	riches
perplexed	tormented, afflicted
peruke	head of hair

pike (at)	by auction
piled	held in a pile
pill	plunder, rifle
piteous	compassionate
plaguey	that affects like a plague, accursed
plain	complain
plaint	complaint
poniard	dagger
policy	prudence, foresight, guile
practise	plot, conspire
prater	person who talks foolishly, braggart
precedent	example
prize	bid for
prove	put to the test, experience
puissance	power

Q

quail	cause to wilt, weaken

R

rampire	rampart
reave (1)	tear or pull up; seize
reave (2)	bereave
rebecome	become again
recure	heal, cure
redoubt	dread, fear (from the French, *redouter*)
re-enforce	make stronger
reform	form again
reft	robbed
regain	win back
remove	move about, change
repair	go
repine at	complain against, grumble
reserve	maintain
rest	remain
retake	take back or again
Romulist	descendant of Romulus, Roman
round	globe
ruminate	meditate, ponder
ruth	sorrow, pity

S

seely	feeble, helpless, pitiable
seld	seldom
self	same (adj.)
semblant	appearance
shake with	shake hands, make a bargain with
shift (make)	manages
shivered	splintered, broken into pieces
signorize	rule over, command
signory	power, dominion
sink	sewage
sith	if, since
slightly	lightly, carelessly, hardly
smoke	give off vapour, steam
smoky	steamy, hot
souspirable	lamentable
spoil	prey, object of plunder
sponge	drain of, divest of
sprite	archaic for spirit
stayless	ceaseless, ever-moving
stays (to practise —)	put a check on, stop
stole	stolen
style	title
succeed	follow (from the French, *succéder*)
succour	aid, assistance
surcease	put a stop to, end
surcloy	surfeit, cloy excessively
suspect	suspicion
swage	assuage
swain	country labourer, shepherd
swift-foot	swift-footed

T

targe	a light shield
target	a small targe or shield
thorn	prick with (or as) a thorn, vex
thorough-pierced	through-pierced
throughly	thoroughly
through-galled	thoroughly harassed
thrall	servitude, bondage

throng	collect in large numbers
tickle	changing, uncertain, fickle
trace	pass, travel
train (1)	follow
train (2)	flatter (v); enticement (n).
training	alluring, seducing
transpose	upset oneself, get beside oneself
travail	work, task; burden.
travailed	burdened, harassed.
trudge	march
touch	concern

U

ulcer	ulcerate
unbroaded	unbraided
under-run	flow beneath
unsupportable	unbearable (from the French, *insupportable*)
unurged	not imposed
unwares (at —)	unexpectedly, by surprise
urge	press forcibly, impose

V

vail	lower
vassalage	servitude
vaunt	boast of, brag
vein	a slight stream of water
venge	avenge
virtue	power, excellence
vouchsafe	grant, allow

W

wax	grow
weal	wealth, possessions; welfare
welter	roll (on the sea)
where	whereas
whilom	formerly
wink	shut one's eyes (in sleep)
wintered	seasoned, experienced
wont to	used to

wonted	usual
wrack	ruin, destruction
wreak	avenge, or revenge
wrench	thrust, drive

Y

you-wards	towards you

NEOLOGISMS AND FIRST OCCURRENCES

This list presents words of which the use in the texts of this edition is the first recorded use (or occasionally predates the first relevant citation) in the *OED*. It includes several unrecorded words. The meaning of the words with an asterisk is explained in the location-specific glossary.

† indicates words that are words that have not been used since (hapaxes).

MARY SIDNEY HERBERT: *ANTONIUS*

*Buriable
*Chamberer
*Enlaced
*Entrapped (earliest use, not recorded in *OED*)
*Frizzed (earliest use, not recorded in *OED*)
*Grow
*Herse
*Impacked (not recorded in *OED* in this sense)
Martyr (trans. verb)
Mother-murdering
*Oared
*Overgrieve
*Piled
*Plaguey (earliest use, not recorded in *OED*)
*Prize
*Rebecome
*Reframe
*Regain
Self-cruel (earliest use, not recorded in *OED*)
Self-forsaken †
Self-succour (not recorded in *OED*)
*Shake
*Thorn
*Ulcer (verb)
*Unbroaded †
*Unsupportable (earliest use, not recorded in *OED*)
Useless
Vintaged (earliest use, not recorded in *OED*)
*You-wards † (not recorded in *OED*)

THOMAS KYD: *CORNELIA*

Calabrian
Carthaginian
*Confirmed
*Control
Dead-grown
*Disgage
*Eaths †
*Fore-game
*Linsel † (earliest and only use in the sense of shroud, not recorded in *OED*)
*Mad
*Madding (earliest use, not recorded in *OED*)
*Neglectly
*Ominous
Orient-pearled (not recorded in *OED*)
*Overmourn
*Pike
Quenchlessly
Romulist
*Round
Slow-paced
*Smile
Souspirable †
*Spoil
*Sponge
Sultry
*Surcloy
*Swift-foot
Thracian
*Through-galled †
*Transpose
*Underground
*Under-run
*Unurged
*Urge
*Wrench

BIBLIOGRAPHY

1. PRIMARY SOURCES

Robert Garnier

Early modern editions:

Cornélie, Tragédie (Paris: Robert Estienne, 1574)

Marc Antoine (Paris: Mamert Patisson, 1578)

Les Tragédies de Robert Garnier Conseiller du Roy, Lieutenant general Criminel au siege Presidial & Senechaussee du Maine (Paris: par Mamert Patisson Imprimeur du Roy, chez Robert Estienne, 1585)

Modern editions:

Marc Antoine, Hippolyte, ed. by Raymond Lebègue (Paris: Belles Lettres, 1974)

Cornélie: Tragédie, ed. by Jean-Claude Ternaux (Paris: Honoré Champion, 2002)

Marc Antoine, ed. by Jean-Claude Ternaux (Paris: Classiques Garnier, 2010)

Mary Sidney Herbert, Antonius

Early modern editions:

Mornay, Philippe de, seigneur du Plessis-Marly, *A Discourse of Life and Death. VVritten in French by Ph. Mornay. Antonius, a Tragoedie written also in French by Ro. Garnier. Both done in English by the Countesse of Pembroke* (London: [John Windet] for William Ponsonby, 1592) [STC 181 138]

Garnier, Robert, *The Tragedie of Antonie. Doone into English by the Countesse of Pembroke* (London [P. Short] for William Ponsonby 1595) [STC 11623]

Modern editions:

The Works of Mary Sidney, Countess of Pembroke, ed. by Robert G. Barnwell (London: John Wilson, 1865), pp. 1–73

The Countess of Pembroke's Antonie (1592), ed. by Alice Luce (Weimar: Emil Felber, 1897)

The Tragedy of Antony, in *Narrative and Dramatic Sources of Shakespeare*, ed. by Geoffrey Bullough (London: Routledge and Kegan Paul; New York: Columbia University Press, 1957–75, 8 vols, 1966.), v, pp. 358–405

Women Writers of the Renaissance and Reformation, ed. by Katherina M. Wilson (Athens and London: University of Georgia Press, 1987), pp. 490–521

Antonius, in *A New Variorum Edition of Shakespeare: Antony and Cleopatra*, ed. by Marvin Spevack (New York: Modern Language Association, 1990) pp. 475–524

Renaissance Drama by Women, ed. by S. P. Cerasano and M. Wynne-Davies (London and New York: Routledge, 2013 [1996]), pp. 13–42

Mary Sidney Herbert: Translation of Philippe de Mornay, A Discourse of Life and Death; Antonius, a Tragedie by R. Garnier, Facsimile. Intr. by Gary F. Waller. 'Vol. 6. The Early Modern Englishwoman: Part One', general editors Betty S. Travitsky and Patrick Cullen (Aldershot: Scolar Press, 1996)

Three Tragedies by Renaissance Women, ed. by Diane Purkiss (London: Penguin, 1998), pp. 39–95

The Tragedy of Antony, ed. by Risa Bear, *Renascence Editions* <http://www.luminarium.org/renascence-editions/antonie.html>, 1998 [accessed 16 June 2016]

The Collected Works of Mary Sidney, Countess of Pembroke, ed. by Margaret P. Hannay, Noel J. Kinnamon and Michael G. Brennan (Oxford: Clarendon Press, 1998), 2 vols, I: *Poems, Translations, and Correspondence*

Selected Works of Mary Sidney Herbert, Countess of Pembroke, ed. by Margaret P. Hannay, Noel J. Kinnamon and Michael G. Brennan (Tempe: Arizona Center for Medieval and Renaissance Studies, 2005), pp. 47–111

Thomas Kyd's Cornelia

Early modern editions:

Cornelia (London: James Roberts, for N[icholas] L[ing] and John Busbie, 1594) [STC 11 622]

Reissued as: *Pompey the Great, his faire Corneliaes tragedie effected by her father and husbandes downe cast, death, and fortune. Written in French, by that excellent poet Ro: Garnier; and translated into English by Thomas Kid* (London: [James Roberts] for Nicholas Ling, 1595) [STC 11 622]

Modern editions:

'Cornelia, A Tragedy. Written by Mr Thomas Kyd', in Robert Dodsley, ed., *A Select Collection of Old Plays*, 12 vols (London: for R. Dodsley, 1744), XI, pp. 65–120

'Pompey the Great, his faire Corneliaes Tragedie: effected by her father and husbandes downecast, death, and fortune. Written in French, by R. G.; and translated into English by T. Kid', in Robert Dodsley and Isaac Reed, eds, *A Select Collection of Old Plays*, 12 vols (London: J. Nichols for J. Dodsley, 1780), II, pp. 231–304

'Cornelia', in *A Select Collection of Old Plays in Twelve Volumes*, ed. by Isaac Reed, Octavius Gilchrist and John Payne Collier, 12 vols (London: Septimus Prowett, 1825), II, pp. 235- 304

'Cornelia', in *A Select Collection of Old Plays, Originally published by Robert Dodsley in the year 1744*, ed. by William Carew Hazlitt, 15 vols (London: Reeves and Turner, 1874), V, pp. 175–252

Cornelia von Thomas Kyd. Nach dem Drucke von Jahre 1594, ed. by Heinrich Gassner (Munich: Wolf, 1894)

'Cornelia',[1] in *The Works of Thomas Kyd*, ed. by Frederick S. Boas (Oxford: Clarendon Press, 1955 [1901]), pp. 101–60, notes pp. 414–36

[1] Boas reproduces the 1595 title page at the beginning of his edition (p. 101) but otherwise calls the text *Cornelia*.

Other Sources

Alexander, Sir William, *The monarchicke tragedies: Crosus, Darius, The Alexandræn, Iulius Cæsar* (London: Valentine Simmes for Ed. Blount, 1607)

Allott, Robert, *Englands Parnassus: or the choysest flowers of our moderne poets* (London: for N[icholas]. L[ing,] C. B[usby] and T. H[ayes], 1600)

Anon., *A conference about the next succession of the crowne of Ingland ... Published by R. Doleman* ([Antwerp: N. Conincx], 1594)

Anon., *The first part of Ieronimo* (London: [William Jaggart] for Thomas Pavier, 1605

Anon., *The tragedy of Cæsar and Pompey. Or Cæsars revenge. Privately acted by the Studentes of Trinity Coledge in Oxford* (London: for Nathaniel Fosbrooke and John Wright, 1607)

Appian, *Roman History, Volumes III and IV*, trans. by Horace White, Loeb Classical Library 4 and 5 (Cambridge, MA: Harvard University Press, 1912)

Ariosto, Lodovico, *Orlando furioso in English heroical verse*, trans. by John Harington (London: Richard Field, 1591)

Ascham, Roger, *The Schoolemaster* (London: by John Daye, [1570]),

[Baldwin, William, et al.], *A myrroure for magistrates* (London: Thomas Marsh, 1559)

——, *The mirour for magistrates* (London: Henry Marsh, being the assign of Thomas Marsh, 1587)

Bartas, Guillaume de Salluste, seigneur du, *La Sepmaine, ou Création du monde* (Paris: Jean Février, 1578)

——, *Bartas: his deuine weekes and workes*, trans. by Joshua Sylvester (London: Humphrey Lownes, 1605)

Bellay, Joachim du, *Les Antiquitez de Rome* (Paris: François Morel, 1558)

Bèze, Theodore de, *A tragedie of Abrahams sacrifice, written in french by Theodore Beza*, trans. by Arthur Golding (London: Thomas Vautroullier, 1577)

The Bible and Holy Scriptures conteyned in the Olde and Newe Testament. Translated according to the Ebrue and Greke, and conferred with the best translations in diuers languges (Geneva: Rowland Hall, 1560)

Bodenham, John, *Bel-vedére, or The garden of the muses* (London: F. K. for Hugh Astley, 1600)

Brandon, Samuel, *The tragicomœdie of the vertuous Octavia* (London: for William Ponsonby, [1598])

Cary, Elizabeth, *The tragedie of Mariam, the faire queen of jewry* (London: Thomas Creed for Richard Hawkins, 1613)

Chapman, George, *The conspiracie and tragoedie of Charles Duke of Byron* (London: N[icholas] O[kes] for Thomas Thorpe, 1625)

Church of England, *The boke of common praier, and administration of the Sacramentes, and other rites and Ceremonies in the Churche of Englande* (London: Richard Grafton, 1559)

Cicero, *On Ends* [*De Finibus*], trans. by H. Rackham, Loeb Classical Library 40 (Cambridge, MA: Harvard University Press, 1914)

——, *On Old Age. On Friendship. On Divination*, trans. by W. A. Falconer, Loeb Classical Library 154 (Cambridge, MA: Harvard University Press, 1923)

C[ovell], W[illiam], *Polimanteia* ([Cambridge and London]: John Legate [and J. Orwin], 1595)

Daniel, Samuel, *A Defence of ryme* (London: for Edward Blount, 1603)

——, *Delia and Rosamond augmented. Cleopatra.* (London: James Roberts and Edward Allde] for Simon Waterson, 1594)

Dekker, Thomas, *A Knight's Conjuring* (London: T[homas] C[reede] for William Barley, 1607)

Dio Cassius, *Roman History, Volume V: Books 46–50*, trans. by Earnest Cary, Herbert B. Foster. Loeb Classical Library 82 (Cambridge, MA: Harvard University Press, 1917)

Drayton, Thomas, *Matilda the faire and chaste daughter of the Lord Robert Fitzwater* (London: John Busby, 1594)

Erasmus, Desiderius, *The Correspondence of Erasmus, 1501 to 1514*, trans. by R. A. B. Mynors and D. F. S. Thomson (Toronto: University of Toronto Press, 1975)

Euripides, *Trojan Women. Iphigenia among the Taurians. Ion*, ed. and trans. by David Kovacs, Loeb Classical Library 10 (Cambridge, MA: Harvard University Press, 1999)

Gager, William, *Ulysses redux tragoedie nova* (Oxford: Joseph Barnes, 1592)

Gosson, Stephen, *The Schoole of Abuse* (London: for Thomas Woodcock, 1579

Greene, Robert, *Menaphon* (London: by T[homas] O[rwin] for Sampson Clarke, 1589)

——, *Philomela, The Lady Fitzvvaters nightingale* (London: Edward White, 1592)

Greville, Fulke, *The Prose Works of Fulke Greville, Lord Brooke*, ed. by John Gouws (Oxford: Clarendon Press, 1986)

Harvey, Gabriel, *A new letter of notable contents with a straunge Sonet, intituled Gorgon, or the wonderfull yeare* (London: for John Wolfe, 1593).

Henslowe, Philip, *Diary*, ed. by W. W. Greg, 2 vols (London: A. H. Bullen, 1908).

Hirtius, Aulus, in Julius Caesar, *The Gallic War*, trans. by H. J. Edwards, Loeb Classical Library 72 (Cambridge, MA: Harvard University Press, 1917)

Homer, *The Iliads of Homer prince of poets*, trans. by George Chapman (London: R[ichard] F[ield] for Nathaniel Butter, 1611)

Horace, *Odes and Epodes*, ed. and trans. by Niall Rudd, Loeb Classical Library 33 (Cambridge, MA: Harvard University Press, 2004)

Junius, Stephanus Brutus [i.e. Mornay, Philippe de, sieur du Plessis-Marly, and Hubert Languet?], *Vindicae, contra tyrannos* (Edimburgi [Basel]: 1579)

——, *Vindicae, Contra Tyrannos*, ed. by George Garnett (Cambridge: Cambridge University Press, 1994)

Kyd, Thomas, *The Spanish tragedie containing the lamentable end of Don Horatio and Bel-imperia* (London: Edward Allde for Edward White [1592])

——, *The Spanish Tragedy* [1592], in *The Works of Thomas Kyd*, ed. by Frederick S. Boas (Oxford: Clarendon Press, 1955 [1901])

——, *The tragedie of Soliman and Perseda* (London: Edward Allde for Edward White, [1592])

Ling, Nicholas, *Politeuphuia, wits common wealth* (London: for Nicholas Ling, 1598)

Lucan, *Lucans first booke translated line for line*, trans. by Christopher Marlowe (London: Peter Short, 1600)

——, *The Civil War (Pharsalia)*, trans. by J. D. Duff, Loeb Classical Library 220 (Cambridge, MA: Harvard University Press, 1928)

Lucretius, *On the Nature of Things*, trans. by W. H. D. Rouse and Martin F. Smith, Loeb Classical Library 181 (Cambridge, MA: Harvard University Press, 1924)

Marlowe, Christophe, *The tragedie of Dido Queene of Carthage* (London: the Widow Orwin for Thomas Woodcock, 1594)

——, *The tragicall history of D. Faustus* (London: V[alentine] S[immes] for Thomas Bushell, 1604)

May, Thomas, *The tragedie of Cleopatra, Queen of Ægypt* (London: Thomas Harper for Thomas Walkley, 1639)

Meres, Francis, *Palladis Tamia. Wits treasurie being the second part of Wits common wealth* (London: Peter Short for Cuthbert Burby, 1598)

——, *Wits common wealth The second part. A treasurie of diuine, morall, and phylosophicall similies, and sentences, generally vsefull* (London: William Stansby, to be sold by Richard Royston, 1634)

Mornay, Philippe de, sieur du Plessis-Marly, *Excellent discours de la vie et de la mort* (n.p.: chez Jean Durant, 1576)

——, *Traité de la vérité de la religion chrétienne* (Antwerp: Christophe Plantin, 1581)

——, *A woorke concerning the trewnesse of the Christian religion, written in French*, trans. by Sir Philip Sidney (London: for Thomas Cadman, 1587)

Mulcaster, Richard, *The first part of the elementarie vvhich entreateth chefelie of the right writing of our English tung* (London: Thomas Vautroullier, 1582)

Norton, Thomas, and Thomas Sackville, *The Tragedie of Gorboduc* (London: William Griffith, 1565)

Ovid, *The heroycall epistles of the learned poet Publius Ovidius Naso In English Verse*, trans. by George Tuberville (London: Henry Denham, 1567)

——, *Heroides. Amores*, trans. by Grant Showerman and G. P. Goold, Loeb Classical Library 41 (Cambridge, MA: Harvard University Press, 1914)

——, *Metamorphoses*, trans. by Frank Justus Miller and G. P. Goold, 2 vols, Loeb Classical Library 42–43 (Cambridge, MA: Harvard University Press, 1916)

——, *Art of Love. Cosmetics. Remedies for Love. Ibis. Walnut-tree. Sea Fishing. Consolation*, trans. by J. H. Mozley and G. P. Goold, Loeb Classical Library 232 (Cambridge, MA: Harvard University Press, 1929)

Plutarch, *The lives of the nobles Grecians and Romanes ... Translated out of Greeke into French by James Amyot ... and out of French into English, by Thomas North* (London: Thomas Vautroullier for John Wright, 1579)

——, *Lives*, trans. by *Bernadotte Perrin*, 11 vols (Cambridge, MA.: Harvard University Press and London: William Heinemann, 1917–26)

Puttenham, George, *The arte of English poesie* (London: by Richard Field, 1589

Seneca, Lucius Anneus, *The sixt tragedie of the most graue and prudent author Lucius, Anneus, Seneca*, trans. by Jasper Heywood (London: Richard Tottel, 1559)

——, *Seneca his tenne tragedies* (London: Thomas Marsh [for Thomas Newton], 1581)

——, *Tragedies*, ed. and trans. by John G. Fitch, 2 vols, Loeb Classical Library 62 and 78 (Cambridge, MA: Harvard University Press, 2002–04)

Shakespeare, William, *The Complete Works*, ed. by Stanley Wells and Gary Taylor (The Oxford Shakespeare, Oxford: Oxford University Press, 1988)

——, *Antony and Cleopatra*, ed. by John Wilders (The Arden Shakespeare, London: Routledge, 1995)

Sidney, Sir Philip, *The Countess of Pembrokes Arcadia* (London: [John Windet] for William Ponsonby, 1593)

——, *The defence of poesie* (London: [Thomas Creed] for William Ponsonby, 1595)

Spenser, Edmund, *The faerie queene* (London: [John Wolfe] for William Ponsonby, 1590)

——, *Complaints. Containing sundrie small poemes of the worlds vanitie* (London: for William Ponsonby, 1591).

Suetonius, *The Lives of the Caesars*, vol. 1, trans. by J. C. Rolfe, Loeb Classical Library 31 (Cambridge, MA: Harvard University Press, 1914)

Tasso, Torquato, *The householders philosophie*, trans. by Thomas Kyd (London: J. C[harlewood] for Thomas Hacket, 1588)

Van der Noot, Jan, *A theatre wherein be represented as wel the miseries & calamities that follow the voluptuous worldlings* (London: Henry Bynneman, 1569)

Virgil, *Eclogues. Georgics. Aeneid: Books 1–6*, trans. by H. Rushton Fairclough and G. P. Goold, Loeb Classical Library 63 (Cambridge, MA: Harvard University Press, 1916)

——, *Aeneid: Books 7–12. Appendix Vergiliana*, trans. by H. Rushton Fairclough and G. P. Goold, Loeb Classical Library 64 (Cambridge, MA: Harvard University Press, 1918)

Webster, John, *The Tragedy of the Dutchesse of Malfy* (London: Nicholas Okes for John Waterson, 1623)

Whitney, Geffrey, *A choice of emblems, and other devises* (Leyden: in the house of Christophe Plantin, by Francis Raphenlengius, 1586)

Yver, Jacques, *A courtlie controuersie of Cupids cautels*, trans. by Henry Wotton (London: Francis Coldock and Henry Bynneman, 1578)

2. CRITICAL WORKS

Aebischer, Pascale, 'The Properties of Whiteness: Renaissance Cleopatras from Jodelle to Shakespeare', *Shakespeare Survey*, 65 (2011), 221–38

Alexander, Gavin, 'Review of *The Collected Works of Mary Sidney Herbert, Countess of Pembroke*, ed. Margaret P. Hannay, Noel J. Kinnamon, and Michael G. Brennan. Vol. I: *Poems, Translations, and Correspondence*; Vol. II: *The Psalmes of David.* Oxford: Clarendon Press, 1998', *Translation and Literature*, 8.1 (1999) 78–91

Ardolino, Frank, 'The Influence of Robert Garnier's *Les Juifves* on Kyd's *The Spanish Tragedy*', *Notes and Queries*, 62.1 (2015), 64–66

Arshad, Yasmin, 'The Enigma of a Portrait: Lady Anne Clifford and Daniel's *Cleopatra*', *The British Art Journal*, 11.3 (2011), 30–37

Arshad, Yasmin, Helen Hackett and Emma Whipday, 'Daniel's *Cleopatra* and Lady Anne Clifford: From a Jacobean Portrait to Modern Performance', *Early Theatre*, 18.2 (2015), 167–86

Barish, Jonas, 'The Problem of Closet Drama in the Italian Renaissance', *Italica*, 71.1 (1994), 4–31

Barker, William, 'Merchant Taylors' School', in *The Spenser Encyclopaedia*, ed. by A. C. Hamilton, P. Cheney et al. (Toronto: Toronto University Press, 1990), pp. 468–69

Barker, Sara, and Brenda Hosington, eds, *Renaissance Cultural Crossroads: Translation, Culture, and Print in Britain, 1473–1640* (Leiden and Boston: Brill, 2013)

Beal, Peter, ed., *Index of English Literary Manuscripts* (London: Mansell; New York: R. R. Bowker Company, 1980), I, 1450–1625

Beilin, Elaine V., *Redeeming Eve: Women Writers of the English Renaissance* (Princeton: Princeton University Press, 1987)

Belle, Marie-Alice, 'Locating Women's Translations in Early Modern England and France', *Renaissance and Reformation*, 35.4 (2012), 5–24

——, '"Comme espics dans les plaines": Patterns of Translation of Robert Garnier's Epic Similes in Thomas Kyd's *Cornelia* (1594)', *Renaissance and Reformation*, 40.3 (2017), forthcoming

Bergeron, David M., *Textual Patronage in English Drama, 1570–1640* (Aldershot: Ashgate, 2006)

Boutcher, Warren, 'The Renaissance', in *The Oxford Guide to Literature in English Translation*, ed. by Peter France (Oxford: Oxford University Press, 2000), pp. 45–55

——, *The School of Montaigne* (Oxford: Oxford University Press, 2016).

Braden, Gordon, *Renaissance Tragedy and the Senecan Tradition: Anger's Privilege* (New Haven and London: Yale University Press, 1985)

——, 'Tragedy', in *The Oxford History of Literary Translation in English, Volume II, 1550–1660*, ed. by Gordon Braden, Brian Cummings and Stuart Gillespie (Oxford: Oxford University Press, 2010), pp. 261–79

Braden, Gordon, Robert Cummings and Stuart Gillespie, eds, *The Oxford History of Literary Translation in English, Volume II, 1550–1660* (Oxford: Oxford University Press, 2010)

Brayman Hackel, Heidi, *Reading Material in Early Modern England. Print, Gender, and Literacy* (Cambridge: Cambridge University Press, 2005).

Brennan, Michael, 'William Ponsonby: Elizabethan Publisher', *Analytical and Enumerative Bibliography*, 7 (1984), 91–110

——, 'The Queen's Proposed Visit to Wilton House in 1599 and the "Sidney Psalms"', *Sidney Journal*, 20.1 (2002), 27–53

——, *The Sidneys of Penshurst and the Monarchy, 1500–1700* (Aldershot: Ashgate, 2006)

Brown, Georgia, *Redefining English Literature* (Cambridge: Cambridge University Press, 2004)

Burke, Peter, and Ronnie Po-Chia Hsia, eds, *Cultural Translation in Early Modern Europe* (Cambridge: Cambridge University Press, 2007)

Cadman, Daniel, *Sovereigns and Subjects in Early Modern Neo-Senecan Drama: Republicanism, Stoicism and Authority* (Farnham: Ashgate, 2015)

——, '"Quick Comedians": Mary Sidney, Samuel Daniel and the *Theatrum Mundi* in Shakespeare's *Antony and Cleopatra*', *Actes des congrès de la Société française Shakespeare*, 33, 2015 <http://shakespeare.revues.org/3536> [accessed 1 March 2016]

Caigny, Florence de, *Sénèque le Tragique en France (XVIe–XVIIe siècles): Imitation, traduction, adaptation* (Paris: Classiques Garnier, 2011)

Cavanagh, Dermot, 'Political Tragedy in the 1560s: *Cambises* and *Gorboduc*', in *The Oxford Handbook of Tudor Literature, 1485–1603*, ed. by Mike Pincombe and Cathy Shrank (Oxford: Oxford University Press, 2011), pp. 488–503

Chardon, Henri, *Robert Garnier, sa vie, ses poésies inédites* (Paris: Slatkine, 1970)

Charlton, H. B., *The Senecan Tradition in Renaissance Tragedy* (Manchester: Manchester University Press, 1946)

Clarke, Danielle, 'The Politics of Translation and Gender in the Countess of Pembroke's *Antonie*', *Translation and Literature*, 6 (1997), 149–66

——, *The Politics of Early Modern Women's Writing* (London: Longman, 2001)

——, 'Translations', in *The Cambridge Companion to Early Modern Women's Writing*, ed. by Laura Lunger Knoppers (Cambridge: Cambridge University Press, 2009), pp. 167–80

——, 'The Psalms of Mary Sidney, Countess of Pembroke', in *The Ashgate Research Companion to the Sidneys, 1500–1700*, ed. by Margaret P. Hannay, Mary Ellen Lamb and Michael G. Brennan (Farnham and Burlington: Ashgate, 2015), II, pp. 295–310

Coldiron, Anne E. B., 'How Spenser Excavates Du Bellay's *Antiquitez*', *Journal of English and Germanic Philology*, 101 (2002), 41–67

——, 'Translation's Challenges to Critical Categories: Verses from French in the Early English Renaissance', *Yale Journal of Criticism*, 16.2 (2003), 315–44

——, *English Printing, Verse Translation, and the Battle of the Sexes, 1476–1557* (Farnham: Ashgate, 2009)

——, 'Form[e]s of Transnationhood: The Case of John Wolfe's Trilingual *Courtier*', *Renaissance Studies*, 29.1 (2015), 103–24

——, *Printers Without Borders: Translation and Textuality in the Renaissance* (Cambridge: Cambridge University Press, 2015)

Collinson, Patrick, 'Ecclesiastical Vitriol: Religious Satire in the 1590s and the Invention of Puritanism', in *The Reign of Elizabeth I: Court and Culture in the Last Decade*, ed. by John A. Guy (Cambridge: Cambridge University Press, 1995), pp. 150–70

Cottegnies, Line, 'The Sapphic Context of Lady Mary Wroth's *Pamphilia to Amphilanthus*', in *Women and the Poem in Seventeenth Century England: Inheritance, Circulation, Exchange*, ed. by Susan Wiseman (Manchester: Manchester University Press, 2013), pp. 60–76

Cox Jensen, Freyja, *Reading the Roman Republic in Early Modern England* (Leiden: Brill, 2012)

Crawford, Charles, 'Belvedere, or The Garden of the Muses', *Englische Studien*, 43 (1910–11), 198–228

Crawford, Julie, *Mediatrix: Women, Politics, and Literary Production in Early Modern England* (Oxford: Oxford University Press, 2014)

Davidson, Peter and Jane Stevenson, 'Elizabeth I's Reception at Bisham (1592): Elite Women as Writers and Devisers', in *The Progresses, Pageants, and Entertainments of Queen Elizabeth*, ed. by Elizabeth Archer, Elizabeth Goldring, and Sarah Knight (Oxford: Oxford University Press, 2007), pp. 207–26

Demers, Patricia, *Women's Writing in English: Early Modern England* (Toronto: University of Toronto Press, 2005)

Demetriou, Tania and Rowan Tomlinson, eds, *The Culture of Translation in Early Modern England and France, 1500–1660* (Houndmills, Basingstoke and New York: Palgrave Macmillan, 2015)

Dobby-Poirson, Florence, *Tyrans et victimes: le pathétique chez Robert Garnier* (Paris: Champion, 2006)

Doran, Susan, and Pauline Kewes, eds, *Doubtful and Dangerous: The Question of Succession in Late Elizabethan England* (Manchester: Manchester University Press, 2014)

Dupont, Florence, *Les Monstres de Sénèque* (Paris: Belin, 1995)

Eliot, T. S., *The Sacred Wood: Essays in Literature and Criticism* (London: Methuen, 1920)

Erne, Lukas, *Beyond the Spanish Tragedy: A Study of the Works of Thomas Kyd* (Manchester: Manchester University Press, 2002)

——, *Shakespeare and the Book Trade* (Cambridge: Cambridge University Press, 2013)

Farmer, Alan B., and Zachary Lesser, 'What Is Print Popularity? A Map of the Elizabethan Book Trade', in *The Elizabethan Top Ten: Defining Print Popularity in Early Modern England*, ed. by Andy Kesson and Emma Smith (Farnham: Ashgate, 2013), pp. 19–54

Ferguson, Margaret, 'Sidney, Cary, Wroth', in *A Companion to Renaissance Drama*, ed. by Arthur Kinney (London: Blackwell, 2002), pp. 482–506

Findlay, Alison, *Playing Spaces in Early Women's Drama* (Cambridge: Cambridge University Press, 2006).

Findlay, Alison, and Stephanie Hodgson-Wright, with Gweno Williams, *Women and Dramatic Production 1550–1700* (London: Longman, 2000)

Fleming, Juliette, 'Changed Opinion as to Flowers', in *Renaissance Paratexts*, ed. by Helen Smith and Louise Wilson (Cambridge: Cambridge University Press, 2011), pp. 48–64

Frappier, Louise, 'Sénèque revisité: la topique de la Fortune dans les tragédies de Robert Garnier', *Études françaises*, 44.2 (2008), 69–83

——, 'L'exemplarité de Jules César dans la tragédie humaniste: Muret, Grévin, Garnier', *Tangence*, 104 (2014), 107–36

Freeman, Arthur, *Thomas Kyd, Facts and Problems* (Oxford: Oxford University Press, 1967)

Freer, Coburn, 'Mary Sidney, Countess of Pembroke', in *English Women Writers of the Renaissance and Reformation*, ed. by Katharina Wilson (Athens, GA: University of Georgia Press, 1987), pp. 481–521

Furnivall, F. J., 'Sir John Harington's Shakspeare Quartos', *Notes & Queries*, s-7.IX (May 1890), 382–83

Gillespie, Stuart, *Shakespeare's Books. A Dictionary of Shakespeare Sources* (London and New York: Continuum, 2004 [2001])

Goodrich, Jaime, 'Returning to Lady Lumley's Schoolroom: Euripides, Isocrates, and the Paradox of Women's Learning', *Renaissance and Reformation*, 35.4 (2012), 97–118

——, *Faithful Translators: Authorship, Gender, and Religion in Early Modern England* (Evanston, Northwestern University Press, 2014)

Green MacDonald, Joyce, *Women and Race in Early Modern Texts* (Cambridge: Cambridge University Press, 2002)

Greg, W. W., *A Bibliography of the English Printed Drama to the Restoration, Volume I* (London: for the Bibliographical Society at the University Press, Oxford, 1939)

Gurr, Andrew, *The Shakespearian Stage 1574–1642* (Cambridge: Cambridge University Press, 2003 [1992])

Hadfield, Andrew, *Shakespeare and Republicanism* (Cambridge: Cambridge University Press, 2005)

——, *Edmund Spenser: A Life* (Oxford: Oxford University Press, 2012)

Hamlin, Hannibal, *Psalm Culture and Early Modern English Literature* (Cambridge: Cambridge University Press, 2004)

Hannay, Margaret P., ed., *Silent But for the Word: Tudor Women as Patrons, Translators, and Writers of Religious Works* (Ohio: Kent State University Press, 1985)

——, '"Princes You As Men Must Dy": Genevan Advice to Monarchs in the *Psalmes* of Mary Sidney', *English Literary Renaissance*, 19.1 (1989), 22–41

——, *Philip's Phoenix: Mary Sidney, Countess of Pembroke* (Oxford: Oxford University Press, 1990)

——, 'Elizabeth Ashburnham Richardson's Meditation on the Countess of Pembroke's *Discourse*', *EMS*, 9 (2000), 114–28

——, 'Mary Sidney and Scribal Publication', in *Women's Writing and the Circulation of Ideas: Manuscript Publication in England, 1550–1800*, ed. by George Justice and Nathan Tinker (Cambridge: Cambridge University Press, 2002), pp. 17–49

——, ed., *Ashgate Critical Essays on Women Writers in England, Volume II*: *Mary Sidney* (London: Ashgate, 2009)

Hannay, Margaret P., Mary Ellen Lamb and Michael G. Brennan, eds, *The Ashgate Research Companion to the Sidneys, 1500–1700* (Farnham and Burlington: Ashgate, 2015), 2 vols

Hill, Eugene, 'Senecan and Virgilian Perspectives in *The Spanish Tragedy*', *English Literary Renaissance*, 15 (1985), 143–65

Hillman, Richard, 'De-centring the Countess's Circle: Mary Sidney Herbert and Cleopatra', *Renaissance and Reformation*, 28.1 (2006), 61–79

——, *The French Origins of English Tragedy* (Manchester: Manchester University Press, 2010)

——, 'The French Accents of Seneca on the Tudor Stage', in *New Perspectives on Tudor Cultures*, ed. by Mike Pincombe and Zsolt Almasi (Newcastle-upon-Tyne: Cambridge Scholars, 2012), pp. 244–62

——, *French Reflections in the Shakespearean Tragic* (Manchester: Manchester University Press, 2012)

Höfele, Andreas and Werner von Koppenfels, eds, *Renaissance Go-betweens: Cultural Exchange in Early Modern Europe* (New York: Walter de Gruyter, 2005)

——, '*A Midsummer Night's Dream* and Mary Sidney', *English Language Notes*, 41.3 (2004), 23–28

Hosington, Brenda, 'Commerce, Printing, and Patronage', in *The Oxford History of Literary Translation into English, Volume II: 1550–1660*, ed. by Gordon Braden, Robert Cummings and Stuart Gillespie (Oxford: Oxford University Press, 2010), pp. 45–57

——, ed., *Renaissance Cultural Crossroads Online Catalogue of Translations in Britain 1473–1641* (<http://www.hrionline.ac.uk/rcc/> [accessed 1 July 2016])

——, ed., *Translation and Print Culture in Early Modern Europe*, special issue of *Renaissance Studies*, 29. 1 (2015)

Hosington, Brenda, and Hannah Fournier, 'Translation and Women Translators', in *The Encyclopedia of Women in the Renaissance: Italy, France and England*, ed. by Diana M. Robin, Anne Larsen and Carole

Levin (Santa Barbara: University of California Press, 2007), pp. 369–73

Hunter, G. K., 'The Marking of Sententiae in Elizabethan Printed Plays, Poems, and Romances', *The Library*, 6.3/4 (1951), 171–188

——, *Dramatic Identities and Cultural Tradition: Studies in Shakespeare and His Contemporaries: Critical Essays* (New York: Barnes & Noble Books, 1978)

Ide, Richard, 'Chapman's "Caesar and Pompey" and the Uses of History', *Modern Philology*, 82.3 (1985), 255–68

Jackson, Macdonald P., 'New Research on the Canon of Thomas Kyd', *Research Opportunities in Medieval and Renaissance Drama*, 47 (2008), 107–27

Johnson, Gerald D., 'John Busby and the Stationer's Trade', *The Library*, 6.7 (1985), 1–15

Jondorf, Gillian, *Robert Garnier and the Themes of Political Tragedy in the Sixteenth Century* (London: Cambridge University Press, 1969)

Jones, Richard Foster, *The Triumph of the English Language: A Survey of Opinions Concerning the Vernacular from the Introduction of Printing to the Restoration* (Stanford: Stanford University Press, 1951)

Ker, James, and Jessica Winston, eds, *Elizabethan Seneca: Three Tragedies* (Tudor and Stuart Translation Series, London: The Modern Humanities Research Association, 2012)

Kerrigan, John, *Motives of Woe: Shakespeare and 'Female Complaint': A Critical Anthology* (Oxford: Oxford University Press, 2013)

Kewes, Paulina '"A Fit Memorial for the Times to Come": Admonition and Topical Application in Mary Sidney's *Antonius* and Samuel Daniel's *Cleopatra*', *The Review of English Studies*, 63.259 (2012), 243–64

Kilgore, Robert, 'Poets, Critics, and the Redemption of Poesy: Philip Sidney's *Defence of Poesy* and Metrical Psalms', in *The Sacred and Profane in English Renaissance Literature*, ed. by Mary A. Papazian (Newark: University of Delaware Press, 2008), pp. 108–31

Krontiris, Tina, *Oppositional Voices: Women as Writers and Translators of Literature in the English Renaissance* (London: Routledge, 1992)

——, 'Mary Herbert: Englishing a Purified Cleopatra', in *Readings in Renaissance Women's Drama: Criticism, History, and Performance 1594–1998*, ed. by S. P. Cerasano and Marion Wynne-Davies (London and New York: Routledge, 1998), pp. 156–66

Kuin, Roger, 'Life, Death, and the Daughter of Time: Philip and Mary Sidney's Translations of Duplessis-Mornay', in *French Connections in the English Renaissance*, ed. by Catherine Gimelli Martin and Hassan Melehy (Farnham and Burlington: Ashgate, 2013), pp. 143–60

Lake Prescott, Anne, 'Mary Sidney's "Antonius" and the Ambiguities of French History', *The Yearbook of English Studies*, 38.1 (2008), 216–33

——, 'Mary Sidney's French Sophocles: The Countess of Pembroke reads Robert Garnier', in *Representing France and the French in Early Modern English Drama*, ed. by Jean-Christophe Mayer (Newark: University of Delaware Press, 2008), pp. 68–89

Lamb, Mary Ellen, 'The Myth of the Countess of Pembroke: The Dramatic Circle', *Yearbook of English Studies*, 11 (1981), 194–202

——, 'The Countess of Pembroke and the Art of Dying', in *Women in the Middle Ages and the Renaissance: Literary and Historical Perspectives*, ed. by Mary B. Rose (Syracuse: Syracuse University Press, 1986), pp. 207–26

——, *Gender and Authorship in the Sidney Circle* (Madison: University of Wisconsin Press, 1990)

Leavenworth, Russell, *Daniel's Cleopatra: A Critical Study* (Salzburg: Universität Salzburg, Salzburg Studies in English Literature n°3, 1974)

Lestringant, Franck, 'Le vers de théâtre au XVIe siècle', *Cahiers de l'Association Internationale d'Études Françaises*, 52.1 (2000), 267–78

Liénard, Clarisse, 'Le suicide dans les tragedies de Robert Garnier: les influences néo-stoïciennes', *Seizième siècle*, 6 (2010), 51–61

Lovascio, Domenico, 'Julius Caesar's "Stony Heart": Thomas Kyd's *Cornelia* and the *Mirror for Magistrates*', *Notes and Queries*, 59.1 (2012), 52–53

Macdonald, Robert H., ed., *The Library of Drummond of Hawthornden* (Edinburgh: Edinburgh University Press, 1971)

Mack, Peter, *Elizabethan Rhetoric: Theory and Practice* (Cambridge: Cambridge University Press, 2004)

Maguin, Jean-Marie, 'Of Ghosts and Spirits Walking by Night: A Joint Examination of the Ghost Scenes in Robert Garnier's *Cornélie*, Thomas Kyd's *Cornelia* and William Shakespeare's *Hamlet*', *Cahiers Elisabéthains*, 1 (1972), 25–40

Maguin, Jean-Marie, and Michèle Willems, eds, *French Essays on Shakespeare and His Contemporaries* (Newark: University of Delaware Press, 1995)

Markscheffel, Thomas, *Thomas Kyds Tragödien* (Weimar: Drück der Hof-Buchdruckerei, 1885)

Martinon, Philippe, *Les Strophes: étude historique et critique sur les formes de la poésie lyrique en France depuis la Renaissance* (Geneva and Paris: Slatkine, 1989)

Matthews, Steven, *T. S. Eliot and Early Modern Literature* (Oxford: Oxford University Press, 2013)

Mayer, Jean-Christophe, ed., *Representing France and the French in Early Modern English Drama* (University of Delaware Press, 2008)

McCabe, Richard A., *'Ungainefull Arte': Poetry Patronage, and Print in the Early Modern Era* (Oxford: Oxford University Press, 2016)

Melehy, Hassan, 'Antiquities of Britain: Spenser's *Ruines of Time*', *Studies in Philology*, 102 (2005), 159–83

——, *The Poetics of Literary Transfer in Early Modern France and England* (Farnham, England: Ashgate, 2010)

Morini, Massimiliano, *Tudor Translation in Theory and Practice* (Farnham: Ashgate, 2006)

Mottram, Stewart, 'Spenser's Dutch Uncles: The Family of Love and the Four Translations of *A Theatre for Worldlings*', in *Translation and the Book Trade in Early Modern Europe*, ed. by José María Pérez

Fernández and Edward Wilson-Lee (Cambridge: Cambridge University Press, 2014), pp. 164–84

Mouflard, Marie-Madeleine, *Robert Garnier (1545–1590): la vie* (La Ferté-Bernard, Sarthe: R. Bellanger, 1961)

Muir, Kenneth, *The Sources of Shakespeare's Plays* (London: Methuen, 1977)

Nelson, Alan H., 'Shakespeare and the Bibliophiles: From the Earliest Years to 1616', in *Owners, Annotators and the Signs of Reading*, ed. by Robin Myers, Michael Harris, and Giles Mandelbrote (London: British Library, 2005), pp. 49–73

Nevalainen, Terttu, 'Early Modern English Lexis and Semantics', *The Cambridge History of the English Language, Volume III: 1476–1776*, ed. by Roger Lass (Cambridge: Cambridge University Press, 1999), pp. 332–458

Norbrook, David, *Writing the English Republic: Poetry, Rhetoric and Politics, 1627–1660* (Cambridge: Cambridge University Press, 1999)

Norland, Howard B., 'Englishing Garnier: Mary Sidney's *Antonie* and Daniel's *Cleopatra*', in *Tudor Theatre: Emotion in the Theatre / L'Émotion au théâtre*, ed. by André Lascombes (Bern: Peter Lang, 1996), pp. 159–76

——, 'Gager's *Ulysses Redux*: Tragoedia Nova', in *'Divers Toyes Mengled': Essays on Medieval and Renaissance Culture*, ed. by Michel Bitot, Roberta Mullini and Peter Happé (Tours: Publications de l'Université François Rabelais, 1996), pp. 199–210

——, *Neoclassical Tragedy in Elizabethan England* (Newark: University of Delaware Press, 2009)

——, 'Neo-Latin Drama in Britain', in *Neo-Latin Drama and Theatre in Early Modern Europe*, ed. by Jan Bloemendal and Howard B. Norland (Leiden: Brill, 2013), pp. 471–544

Oberth, Iris, 'Appropriating France in Elizabethan Drama: English Translations of Robert Garnier's Plays', in *Elizabethan Translation and Literary Culture*, ed. by Gabriela Schmidt (Berlin and Boston: De Gruyter, 2013), pp. 275–98

Paleit, Edward, *War, Liberty, and Caesar: Responses to Lucan's 'Bellum Ciuile', ca. 1580–1650* (Oxford: Oxford University Press, 2013)

Parrot, Thomas, 'The "Academic" Tragedy of "Caesar and Pompey"', *The Modern Language Review*, 5. 4 (1910), 435–44

Pender, Patricia, *Early Modern Women's Writing and the Rhetoric of Modesty* (London: Palgrave Macmillan, 2012)

Pentland, Elizabeth A., 'Philippe Mornay, Mary Sidney, and the Politics of Translation', in *Women's Writing / Women's Work in Early Modernity*, *Early Modern Studies Journal*, 6 (2014), 66–99

Perry, Curtis, 'The Uneasy Republicanism of Thomas Kyd's *Cornelia*', *Criticism*, 48.4 (2008), 535–55

Pettegree, Jane, *Metaphor and National Identity: Foreign and Native on the English Stage, 1588–1611* (London: Palgrave Macmillan, 2011)

Raber, Karen, ed., *Dramatic Difference: Gender, Class, and Genre in the Early Modern Closet Drama* (Newark: University of Delaware Press, 2001)

Rhodes, Neil, *Shakespeare and the Origins of English* (Oxford: Oxford University Press, 2004)

——, 'Status Anxiety and English Renaissance Translation', in *Renaissance Paratexts*, ed. by Helen Smith and Louise Wilson (Cambridge: Cambridge University Press, 2011), pp. 107–20

——, 'Shakespeare's Popularity and the Origins of the Canon', in *The Elizabethan Top Ten: Defining Print Popularity in Early Modern England*, ed. by Andy Kesson and Emma Smith (Farnham: Ashgate, 2013), pp. 101–22

Rhodes, Neil, with Gordon Kendal and Louise Wilson, eds, *English Renaissance Translation Theory* (Tudor and Stuart Translation Series, London: The Modern Humanities Research Association, 2013)

Roberts, Josephine A., and James F. Gaines, 'Kyd and Garnier: The Art of Amendment', *Comparative Literature*, 31.2 (1979), 124–33

Russel, Anne, 'The Politics of Print and *The Tragedie of Antonie*', *Research Opportunities in Renaissance Drama*, 24 (2003), 91–100

Sanders, Eve Rachele, *Gender and Literacy on Stage in Early Modern England* (Cambridge: Cambridge University Press, 1998)

Schanzer, Ernest, '*Antony and Cleopatra* and the Countess of Pembroke's *Antonius*', *Notes & Queries*, 201 (1956), 152–54

Schmidt, Gabriela, ed., *Elizabethan Translation and Literary Culture* (Berlin and Boston: De Gruyter, 2013)

Schurink, Fred, ed., *Tudor Translation* (Basingstoke: Palgrave Macmillan, 2011)

Skretkowicz, Victor, 'Mary Sidney Herbert's *Antonius*, English Philhellenism and the Protestant Cause', *Women's Writing*, 6.1 (1999), 7–25

Smith, Helen, and Louise Wilson, eds, *Renaissance Paratexts* (Cambridge: Cambridge University Press, 2011)

Soellner, Rolf, 'Shakespeare's *Lucrece* and the Garnier-Pembroke Connection', *Shakespeare Studies*, 15 (1982), 1–20

Spearing, E. M., *The Elizabethan Translations of Seneca's Tragedies* (Cambridge: Hefper and Sons, 1912)

Spiegel, Glenn S., 'Perfecting English Meter: Sixteenth-Century Theory and Practice', *Journal of English and Germanic Philology*, 79 (1980), 192–209

Stapleton, Michael L., 'Edmund Spenser, George Tuberville, and Isabella Whitney Read Ovid's *Heroides*', *Studies in Philology*, 105.4 (2008), 487–519

Stillman, Robert E., *Sir Philip Sidney and the Poetics of Renaissance Cosmopolitanism* (Aldershot and Burlington: Ashgate, 2013).

Straznicky, Marta, 'Recent Studies in Closet Drama', *English Literary Renaissance*, 28 (1988), 142–60.

——, '"Profane Stoical Paradoxes": *The Tragedie of Mariam* and Sidneian Closet Drama', *English Literary Renaissance*, 24.1 (1994), 104–34

——, 'Closet Drama', in *A Companion to Renaissance Drama*, ed. by Arthur F. Kinney (Oxford: Oxford University Press, 2002), pp. 416–29

——, *Privacy, Playreading, and Women's Closet Drama, 1550–1700* (Cambridge: Cambridge University Press, 2004)

Tricomi, Albert H., 'Philip, Earl of Pembroke and the Analogical Way of Reading Political Tragedy', *Journal of English and Germanic Philology*, 85 (1986), 332–45

Trill, Suzanne, 'Sixteenth-Century Women's Writing: Mary Sidney's Psalmes and the "Femininity of Translation"', in *Writing and the English Renaissance*, ed. by Suzanne Trill and William Zunder (London: Longman, 1996), pp. 140–58

Uman, Deborah, *Women as Translators in Early Modern England* (Newark: University of Delaware Press, 2012)

Vickers, Brian, 'Thomas Kyd, Secret Sharer', *TLS*, April 18, 2008, 13–15

Weiner, Seth, 'The Quantitative Poems and the Psalm Translations: The Place of Sidney's Experimental Verse in the Legend', in *Sir Philip Sidney: 1586 and the Creation of a Legend*, ed. by Jan van Dorsten, Dominic Baker-Smith, and Arthur F. Kinney (Leiden: Brill, 1986), pp. 193–220

Weller, Barry, 'Mary Sidney Herbert, Countess of Pembroke: *Antonius* (1592)', in *The Ashgate Research Companion to the Sidneys, 1500–1700*, ed. by Margaret P. Hannay, Mary Ellen Lamb and Michael G. Brennan (Farnham and Burlington: Ashgate, 2015), II, pp. 199–210

Wesley, John, 'Mulcaster's Boys: Spenser, Andrewes, Kyd', unpublished PhD Thesis, University of St Andrews, 2008

Williams, Deanne, *The French Fetish from Chaucer to Shakespeare* (Cambridge: Cambridge University Press, 2004)

Wilson-Lee, Edward, 'Women's Weapons: Country House Diplomacy in the Countess of Pembroke's French Translations', in *The Culture of Translation in Early Modern England and France, 1500–1660*, ed. by Tania Demetriou and Rowan Tomlinson (Basingstoke: Palgrave Macmillan, 2015), pp. 128–44

Winston, Jessica, 'Expanding the Political Nation: *Gorboduc* at the Inns of Court and Succession Revisited', *Early Theater*, 8.1 (2005), 11–34

Witherspoon, Alexander M., *The Influence of Robert Garnier on Elizabethan Drama* ([Hamden]: Archon Books, 1968 [1924])

Worden, Blair, *The Sound of Virtue: Philip Sidney's Arcadia and Elizabethan Politics* (New Haven: Yale University Press, 1996)

Woudhuysen, Henry R., *Sir Philip Sidney and the Circulation of Manuscripts, 1558–1640* (Oxford: Clarendon Press, 1996)

INDEX

www.ingramcontent.com/pod-product-compliance
Lightning Source LLC
Chambersburg PA
CBHW061427300426
44114CB00014B/1570
* 9 7 8 1 9 0 7 3 2 2 6 7 9 *